*More Blues Singers*

ALSO BY DAVID DICAIRE

*Blues Singers: Biographies of 50*
*Legendary Artists of the Early 20th Century*
(McFarland, 1999)

# MORE BLUES SINGERS

*Biographies of 50 Artists
from the Later 20th Century*

by DAVID DICAIRE

McFarland & Company, Inc., Publishers
*Jefferson, North Carolina, and London*

To Mom and Dad,
Lou Anne and Peter,
and Alex and Brendan

**Library of Congress Cataloguing-in-Publication Data**

Dicaire, David, 1963–
    More blues singers : biographies of 50 artists from the later
20th century / by David Dicaire.
      p.   cm.
    Includes bibliographical references, discographies, and index.
    ISBN 0-7864-1035-3 (softcover : 50# alkaline paper)   ∞
    1. Blues musicians—Biography.   2. Blues (music)—History
and criticism.   I. Title.
ML394 .D53  2002
781.643'092'273—dc21
  [B]                                   2001044839

British Library Cataloguing-in-Publication data are available

Manufactured in the United States of America

*McFarland & Company, Inc., Publishers
  Box 611, Jefferson, North Carolina 28640
   www.mcfarlandpub.com*

# *Contents*

# Introduction

The evolution of the blues is one of the most fascinating chapters in the annals of American and international music. The development of this music from its deep African roots and varied origins—the work songs and field hollers, church and gospel hymns, medicine shows, minstrel shouts, ragtime and string bands—to the mature sound of the modern blues involves many changes. But however growth has taken place, the roots of the blues remain intact, and are the primary building blocks of the modern blues sound.

The term "modern blues" is an eclectic one, encompassing a variety of musical styles—rock, pop, soul, jazz, funk, country, Cajun, rockabilly, psychedelic, classical, gospel, and folk. Ironically, while the blues served as the foundation for many of the new musical directions in the past century, it in turn absorbed the finer points of each form along the way. The expansion of the blues' parameters has enabled the genre to appeal to new generations of blues fans while retaining the fire and magic of the original strains.

The roots of the modern blues sound began to take shape at the turn of the twentieth century. The consolidation of African roots, gospel, and individual expressionism into a cohesive sound resulted in the regional down-home blues of Mississippi, Texas, Louisiana, Georgia, Tennessee, North and South Carolina, and Florida. For the most part, these regional down-home blues idioms were pure strains, with the exception of the Texas sound: From the very beginning, the Texas blues were a hybrid of the many diverse musical styles found in the Lone Star State.

By the early 1920s, the regional down-home blues in each respective population pocket were established and flourished with great pride. Each particular strain boasted a champion. Charley Patton was the king of the Delta blues; Blind Lemon Jefferson was the Father of the Texas sound; Blind Willie McTell was the dean of the Atlanta blues; and the obscure Blind Blake was the hero of the Virginia-Piedmont area.

It was also during this decade that the world was first treated to the

1

recorded blues. The classic female blues singers dominated the "race" market as millions of blues records were sold, clearly establishing the potent commercial appeal of the genre. But, at the height of its newly found power, the record industry was practically decimated by the stock market crash of 1929.

The 1930s were a decade of decided change. It was at this point that the regional down-home blues styles were split down the middle. The migration north in search of better economic prospects included many blues singers with a traveling bone. Those who made the trek out of the south settled in Chicago, Detroit, New York, Los Angeles, and Gary, Indiana. Those who stayed behind made Memphis into the new Southern blues Mecca.

In the cosmopolitan cities of Chicago, New York, Detroit, Los Angeles, St. Louis, Milwaukee, and Gary, the blues adopted a more urban sound in order to appeal to the metropolitan populace. With the advent of the electric guitar at the tail end of the decade, the urban blues took on a more raucous, brash sound that further distanced it from the Memphis blues.

The Memphis blues, meanwhile, were also evolving into a more modern sound. There were essentially two main components of the Memphis sound. The first was the jug band, which clung to the more traditional Southern country-blues; the second was its own brand of electric blues. Both styles shared one important characteristic: Specific guitar duties — solo and rhythm—were designated to specific individuals within the band ensemble. This is a trademark that still exists in the modern blues form, as well as in rock and roll, jazz, soul, and country.

By the beginning of World War II, the blues were a dominant musical force despite being overshadowed by the hot, sassy sound of jazz. Jazz, a direct outgrowth of the blues, shared many of the same characteristics, such as individually assigned parts to the guitarists in the band, single-string solos, horn sections, thumbing pianos, and a swing feel. The blues and jazz borrowed heavily from each other, expanding their boundaries and, in turn, their commercial appeal.

Rhythm and blues was born from the union of the blues and jazz; it was a sound with strong blues roots and tinges of jazz. Originally, rhythm and blues covered all music that was not considered blues or jazz. Rhythm and blues would become an important precursor to the musical explosion that was just on the horizon.

Although all of the essential elements of rock and roll had been in place for some twenty years, it wasn't until the mid–1950s that the genre was truly born. The rock-and-roll efforts of Chuck Berry, Elvis Presley, Bo Diddley, Little Richard, Carl Perkins, Fats Domino, Buddy Holly,

Roy Orbison, Eddie Cochran, Bill Haley and the Comets and numerous others were nothing more than up-tempo blues. Chuck Berry and Bo Diddley even recorded many of their early rock-and-roll classics at Chess Studios, the home of the urban Chicago blues. Rock and roll, as an outgrowth of the blues, brought the latter genre directly to a white audience for the first time. Sadly, the rule of the first generation of rock and rollers was like a meteor in the sky—their presence was powerful, but very brief.

One of the greatest changes in the unfolding of the blues story has been in the racial constitution of its practitioners. Once the exclusive expression of the African American experience, the blues have become predominantly white in the past forty years. Many young African Americans considered the blues the music of their parents and grandparents. While there remained a small, dedicated army of African American blues enthusiasts, many explored different, new and exciting variations of blues roots. This particular shift, which began with the first generation of rock-and-roll singers, gained momentum in the 1960s as the blues fueled a multitude of new musical directions.

The first half of the decade witnessed a folk music revival sparked by white college students. It was an opportunity for forgotten acoustic blues artists such as Sam "Lightnin'" Hopkins, Mississippi John Hurt, Mississippi Fred McDowell, Eddie "Son" House, Skip James, and others to rekindle their careers.

Out of Detroit—a northern blues Mecca—emerged the Motown sound, a variation of rhythm and blues. Along with the creation of soul music—yet another derivative of the blues—the Motown sound served as the soundtrack of a generation. The rhythm-and-blues elements of the Motown sound, and soul, would eventually fuse to create funk, rap, and hip-hop.

With the demise of the careers of many of the first generation of rock and rollers, the genre lay dormant for the first few years of the 1960s. Not until the Beatles, the Animals, the Yardbirds, and the Rolling Stones gave back to rock and roll its strength and vitality did the genre regain its popularity. They did it by fusing the blues with rock and roll.

The marriage between the blues and rock and roll brought the blues to the international stage, along with the artists who had toiled in relative obscurity. It was a grand love affair that changed the course of modern blues as well as modern music. Every blues scholar to emerge from England in the 1960s had a secret agenda to repay the debt they all felt they owed to the old blues masters who had sparked the initial fire.

When the blues-rock marriage began to dissolve in the late 1970s, the fortunes of the blues ebbed lower. The disco and punk-rock adventures of the 1970s pushed the blues even farther away from the interests of mainstream music fans. But the blues' downward turn in popularity would not last long.

While the early 1980s brought about a confusion of musical styles, underneath it all was a blues tidal wave that was about to rise up and destroy everything in its path. It was a force that emerged from Texas; and like everything else from Texas, it was big, very big. The 1980s blues explosion was spearheaded by a young Texan named Stevie Ray Vaughan. The most spectacular electric guitarist to arrive on the scene since the departure of Jimi Hendrix, Vaughan almost single-handedly catapulted the blues back into the forefront of popular music. Overnight, old blues fans who had drifted away returned, and a whole new generation of fans discovered the blues.

The 1990s were known as the post–Stevie Ray Vaughan era, and his ghostly presence continues to influence blues tastes and artists. The 1980s blues revival was a party; the happy hangover continues more than a decade later. In many ways, the blues have not enjoyed this kind of popularity since their golden age of the 1920s. There are numerous blues clubs in every major city and small town in North America. Blues festivals are common summer events, and the opportunities for blues musicians have never been better. Not only are the blues thriving in North America and Great Britain; the raging fever has spread throughout the world. The blues are a genuine global musical force.

In my first book, *Blues Singers*, I paid tribute to the pioneers, innovators, superstars, and cult heroes born prior to 1940. This second installment is dedicated to the blues singers born after 1940 who have wholeheartedly carried on the tradition of the earlier blues influences.

Like the first volume, this book is divided into five separate sections to give the names some semblance of order. The first part is called "Modern Acoustic Blues" and examines those blues singers who have continued where Charley Patton, Son House, and Robert Johnson left off. "Contemporary Chicago Blues" spotlights those who continue to deliver amplified, citified, gritty blues in the tradition of Muddy Waters, Buddy Guy, Howlin' Wolf, Elmore James, and dozens of others. The third section is "Modern American Electric Blues," taking up where the "Texas Blues Tradition" left off in the previous volume. It includes some Texas blues singers like Stevie Ray Vaughan, Jimmie Vaughan, and Johnny Winter, but it also is a reflection of how the blues have spread throughout the entire continent. "Contemporary Blues Women" is a tribute to the contributions of the new generation of women blues artists. The last section is an extension of the first book's "Blues Outside the Delta." Called "Blues Around the World," it introduces blues singers from four different continents and a dozen different countries, and is further proof of the widespread appeal of all types of blues.

It was eighty years ago that Mamie Smith stunned the world with her "Crazy Blues." Since then the blues have undergone many changes, but the genre has survived and prospered. The history of the blues is a truly rich tradition; it boasts an assortment of colorful, talented individuals who have expanded the original blues to include many different musical styles, ideas, and tastes. Yet, despite the assimilation of so many disparate elements, and no matter what term is used, the fire and magic are undeniable. In the end, the blues are still the blues.

# PART ONE

# Modern Acoustic Blues

The acoustic blues tradition is more than a century old. It was one of the earliest recorded forms of the blues, and, as such, served as the musical well from which many artists drew their inspiration. The country-blues masters who shaped the music that sparked the fire became legends around the globe. Despite its revered status, the acoustic genre has suffered through lean periods when it was practically forgotten in favor of other types of blues, and other styles of music.

In the 1920s and 1930s, the acoustic blues reigned supreme, but the introduction of the amplified guitar in the early 1940s forced the acoustic blues into the background. The genre rebounded during the late 1950s and early 1960s, however, during the feverish folk/blues revival. Then the marriage of the blues and rock and roll once again consigned the acoustic blues to a background position.

The deaths of Mississippi John Hurt (1966), Skip James (1969), Lonnie Johnson (1970), Mississippi Fred McDowell (1972), Rev. Gary Davis (1972), Mance Lipscomb (1976), Bukka White (1977), Sleepy John Estes (1977), Big Joe Williams (1982), Lightnin' Hopkins (1982), Sonny Terry (1986), Son House (1988), Johnny Shines (1992), and Brownie McGhee (1996) left the acoustic blues tradition in disrepair. There were only a handful of artists left who had dedicated themselves to the acoustic blues tradition, including John Hammond, Jr., John Mooney, Paul Geremia, Lonnie Pitchford, Lonnie Shields, Rory Block, and, in their early careers, Taj Mahal and Bonnie Raitt. Both Mahal and Raitt had explored different musical paths, eventually leaving the acoustic format behind.

But in the past decade the acoustic blues has enjoyed a true resurgence, due in large part to a proud African American presence. In an era when many young African American artists have turned their backs on the blues—their musical heritage—in favor of different styles, a small army of acoustic blues warriors have almost single-handedly rejuvenated the acoustic blues spirit. The acoustic blues tradition remains a viable form, and, considering the quality of young talent dedicated to keeping the flame alive, the future appears very promising.

The following are some of the major players on the acoustic blues scene today.

Taj Mahal was one of the modern acoustic blues singers to revive the country-derived styles of blues during the blues-rock era. An anomaly at the time, his work inspired later blues artists to explore the rich vein of regional down-home blues handed down from the old masters.

John Hammond, Jr., is one of the main proponents of the modern acoustic blues movement. Along with Taj Mahal, Hammond gave the genre back the respect it deserved, and inspired others to follow in his path.

Paul Geremia is a modern acoustic performer who first caught the fever during the folk revival in the early 1960s and has never departed from this path.

Kelly Joe Phelps has followed in the footsteps of Hammond and Geremia. He has left no doubt that one does not require an authentic Mississippi blues certificate to play genuine, gritty Delta blues.

Keb' Mo' is one of the new generation of acoustic blues performers who has delved into the past of the great country-blues singers to create his own sound.

John Mooney plays furious acoustic blues reminiscent of his mentor, Son House, and Big Joe Williams.

Alvin Youngblood Hart, like Keb' Mo', is part of the same movement that heralds the old acoustic masters while delivering a fresh take on the acoustic blues. A pure gem, Hart sounds as if he inherited the best elements of Charley Patton, Robert Johnson and Skip James.

Corey Harris is an integral artist in the modern acoustic blues revival. Along with Hart and Keb' Mo', Harris has returned the pride and joy to the down-home African American blues sound.

These eight acoustic blues performers are a fair representation of the modern acoustic blues movement. However, the efforts of Lonnie Shields, Ben Harper, Sonny Rhodes, Terry Garland, Roy Book Binder, Cephas and Wiggins, Guy Davis, and Roy Rogers should never be ignored.

# TAJ MAHAL

## *The Blues Scholar*

The study of the blues is a long, complicated process, thanks to the vast depth and subtle nature of the music. In the past hundred years a legion of musicians have dedicated themselves to unraveling the secrets of the blues; and, while some have been more successful than others, one blues musician has earned the distinction of being the premier scholar of African American roots music. This musicologist is none other than Taj Mahal.

Taj Mahal was born Henry St. Clair Fredericks on May 17, 1942, in New York City. Henry grew up in Springfield, Massachusetts, in a musical environment: his mother was a schoolteacher who sang in a local gospel choir, and his father was a West Indian jazz arranger who played the piano. The house was filled with different types of music—via a short-wave radio—that exposed little Henry to the international flavor of rhythms and harmonies that existed in various cultures. It was this understanding and appreciation for world music that would later enable Henry to develop his expansive musical vision.

A large part of his early musical education consisted of studying the intricate styles of some of his favorite blues singers, including Jimmy Reed, Howlin' Wolf, Big Mama Thornton, Sleepy John Estes, Son House, Mississippi John Hurt, and Sonny Terry. While attending the University of Massachusetts he undertook further study of the ethnomusicology of rural black styles, which led him to the folk music of the Caribbean and West Africa.

Although Mahal would embrace the entire spectrum of African American roots music, including jazz, folk, rhythm and blues, gospel, and New Orleans zydeco, it was the authentic, down-home, country-blues that served as the foundation of his unique sound throughout his entire career.

His thirst for knowledge was unquenchable as he devoured blues history, storing the information for later use. In his scholarly approach to becoming a connoisseur of African American roots music, he left no stone unturned; he also kept abreast of the burgeoning rock, pop, and soul movements of the early 1960s.

While a student, he also expanded his musical horizons by learning to play the piano, acoustic guitar, banjo, mandolin, dulcimer, harmonica, and assorted flutes. It was also during this period that he formed his first band, Taj Mahal and the Elektras, performing in Boston coffeehouses and at college dances.

Although he was proud of his birth name, Henry St. Clair Fredericks, it did not reflect what he was trying to accomplish as a musician. He needed a name that suggested a broader vision, a name that was unique yet instantly recognizable. The moniker Taj Mahal fit the bill perfectly. It was an exotic name, one of grandeur and splendor; but, more importantly, it represented a balance between his love of the country-blues and world music.

In 1964, after graduating from the University of Massachusetts with a B.A. in agriculture and animal husbandry, Mahal moved to the West Coast. In Los Angeles, he frequented the blues clubs on the city's poorer south side. He wasn't long in the city of angels before he found a kindred spirit in Ry Cooder.

Cooder, a native of Los Angeles, had also discovered the blues at an early age and developed a deep affection for its thumping rhythms and mojo moans. He had cultivated a searing slide-guitar style in the tradition of Son House and Robert Johnson. A journeyman who never enjoyed great commercial success, Cooder became one of the ace session men in all of rock with his blues-flavored guitar style.

Mahal and Cooder formed a band called the Rising Sons, which, despite their ambitions, did not last long; they released only one single during their time together. Years later, long after they had gone their separate ways, a greatest-hits package surfaced that contained twenty-five tracks. The collaboration between Cooder and Mahal was a promising one and it would have been interesting to hear the band develop and mature musically.

In 1968, Taj Mahal released his self-titled debut album for Columbia. It contained such familiar classics as "Statesboro Blues," "Dust My Broom," and "Walkin' Blues." Despite the marked presence of the country-blues, there was an eclectic flavor to the album, a hint of other styles including folk, rock, and universal rhythmic ideas not usually found in a folk/blues record. The album served as a blueprint for Mahal's later musical adventures.

A prolific songwriter, Mahal recorded several albums in the late 1960s and early 1970s for Columbia in the folk/blues vein that showcased his country-blues fingerpicking style and his laid-back vocals. The albums *Giant Step/De Ole Folks at Home* and *The Real Thing* were double sets. By 1975 Taj began to widen his musical boundaries with a series of albums that stretched his creative muscle and tested his encyclopedic knowledge of roots music. The first such album, *Music Keeps Me Together*, focused on West Indian cultural harmonies and revealed Mahal's incredible diversity as a musician, a bandleader, and a songwriter.

Throughout the remainder of the 1970s, Mahal's albums featured a mixture of country-blues, West Indian roots music, bluegrass, soul, R&B, reggae, and Caribbean polyrhythms. A composer of genius, he was able to weave elements of each style into a beautiful tapestry of musical expression. His fertile imagination and talent as a multi-instrumentalist enabled him to create his personal vision of world music.

While he remained very active throughout the 1980s, after the release of *The Best of Taj Mahal, Live*, in 1981, there was no new Mahal studio material available until *Taj* in 1986. That five-year span represented the longest period of recorded inactivity in his brilliant career. Because of his lack of releases, by the end of the decade his recording career was on a downturn and a musical transfusion was needed.

He returned to the country-blues idiom and enjoyed a renaissance with a string of strong albums for the Private Music label. *Phantom Blues*, *Dancing the Blues*, and *Señor Blues* all demonstrated that Mahal had not lost his blues identity. They also shared the common concept of paying homage to the origins of much of the trendy music of the day. Of the three, *Señor Blues*, which won a Grammy Award in 1997, proved to be the most interesting and diversified.

The album started off with a slamming version of "Queen Bee," an original Mahal composition that had been a concert favorite since his earliest days. The song "Think" featured the street-tough funk of James Brown, while at the other end of the spectrum "Irresistible You" reflected Mahal's fondness for the New Orleans party-type tune. He swung from hard blues on "Real Bad Day" to progressive jazz with the title track, "Señor Blues." The driving "Sophisticated Mama" demonstrated that Taj had not lost his taste for rock and roll; and the gospel-flecked "Crazy Up in Here," was a tribute to church music. He reached back five decades and delivered the T-Bone Walker gem "I Miss You Baby" on a silver platter. He extended his blues/jazz excursion to include "You Rascal You," recorded in a Louis Jordan vein. The song "Mind Your Own Business," an old Hank Williams standard, was a tip of the hat to country music, which had made a big comeback in the beginning of the 1990s. The last three songs, "21st Century Gypsy Singin' Lover Man," "At Last," and "Mr. Pitiful," were clear examples of Mahal's soul side.

This eclectic album reintroduced Mahal's unique scope of world music that underlined many of his recorded efforts in the 1990s. Some of his best efforts in uniting the country-blues and world roots music have occurred in this decade.

Mahal, a resident of Hawaii for over a decade, had always been enchanted with the sweeping, magical sounds of the islands. It had been a lifelong dream to blend the complex rhythms and melodies of the various island tribes with his passion for African American roots music. The eventual result was *Sacred Island*, the kind of ambitious project that Mahal thrived on.

The adventure combined two of Mahal's greatest interests, the art of mixing different forms of music into one cohesive sound and the joy of working with different musical personalities. Just a sampling of the different ingredients that created this rich stew of musical flavors included fingerpicking country-blues, bluegrass banjo, slide guitar, soul, R&B, reggae, the Caribbean polyrhythms, and of course the majestic sounds of Hawaiian folk music. The International Rhythm Band and the Intergalactic Soul Messengers Band, as well as an interesting cultural mix of musicians of Afro-Caribbean, Afro-American, Pacific-Islander, Native-American, and Portuguese descent contributed to the final product.

The eclectic nature of the songs reflected the diversity of the group. The song "Calypsonians" was a blend of Calypso and country-blues with a Hawaiian touch. "The New Hula Blues" threatened to start a revolution in musical styles with its soft, soothing polyrhythms. The title song, "Sacred Island (Moku La'a)," was a funky number hinting at some secret system of coded musical messages that took the listener away to a different universe. "No No Mann" was a heavily reggae-influenced tune that was a bold representation of the regional down-home folksy feel that ran through the entire collection of songs.

Perhaps the most complex and diverse album of Mahal's career (thus far) was the *Kulanjan* project that saw him unite his love of country-blues with the rich musical traditions of the Mali of West Africa. The record featured the use of intricate instruments such as the Kora, a 21-string harp-lute, the ngoni, also a lutelike instrument, the kamalengoni, a type of harp, and the Mande balafon, related to the xylophone. The combination of Mahal and seven Mali musicians including Toumani Diabate, the foremost exponent of the Kora, put a new spin on such classics as "Queen Bee," "Catfish Blues," "Mississippi-Mali Blues," and "Let's Get Together." Only Mahal, with his deep and broad knowledge of other types of root music, could have pulled off such an ambitious project.

Mahal's latest release, *Shoutin' in Key*, is a live recording that occurred at The Mint, in Los Angeles, one of his favorite venues. Along with his current band, the Phantom Blues, Mahal has fun working through thirteen tracks that include some originals and some standards. The passion he burns into the grooves of "Mailbox Blues," "Corrina," "EZ Rider," and ten other songs is classic Mahal. A musical chameleon, he explores blues, soul, funk, rock, reggae, Caribbean rhythms, New Orleans second-line beat, and West African folk sounds on this album. It is an interesting project and deserves a long and close listen.

Today, Mahal is a respected member of the acoustic blues circle as well as an important spokesman for world music. He tours frequently with the Phantom Blues band and his concerts remain fun and informative.

Taj Mahal is a blues encyclopedia. He is the foremost authority on African American roots music, and his understanding of the entire spectrum, including the blues, Caribbean, Hawaiian, African, jazz, pop, rock, and reggae, is second to none. His ability to assimilate various styles and rhythms into one cohesive sound is the yardstick for other modern blues musicologists. He is a true master musician of world music. His career spans an incredible thirty-five years, in which time he has done much to educate blues fans to the fact that the genre exists in many different forms around the world. He is that rare artist who has never made the same album twice.

But, despite a well-deserved reputation as a modern musical chameleon, Mahal has never really strayed from his country-blues base. He has experimented with the genre, expanding its parameters to create his vision of world music. Yet, despite his tinkering, Mahal has remained a champion of the country-blues by preserving the tradition while updating it to a contemporary sound.

Along with John Hammond, Jr., Mahal has kept the country-blues form vital long after the deaths of Mississippi John Hurt, Skip James, Big Joe Williams, Lightnin' Hopkins, and Sonny Terry threatened to make the style extinct. In turn, Mahal has been the inspiration for the modern acoustic blues revival that has taken place in the 1990s. Young artists like Keb' Mo', Alvin Youngblood Hart, Corey Harris, Joanna Connor, Kelly Joe Phelps, Guy Davis, and Ben Harper have picked up the threads of the country-blues tradition and strengthened those fibers to weave a strong musical fabric.

Mahal has shared the stage with a variety of musicians, including Etta James, Ry Cooder, Eric Clapton, Bonnie Raitt, Lightnin' Hopkins, Pete Seeger, the Pointer Sisters, Toumani Diabate, and many others. Over the years Mahal has added his expertise as a multi-instrumentalist to the recorded efforts of an incredible variety of artists. A partial list includes Rock Machine, B. B. King, Michael Bloomfield, Pamela Polland, Bonnie Raitt, Wendy Waldman, Rory Block, Noble "Thin Man" Watts, Michelle Shocked, Vinx, Ali Farka, Cedelia Marley-Booker, Carly Simon, Alvin Youngblood Hart, Mike Reilly, Quint Black, Salmon Leftover, and Marty Grebb.

A man of incredible energy, Mahal has always demonstrated an unbounded eagerness to take on new projects. His endeavors include scores for television, movies, and the theatre. A list of the credits that appear on his résumé include the movies *Phenomenon*, *The Mighty Quinn*, *Once Upon a Time When We Were Colored*, *Sounder I* and *II*, *Brothers*, and *Scott Joplin—King of Ragtime*. There are television shows: "The Man Who Broke a Thousand Chains," and "Br'er Rabbit," a tale for children. He has recorded several children's albums and provided the voice for the cartoon character Sage in the animated series *The Blues Brothers*. He also composed authentic music for the Broadway production of *Mule Bone*, a Langston Hughes/Zora Neale Hurston play that starred Louisiana bluesman Kenny Neal.

His live appearances are a night of world music as he takes the audience on a splendid journey through the entire spectrum of African American blues roots. His warm stage personality, his wit, and his incredible knowledge help him educate as well as entertain his fans. The blues professor is able to deliver his lessons in a way that is both fun and exciting.

His recorded catalog is an audio encyclopedia of blues roots and folk music. A crafty songwriter whose songs have both depth and breadth, Mahal has also carved out a reputation as one of the premier cover artists of the modern era. He has always been able to give a song the musical respect it deserves while stamping it with his own distinct voice and playing. His ability to bring out the highlights, tones, colors, dynamics, and tension of a song without losing its originality is sheer brilliance.

The richness of his music requires an open mind in order to understand his vision. A multi-instrumentalist, Mahal displays a pronounced intellectual approach; he plays each instrument with the serious intensity of a proud student. The focus that he has always brought to bear on his undertakings is one of the main reasons for his wide success.

With a career that spans over thirty years, Taj Mahal is clearly one of the most important and respected modern musicians. His knowledge, personality, creativity, and ability have earned him several awards that are just part of his vast accomplishment. While Taj Mahal was honoring roots music from cultures all over the world, he was also establishing his credentials as the ultimate blues scholar.

## Discography

*Taj Mahal*, Columbia 2779.
*Natch'l Blues*, Columbia 9698.
*Giant Step/De Old Folks at Home*, Columbia CGK-18.
*Happy to Be Just Like I Am*, Mobile Fidelity MCFD 10-00765.
*Recycling the Blues and Other Related Stuff*, Mobile.
*Fidelity* MCFD-764.

*The Real Thing*, Columbia 30619.
*Sounder*, Columbia 70123 (soundtrack).
*Ooh, So Good 'n' Blue*, Columbia 32600.
*Mo' Roots*, Columbia CK-3305.
*Music Keeps Me Together*, Columbia 33801.
*Satisfied 'n' Tickled Too*, Columbia 34103.
*Music Fuh Ya*, Warner Brothers 2994.
*Brothers*, Warner Brothers 3024.
*Evolution*, Warner Brothers 3094.
*Taj Mahal & Int'l Rhythm Band Live*, Crystal 5011.
*Taj*, Grammavision R2-79433.
*Live & Direct*, Laserlight 15297.
*Shake Sugaree*, Warner Brothers 42502
*Like Never Before*, Private Music 2081-2-P.
*Mule Bone*, Grammavision R2-79432.
*Don't Call Us*, Atlantic PDJ810002.
*Taj's Blues*, Columbia/Legacy CK-52465.
*World Music*, Columbia CK-52755.
*Dancing the Blues*, Private Music 82112.
*Taj Mahal*, 1980, Just A Memory 3.
*Muntaz Mahal*, Waterlily Acoustics 46.
*Live at Ronnie Scott's*, London, DRG 1441.
*Phantom Blues*, Private Music 82139.
*An Evening of Acoustic Music*, RFR 1009.
*Señor Blues*, Private Music 82151.
*Shakin' a Tailfeather*, Rhino 72940.
*Sacred Island*, Private Music 82165.
*Taj Mahal & the Hula Blues*, Tradition and Moderne 009.
*Kulanjan*, Hannibal 1444.
*Shoutin' in Key—Live*, Hannibal 1452.

# JOHN HAMMOND, JR.

## *White Country Blues*

Most of the old acoustic blues masters of the 1920s and 1930s were long forgotten by the time the first generation of rock-and-roll stars were fading from the musical scene. But the folk/blues revival of the late 1950s and early 1960s—spearheaded by the enthusiasm of white college students—recaptured the lost spirit of the Delta musicians of years gone by. From this acoustic blues renaissance emerged a host of inspired new performers, including the single most important white country-blues artist, who forged his own distinct, rich style. His name is John Hammond, Jr.

Hammond was born on November 13, 1942, in New York City. His father was John Hammond, the man responsible for signing Billie Holiday, Bob Dylan, Bruce Springsteen, and Stevie Ray Vaughan to Columbia Records. The young Hammond discovered the country-blues in high school and began to teach himself the guitar and the harmonica by listening to the records of Robert Johnson and Jimmy Reed.

After a one-year stint at Antioch College in Ohio, Hammond decided to pursue a career as a country-blues musician. He moved back to New York and began to work the coffeehouse circuit. Hammond's timing could not have been better; his decision coincided with the acoustic blues explosion. He shared the stage with Mississippi John Hurt, Skip James, Rev. Gary Davis, and Lightnin' Hopkins, who had recently been "discovered" by white blues pundits.

In 1963 Hammond's self-titled debut album was released on the Vanguard label and included the classics "See That My Grave Is Kept Clean" and "Crossroads Blues." It was evident from the opening bars that Hammond was no mere interpreter; he was an original performer who was capable of taking the past and molding it into a contemporary sound, making every cover song his own. It was this special ability that separated him from all the other practitioners of the country-blues form at that time.

He was equally brilliant in concert, and his performances drew rave reviews from some of the leading music magazines of the day. He toured England and Canada, building up a sizable following outside of the United States. At home, he was a permanent fixture on the Greenwich Village scene as well as at folk/blues festivals throughout the land. His live material was a mixture of his own compositions and the extensive catalog of Robert Johnson, Jimmy Reed, Skip James, Son House, and Blind Lemon Jefferson.

At the start of Hammond's recording career, each successive album emphasized a certain theme. *Big City Blues* was a collection of songs that had first been recorded by artists on Chess Records. His cover versions of Chuck Berry, Willie Dixon, and Bo Diddley originals demonstrated that Hammond was capable of handling both the country and urban blues styles with relative ease.

His next effort, *Country Blues*, concentrated on the down-home blues of Robert Johnson, Blind Willie McTell, and Sleepy John Estes, as well as the electric rhythmic thumping of John Lee Hooker, the sweet blues of Jimmy Reed, and the more citified blues of Willie Dixon. By this time Hammond had begun to record his albums as a solo artist, playing the guitar and harmonica and handling all the vocal chores.

The *So Many Roads* release was a landmark album. It featured appearances by Robbie Robertson and members of the Band when they were known as the Hawks. It also included a young Charlie Musselwhite, and Michael Bloomfield on piano. It was a dedicated tribute to the Chicago blues style made famous by Muddy Waters, Willie Dixon, Howlin' Wolf and the entire galaxy of Windy City bluesmen. On this album Hammond played mostly electric guitar as his acoustic instrument was put aside.

Although he had gained a well-deserved reputation as a prime solo performer, Hammond also recorded a few albums with the help of others. On the *I Can Tell* album he was backed by bassist Bill Wyman of the Rolling Stones and by Robbie Robertson. The album *Southern Fried* featured Duane Allman on slide guitar. (Hammond, like all good country pickers, was a very capable slide guitarist, but stepped aside so Allman could shine.) The album *Triumvirate* featured the mystical Dr. John. The *Footwork* effort featured the legendary Roosevelt Sykes on piano. On *Hot Trails*, Jimmy Thackeray and his band the Nighthawks backed Hammond, creating an interesting sound.

On the *Got Love If You Want It* CD, he was backed by Little Charlie and the Nightcats, one of the new bands on the scene. The combination of Hammond's undeniable talent and the fresh approach of Little Charlie and the Nightcats was a genuine treat for blues fans. Although they are one of the zanier acts on the blues circuit, Little Charlie and the Nightcats are true professionals and their musicianship is first rate. The two diverse acts would collaborate once again on the *Trouble No More* CD.

Throughout the 1980s Hammond continued to record regularly for a variety of labels and played small-to-medium-sized venues, often as a solo artist. While his popularity had decreased significantly from his heyday in the early 1960s, Hammond had no intention of abandoning his acoustic blues identity.

The winds of change blew again in the early 1990s, with the release of Eric Clapton's *Unplugged* album. Within a few years a whole new cohort of acoustic blues players were releasing albums and performing all over the country. Many of these new artists traced their own roots back to the dedication, spirit, and longevity of Hammond's career.

John Hammond, Jr., continues to record. His lengthy discography is the yardstick for all new acoustic blues players on the scene. He continues to perform in small and mid-sized venues, as well as at folk/blues festivals in the United States, Canada, and Europe. His concerts are major events that never draw the attention they deserve.

John Hammond, Jr., is a blues traditionalist. Along with Taj Mahal, Paul Geremia, and John Mooney, he has kept alive songs from the 1920s, 1930s, 1940s, and 1950s that would otherwise be forgotten. While he has continued to champion the acoustic blues form, he has also carved out a reputation as a performer with an individual sound. It was Hammond who proved that the past could be modernized without losing any of its beauty, emotion, or depth.

Hammond is truly underrated as a musician; his guitar work is exceptional. He studied the old masters closely (particularly Robert Johnson) and developed an authentic sense of rhythm and feel. He is a sound finger-picker, able to hit the thumping bass notes in perfect time to make his lone instrument sound like a whole orchestra of guitars. His strumming technique ranges from the feverish pitch of a Big Joe Williams to the color tones of Robert Junior Lockwood and Eddie Taylor. Hammond is comfortable playing acoustic six-string and twelve-string, as well as electric, guitars. He has been able to play both acoustic and electric guitar without changing his style. Over the years he has developed a hypnotic slide guitar technique, and demonstrates this ability on a National Steel guitar in concert.

He is also an accomplished harmonica player, his style derived from listening to Jimmy Reed albums. He uses the harmonica as the second prong of his musical attack, coupling it with his smooth guitar powers and quality vocals. His ability to blend his masterful guitar touch, his well-spaced harmonica lines, and unique voice into one cohesive charge makes him an interesting performer.

In concert, Hammond creates his own blues universe and entices the crowd to enter at their own risk. Hammond possesses the pure ability to take the listener on a special trip, with his renditions of Robert Johnson, Son House, Big Joe Williams, and Charley Patton tunes. He conjures up grainy images of the Mississippi Delta in the 1920s, of some juke joint on a sultry summer night with a crowd gathered around the stage listening to the haunting sounds of the beginning of the blues. He can take you to the Chess studios of the 1950s, home of the recorded urban blues, with his thumping rhythms, wailing harmonica, and powerful vocals. He evokes the past, but is capable of making it sound fresh and new.

Because Hammond boasts a repertoire that is as deep as the history of the blues, no two concerts are exactly alike. His intuitive skill for feeling out a song allows him to choose each offering with the calculated care of a seasoned blues master. He can make each song sound distinct, yet all the songs fit together like a long symphonic piece. Hammond, who shunned the group format for that of solo performer a long time ago, stings his audience with his percussive guitar style, precise harmonica licks, and recognizable voice.

Like the Rolling Stones, Cream, Led Zeppelin, the Animals, the Yardbirds, and the Paul Butterfield Blues Band, Hammond is frequently an introduction to the blues for many new fans. His cover versions often inspire curious blues fans to trace the original sources of the songs, thus enabling the music of the old country-blues masters to remain vibrant and current.

The name John Hammond evokes different responses from different generations. Those who were around and musically aware in the 1960s remember Hammond with a soothing familiarity. Later generations, unless they are true blues scholars, are often unfamiliar with him and the vast contributions he has made to the acoustic blues.

In some ways, John Hammond is the Ernest Hemingway of modern acoustic blues guitarists. Hemingway, who has often been cited as a perfect vehicle to teach students the rudiments of the English language, wrote in a very simple yet effective style. His writing was accessible, could be broken down easily, and was always grammatically solid.

The same can be said of Hammond in a musical sense. His style is soundly structured and is easy to decipher, helping aspiring musicians to grasp the concept of the country-blues idiom. Hammond's tasteful guitar and harmonica work is an audio-Bible and his reworking of old blues songs provides a perfect "classroom" for all students interested in building on the foundation established by Robert Johnson, Sleepy John Estes, and John Lee Hooker. Also, like Hemingway, Hammond is a pure American original.

Along with Taj Mahal, John Mooney, Paul Geremia, and Lonnie Pitchford, Hammond has maintained an interest in the acoustic blues that began the whole process. Today, with the emergence of young, dedicated country-blues players like Keb' Mo', Alvin Youngblood Hart, Corey Harris, Kelly Joe Phelps, and Ben Harper, the renewed revival of acoustic blues is a true event. Although it wasn't easy, Hammond has managed to prolong a career in a genre that has suffered its fair share of low popularity levels in the last thirty years.

But what separates Hammond from the hundreds of other white blues musicians who took up the country-blues tradition in the early 1960s is that Hammond developed a unique sound that was his very own. He was more than just an interpreter; he understood the textures of the country-blues so deeply that he was able to incorporate them into his own style without losing the authenticity of the old music. He didn't try to play every song he covered note for note, but instead concentrated on capturing the essence of each individual tune.

Hammond's dedication to the old country-blues tradition is heartwarming. A talented individual who could have made a more comfortable living playing electric blues and leading his own band, Hammond has remained faithful to the acoustic tradition. After almost forty years of delighting audiences with his personal brand of country-blues, Hammond is entitled to more acclaim than he currently receives from most music fans. But those who are aware of his vast body of work are part of the secret society of blues fans who appreciate the man most responsible for keeping the acoustic flame burning with his white country blues.

## Discography

*John Hammond* (1963), Rounder 9132.
*John Hammond* (1964), Vanguard 2148.
*Big City Blues*, Vanguard 79153.
*Country Blues*, Vanguard 79198.
*So Many Roads*, Vanguard 79178.
*Mirrors*, Vanguard 79245.
*I Can Tell*, Atlantic 82369.
*Sooner or Later*, Atlantic 8206.
*Southern Fried*, Atlantic 8251.
*Source Point*, Columbia 30458.
*When I Need*, Columbia 30549.
*I'm Satisfied*, Columbia 31318.
*Triumvirate*, Columbia 32172.
*Can't Beat the Kid*, Capricorn 0153.
*John Hammond Solo* (Live), Vanguard 79380.
*Footwork*, Vanguard 79400.
*Hot Trails*, Vanguard 79424.
*Mileage*, Rounder 3042.
*Frogs for Snakes*, Rounder 3060.
*Hits for the Highway*, Aim 54.
*Spoonful*, Edsel 129.
*Nobody but You*, Flying Fish FF 502.
*Live*, Rounder 3074.
*Gears/Forever* Taurus, BGP 37.
*Got Love, If You Want It*, Charisma 92146-2.
*You Can't Judge a Book by the Cover*, Vanguard VCD-9472.

*Trouble No More*, Pointblank V2-88257.
*Found True Love*, Virgin 40655.
*Long as I Have You*, Virgin 45514.
*John Hammond*, Rounder 11532.
*My Spanish Album*, Caytronics 1493.
*The Best of John Hammond*, VCD 11/12.
*The Best of the Vanguard Years*, Vanguard 79555.
*The Search for Robert Johnson*, Sony 49113.

# PAUL GEREMIA

## *Gamblin' Woman Blues*

The acoustic blues, the guitar-driven form of the blues that first gained attention, has featured some of the greatest blues singers in the genre. Charley Patton, Eddie "Son" House, Robert Johnson, Skip James, Big Joe Williams, Mississippi Fred McDowell, Mississippi John Hurt, Bukka White, and many more lived and died for their art. Despite their breadth and depth of talent, determination, and perseverance, few earned fortunes; many of them lived a hand-to-mouth existence and died poor. With more media resources available to them, today's modern acoustic blues singers have a much better chance to make a decent living. Despite these advantages, however, some modern acoustic artists continue to struggle financially even though they remain fiercely dedicated practitioners of the country-blues tradition. One of these is the man with the Gamblin' Woman Blues; his name is Paul Geremia.

Paul Geremia was born on April 21, 1944, in Providence, Rhode Island. As a child he moved across the country, calling several places home; the experience nurtured a love of traveling in him that he still possesses to this day. The unforgettable images of the majestic Rocky Mountains, the sweeping Plains, the crowded, charismatic cities of the East Coast, the stark beauty of the open Southwest, and the bountiful California valleys burned a deep hole in his soul. It was these early experiences that would provide the raw material for his extensive song catalog.

Geremia absorbed the rhythms and patterns of different American lifestyles by listening to the regional folk music of the respective cross sections of the American people. But it wasn't until the folk revival of the 1960s—he saw Mississippi John Hurt perform at the Newport Folk Festival in 1964—that Geremia was pointed in a decided direction. He dropped out of college and began to teach himself how to play the guitar and harmonica.

Once he had become proficient on both instruments, Geremia began to play the small coffeehouses around Providence, Boston, Cape Cod, and eventually all over the Atlantic states. When the folk/blues craze subsided he could easily have switched to electric guitar, but continued in the acoustic vein. It was at this point that Geremia abandoned all other sources of income living solely on the standard earnings from his performing career.

In 1968, after paying his blues dues as a live performer, he was given the chance to record his own material. With the release of two albums that year—*Just Enough*, and the self-titled *Paul Geremia*—his career began to gain momentum. Both long playing discs featured many distinct characteristics that would become Geremia trademarks.

He covered songs from the vast repertoire of the early blues masters of the 1920s, 1930s, and 1940s. But Geremia did more than just create imitations; he reworked the lost gems into a modern style that sounded as if he were some reincarnated lost blues soul from the Delta of the 1930s. His dedication to authenticity was underscored by his cover of the Muddy Waters classic, "I Can't Be Satisfied." Geremia recorded the song in its original name, "I Be's Troubled," and made it sound as if he were back on the Stovall Plantation.

Although the majority of his performance gigs were in Rhode Island and Massachusetts, he also played in Chicago, as well as in Greenwich Village at places like the Gaslight. The Gaslight was an important venue, not only because Bob Dylan had played there, but also because the shows at the clubs in the Village were for real pay. Geremia was earning a living as a genuine acoustic blues singer.

From this point on Geremia did what he was born to do: play the acoustic blues for interested audiences. As his reputation grew, so did the number of bookings. Never interested in securing the services of a manager or a crew, Geremia took it upon himself to perform all of the tasks of bookkeeper, roadie, booking agent, tour manager, and all-around gopher. Geremia was a throwback to the country-blues singers of the 1920s and 1930s who traveled the South, often alone, without a management team and with no corporate backing. Like the old blues masters, Geremia played for his love of the blues and not for financial security.

Throughout the lean years of the 1970s when there was very little interest in folk blues music, Geremia continued to ply his trade. He covered hundreds of thousands of miles every year, driving through winter blizzards and summer storms, always eager to make his appointed show whether there were a thousand people, a couple of hundred, or just a handful of paying patrons.

After his banner year of 1968, there was no new Geremia material available to the public until 1973. *Hard Life Rockin' Chair*, released that year, was a solid effort with the usual assortment of cover songs, including Big Bill Broonzy's "Long Tall Mama," and Blind Blake's "Early Morning Blues." The album also featured some of his original compositions, which showed maturity in his songwriting. In between the releases of his infrequent studio albums, Geremia, an exciting performer, kept his name fresh in the minds of hard-core blues fans and promoters through extensive touring.

It would be another nine years before Geremia's next studio release. The long-awaited *I Really Don't Mind Living* was recorded on the Flying Fish label. In a departure from his earlier albums, it included no cover versions, only Geremia originals. Although there was a marked maturity in his songwriting as well as his playing, it was evident that he had not yet captured the attention of the commercial blues audience with his own songs.

Four years later *My Kinda Place* was available to the public. It contained covers of Blind Willie McTell's "Savanna Mama" and "Broken Down Engine Blues." Geremia, who traveled in a dilapidated van, sang the latter song with genuine conviction. He also included Blind Lemon Jefferson's "Shuckin' Sugar Blues," Leadbelly's "Silver City Bound," and a couple from Scrapper Blackwell, "Artificial Blues" and "Back Door Blues." The self-penned "Big Walter" was a touching tribute to Big Walter Horton, and was Geremia's way of giving back to one of the early blues artists who had had a profound effect on his early development as a musician.

While the 1970s and the 1980s saw only three new album releases from Geremia, the 1990s were much more productive. The album *Gamblin' Woman Blues*, for Red House, boasted cover versions of Barbecue Bob's "She Moves It Just Right," Blind Lemon Jefferson's "Cheater's Spell," Blind Willie McTell's "Blues Around Midnight," and Skip James's "Special Rider Blues." On this album, Del Long backed him on piano and Roy McLeod on bass.

The *Self-Portrait in Blues* effort was another acoustic blues gem. Apart from the strong Geremia compositions, a lively rendition of the Skip James classic "Devil Got My Woman," Charley Patton's "Shake It, Break It," Blind Willie McTell's "Drive Away Blues," Leadbelly's "Leavin'

Blues," and Leroy Carr's "Midnight Hour Blues" graced the CD. The disc was also special because it featured the talented Harvey Armstrong on mandolin and violin.

Since Geremia had earned his living primarily through live appearances, it was only fitting that he release *Live from Uncle Sam's Backyard* next. The album was a more-than-fair representation of Geremia in his natural state—in front of an audience. There were many outstanding cuts on the album, including two vignettes of Hambone Willie and Son House. There was also a live version of Robert Johnson's "Travelin' Riverside Blues," and Blind Willie McTell's "Dying Crapshooter's Blues."

*The Devil's Music*, also on the Red House label, gained Geremia praise that was long overdue; it received rave reviews from journals around the country. It was a well crafted work that contained the Percy Mayfield gem "Lost Mind," Blind Lemon Jefferson's "Stocking Feet Blues," Robert Johnson's "Terraplane Blues," and Blind Boy Fuller's "Fuller's Walking Blues." As usual, his priceless cover versions were balanced by his self-penned poetic masterpieces. The use of the six-string and the twelve-string, an army of harps, and a piano—all played with expertise by Geremia—only enhance his reputation as one of the leading, if not the best, acoustic blues singers on the circuit today.

He continues to perform and to record sporadically.

Paul Geremia is a blues troubadour. He has traveled the country and the world delivering his Delta/Piedmont acoustic blues to eager audiences. He has not made a vast fortune from his concerts, nor is he a household name. Yet, he has managed to stretch out a career in a business that chews up and spits out acts effortlessly and regularly. There are many keys to Geremia's survival.

First, there is the rich authenticity of his musical approach. Geremia, who deeply studied all of the old masters, took his cue from Rev. Gary Davis and plays his guitar as if it were a piano. He uses his thumb of his picking hand to pick the bass notes like a pianist's left hand, and the other fingers play the melody like a pianist's right hand. His fingerpicking ability is first-rate; he is capable of rhythmic flourishes and stunning single-line runs, all accompanied by impressive harmonica solos.

His harmonica playing, often raw and untrained, is a reflection of his self-taught method after having watched Big Walter Horton in concert. He is not as good as the great Horton, but can more than hold his own. But Geremia never makes his harmonica the focus of attention; instead, he uses the instrument as an extension of his voice and to complement his excellent guitar skills. His harmonica adds tones, colors, and an accessible dimension to his entire musical package.

While he has not gained national attention, Geremia has gained the respect of the blues community and of modern acoustic players in particular. Along with Taj Mahal, John Hammond, John Mooney, Lonnie Pitchford, and Dave Van Ronk, Geremia has kept the acoustic blues tradition alive. A traditionalist in the purest sense, Geremia has always showed a genuine love for the old blues songs and has dedicated his career to making sure they were never forgotten. He has done so with the sweat of his brow, his unique talent, and his unwavering focus.

In concert, Geremia's authenticity shines through like an original Delta tune. He has an immense repertoire to choose from, so no two concerts are exactly the same. After tuning up he proceeds to the bandstand and immediately begins to entertain the crowd. He might open up with "Stomped Down Rider" or "Broke Down Engine," both Willie McTell songs. He might play some other well-known song from the Piedmont category of such blues legends as Pink Anderson, Brownie McGhee, Blind Blake, and Blind Boy Fuller, or he might start off with an obscure Blind Lemon Jefferson composition like "Jack o' Diamonds."

His hearty interpretations of raw country-blues and jazzy rags like the "The Death of Ella Speed," "Stones in My Pathway," and "The Way to Get the Lowdown," are crowd favorites that elicit a warm round of applause. He delivers his distinct acoustic blues sets while switching between his beloved Gibson six-string and the twelve-string Stella that he rescued from the scrap heap. He plays both guitars in a variety of tunings that create an atmosphere of sound. He also plays the harmonica and creates a strong interplay among the guitars, harmonica, and his rich, expressive voice. If there is a piano in the corner, Geremia will pull it out of its nest and give it a good working over, pounding expert boogie-woogie chords and barrelhouse fun.

His engaging storytelling ability enables him to draw the audience into his wonderful universe of blues history and musical power. He introduces each song with a brief anecdote that breaks the ice with the paying customers. If his first number of the night doesn't get them, then his second effort will certainly capture their imagination.

Although he plays a lot of cover tunes, Geremia also finds space for one of his own original compositions. His style of writing is a reflection of the music that has inspired him for the past thirty years, but he is no mere imitator; Geremia has the ability to write an original song that sounds as if Blind Willie McTell, Blind Lemon Jefferson, Pink Anderson, or some other of his musical heroes created it. He has given the world the rich, original compositions "I Just Roll Along," "Stone Sober Blues," "See Saw Blues," "My Kinda Place," "I Really Don't Mind Livin'," "Cocaine Princess," "Things That Used to Matter," "Kick It in the Country," "Henry David Thoreau," "Live Wire Blues," "Where Did

I Lose Your Love?" "Same Old Wagon," and "Farewell Street Rag," among others.

There are no pretensions in Geremia or his music. He is a genuine acoustic blues performer, often solo, who plays beaten up guitars, harmonicas, and pianos. To the ears of the true blues fans his sound is enthralling. Geremia is a breath of fresh air in a business of over-produced, publicity-engineered musical figures who are here today and gone before the ink can dry on their too-rich contracts.

Thirty years later, while countless musical styles and their practitioners have been dumped for the new flavor of the month, Paul Geremia, acoustic blues player with a Mississippi heart and a Delta soul, is still around. His concerts are not million-dollar makers; he does not travel by jet or limousine; he is not a household name; but he has survived. Because of his sincerity, talent, and commitment, there will always be a place for Paul Geremia and his Gamblin' Woman Blues in blues circles.

## Discography

*Just Enough*, Folkways FTS 31023.
*Paul Geremia*, Sire SI-4902.
*Hard Life Rockin' Chair*, Adelphi AD 1020.
*I Really Don't Mind Living*, Flying Fish 270.
*My Kinda Place*, Flying Fish FF 395.
*Gamblin' Woman Blues*, Red House CD RHR 54.
*Self-Portrait in Blues*, Red House CD RHR 77.
*Live from Uncle Sam's Backyard*, Red House CD RHR 101.
*The Devil's Music*, Red House CD RHR 127.

# KELLY JOE PHELPS

## *Hosanna Blues*

The country-blues, a form that was once thought to be in complete disarray, rebounded in the 1990s when a small, devoted group of blues singers took up the cause. Drawing their inspiration from the music of the old masters, this new breed of acoustic players rekindled interest in the country-blues to the point that it is once again a dominant branch of the genre. One of the artists responsible for this renaissance is the man singing his Hosanna blues. His name is Kelly Joe Phelps.

Kelly Joe Phelps was born on October 5, 1959, in Sumner, Washington, a small farming town east of the Cascades. He was introduced to music in a most natural way through his family. His father, mother, and brother were all musically inclined; his father and mother were multi-instrumentalists. Kelly himself developed a love for music at an early age and played the drums in the school band—just the beginning of a long and colorful journey from curious youngster to national acoustic blues act.

Phelps, a resident of Washington his entire life, began his musical evolution by embracing the hard-rock/blues-drenched/folk sounds of Led Zeppelin in the band's formative years. Phelps, just entering his teens at the time, was like a canvas waiting to be painted with the vast array of musical influences.

A couple of years later his imagination was captured by the folk music of Bert Jansch, Leo Kottke, and John Fahey. Jansch had been one of the main inspirations for Jimmy Page's love of acoustic music. The acoustic players taught Phelps how to balance his voice with his developing guitar skills. The weaving of the two into an intricate mixture of beauty and tension was a lesson that Phelps worked hard to incorporate into his still-developing sound.

The free-form style of folk music eventually led Phelps to the world of jazz. Great jazz names like Charlie Parker, Miles Davis, Thelonious Monk, and Dexter Gordon replaced the folk singers as his main musical heroes. Overnight he became a jazz fanatic, devoting all of his waking time to the unlocking of the mysteries of the form. After a ten-year voyage in the land of jazz, by which time he had explored all of the angles of the music, Phelps was at wits' end. He craved a new musical direction, and it was then that he discovered the folk/acoustic blues.

It was a true rebirth. He was able to collect all the lessons that he had carefully learned during his rock/folk/jazz days and incorporate them into this new direction. The voyage that he had begun as a youngster was now complete. Phelps embraced the folk blues of Robert Pete Williams, Skip James, Blind Willie Johnson, Joe Callicott, and the entire list of country-blues artists. He began to play in small coffeehouses, folk clubs, on street corners and wherever else he could be heard. His spirit was renewed; his vision now focused and clear.

In 1994, after he had honed his guitar skills to blend with his coarse singing voice, Phelps was ready to make records. His first effort, *Lead Me On*, was recorded for Burnside Records, a small label based in Portland, Oregon. His many years of practicing and constantly developing his musical voice paid off handsomely. The album contained six originals and six songs derived from his musical heroes, including "Hard Time Killing Floor Blues," by Skip James. The album gave notice to the acoustic country-blues community that a new talent had arrived on the scene and he was not to be ignored.

Phelps was featured in such important national magazines as *Billboard*, *Blues Wire*, and *People*, which helped spread his name to a larger audience. His album was a fresh-sounding effort that featured a simple formula: Kelly Joe and his guitar. Phelps, a lap slide-guitar player (his left wrist was damaged during a childhood accident), accompanied his driving guitar work and tough, blue-collar voice with his stomping foot.

It was three years before Phelps returned to the recording studio, but the wait was well worth it. His second effort, *Roll Away the Stone*, on Rykodisc, catapulted him into the national and international acoustic blues spotlight. Phelps began to tour extensively outside the United States, in Canada, Europe and Australia. His success linked him undeniably with the new acoustic blues movement that was gaining momentum. Roll Away the Stone was a logical extension of his first effort, Lead Me On, and featured the same formula as on his first record. The new album included some originals as well as cover versions of old blues standards. There was a haunting version of Blind Lemon Jefferson's "See That My Grave Is Kept Clean," and an interesting take on "Cypress Grove," an old Skip James chestnut. There were also rearrangements of the traditional songs "When the Roll Is Called Up Yonder," "That's All Right," and The Doxology. His own "Footprints," "Hosanna," "Without the Light," and the title song "Roll Away the Stone" demonstrated a uniquely talented man with a firm vision of the depth and breadth of the long-standing country-blues tradition. He was bringing alive the spirits of the old country-blues masters—Skip James, Blind Lemon Jefferson, Robert Pete Williams, Blind Willie Johnson, Mississippi Fred McDowell, Mississippi John Hurt—through his music.

Phelps began to tour extensively throughout the United States in support of B. B. King, Leo Kottke, Keb' Mo', Robben Ford and Little Feat. He also appeared at the Chicago Blues Festival and spread his message even further with a spot on the public radio show *A Prairie Home Companion*. Soon after that he headed off on a tour of several European countries. With his first two albums, Phelps had managed to become one of the leading lights in the country-blues revival.

In 1998 his third album, *Shine Eyed Mister Zen*, was released for the public's enjoyment. It contained some of his best songwriting—"Hobo's Son," "Katy," "Wandering Away," "Piece by Piece"—as well as traditional arrangements of "July House Carpenter," "Train Carried My Girl from Town," and the Leadbelly classic "Goodnight Irene." Phelps proved once again that he had a definite grasp of the country-blues tradition.

Since then Phelps has added to his burgeoning reputation as one of the most entertaining country-blues artists by performing at outdoor festivals and many other venues around the world.

Kelly Joe Phelps, though not yet a blues superstar, is rapidly heading in that direction. His meteoric rise from the coffeehouses of the Northwest to headlining some of the major blues festivals in the country is nothing short of astounding. His devotion to and clear vision of what the acoustic blues are all about rank him with the best of any generation. He has been able to draw tremendous inspiration from the old masters and has channeled their energy and spirit through his own playing.

Although he is known as a leading exponent of the acoustic blues idiom, Phelps also mixes in tinges of gospel and country music with the free-flowing attitude of a jazz player. He is a prime example of the modern blues singer. His music is not a reworking of old blues clichés, but the definite new direction of the acoustic blues movement. Along with Keb' Mo', Alvin Youngblood Hart, Taj Mahal, and Corey Harris, Phelps has rekindled interest in the richest of all blues styles.

Phelps plays six-string and twelve-string lap slide guitars in multiple tunings. He picks and slides at the same time, using his right hand on the body of the guitar to create a percussive, ringing rhythm. His smoky voice, tailor-made to sing the country-blues, blends with his intricate guitar style to create a truly individual sound.

Like his predecessor Skip James, Phelps invents his own worlds of foggy, somber Northwest mornings; crisp autumn days of clear sunshine and beautiful colors; summer days of warm breezes with the roar of the ocean nearby; and lonely days spent listening to the dancing rhythm of the raindrops.

His Hosanna blues is a direct link to the raw material that the old country-blues artists used to shape their songs. Phelps has brought the black-and-white images of a century ago alive in full-blown color with his inspirational singing, playing and songwriting.

His undisputed talent has not gone unnoticed. He has also made appearances on Greg Brown's album *Further In*, Tony Furtado's *Roll My Blues Away*, and Townes Van Zandt's *Martin Simpson and Louise*. While the list of his peerless contributions to the efforts of other artists is rather slim, over time there is no doubt that the list will grow much longer.

Kelly Joe Phelps is now a mainstay on the acoustic blues stage. He has inspired others with his cleverly executed style and will continue to do so for years to come. While other modern blues singers are busy grooving on Chicago-style blues, blues-rock, blues-soul and other types of blues styles, Phelps is content playing and singing his Hosanna blues and the world is a better place for it

## Discography

*Lead Me On*, Burnside 15.
*Roll Away the Stone*, Rykodisc 10393.
*Shine Eyed Mister Zen*, Rykodisc 10476.

====

# KEB' MO'

## *The Rainmaker*

The country-blues is the root music of all contemporary blues artists. The fire sparked by Charley Patton, Son House, Robert Johnson, Skip James, Big Joe Williams, Mississippi Fred McDowell, Sleepy John Estes, Mississippi John Hurt, and many others continues to fuel today's music. The originators were able to create new worlds with their guitars and voices that delivered them from the harsh and grim reality of daily life. With the ability to invent landscapes of vivid natural imagery and sharp detail, the Rainmaker revisits the old days through a modern voice. His name is Keb' Mo'.

Keb' Mo' was born Kevin Moore on Oct 3, 1951, in Los Angeles, California. As a young boy growing up, he was fed a steady diet of gospel and blues by his parents, who were originally from the Texas/Louisiana area. Moore discovered the power of music at an early age, developing an insatiable appetite for rhythm, harmony, and melody. In an effort to replicate the sounds that stirred deep emotions inside him, Moore picked up the guitar, opening up a magical world that could not compare to anything else; he was swept away by the beauty and the mystery of the instrument.

Moore jammed around his home in Los Angeles with a variety of garage bands whose members dreamed of becoming big stars some day, but none of whom possessed the determination, stamina, or talent that Keb did. When he was twenty-one, having played around the Los Angeles area for a number of years, he landed a spot in his first major group, the Papa John Creach Band. Moore stayed with the group for three years, during which they opened for such headliners as the Mahavishnu Orchestra, Jefferson Starship, and Loggins & Messina. The experience helped Moore develop his musical vision and capabilities.

He then moved on to work for Almo Music, a division of A&M Records. At Almo, Moore served as contractor and arranger for the company's demo sessions. In 1980, Moore was finally given a chance to record his own material for Chocolate City, a subsidiary of Casablanca Records. The album, *Rainmaker*, was an R&B-flavored work that hinted at Moore's ability and talent as a musician. Unfortunately, the label collapsed and Moore was left out in the cold. Some time later, Moore joined the Whodunit Band, led by Monk Higgins, gaining valuable performing experience. It was at this juncture in his blossoming career that he met and played with some of the greatest bluesmen, including Big Joe Turner, Jimmy Witherspoon, Pee Wee Crayton, and Albert Collins.

Moore spent the rest of the decade with the Rose Brothers, playing in and around the Los Angeles area. Somewhat frustrated by the music business and his lack of success, Moore turned to acting. He played the role of a Delta bluesman in a play called *Rabbit Foot*, served as an understudy for the play *Spunk*, and later portrayed the mysterious Robert Johnson in *Can't You Hear the Wind Howl?*

After a brief stint in Quentin Dennard's jazz band, Moore was finally able to record his first true solo album. The self-titled *Keb' Mo'* was everything a first record should be. It contained eleven songs written and co-written by Moore, along with two Robert Johnson covers, "Come on in My Kitchen" and "Kindhearted Woman." With his album Moore established himself as one of the main proponents of the modern acoustic blues movement. The collection of gritty blues songs ran together with the power of a hurricane-force wind raging across the open cotton field. He clearly demonstrated that he was an accomplished singer, guitar player, and songwriter.

As a result of this award-winning debut CD, Keb' Mo' became an in-demand performer and appeared at the Newport Folk Festival and other such blues events all over the country. His excellent driving set at the Newport Folk Festival in 1995 opened up a whole new world for him. The country-blues, once considered a dormant format, was making a strong comeback and Moore played a leading role. His long apprenticeship in the various Los Angeles jazz and R&B bands in the early part of his career was starting to pay off.

Moore's follow-up CD, *Just Like You*, was another strong outing that saw him stretch his creativity and expand his blues base to include different styles. While the thirteen tracks on the album—including four self-penned and eight co-written songs—did not have the naturalness of his first release, some of his more interesting compositions were found on this album, including the pop/soul-flavored "Angelina" and "She Just Wants to Dance." "Anybody Seen My Girl?" was a tender blues ballad that could have been sung by Charles Brown. The composition "Am I Wrong" was a tough, funky blues number. The tune "Tell Everybody I Know" melded light Caribbean rhythms with the traditional blues. The record also contained a Robert Johnson cover "Last Fair Deal Going Down."

As a side note, the vocal contributions of Bonnie Raitt and Jackson Browne signified the musical community's rapidly increasing respect for Keb' Mo'. Although his dabbling in rock and other forms was an interesting side project, there was no denying the fact that Moore was at his best playing modern country-blues.

By the time of his third release, *Slow Down*, Moore was regarded as one of the new leading blues lights. His dominating guitar work, emotional vocals, and contemporary songwriting abilities had won him a legion of fans. There was no doubt that Keb' Mo' was held in high regard in the blues community. However, as in his previous effort, Keb' Mo' was exploring a different end of the country-blues spectrum.

*Slow Down* was a contemporary blues record with introspective lyrics and a variety of musical styles. It contained some funky blues pieces like "Muddy Water" and "As Soon as I Get Paid." A pop element could be found in "I Was Wrong" and "I'm Telling You Now." There was a jazz feel to "Rainmaker," and a definite gospel touch in "God Trying to Get Your Attention." There was also a soulful side in the tunes "Henry," "A Better Man," and the title cut, "Slow Down." He also slipped in a Robert Johnson song to keep the tradition of the previous two CDs alive. His delivery of "Love in Vain" was a spectacular, heartfelt rendition. The blues ballad "I Don't Know" was another slow, soul-filled number. *Slow Down* was a collection of songs that definitely satisfied the palate of a certain segment of the blues population.

Keb' Mo' continues to record and perform all over the United States and Europe.

Keb' Mo' is a fantastic blues discovery. His sweeping guitar style, passionate vocals, and polished songwriting have created a renewed excitement in all blues circles. An extremely talented individual, he has the ability to experiment and stretch the parameters of the country-blues form without compromising his acoustic blues voice. He has taken the fundamentals of country-blues and shifted them into territory that others have not yet explored. He is certainly one of the more intriguing contemporary blues artists on the circuit.

Keb' Mo' is an accomplished guitar player capable of creating special worlds with his acoustic, electric, and slide-guitar powers. His years of playing in jazz bands gave him the ability to improvise, a trait that was one of the striking characteristics of the early country-bluesmen. His versatility as a guitarist enables him to cover a variety of styles from gritty country-blues to blues with a harder rock edge and blues with a pop/soul element.

Keb' Mo' sings as if he had inherited the vocal genes of both Robert Johnson and Robert Cray. There is a plaintive, yet assured power in Mo's voice that is reminiscent of Johnson. But Mo's voice also possesses smoothness, a polished control that has been developed listening to Robert Cray albums. It is an interesting voice, capable of taking a song in different directions, and one that transcends time.

Keb' Mo' is a superb bandleader who knows how to get the best out of his band members. After years of being part of a band, Keb' Mo' formed his own group. It includes Laval Belle on drums, Joellen Friedkin on keyboards, and Reggie McBride on bass. They are all veterans of the Los Angeles club scene and this is where they met Moore. They all contribute song ideas as well as backing Mo' up in the studio and on tour. On some concert dates Clayton Gibb adds his expert banjo licks to the exciting ensemble.

Like Robert Junior Lockwood, Johnny Shines, and Elmore James, Keb' Mo' is also a Robert Johnson disciple. However, unlike Robert Junior Lockwood, Moore was never given private lessons. Also, Keb' never had the chance to travel with the shadowy Johnson through the bare Delta landscape the way Johnny Shines did. While he has included at least one Robert Johnson composition on his first three albums, he has not built his career on a Johnson classic as Elmore James did with "I Believe I'll Dust My Broom." But Moore has drawn heavily on the old-fashioned country-blues style of Robert Johnson, using the heavy Delta sound with its catchy turnarounds, thumping bass lines, and percussive ringing guitar sound.

Keb' Mo' has in a short time carved out a special place for himself in the blues world. Although he has been able to absorb the magic of the country-blues—especially that of Robert Johnson—he has no genuine precedents and will no doubt inspire a host of imitators. As he continues to evolve and mature as a musician, bandleader, and songwriter, he will only get better. It is thrilling to think of the delightful music that the Rainmaker will provide us with in years to come.

**Discography**

*Keb' Mo'*, Okeh 57863.
*Just Like You*, Okeh 67316.
*Slow Down*, Sony 69376.

---

# JOHN MOONEY

## *Workingman's Blues*

The country-blues—the guitar-driven down-home regional style—
has always been regarded as the music of common, hard-working people
with unbreakable ties to the (stark, unforgiving) landscape of their surroundings. This spirit of the country-blues lives in the heart of every performer who is keen on continuing the tradition that has existed for over
a century. With his workingman's blues, one modern acoustic blues singer
has not forsaken the roots of his predecessors. His name is John Mooney.

John Mooney was born on April 3, 1955, in East Orange, New Jersey, but grew up in upstate New York. He discovered the guitar at an early
age and developed his skills by listening to country and popular folk songs
on the radio. One day he heard the hypnotic, slithering style of Son House.
House, one of the original Delta slide-guitar masters, made a life-changing impact on young Mooney. House, who had moved to Rochester years
before, lived near Mooney. Upon their initial meeting the pair discovered
that they were like two long-lost blues brothers, and House quickly
became Mooney's mentor. After a long internship Mooney was playing
alongside House at local gigs. The experience was the envy of every aspiring bluesman who had ever dreamed of embarking on a musical career.
The pair traveled together and Mooney learned everything he could from
this elder statesman of the blues who had been the inspiration for both
the legendary Robert Johnson and Muddy Waters. Once he had absorbed
everything House could teach him, Mooney began his solo career.

He spent time in Arizona and California, where he hosted a radio
show before pushing on to New Orleans. It was in the Crescent City
that he learned about the second-line rhythms from blues stalwarts like
Professor Longhair and the Meters. He often shared the stage with

Professor Longhair, Earl King, Clarence "Gatemouth" Brown, Snooks Eaglin, Dr. John and James Booker. Occasionally, he opened for the great Bonnie Raitt.

He spent much of the 1970s as a rambling acoustic blues player, hoboing around the country with his National steel guitar, playing small clubs, coffeehouse, and middle-sized venues. He lived the life of a renegade blues singer, surviving from one gig to another. He was one of only a handful of young performers on the blues circuit dedicated to keeping the down-home country-blues tradition alive.

In 1981, he formed his band Bluesiana, which at times featured bass guitarists George Porter, Jr., and Glenn Fukunaga, and drummers John Vidacovich and Kerry Brown. Their repertoire consisted of Delta toughness and the second-line rhythm shuffles of New Orleans. Mooney and his band toured throughout the United States, Europe, and Japan. He appeared at numerous folk/blues festivals across the country, including an annual spot at the New Orleans Jazz and Heritage Festival.

Along the way, Mooney recorded a few albums. His debut, *Comin' Your Way* on the Blind Pig label, drew rave reviews. From the beginning it was evident that Mooney was interested in playing workingman's blues. His distinct Delta/New Orleans–inspired guitar lines and coarse, hearty vocals were stamped on every song on the record. There were originals like "Ain't Gonna Get Drunk No More," "Take A Walk Around the Corner," "Shout Sister Shout," and "I'm Mad." There was Mooney's version of the old Charley Patton chestnut, "Pony Blues." There were songs that clearly demonstrated his New Orleans influence: "Hot Tub Mambo," "Move to Louisiana," and "Stop That Thing." It was an impressive debut.

The album *Testimony* was another strong effort. It featured John Vidacovich on drums and George Porter, Jr. (from the Meters), on bass. But again the focus of the record was Mooney's intense guitar work and disturbing vocals. The emotion he injected into each song turned what would have been an ordinary CD into something special. *Testimony* sizzled like hot grease on a burning grill with a mixture of blues classics, including "Lil' Queen of Spades," "In the Night," and "Levee Camp Moan." There were also seven Mooney originals. With *Testimony*, Mooney clearly indicated that he was more than a protégé of Son House and Professor Longhair; he possessed his own blues identity and was capable of delivering a modern blues record that burned with an unusual power.

In 1996 Mooney delivered the album *Against the Wall*, a blues *tour de force* that combined his chilling slide-guitar work with the Delta voice of someone who had witnessed too much. The opener, "Sacred Ground," set the tone for the entire product, a haunting reminder that to play the blues was to walk among ghosts that weren't always friendly. The jungle rhythms enhanced the mood that Mooney was trying to create. He took the listener to the dark side of the blues, the very heart of the Crossroads legend that had induced whisperings for over a hundred years and still does to this day. The stark boldness of *Against the Wall* placed Mooney in a totally different dimension; he was walking down the same dusty blues road as Son House, Charley Patton, Johnny Shines, and of course, Robert Johnson.

His eighth album, *Dealing with the Devil*, was a recording from a concert he performed in Bremen, Germany, in front of a small but very enthusiastic crowd who were enchanted by this authentic American bluesman. It contained such blues classics as Robert Johnson's "Travelin' Riverside Blues," Big Joe Williams's "Baby Please Don't Go," and Sleepy John Estes's "New Someday Baby." There were originals like the six-minute "It Don't Mean a Doggone Thing" and "Grinnin' in Your Face" that proved he could pen a modern blues tune with the best of them. While his playing and singing were exemplary, it was his live-and-die-for-his-art attitude that gave the album its unusual passion and fire.

*Gone to Hell*, his latest effort, demonstrates Mooney's genuine maturity and is the best example to date of his ability to meld his two biggest influences, the Delta grit of Son House and the stomping New Orleans rhythms of Professor Longhair. There are two House covers, "Dry Spell Blues" and "Down South Blues," as well as the Leroy Carr chestnut, "How Long Blues." From the very first track, "Gone to Hell," this album—easily one of Mooney's best—rocks like a New Orleans house party spiced with Delta fury. Mooney's songwriting, urgent vocals, and exceptional slide-guitar work all combine to deliver a great record from a major blues artist. The inclusion of Dr. John on four tracks ensures the album's credibility.

Mooney continues to bring his distinct brand of blues to live audiences as his tour card is always filled. In the spring and throughout the summer of 2000, he entertained crowds at festivals in the southern, western, and eastern parts of the United States, as well as Canada. His next studio album is eagerly anticipated.

John Mooney is a blues knight. He has, over his long career, fought gallantly for the blues cause. His battered electric and acoustic guitars serve as his lance and shield, his hard-boiled voice as his battle cry, and his blues enthusiasm as his badge of honor. He is a modern blues musician who has managed to keep the spirit of the old blues alive.

The two greatest influences on Mooney were Son House and Professor Longhair. In many ways Mooney is a modern day Son House. He travels the countryside captivating audiences with his intense slide work that is as chilling as waiting for Papa Legba at the crossroads on a moonless night. He has kept the spirit of the stark Delta blues alive not by imitating the great Son House, but by channeling all of the House trademarks into his own playing and adding his own individualism. Although Mooney has enjoyed a more prolific recording career than House, he still remains one of the best-kept secrets in the blues. The name of Son House, who never received the credit he deserved, has been elevated to a higher status through the music, vision, and power of John Mooney.

The enjoyable, party-like quality of Mooney's blues is a direct result of listening and acquiring Professor Longhair's infectious blues spirit. When the Professor was at the piano, a good time was guaranteed for all in attendance. Mooney has been able to create the same kind of magic for his audience, and in turn celebrates the wonderful blues talent that was Professor Longhair. The interplay of Mooney's voice, guitar work, and rhythm backing is the foundation of his sound. Arguably one of the best, if not the best, slide guitarists today, Mooney learned from one of the greats, Son House. Mooney manages to create different textures by juxtaposing his tough workingman voice with his eerie slide work. He creates a three-way conversation with the growl of his slide-guitar work, his hard-edged vocals, and a rhythm that drives everything along like a fine-tuned engine.

John Mooney—like other traditional country-blues guitarists—has developed his own unique style, a workingman's blues that is a throwback to the music of the 1920s and 1930s. He demonstrates the vigorous energy of a Big Joe Williams, strumming his guitar hard; his attack is a ferocious flow of energy that erupts from deep inside into a deluge of hot-spiked notes. He combines this volcanic energy with a sincerity for the music he loves so profoundly.

Mooney blends his power-packed guitar approach with a forceful voice that makes the listener sit up and take notice. Perhaps his voice is not as commanding as that of Muddy Waters, but it has the right amount of Delta grit. At the same time, there is a liquid subtlety and quality of tone in his voice that combines perfectly with his gritty Mississippi growl. There are essentially two sides to John Mooney. The human being offstage is a friendly, amiable character with a wide smile and a solid handshake. But when he performs he assumes a totally different persona: he is dynamic, energized, vibrant, a man possessed. It is as if the ghosts of the Mississippi Delta bluesmen were haunting his spirit when he is on stage.

There is originality to his music. Mooney draws from his many adventures, genuine blues spirit, and keen observations of everyday life to write his own material. His versions of various cover songs are more than just imitations of his blues heroes. Every reworked tune has the John Mooney touch; the arrangements flow from his creative genius and his big blues heart. No one can ever accuse him of being a simple interpreter of the music that runs so forcefully through his veins.

Although he has enjoyed a steady recording career, Mooney has never been able to sign on with a major record company for a long period of time. His work appears on a variety of labels. Despite the apparent disarray of his discography, Mooney has managed to instill each recording with excellent slide work, rough vocals and his essential blues touch. His recorded efforts are fun, accessible, and guaranteed to inflict blues fever on anyone who has not yet been stung by the music.

Although there are more commercially successful modern bluesmen than Mooney, he remains one of the brightest lights. Mooney has managed to carve a proud career for himself playing his deep acoustic and electric blues. With his sheer talent and dedication to the lessons learned from Son House and Professor Longhair, Mooney is one of the most entertaining blues performers on the circuit today. His workingman's blues are both a tribute to past blues legends and an important element of the modern acoustic blues movement.

## Discography

*Comin' Your Way*, Blind Pig BP-70779.
*Late Last Night*, Bullseye Blues BB-9505.
*Telephone Blues*, Powerhouse POW 4101.
*Telephone King*, Blind Pig BP-1383.
*Testimony*, Domino 001.
*Travelin' On*, Blue Rock'it 123.
*Against the Wall*, House of Blues 87006.
*Dealing with the Devil*, RFR 1015.
*Gone to Hell*, Blind Pig 5063.

# ALVIN YOUNGBLOOD HART

## *Thunder in His Hands*

In the time-honored tradition of the Mississippi Delta acoustic blues the guitar holds a prominent position. Starting with the earliest performers—Charley Patton, Eddie "Son" House, Skip James, Robert Johnson, and Big Joe Williams—blues singers were able to create magic with their primitive instruments. The genre remains vibrant today because new groups of acoustic players have emerged to continue the practice of the old masters, but with new contemporary power. One individual's passion has been fueled so much by the past blues legends that when he plays he sounds like he has thunder in his hands. His name is Alvin Youngblood Hart.

Alvin Youngblood Hart was born George E. Hart, in Oakland, California, on March 2, 1963. The nicknames "Alvin" and "Youngblood" would be acquired later on. His father, a traveling salesman, moved the family around and Hart was able to call many places home. During his teens the family resided in Chicago, which allowed Hart ample opportunity to hang out at the famous Maxwell Street scene. But the most cherished sojourns were at his grandmother's house in the hill country of northern Mississippi. Those visits connected Hart with the roots of primal country-blues and made a lasting impression on him. When he began to study the guitar in his early teens, Hart had already decided to make the Delta country-blues the foundation of his overall sound.

In 1986, he joined the Coast Guard and was stationed in Natchez, Mississippi. By this time he had already begun his lifelong dedication to the study of the acoustic blues form. He performed with local bands when his schedule allowed for it. Hart, a self-taught guitarist, was paying his dues and paving the way for a career as a country-blues revivalist long before the genre would regain the respect it had lost in the face of various pop genres.

In 1991, thanks to a chance meeting with Joe Louis Walker—an important West Coast blues singer—Hart was given his first big break, an appearance at the San Francisco Blues Festival. He made the most of his good fortune and delivered an impressive set that hinted at his vast talents. He built upon this opportunity to play other festivals and began to weave his magical blues spell.

After his duties in the Coast Guard had been fulfilled, Hart poured every ounce of his time and energy into building his musical career. One night, he opened up for the blues scholar, Taj Mahal, in Oakland. His passionate performance of acoustic blues classics and self-written material caught the attention of Bob Weir and David Murray, who became his managers. From that point on things happened fast for Hart, who had by now adopted the stage name Alvin Youngblood Hart. The name Alvin was taken from the lead character on the cartoon television show "Alvin and the Chipmunks." The name Youngblood was a nickname that he had been tagged with by the grizzled blues veterans he jammed with on the streets of Mississippi.

Hart's first release, *Big Mama's Door*, was a financial and critical success. The CD earned him three Living Blues Critics Poll Awards, for best blues album, best debut album, and best traditional album of the year. *Big Mama's Door*, an affectionate name that reminded him of the vacations to his grandmother's place, contained some brilliant original compositions. It also demonstrated Hart's ability to rework old classics like Charley Patton's "Pony Blues," Leadbelly's "When I Was a Cowboy (Western Plains)," Blind Willie McTell's "Hillbilly Willie's Blues," and an interesting interpretation of "Gallow's Pole" in a modern context. The album was dedicated to Brownie McGhee, who had just passed away. Hart, in support of Mickey Hart (no relation), played in thirty-one dates across the country—his first major tour—to promote *Big Mama's Door*.

His debut effort not only established Hart as one of the bright young blues stars, but it also earned him a W. C. Handy award as best new blues artist. It also served notice that the Delta blues style was not a forgotten art, but burned with an endless intensity. The torch had been passed to Hart and he carried it high with pride and dignity.

From that point on, Hart became a globetrotting bluesman, appearing at festivals throughout the United States and all over Europe. He shared the stage with a number of acts, including blues legends John Lee Hooker, Buddy Guy, Clarence "Gatemouth" Brown, and Taj Mahal. He also was a supporting act for Neil Young, Los Lobos, Richard Thompson, and the revitalized Allman Brothers. His taste for traveling took him to such faraway places as Australia and Norway.

It was with great confidence that Hart returned to the studio to begin work on his second release. This new CD, *Territory*, not only enhanced his already strong credentials, but also showed his maturity as an artist and a person. It included such classics as "Illinois Blues." While *Big Mama's Door* had been strongly rooted in the Delta acoustic blues, *Territory* was more adventurous. It included the obligatory roots and blues, "John Hardy" and "Mama Don't Allow," a western swing, "Tallacatcha," ska, and a Captain Beefheart composition, "Ice Rose." On *Territory* Hart could be heard fingerpicking his acoustic Stella six-string and his old reliable Fender Stratocaster.

*Start with the Soul*, his latest release, threatened to duplicate the success of his previous efforts. However, the CD has a different, hard-edged flavor. The opening song, "Fightin' Hard," is a genuine rocker and a tribute to the late Phil Lynott, leader of Thin Lizzy, one of the bands that had a significant influence on Hart. There is also a reworking of the Chuck Berry classic, "Back to Memphis." Berry, one of the greatest musicians of the past half-century, recorded his early material at Chess Records, home of the urban blues. Hart, like Berry, pushed the citified blues in a new direction by adding a rock-and-roll edge. Although Hart has traveled a long way musically from his *Big Mama's Door*, he has never forsaken his acoustic blues roots. His ability to forge defined styles into a contemporary mold is pure musical genius.

Hart, a breath of fresh air, continues to record and perform.

Alvin Youngblood Hart is a blues original. An artist who has never worried about copying the latest trends, he has blazed his own path by following his heart. As a result his music flows with the fire and magic of the old masters. Hart has been able to build on the rich foundation of acoustic country-blues and put his own stamp on it at the same time.

Hart, who stands well over six feet and sports dreadlocks that have taken on a life of their own, looks more like a reggae enthusiast then a dedicated acoustic blues devotee. But an intensity burns in his eyes and deep within his soul, and emerges through his music. He is equally comfortable on acoustic and electric guitar. This versatility allows him to explore the many avenues of his fervid imagination.

To understand Hart, or any artist for that matter, one must examine their musical influences; in Hart's case they are deep and wide. They include the Delta blues of Charley Patton, Skip James, Bukka White, and the regional flavor of Leadbelly, Brownie McGhee, and Blind Willie McTell. But there are other musical dimensions to the Hart sound. They include the gritty Chicago blues of Muddy Waters and Howlin' Wolf; the soul world of Wilson Pickett; the raunchy rock of Frank Zappa; the originality of Captain Beefheart; the western swing of cowboy Bob Willis; the commercialism of Eddie (Guitar Slim) Jones; the modern blues vision of Jimi Hendrix; and the uniqueness of Link Wray. He has taken bits and pieces of each performer mentioned above and woven everything together to create his own solid musical fabric.

But two of the musicians in Hart's blossoming career who had a direct effect on his playing and vision as an acoustic blues artist are Joe Louis Walker and Taj Mahal. It was Walker who gave Hart his first big break when the latter was in San Francisco. Walker not only let Hart open up for him on some concert dates, but he also kept a close eye on his development.

Hart is continuing not only the tradition of Robert Johnson and other Mississippi Delta singers, but also the work of modern acoustic blues singers like his mentor Taj Mahal. Mahal, who was one of the first country-blues revivalists back in the 1960s, is a prime inspiration for someone like Hart. Mahal played on Hart's first album, *Big Mama's Door*, and contributed some liner notes. Mahal boasts of Hart like a proud father talking about his beloved son.

Already in his short career Hart has covered much territory. He has played at numerous outdoor festivals throughout the continental United States, Eastern Europe, and other faraway places. He contributed two tracks ("Sway" and "Moonlight Mile") to the Rolling Stones tribute album, *Paint It Blue.* He has turned out a version of the classic Led Zeppelin song "Heartbreaker" for the Whole Lotta Love project, a tribute to the British blues-rock band's music. Hart has also worked with Chris Siebert, Jay Newland, and Bill MacBeath. He has appeared on numerous albums for other musicians, including Junior Wells' *Come on In This House*, Joe Louis Walker's *Silvertone Blues*, and *Hound Dog Taylor: A Tribute*.

Another interesting project that Hart is involved in is the Robert Johnson film that explores the late, great bluesman's controversial life. Hart, along with his mentor Joe Louis Walker, makes a cameo appearance. Hart's involvement in the film is his way of giving back to the world of blues that has given him so much. Before the screening of the film at the Mill Valley Film Festival, Hart demonstrated how strong an influence Johnson had on his playing, singing, and songwriting by appearing on stage and delighting the crowd with a strong set.

Almost as interesting is Hart's guitar collection. A self-confessed vintage-guitar nut, he owns quite a collection. It includes a National brass-bodied guitar, a wooden National with an aluminum resonator, a pre–World War II Regal 12-string, a Bay State 6-string from the 1920s, and a Harmony 12-string, from the 1960s. Interestingly, the guitars best suited to his ferocious attack are the Stellas from the 1920s and 1930s, the same kind used by Charley Patton, Son House, Skip James, Big Joe Williams and other Delta players. The Stellas, with their thin necks, are easier to strum, and Hart has an incredibly powerful strum motion. Not only does he collect guitars, Hart, along with his wife, restores them. The same pride that goes into writing and performing his music is evident in his reconstruction of guitars in order to honor the past through the present.

In concert, Hart is a human dynamo, delivering as much music with just his battered guitars and his stomping foot as most bands can muster with a full lineup. He is one of the better acoustic guitarists and has the ability to create a unique blues universe from one note, one idea, one chord.

An Alvin Youngblood Hart concert is more than just a couple of hours of music. It is a history lesson, a social lesson, and a life lesson. He plays music that stretches from the beginning of the Delta blues to the current tastes of modern blues and everything in between. He teaches his audience, without preaching to them, that music is the strongest force in uniting people of different races. Hart, through the versatility of his music, presents his personal vision of how people, communities, and the world should be one. He transcends the lines of culture and race to appeal to everyone, demonstrating that music is an international language that celebrates the spirit of all humanity.

There are many dimensions to a Hart concert. He jokes around with his audience, tells them stories, and interacts with them on a personal level. Like few other artists, Hart is able to connect with every single member in attendance on an individual basis. An Alvin Youngblood Hart concert can be a life-changing experience. And, if he were to play the same set list on two consecutive nights, the concerts would be completely different. Hart's performance is fueled by the response of the audience. A master performer, he is able to draw his audience into his private world and guide them through his beloved blues with an uncommon precision.

Hart, along with Corey Harris and Keb' Mo', is one of only a handful of African Americans interested in keeping the acoustic tradition alive. While other young African Americans consider the country-blues to be stale, and have forsaken their musical legacy in favor of rap and hip-hop, Hart carries the country-blues fever in his heart with all the pride of a Muddy Waters. The flame of the country-blues that was in danger of being extinguished just a few short years ago now burns with a fierceness that hasn't been seen in a very long time.

Hart uses the Delta acoustic base to explore different avenues. While other blues singers are content to stay within the confines of one particular blues style, Hart is busy fusing different musical ideas and textures together. He is like a scientist in a lab creating with his guitar and voice different musical potions guaranteed to captivate the listener.

Hart has been able to capture the spirit of the old country-blues. He is no mere interpreter, but an original and creative individual who has tapped into the same energy source as those before him. To hear him play is to listen to the ghosts of former blues legends. Perhaps the greatest test of his original material is to compare it to the traditional numbers that he performs.

Although he is an astonishing musician, music is only part of Hart's life. He is a family man, married with a child, and intent on creating a better world for his child to live in. The Harts live in Memphis, which gives Alvin ample opportunity to explore different musical scenes, including jazz, rumba, pop, and soul. He has a special affection for the rhythms of the New Orleans second-line marching bands.

Although his discography is small, Hart has a bright future ahead of him. He is a marvel to watch and listen to on stage. The future of the acoustic blues is bright and healthy as long as there are dedicated musicians like Hart to keep the interest alive. While he may never be fingered as the new trend by industry publications, no matter what stage he is performing on, or what guitar he is playing, Hart always leaves the impression that he has thunder in his hands.

## Discography

*Big Mama's Door*, Okeh 550.
*Territory*, Hannibal 1431.
*Start with the Soul*, Rykodisc 1449.

================

# COREY HARRIS

## *High Fever Blues*

Seventy years ago, Charley Patton gave the world his "Pony Blues," which quickly became a Delta classic. A few years later, Robert Johnson arrived on the scene and, though he left us too early, delivered a number of classics, including his "Crossroads Blues." Sixty years later, after the acoustic blues tradition had undergone rises and falls in popularity, a contemporary bluesman arrived on the scene and gave the world his "High Fever Blues." His name is Corey Harris.

Corey Harris was born on February 21, 1969, in Denver, Colorado. Although Denver is not known as a prime blues community, it didn't stop Harris from developing a keen interest for the genre. He picked up the guitar when he was twelve and immediately began to teach himself the music that inspired him—most notably from the records of R. L. Burnside, Big Jack Johnson, John Jackson, Son House, Mance Lipscomb, Charlie Patton, and Sam Lightnin' Hopkins. Although he was touched by several of the old blues masters, it was Lightnin' Hopkins who made the greatest impact on Harris.

But Harris did not limit his musical education to just the blues. He listened to country, soul, and rock, adopting the best parts to incorporate into his own developing style. Sometimes the music came easily; when it didn't he just practiced harder. He sang in church groups; he also played the trumpet and the trombone in his junior high school marching band. In high school, he joined a rock band.

While music was a definite career option, he attended Bates College in Maine, eventually earning a teaching degree. In 1991, he went to Cameroon in West Africa, where he developed a deep respect for the indigenous rhythms of the people's folk music. The intense, coded drumming was a new musical language to Harris, who immediately added it to his guitar vocabulary. The time he spent in West Africa had a great influence on Harris as a human being and as a musician.

He returned to Louisiana, where he taught French and English to rural students. At night and on weekends he pursued his musical ambitions in New Orleans, playing his guitar on street corners as many of the blues legends had done in another dimension of time. His days as a street performer taught him some valuable life lessons and further shaped his perspective as an aspiring musician. He graduated from street corners to coffeehouses to college campuses to clubs in a relative hurry.

By 1994, Harris had paid his dues and was ready to make records. He had developed an intense rhythmic and slide-guitar style acquired from the constant practice of his formative years, the eye-opening African experience, and the time spent performing in various venues. With a voice tailormade for the acoustic blues, Harris caught the attention of Bruce Iglauer, the president of Alligator Records, and was signed to a recording contract. Corey's first CD, *Between Midnight and Day*, was released in 1995 and ushered in a new era of acoustic blues. It contained a few original compositions, including the title song and "Roots Woman," and "Bound to Know Me." The remainder of the CD was made up of old Delta and Piedmont classics, but Harris was no mere imitator. He pumped new life into "Pony Blues," "Rattlesnakin' Daddy," "Going to Brownsville," "I Ain't Gonna Be Worried No More," "Feel Like Going Home," and "She Moves Me," playing them not the way the originators had played them, but the way he, Harris, heard and felt them. His ability to put a new spin on an old tune only enhanced his growing popularity.

It was a stunning debut that had critics raving and fans flocking to buy the album. But more importantly Harris gained the admiration and respect of his fellow musicians. Natalie Merchant, upon hearing Harris, immediately invited him to tour with her. Later, Harris appeared on stage with Buddy Guy, B. B. King, and the Dave Matthews Band. He played all over the United States, Europe and Japan. He had served notice that there was a new bluesman on the scene who had taken up the cause of the country-blues style. Corey Harris had arrived.

In the studio, Harris was a solo performer in the grand tradition of the Delta bluesmen, but was never alone when he recorded *Between Midnight and Day*. The spirits of Robert Johnson, Charley Patton, Muddy Waters, Son House, Big Joe Williams, Sleepy John Estes, Mississippi Fred McDowell, and other Delta bluesmen were present, as well. Harris was making the old blues legends proud with his determination and genuine heartfelt love of the music that sparked the original fire.

With *Fish Ain't Bitin'* Harris managed to strike gold a second time, despite changing some of the formula of the first album. He augmented his lone, crying guitar with a sassy New Orleans brass section on four tracks, creating an interesting and very different sound than in his first effort. His songwriting also took on more of a social aspect on this second album. The CD earned Harris respect throughout the blues community from his peers, from critics all over the country, and most importantly from the fans. Harris was rewarded when *Fish Ain't Bitin'* won the W. C. Handy award for best Acoustic Blues Album of the Year.

Harris followed up the success of his second album with classic solo appearances at festivals and clubs that enhanced his burgeoning reputation. His spectacular performances earned the attention of a variety of people, including Billy Bragg, who was putting together a tribute to Woody Guthrie. Harris played and sang on a few numbers; it was a rich, rewarding experience for the young blues musician.

Harris's third release, *Greens from the Garden,* saw him stretch out to include more than just traditional blues; it was a melting pot of Caribbean rhythms, mambos, blues, reggae, and ragtime. Although the album could have sounded disjointed, it didn't. Harris was able to blend all of the various "greens" from his musical garden to create a tasty repertoire of exciting songs.

Harris's fourth release, *Vu-Du Menz,* was another power-packed collection of Delta acoustic grit and New Orleans strict rhythms. He was accompanied by Henry Butler on the piano and the two evoked memories of other famous blues duos, including Scrapper Blackwell and Leroy Carr, Tampa Red and Georgia Tom, and Snooks Eaglin and Professor Longhair. However, Harris and Butler offered a thoroughly modern sound with the energy they burned into the fifteen tracks. The songs written individually or as partners included "King Cotton," "Let 'Em Roll," "Voodoo Man," "Sugar Daddy," and "Shake What Your Mama Gave You."

He is currently on tour promoting the new album to enthusiastic revues.

Corey Harris is a rising blues star. He has managed to remind the music world of the magic created by Charley Patton, Robert Johnson, Son House, Willie Brown, and all the old Delta masters. In a very short time he has created his own musical universe, which he shares with audiences through his recorded material and live performances. Harris brings the secrets of the blues to the international stage with a youthful enthusiasm, a powerful passion, and an unmatched style.

Corey Harris, along with Keb' Mo' and Alvin Youngblood Hart, is among the small coterie of the new breed of young African American blues performers who have embraced the traditional acoustic style that dates back to the turn of the century. They have made the country-blues fashionable again to young African Americans. But they are not a new wave or a trend; they are continuing the proud tradition to ensure it remains strong and true. Traditions are to be protected, savored, and enjoyed. Harris has helped to bring back to the acoustic blues tradition the respect that had been absent for some years.

He is a talented guitar player who plays more than note-infested solos. With his uncanny sense of polyrhythms, Harris has managed to develop an accessible, rhythmic shuffle. Like his contemporary, Kelly Joe Phelps, Harris sounds as if he were in a room full of musicians during his solo workouts. He has developed a ringing percussive beat on the guitar, augmented by the stomping of his right foot in perfect time.

The undeniable influences of Robert Johnson, Charley Patton, and Son House are part of the Harris sound, as are the second-line rhythms of the popular marching bands of New Orleans. Professor Longhair, with his rocking, party rhythms, was a special influence on Harris. Instead of the note-bending, heavy guitar style of the Kings—Freddie, Albert, and B. B.—Harris has opted for the traditional acoustic power of a Lightnin' Hopkins.

He is the complete musician, with the ability to play hard-strumming rhythm and accurate slide guitar. Unlike some of the Delta bluesmen, Harris is also able to sing convincingly the songs that he writes and those that he fashions into his own. He has been able to combine his developed talent with the special skill of making his songs sound as if they were recorded seventy years ago. Harris's unique approach has gone a long way to explaining why he has attained the level of popularity that he currently enjoys in such a short time.

Corey Harris is a spirited bluesman with an incredibly bright future ahead of him. He has made a major impact on the blues with his brash guitar style, hard-edged vocals and surprising songwriting abilities. He has established himself as well as any other young bluesman in the business. There is no telling what heights this very talented young man will scale with his high fever blues.

### Discography

*Between Midnight and Day*, Alligator AL 4837.
*Fish Ain't Bitin'*, Alligator AL 4850.
*Greens from the Garden*, Alligator AL 4864.
*Vu-Du Menz*, Alligator AL 4872.

# PART TWO

# Contemporary Chicago Blues

The Chicago blues style—the burning guitar licks, the hard rocking piano rhythms, the wailing harmonicas—of Muddy Waters, Tampa Red, Howlin' Wolf, Little Walter, Elmore James, Buddy Guy, Otis Rush, Sonny Boy Williamson II, continues to thrive at the hands of its current practitioners. The contemporary Chicago blues sound has retained the genuine houserocking feel and is renowned throughout the world.

The Chicago blues tradition can be divided into three separate eras. The first period of Chicago Blues (1934–1948) is fondly known as the Bluebird sound, because many of the artists of that era recorded for the Bluebird label.

The second period of Chicago Blues (1948–1965) is considered the golden age and is known as the Chess years; many of the mainstays of the blues scene in those years recorded for Chess Records. They played raw, amplified blues that included a driving rhythm section, setting the standard for all modern blues and its outgrowths to follow.

But by 1965 the golden era of the Chess years was over. The Chicago blues was taking on a different face as a new generation of musicians— many of whom had been born in the Windy City—took up the cause. The biggest difference was that the new bluebloods were white players, including Paul Butterfield, Mike Bloomfield, Elvin Bishop, and Mark Naftalin. They introduced the Chicago blues style to the rock-and-roll crowd, thus gaining the genre more exposure; and they helped create modern American electric blues.

The third period of Chicago Blues (1972–present) is known as the Alligator years, in honor of the now-famous label, created as a one-project adventure that blossomed to become the top record company in Chicago and one of the best in the world. The contemporary Chicago blues sound is a mixture of familiar elements laced with rock, jazz, pop, soul, and other styles. While the eight singers in this book represent the elite of the contemporary Chicago blues scene, other names of note on the scene include Maurice John Vaughan, Big Bill Morganfield, Donald

Kinsey, Fernando Jones, Bernard Allison, Ronnie Brooks, and Fenton Robinson.

Son Seals has been a mainstay on the Chicago blues scene for more than a quarter of a century. A dynamic live performer who never fails to give his audience their money's worth, he has raised the Chicago blues flag high above his head.

Paul Butterfield was one of the first white proponents of the Chicago blues and was an essential link between the genre and rock and roll. His contribution has spurred many future blues rockers.

Mike Bloomfield, who starred in Butterfield's band in the mid-sixties, established a reputation as one of the best electric guitarists in the annals of the blues. His fiery guitar solos continue to inspire musicians around the world.

Charlie Musselwhite took his cue from Little Walter, Big Walter Horton, James Cotton and Sonny Boy Williamson I, to become one of the best harmonica players on the Chicago blues scene.

Billy Branch is one of the new Chicago blues harmonica stylists whose expertise has enabled the genre to remain a dominant force in blues circles.

Lurrie Bell is just one of many Chicago-style blues singers who can claim authentic roots. His father, Carey Bell, is a noted Chicago bluesman who spent time in Muddy Waters' band.

Lil' Ed Williams is a slide guitarist in the mold of Elmore James who has continued to uphold the dangerous style of Chicago blues. The party is always on when Lil' Ed and his band are onstage.

Melvin Taylor is a perfect example of the urban blues singer. He has been able to meld the traditional Chicago blues sound with his own unique expressiveness into something new and exciting.

# Son Seals

## Bad-Axe Blues

The fiery Chicago blues guitar style—the legacy of Tampa Red, Earl Hooker, Muddy Waters, Jody Williams, Hubert Sumlin, Elmore James, Buddy Guy, Magic Sam, Otis Rush—remains vibrant and alive today as a new generation of riveting Chicago blues guitarists has taken up the cause. In the numerous clubs and streets of the south and west sides of the Windy City, the screaming blues guitars fill the air. While there are many noteworthy guitar slingers on the Chicago blues scene today, only one of them, with his scorching, bleeding guitar work, has earned the well-deserved moniker Bad Axe. His name is Son Seals.

Frank "Son" Seals was born August 13, 1942, in Osceola, Arkansas. Osceola, a strong blues community, provided Seals with an excellent blues education. Son's father Jim was the proprietor of the Dipsy Doodle, a regular tour stop for legendary blues artists Sonny Boy Williamson II, Albert King (who lived in Osceola), and Robert Nighthawk, among others. The elder Seals, a serious musician in his own right, played the piano, trombone, guitar and drums, and had appeared with the great Bessie Smith and Ma Rainey in the Rabbit Foot Minstrels in the 1920s. With the blues ringing in his ears, Seals's career choice was an easy one.

With his father as his mentor, Son's deep talent was nurtured like that of someone training to be a future athlete. By his late teens Seals was something special on the guitar. On the weekends he fronted his own band, playing all over the Arkansas area; during the week he jammed with the bands appearing in his father's club. Like most true bluesmen, Seals was born with a traveling bone; he left home when he was eighteen to play in Earl Hooker's band. Sometime later Seals joined Albert King's band before settling in Chicago.

Once in Chicago, Seals lost no time in immersing himself in the local blues scene. He jammed with Otis Rush, Buddy Guy, Koko Taylor, Junior Wells, James Cotton, Muddy Waters, and Hound Dog Taylor on a regular basis. He eventually landed a regular gig at the Expressway Lounge, one of Chicago's finest blues clubs.

While his credentials as a live performer had been established, his recording career moved along at a slower pace. In 1973, Seals, by then a well-seasoned blues performer with an impressive résumé, was finally given a chance to record by Alligator Records. Alligator, which has since become to the newer generation of Chicago blues singers what Chess Studios was to Chicago bluesmen in the 1950s, was a small, struggling label when Seals recorded the album *The Son Seals Blues Band*.

The ten tracks on the record burned with a fierce intensity that assured Son's immediate high ranking in Chicago's blues hierarchy. Songs such as "Mother-in-Law Blues," "Your Love Is Like a Cancer," "Going Home Tomorrow," and "Cotton Picking Blues" made people take notice. Seals was joined by Johnny "Big Mouse" Walker on keyboards, while Charles Caldwell and John Riley provided the rhythm section. The success of the record served notice that the Chicago blues was still burning with a pure passion.

But the album was important for another reason. Ever since the marriage between the blues and rock and roll in the middle of the 1960s, many of the most popular blues singers on the circuit were white. Traditional blues performers had turned their backs on the genre in favor of other styles. Like Melvin Taylor, Billy Branch, Lurrie Bell, and Ed Williams, Seals kept an African American presence on the Chicago blues scene. Overnight, it seemed that the blues torch was handed down to Seals to carry; he did not disappoint.

After the release of his first album he began to tour extensively throughout the country, playing in clubs, on college campuses, and at blues festivals. He brought his bad-axe blues to every town he visited and left the stage a heap of smoldering ashes. However, it was at this point that the marriage with rock and roll began to unravel and the blues suffered a sharp decline in popularity.

But Seals was not deterred by the lack of recognition blues artists were receiving. In 1976, he released *Midnight Son*, which generated an incredible amount of interest in his dynamic blues talent. Track by track, there was no denying the power of the blues grooves on this album. Seals wrote many of the songs, including the burning "I Believe," "No, No Baby," "Don't Fool with My Baby," "Telephone Angel," and "Don't Bother Me." His songwriting ability had attained a level of maturity rarely seen on someone's second release. Son's pace was relentless. His recording career was in full bloom and his name was on the lips of every concert promoter in the country. Son was the real thing and he delivered hard crunching blues that left his audience agape. His powerful hands and dexterous fingers worked the guitar fret board with an expert and crisp touch.

In an effort to combine the power of his live appearances and the winning touch of his studio releases, Seals recorded *Live and Burning* at the Wise Fool's Pub in his home base of Chicago. The Wise Fool's Pub was a favorite haunt of Seals and his rocking Chicago blues band. The album, available to the public in 1978, complemented his two previous efforts and provided blues fans with a delicious audio taste of his live show. The pure skill demonstrated on "I Can't Hold Out," "The Woman I Love," "Hot Sauce," and "Funky Bitch," made *Live and Burning* one of the best live blues albums of the decade. The album provided many highlights, including an appearance by A. C. Reed blowing his hot, sweaty sax sounds and adding a perfect counterpoint to Seals screaming guitar. The raw energy of the performance sparked a special rapport between Seals and the rabid crowd, and the magic was captured for eternity.

Son's touring schedule took him all over Europe and across North

America. He appeared with his band, consisting of Steve Plair on rhythm guitar, Snapper Mitchum on bass, Bert Robinson on drums, and Albert Gieanquinto on keyboards. All of them were veterans of the Chicago blues scene and complemented Son's musical gifts nicely. A true road band, they spent hours driving from one gig to another—often all night, stopping briefly for coffee and other on-the-road staples and necessities.

Son's next effort, *Chicago Fire*, only added to his blossoming reputation. This album featured Son experimenting with his gritty, straight Chicago blues sound by adding horns. Although Seals wrote nearly all of the songs on the album, a practice that he had established from his first album, he did sneak in the Steve Cropper and Wilson Pickett composition "I'm Not Tired," which demonstrated Son was very capable of handling outside material. With songs like "Buzzard Luck," "Landlord at My Door," "Watching Every Move You Make," and "Crying Time Again," it was easy to understand why he was regarded as one of the top contemporary blues singers at the beginning of the 1980s. While much ado was being made over punk rock bands and the emerging British techno-pop sound, the real deal was in Chicago and his name was Son Seals.

His next effort, *Bad Axe*, released in 1984, was a logical follow-up to his previous album. Although it did not include horn arrangements, *Bad Axe* was the work of a national blues act, giving the listener a solid forty-five minutes of exciting contemporary Chicago blues. He truly was the bad axe of the Chicago blues scene and proved it with his searing, controlled playing throughout the album. The songs "Just About to Lose Your Clown," "Cold Blood," "I Think You're Fooling Me," "Out of My Way," and "I Can Count on My Blues," all contained the Seals trademark—the excellent, heavy blues guitar, the gruff, controlled vocals, the poignant songwriting—that had made him one of the leading blues singers in the country and around the world.

After five successful albums with Alligator, Seals took a break from recording. Instead he concentrated on his touring, which regularly took him to Europe and across North America, where he headlined outdoor blues festivals, played cozy college campuses and demolished small, smoke-filled clubs with his thrashing, bad-axe Chicago blues. Although he did stay in the news based solely on his live appearances, much of the momentum he had built up with his string of strong recordings was lost.

In 1991, Son returned to Alligator Records and recorded *Living in the Danger Zone*. Despite the long layoff there seemed to be no ill effects. The bad axe was back with his knife-sharpened guitar sound, street-tough vocals, and workingman blues songs. Although the content included more outside material than his previous efforts, there were four Seals originals on the album: "Woman in Black," "Bad Axe," "My Life," and "My Time

Now." The addition of Red Groetzinger on tenor sax and flute, and Sugar Blue on harmonica, added new dimensions to Seals's hard-boiled blues.

Three years later, *Nothing but the Truth*, Son's seventh album on Alligator Records, was released. The self penned "Life Is Hard," "I'm Gonna Take It All Back," "Frank and Johnnie," and "Little Sally Walker," along with cover songs "Before the Bullets Fly" and "Tough as Nails," bore the mark of a veteran Chicago bluesman who knew how to deliver a first-class CD. The lineup for this album included John Randolph on rhythm guitar, the horns of Red Groetzinger and Dan Rabinovitz, Tony Zamagni on keyboards, Noel Neal on bass, bass player Johnny B. Gayden on a handful of songs, and David Russell on drums.

Son's next release, *Live—Spontaneous Combustion*, was recorded in the friendly atmosphere of a hometown crowd at Buddy Guy's Legends. Seals, always a dynamic live performer, delivered a power-packed show that stung the listener with a fierce attack of greasy Chicago blues. Son and his all-star Chicago band tore through the twelve songs—"Crying for My Baby," "No, No Baby," "Your Love Is Like a Cancer," "Landlord at My Door," and the Tampa Red classic "Don't Lie to Me" among them—with an unequaled ferocity.

After eight albums with Alligator, Seals moved over to the Telarc label to record his next album, *Lettin' Go*. Although he switched record companies, Seals didn't change his style. The fourteen tracks on the album burned with a funky blues groove that was pure Son Seals. He wrote or co-wrote ten of the songs on the record, including "Bad Blood," "Give the Devil His Due," "Doc's Blues," "Rockin' and a Rollin' Tonight," and a remake of "Funky Bitch." Al Kooper and the Vivino brothers, Jimmy on acoustic rhythm guitar and Jerry on tenor saxophone, supported Seals on the album. Seals cemented his position as one of the top acts on the Chicago blues scene with *Lettin' Go*.

Son Seals continues to record and perform.

Frank "Son" Seals is one of the best Chicago-style blues singers of the modern era. He has incorporated the teachings of past Chicago blues masters into his own playing and given them a modern twist. He is a veteran of the Chicago blues scene and one of the most important links between the first and second generations. He has taken the Chicago blues into a dimension of his own creation by fusing the past with the future.

Seals's arrival on the Chicago blues scene had impeccable timing. He broke through just a few short years after the sad passing of Magic Sam. In many respects, Seals carried on where Magic Sam left off. Seals shares with Buddy Guy and Otis Rush the distinction of being the main proponents of the second generation of fine Chicago blues guitarists.

Though he has not attained the same level of popularity as Buddy Guy, his recording career is much more impressive than that of Otis Rush.

Seals possesses all of the attributes that any Chicago blues guitarist needs to be successful. His playing style is an example of simplicity. There are no toys, no electric devices to mess up the signal. Son's guitar playing is a genuine and calculated release of pure emotion. He plays burning licks with a passion and an intensity that are pure sweetness. He is a talented guitar player capable of unleashing a blistering attack of notes that leaves the listener stunned. He can also rock with the best, hammering out hard riffs of pure blues fire. His combination of soul, speed, timing and intensity sets him apart from other guitar players on the Chicago blues scene.

When Son Seals sings, people immediately take notice. He does not soften the lyrics; he barks them out in true Chicago blues form. But he is more than a mere shouter; he is capable of stressing a certain word or syllable to achieve the effect he desires. A growling bluesman who always seems to be in a bad mood when he sings, Seals is able to tease the audience with his improvisations or raise the little hairs on the backs of their necks with his strong pipes.

He combines his gut-wrenching guitar ability with his intense vocals to create a wall of sound. A seasoned performer, Seals long ago mastered the ability to create a conversation between his gritty guitar work and his equally rough sandpaper vocals. Whether he combines the two or sets them up against each other, Seals creates a special world for the audience.

In the beginning, when he was paying his blues dues, Seals was a true road warrior, covering thousands of miles in order to carve out a name for himself in the cutthroat music business. In the past few years he has abandoned the guise of road warrior and remained in the Chicago area. His preference for home turf is unfortunate, because it denies others around the country the opportunity to witness his fiery stage act. He has, instead, become a weekend fixture in the blues clubs in the city with his group Son Seals and the Chicago Fire Blues Band.

Seals won the award as best Chicago artist in 1997, one that was long overdue. He has gained the respect of the blues community and his contemporaries. He has played with the cream of Chicago blues artists over his career, including Buddy Guy, Koko Taylor, Otis Rush, Junior Wells, Melvin Taylor, Lil' Ed Williams, Hubert Sumlin, Charlie Musselwhite, Billy Branch, Lurrie Bell, James Cotton, and Carey Bell. While the awards have not fallen down like rain around his feet, Seals is secure in the knowledge that he possesses a large fan base that is always eager to hear him play.

Although he has suffered personal problems in the past few years—

most notably a bout with diabetes that cost him part of his leg, and being shot in the jaw by his enraged wife—Seals remains a fierce blues power. Whatever his troubles may be, there is no denying Seals's place among the most respected Chicago blues singers of the modern era. He has managed to keep the flame lit and even turned up the burner a couple of notches with his own contributions. There is no doubt that Son Seals has entertained and will continue to entertain the entire world with his bad-axe blues.

## Discography

*The Son Seals Blues Band*, Alligator 4703.
*Midnight Son*, Alligator 4708.
*Live and Burning*, Alligator 4712.
*Chicago Fire*, Alligator 4720.
*Bad Axe*, Alligator 4738.
*Living in the Danger Zone*, Alligator 4798.
*Nothing but the Truth*, Alligator 4822.
*Live—Spontaneous Combustion* [live], Alligator 4846.
*Lettin' Go*, Telarc 83501.

# PAUL BUTTERFIELD

## *Hot Buttered Blues*

The white blues explosion of the 1960s featured many different styles. The big rave was the white acoustic blues; but there was a small coterie of enthusiastic white blues singers who were determined to bring the urban, amplified sound of the Chicago blues school to the attention of the world. One of the first and most important white blues players on the scene was the man who gave the world his hot buttered blues. His name was Paul Butterfield.

Paul Butterfield was born on December 17, 1942, in the Hyde Park section of Chicago, Illinois. The Windy City, the second largest metropolis in the United States at the time, was a melting pot of cultural influences; the various musical styles were thick and heavy. Initially,

Butterfield leaned towards classical and jazz music. His first instrument was the flute and he became proficient enough to study under the first chair flutist of the Chicago Symphony Orchestra.

Butterfield, who was also a promising athlete, suffered a severe knee injury that dashed any chances of an athletic scholarship at Brown University. From that point on, Butterfield focused on a musical career, and he began to absorb the music around him. He also started to teach himself the harmonica and the guitar.

There were few white enthusiasts of the urban, electrified blues in the late 1950s. The South Side of Chicago, predominately black, was one of the roughest parts of town and was shunned by most white people. But, after meeting Nick Gravenites, Butterfield started hanging outside the blues clubs with his new friend, listening to the sounds of Muddy Waters, Howlin' Wolf, Buddy Guy, and Sonny Boy Williamson II floating out into the street.

The bond between Gravenites and Butterfield went beyond the color of their skin; they were both blues aficionados. The two started to play together at various college campuses and their collaboration gave Butterfield his first taste of a group outfit. Their musical dream was temporarily put on hold when Butterfield enrolled in the University of Chicago, but his academic pursuits soon lost out to his passion for playing the blues.

At this point in his musical development Butterfield had received formal lessons on several different instruments; however, from this time on his education in the harmonica took on more importance. Butterfield practiced long hours by himself at the foot of Lake Michigan. He blew his harp against the roar of the sharp waves that crashed against the rocks; he played softly on calm days; he whistled eerie notes on lonely, foggy mornings when his only companion was a lost gull. It was around this time in his life that he met Elvin Bishop.

Bishop, who was from Oklahoma, had enrolled at the University of Chicago on a scholarship and had discovered the city's thriving blues community. A fluid guitarist, Bishop was enthralled at the many blues venues that were available to him. He and Butterfield quickly hit it off, sharing a love of booze and blues.

After playing parties in the neighborhood, Butterfield and Bishop would work up the nerve to go down to the clubs where the best blues players that Chicago had to offer were playing. This list included Buddy Guy, Junior Wells, Howlin' Wolf, Otis Rush, Magic Sam, and the great Muddy Waters. Although they were the only two white faces in a sea of black ones, they were accepted by the blues stars of the day. Waters and all were impressed with the pair's determination, ability, and dedication to learning urban, amplified Chicago blues. They were more than mere imitators; they were the real thing.

This initiation into the blues clubs of the South Side enabled Butterfield and Bishop to gain valuable lessons firsthand. Butterfield, Bishop, and other white blues players in Chicago had a decided advantage over their blues mates from across the Atlantic, because they were given the opportunity to talk shop, swap guitar licks, study closely, and sit in with the legends of Chicago blues. All of the British blues artists of the time—the Rolling Stones, the Yardbirds, the Animals, Fleetwood Mac—had to learn their blues by listening to records.

When Butterfield was offered the chance of becoming the house band at Big John's on the north side of the city, he knew it was time to form a group. He managed to lure Jerome Arnold (bass) and Sam Lay (drums) from Howlin' Wolf's band, adding his own masterful harmonica playing and Bishop's stinging blues guitar to this experienced rhythm section. Thus the first true, official version of the Paul Butterfield Band was born.

The racially mixed Butterfield band, a rarity on the Chicago blues circuit at the time, received rave reviews for its sincerity and ability. All four—Butterfield, Bishop, Arnold, and Lay—had cut their teeth on Chicago blues and boasted valued experience. When it came time to make an album, the group added Mike Bloomfield, as a second lead guitarist, and keyboard player Mark Naftalin.

The band's self-titled first album for Elektra Records was one of the strongest debuts in modern blues history. The record captured a white blues band in heat; all members shined with equal brilliance. That first album was a harbinger of the direction that blues music would take in the next five or six years.

The band's second album, *East-West*, was a testimony to the talent and musical tastes of the individual members of the group. It showed more of an eastern influence and included dazzling, extended solos. One of the reasons for this change of direction was that Billy Davenport had replaced Sam Lay on drums and had brought along his jazz and rock rhythms. The band used the blues as their musical foundation to explore different textures.

The Paul Butterfield Blues Band's time in the sun was short-lived. Just when they had appeared on the scene, it seemed, the group broke up. Mike Bloomfield left (*see* Mike Bloomfield: Blues All Around), and after the group's third album was recorded Mark Naftalin also left to pursue various projects.

That third album, *The Resurrection of Pigboy Crabshaw*, preserved some of the blues direction of the original group; but the addition of a horn section further clouded the once lucid blues sound that had earned the band such a devoted following.

Butterfield continued to record albums, but the magic had gone from the group. The last two albums that he released under the name the Paul Butterfield Blues Band, *In My Own Dream* and *Keep on Moving*, were desultory efforts that were far removed from the brilliance of the first three. In 1972, Butterfield dissolved the group and formed Better Days, with Billy Rich on bass, Chris Parker on drums, Ronnie Barron on piano, Amos Garrett on guitar, and Geoff Muldaur as a second vocalist.

The name Better Days proved to be an ironic one for his new band. After recording two albums—*Paul Butterfield's Better Days* and *It All Comes Back*—which failed to capture the imagination of the public, Butterfield disbanded the group.

Butterfield slipped into obscurity, emerging periodically to participate in special projects, including The Band's farewell concert, as well as the accompanying documentary, "The Last Waltz." He later toured with a couple of members of The Band. He also recorded a couple of comeback albums—*Put It in Your Ear* and *North/South*—both of which fizzled miserably.

Butterfield battled drug and alcohol addiction for the entire decade of the 1980s. On May 3, 1987, in Los Angeles, California, Paul Butterfield died of drug-related heart failure. He was 44 years old.

Paul Butterfield—along with the members of his band—was a blues pioneer. Always ahead of his time, Butterfield set the direction that the modern blues-rock movement would take throughout the 1960s and much of the 1970s. With his band he blazed the trail for many other rock-blues bands—the J. Geils Band, Foghat, The Fabulous Thunderbirds, The Doors, Canned Heat, Ten Years After, Led Zeppelin, the Jeff Beck Group, Savoy Brown—to follow. The influence of the Paul Butterfield Blues Band continues today, and can be heard in the styles of The Fabulous Thunderbirds, The Ford Blues Band, Roomful of Blues, Little Mike & the Tornadoes, Rod Piazza and the Mighty Flyers, and the Prime Movers, to name just a few.

Paul Butterfield was a blues original. A talented harmonica player, he was more interested in developing his own style than in imitating harp legends like Little Walter, Sonny Boy Williamson I, Shaky Horton, Junior Wells, and Sonny Boy Williamson II. When all is said and done, Butterfield deserves to be on the same list with all the great harmonica practitioners of the Chicago-style blues.

Butterfield is perhaps the greatest white blues harmonica player in the history of the genre. Only William Clarke, Kim Wilson, Rod Piazza, and Magic Dick (of the J. Geils Band) are in the same league. Although the harmonica never became as dominant an instrument in white blues as the guitar, there is no doubt that Butterfield influenced a generation of harp players. Certainly Kim Wilson of The Fabulous Thunderbirds and Magic Dick were two players to benefit from Butterfield's achievements.

Much of Butterfield's influence can be traced to his unique talent. Like most Chicago-style amplified harmonica players, Butterfield played the instrument like a horn—a trumpet. Although he sometimes used a chromatic harmonica, Butterfield mostly played the standard Hohner Marine Band in the standard cross-position. But Butterfield was a left-handed player who held the harp in his left hand, in the standard position with the low notes facing left. He tended to play single notes that punctuated the air with a stinging resonance. He preferred the attack of the single note to bursts of chords. His harp playing was always intense, understated, concise, and serious. His expert choice of notes has often been compared to the style of Big Walter Horton.

The Butterfield Blues Band alerted America to the intense music that was being created in their proper backyard. While most aspiring blues musicians had first acquired a taste for the music through cover versions by bands like the Rolling Stones, the Animals, the Yardbirds, and other British R&B groups, the Butterfield band was American. The Butterfield band introduced the modern Chicago blues to mainstream white audiences.

The Butterfield band not only blazed the trail for other white blues acts to follow, they also reflected some of the spotlight on their mentors. Butterfield was the first American musician to champion the blues that Muddy Waters and the rest of the Chicago-style bluesmen played in relative obscurity. The Butterfield Band broke down racial barriers and proved that the blues were not about skin color, but about emotion and power.

But the Butterfield band did more than influence aspiring blues artists. With its Eastern Indian ragas, its passion for the extended solo, and its use of horns, the band was at the root of many musical movements. It had a hand in the fusion of East-West music, the psychedelic acid rock that became so predominant in the late 1960s, and the jazzy, horn-driven sound of future bands like Blood, Sweat & Tears and Chicago Transit Authority.

In many ways Paul Butterfield never received the credit he deserved for his pioneering ways. He is a sometimes forgotten figure in blues history because of his relatively short time in the spotlight, but the importance of Butterfield's influence can not be overstated. Without a doubt Butterfield wrote an important chapter in the modern blues era with his hot buttered blues.

## Discography

*An Offer You Can't Refuse*, M.I.L. 6115.
*The Paul Butterfield Blues Band*, Elektra 7294-2
*East-West*, Elektra 7315-2.
*East-West Live*, Winner 447.
*The Resurrection of Pigboy Crabshaw*, Elektra 74015-2.
*In My Own Dream*, Elektra 74025.
*Keep on Moving*, Electra 74053.
*Sometimes I Feel Like Smilin'*, Elektra 75013.
*Paul Butterfield's Better Days*, Rhino R21Y 70877.
*It All Comes Back*, Bearsville R2-70878.
*Put It in Your Ear*, Bearsville 6960.
*North/South*, Bearsville 6995.

# MIKE BLOOMFIELD

## *Blues All Around*

There are basically four ways to learn how to play guitar. The first method is lessons, which can be tedious, but offer help in deciphering the guitar fret board and its intricate secrets. Another way to learn is self-study through guitar books. This is an acceptable approach, but also quite slow. Another way to learn is from previous recorded material, which is fine if one has an ear for music. For the blues guitar, the best way is the fourth way: in the bars, clubs, outdoor jams, rent parties, trains, band busses, backstage areas, and studios where bluesmen trade licks, tricks, and ideas. These unconventional classrooms have produced many of the greatest blues guitarists. One of the premier modern blues stylists grew up in Chicago with the blues all around him. His name was Mike Bloomfield.

Michael Bernard Bloomfield was born July 28, 1943, in Chicago, Illinois. A Jewish boy who had little interest in school or its extracurricular activities, he instead immersed himself in the glorious world of music, which became his sanctuary. He received his first guitar when he was thirteen and marveled at the secrets it held. Although he was first influenced by the rock and roll of Elvis Presley and counted Elvis's guitar player

Scotty Moore as one of his early guitar heroes, it wasn't long before Bloomfield discovered the music that was being played on Chicago's South Side.

By the time he was fifteen, Bloomfield was sneaking into blues clubs to hear the authentic Chicago blues, the amplified, raw-edged, thick sound practiced by Muddy Waters, Howlin' Wolf, and Elmore James. Bloomfield met Muddy Waters, as well as Little Walter, Otis Spann, Howlin' Wolf, Magic Sam, Buddy Guy, and Otis Rush. Initially an outcast in the blues community, he was slowly accepted by the veteran Chicago bluesmen. Not only was he a novelty, a lonely white face in a sea of African Americans, but he was also a solid blues guitarist who showed an eagerness to learn what the older musicians were willing to teach him. So instead of having to learn the blues through books, or records, Bloomfield received a first-hand education at the feet of Muddy Waters and other Chicago blues singers.

Eventually, Bloomfield found some kindred spirits in Paul Butterfield, Nick Gravenites, Charlie Musselwhite, and Elvin Bishop. They were white students of the blues who had rejected the music the record executives tried to shove down their throats in favor of the hard-driving, pulsating rhythms and riffs that opened the catacombs of their musical imaginations. But Bloomfield and the others were more than just enthusiastic fans; they wanted to take the music of Muddy Waters and the others to the international stage.

By his late teens Bloomfield was playing blues guitar in and around the clubs on the south and west sides of Chicago. He had blossomed into a riveting guitarist who played straight Chicago blues as well as any established star of the day. He learned from a large cast of blues artists, including Sleepy John Estes, Yank Rachell, Little Brother Montgomery, and Big Joe Williams. In addition to jamming on stage with all of his musical heroes, he also managed a folk/blues club in Chicago called the Fickle Pickle. As the director of the acts that appeared on stage, Bloomfield hired many of the blues singers who had a hard time getting a gig. He even traveled with some of his blues heroes, including Big Joe Williams.

He eventually signed a recording contract with CBS, but nothing much happened. At about this time he was approached to play on the sessions with the Paul Butterfield Blues Band; he promptly accepted the offer.

Butterfield and Bloomfield fit together like the lyrics and harmony of a good blues song. They inspired and challenged each other, trading riffs and musical ideas to generate an explosive, hot sound. The chemistry between the two was magical, and reminiscent of the affinity that Muddy Waters and Little Walter had enjoyed together. They were able to play extended jams together, improvising on one-note riffs as the music flowed like an electric charge between the harmonica player with the funky notes and the guitarist with the hot licks.

It was at this point that Bloomfield's stunning guitar ability caught the attention of a wider circle of people. He backed up Bob Dylan on the latter's classic album, *Highway 61 Revisited*. Bloomfield also appeared with Dylan at the Newport Folk Music Festival in 1965, the famous concert where Dylan shocked the folk-music diehards by plugging in. Although being in Dylan's band was a thrilling experience, Bloomfield declined an offer to be a permanent member because of his commitment to Butterfield. The release of their third album, a live set, was the apex of the Butterfield/Bloomfield musical partnership. Shortly afterward, Bloomfield left the band to begin his solo career.

After his departure from the Butterfield band, Bloomfield formed his own blues outfit, The Electric Flag, with Barry Goldberg on keyboards, Nick Gravenites on vocals, Harvey Brooks on bass, and a young Buddy Miles on drums. An immensely talented band, the group made its debut at the Monterey Pop Festival and boasted a bright future. They played Chicago blues with a horn section that entertained the crowd and laid the groundwork for such future bands as Blood, Sweat & Tears and Chicago Transit Authority. Despite the promise of the band, however, it all fell apart a year later.

After the demise of The Electric Flag, Bloomfield relocated to San Francisco to recoup. He found work writing scores for movies, producing other artists, and playing studio sessions. One of these sessions included a superstar jam with revered keyboard ace Al Kooper. Although the initial album, as well as a second produced from his association with Kooper, proved successful, Bloomfield grew disenchanted with the entire project and retreated into seclusion. The title of superstar guitarist, earned from his days in the Paul Butterfield Blues Band, haunted him. It generated an uncomfortable amount of pressure that alienated him even further from the thriving musical scene. His reluctance to be someone he wasn't, plus health problems brought on by the heavy use of drugs, only added to his mounting troubles.

Throughout the seventies he played occasional gigs in the San Francisco area backed by his band, which included Mark Naftalin and Nick Gravenites, among others. He was also active as a session guitarist and played on many studio albums. The solo projects that he released during this period were of an inferior quality that only further tarnished a fading image. A reunion of Electric Flag proved to be a fruitless venture.

In 1980, he enjoyed a successful tour of Italy and was joined by

Woody Harris and Maggie Edmonston on stage. Later that year, Bloomfield joined Bob Dylan in concert, bringing back memories of the good
old days long behind him. After years of drug abuse, increasing health
problems, and a lack of direction, Bloomfield was only a shell of the man
who had inspired a generation of guitarists with his burning style as a
member of the Paul Butterfield Blues Band.

On February 15, 1981, in San Francisco, Michael Bloomfield was
found dead in his car of a drug overdose. He was 36 years old.

Mike Bloomfield is one of the premier blues stylists of the modern
era. A guitarist possessed of an incredible amount of talent, he inspired
many modern blues players with his brilliant display of vibrato and sheer
intensity. Bloomfield was able to hold his own with such blues stalwarts
as Albert King, B. B. King, Albert Collins, Buddy Guy, Otis Rush, and
Magic Sam. In his heyday, Bloomfield was rightly called the greatest white
blues guitarist in the world. Along with his band mate Paul Butterfield,
he was responsible for bringing the Chicago-style blues of Muddy Waters,
Howlin' Wolf, Willie Dixon and others to the rock-and-roll stage. In the
era of emerging guitar heroes, Bloomfield ranked with the best.

Despite his acclaimed brilliance, Bloomfield never fulfilled his full
potential. After his departure from the Paul Butterfield Blues Band, his
career took a downward turn from which it—and he—never recovered.
He shunned the spotlight, and his preference for a low profile only defiled
his once well-earned accolades. An unresolved heavy drug dependency
that contributed to various health problems did him no favors.

A keen student of B. B. King, Bloomfield could play in any style,
including those of Muddy Waters, T-Bone Walker, Big Bill Broonzy, and
Freddie King. But he was more than just an imitator; like Magic Sam,
Buddy Guy, and Otis Rush, Bloomfield absorbed the lessons of the old
masters but added his own personal touch to create something new and
fresh. Whether he played his ringing Telecaster or his heavy Les Paul,
Bloomfield played a distinct brand of Chicago blues. His solos were masterpieces of fast flurries of notes and incredible string bending, coupled
with an uncanny sense of timing. His ability to create tension by holding notes for sustained periods of time and then releasing them just as it
seemed his guitar was about to erupt was one of his prime trademarks as
a guitarist. His precise attack, a calculated display of raw energy, and split-
second decisions made him the guitar player to copy.

Mike Bloomfield opened doors for many white blues guitarists who
followed him in the next three decades. Many of the blues rockers of the
sixties, including Johnny Winter, Jeff Beck, Jimmy Page, Duane Allman,
and Kim Simmons, owe a large debt to Mike Bloomfield. Ronnie Earl,
Tinsley Ellis, Duke Robillard, Jonny Lang, and Kenny Wayne Shepherd

all followed the path blazed by Bloomfield. With the exceptions of Stevie Ray Vaughan and Eric Clapton, Bloomfield must be considered the most important white blues guitar player of the past thirty-five years.

In addition to his solo recordings and the many group projects he was associated with, Bloomfield was a busy session man who left a trail of achievements scattered through the blues-rock world. A partial list of the artists he worked with includes Bob Dylan, Mitch Ryder, Janis Joplin, Chuck Berry, Beaver and Krause, Sleepy John Estes, Barry Goldberg, James Cotton, Woody Herman, and Brewer and Shipley. While inconsistency was something he struggled against his entire life, Bloomfield was capable of demonstrating moments of pure brilliance.

Bloomfield was one of the first blues singers to work on soundtracks for movies, once again creating opportunities for other blues artists. A short list of the soundtracks he worked on includes *Medium Cool*, *Medium Cool Sneakers*, *Steelyard Blues*, *The Trip*, *You Are What You Eat*, and additional scores for pornographic films. He also made several documentary and television appearances, including "Bongo Wolf's Revenge"; "Blues Summit in Chicago" with Muddy Waters, Nick Gravenites, and others (Festival); "Ready, Steady, Go" (BBC, 1966); and "The Paul Butterfield Blues Band at the Speakeasy." He also appeared with Al Kooper on *Don Kirshner's Rock Concert*, a 1970s TV show.

Whatever his shortcoming in the latter part of his career, there is no denying Bloomfield's place among the greatest blues guitarists of all time. He played from his heart and when he was on he was one of the best. He carried the torch that had been passed directly to him with pride and dignity. Although he might never have fulfilled his enormous potential, Bloomfield had a serious impact on blues history, and his place as one of the pioneers of the blues-rock wedding cannot be denied. For Bloomfield, there was never a doubt that the blues were all around.

## Discography

Michael Bloomfield Solo:

*American Hero*, Thunderbolt THBL-100.
*Analine*, Takoma B-1059.
*Between the Hard Place and the Ground*, Takoma 7070.
*Bloomfield—A Retrospective*, Columbia C2-37578.
*Count Talent and the Originals*, Clouds 8005.
*Cruisin' for a Bruisin'*, Takoma 7091.
*If You Love These Blues, Play 'Em as You Please*, Guitar Player 3002.
*I'm with You Always*, Demon Fiend-92.

*It's Not Killing Me*, Columbia KH-30395.
*Live Adventures* (Masters 20784), bootleg, Dutch release of *American Hero*.
*Live in Italy*, Mama Barley 001.
*Living in the East Lone*, Waterhouse 11.
*Michael Bloomfield*, Takoma 7063.

With the Paul Butterfield Blues Band:

*East-West*, Elektra EKS-7315.
*The Paul Butterfield Blues Band*, Elektra K-294.
*Golden Butter*, Elektra 2005.

With The Electric Flag:

*A Long Time Comin'*, Columbia CS-9597.
*The Band Played On*, Atlantic SD-18112.
*The Trip*, Sidewalk/Tower ST 5908.

Mike Bloomfield/Al Kooper:

*The Live Adventures of Mike Bloomfield and Al Kooper*, Columbia KGB-6.
*Super Session*, Columbia CS-9701.

# CHARLIE MUSSELWHITE

## *Ace of Harps*

The harmonica is a fascinating instrument. It is light, requires very little maintenance, is the hit at a party, fits snugly in one's pocket, and is a traveling bluesman's best friend. From this tiny instrument, which looks like a hunk of metal that has been attacked by a mad person with a drill, issues most wonderful music; it can be sweet and soft or harsh and heavy. It can create moods of lonely, rainy autumn days, of cold, melancholy winter times, of sunny, happy spring joy, of endless, lazy summer dreams. Some of the greatest musicians in blues history have made the harmonica their instrument of choice. On this distinguished list is the ace of harps. His name is Charlie Musselwhite.

Charlie Musselwhite was born on January 31, 1944, in Kosciusko, Mississippi, but grew up in Memphis where he first heard the music that would be an integral part of his life. A true blues spirit right from the beginning, Musselwhite, of Choctaw ancestry, investigated the source of this blues music that so intrigued him and in the process met Will Shade and Furry Lewis, two of the biggest names in Memphis blues at the time. It wasn't long before Musselwhite was learning the secrets of the blues directly from Lewis and Shade. By his mid-teens he was adept at both the guitar and the harmonica.

Like other southern bluesmen before him, Musselwhite was convinced that Chicago was a mythical town of golden opportunities for aspiring blues singers, and he made his way there after high school graduation. At first he played street corners for spare change before getting his foot into the competitive club scene of the South Side. He eventually met and jammed with the leading harmonica players in the Windy City at the time, including Little Walter, Big Walter Horton, Carey Bell, and Sonny Boy Williamson II. Although he sat in on a few recording sessions with Horton and with John Hammond, Jr., Musselwhite wasn't able to record his own songs until 1966 for the Vanguard label. The seminal *Stand Back! Here Comes Charlie Musselwhite's Southside Blues Band* was a thrilling album and successfully ushered him into the blues fold.

Part of the charm of *Stand Back! Here Comes Charlie Musselwhite's Southside Blues Band* was the rough-edged work of Musselwhite, then a twenty-two-year-old recording novice, who belted out the songs in a harsh, almost strained voice. His harmonica playing was a different story, however, especially on songs like "Baby Will You Please Help Me," "Cha Cha Blues," "My Baby," and "Christo Redemptor," which last would become a Musselwhite concert staple and be recorded more than once during his career. Harvey Mandel's guitar work challenged Musselwhite's daring harmonica style.

He released three more albums on the Vanguard label, *Stone Blues*, *Charlie Musselwhite*, and *Tennessee Woman*. His next two albums, *Louisiana Fog* and *Blues from Chicago*, appeared on Cherry Red Records. Besides his recordings, Musselwhite was an in-demand performer and appeared at many of the rock venues of the time, including the Fillmore West and the Fillmore East, the Kinetic Circus in Chicago, and major rock festivals throughout the country. In the late 1960s, feeling the need for a change, Musselwhite moved to San Francisco.

In San Francisco, Musselwhite found steady work and carved out a name for himself in the city's club circuit. His Memphis and Chicago-style blues harmonica was very popular in the late 1960s and the early 1970s. He cut two albums for Arhoolie, *Takin' My Time* and *Memphis Charlie*. For the remainder of the 1970s Musselwhite could be found in one of San Francisco's many fine clubs, in the recording studio, or touring the world delivering his hypnotic brand of harp blues.

During the 1980s Musselwhite continued to record and perform on a regular basis, though his popularity had waned from its height of the late 1960s and early 1970s. Despite the blues boom of the 1980s, he was unable to revive his sagging career. He was fighting the battle of the bottle and, unfortunately for blues fans, he was losing. He recorded half a dozen forgotten albums on a host of labels. His concert performances became erratic.

However, in the midst of one of the slackest periods in his extensive career, he did release *Memphis Tennessee* in 1984. The album, his recording highlight of the decade, featured bass player Jack Myer and pianist Skip Rose as his back-up band. One of the hardest rocking editions of all of Musselwhite's bands, the trio created genuine excitement with a dynamic cover of Muddy Waters' "Trouble No More." A definitive version of "Arkansas Boogie" was also one of the stronger tracks on the album, as was the slow, mournful "Willow Weep for Me."

The year 1990 ushered in a new decade, a new attitude, a renewed blues spirit, and a new recording contract for Musselwhite, with Alligator Records. *Ace of Harps* was a hard-driving collection of urban blues songs. His band, consisting of Thomas Hill on drums, Andrew "Jr. Boy" Jones on guitar, Artis Joyce on bass, and Jimmy Pugh on keyboards, backed him up. Musselwhite blew some of the fiercest harp of his career on this album and also took on the unusual role of solo guitarist on the track "My Road Lies in Darkness." The album revived Musselwhite's career and he began a steady climb back to the respectability that had slipped away from him during the previous decade.

Musselwhite followed up his smash hit *Ace of Harps* a year later with the album *Signature*, which reinforced the fact that Musselwhite was back. A solid album of urban blues, *Signature* featured Musselwhite's furious and energetic blues harp as well his backing band, a horn section, and a special guest appearance by the boogie master John Lee Hooker. On this jazzy, funky album, Musselwhite was at his sharpest and answered all of his detractors the best way possible—with his harp playing. It was a riveting performance that earned him a Grammy nomination.

The rebound that had begun with *Ace of Harps* accelerated further with *In My Time*, Musselwhite's third album for Alligator Records. *In My Time* demonstrated the many sides of Charlie Musselwhite the artist. On a couple of tracks he played guitar, a pure compliment to the Delta tradition. He included two gospel numbers on the album, with help from the group Blind Boys of Alabama. Musselwhite also offered three jazz selections that were driven by his horn-like harmonica wizardry. But it was the blues songs "If I Should Have Bad Luck" and "Leaving Blues" that held the album together.

Despite his success on Alligator, Musselwhite moved elsewhere to record four more albums in the 1990s, all featuring his distinctive harp playing, a wealth of solid material, and the dedication of a blues professional. His album *Continental Drifter* carried on the success he enjoyed at the beginning of the 1990s. A solid effort with Musselwhite at his leanest and meanest, the eleven tracks burn with his typical frenetic energy, especially on cuts like "Edge of Mystery," "Voodoo Garden," "Blues up the River," and "No." It was a strong collection characterized by powerful performances on each cut.

Today Charlie Musselwhite tours regularly and is a fixture on the blues festival circuit. Wherever he goes, Musselwhite is well received and always delivers smashing, dynamic harmonica blues that leave the audience wanting more.

Charlie Musselwhite is a blues survivor. He broke in during the blues-rock era and, along with Paul Butterfield, generated the interest in Chicago blues. His career continued to advance despite suffering a dip in popularity in the late 1970s and much of the 1980s. He has emerged in the last ten years to reclaim his crown. Musselwhite is a constant in the blues circuit, a steady performer who has had an interesting career.

He is one of the best modern harmonica players, with few peers. He was able to apply the lessons of the old masters to his contemporary musical ideas to create an interesting synthesis of sound. The Musselwhite delivery—sharp, beefy notes that create infinite waves like a pebble dropped in a pool—has been his badge of honor since the beginning. His sound is rooted deeply in the Memphis/Chicago-style blues, but Musselwhite also infuses his playing with large doses of hard rock and funky soul. A creator of moods, he is able to take someone on a fantastic journey through blues history from the appearance of the Memphis jug bands to the harmonica sound of today.

Musselwhite can, with just a handful of notes, introduce the basic rhythm and harmony of a song. His style is sparse, almost eerie, yet he can also blow a furious run of searing notes that melts the outside world. He plays his harmonica like a horn, creating a driving rhythm, but is capable of attention-getting solos. His wide range of abilities on the instrument makes him one of the best.

Over his long career he has played with many of the greatest blues artists. He has an incredible résumé, most notably as a superb bandleader. Under his direction such greats as Harvey Mandel, Freddie Roulette, Luther Tucker, Louis Myers, Robben Ford, Fenton Robinson, and Junior

Watson have made immense contributions to the blues world. Many of these musicians have matured enough under his guidance to go on and form their own eponymous blues outfits. Musselwhite, a relaxed individual with an easygoing character, has always allowed the members of his band to explore the entire range of their abilities.

Charlie Musselwhite is a blues drifter, like a Louisiana fog that floats in, stays a while, and then moves on. He has strung together a career that has lasted more than thirty-five years, one that has seen its fair share of both good and hard times. But no matter how low his popularity dipped, he was always present. On the twenty-fifth album of his career, *Continental Drifter*, the closing song is "Please Remember Me." There is no doubt that, with the wealth of music and fond memories that Musselwhite has presented to the world in his many years as a standout musician, the ace of harps will never be forgotten.

## Discography

*Stand Back! Here Comes Charlie Musselwhite's Southside Blues Band*, Vanguard 79732.
*Blues from Chicago*, Cherry Red 5104.
*Stone Blues*, Vanguard 79087.
*Louisiana Fog*, Cherry Red 5102.
*Chicago Blues Star*, Blue Thumb 8809.
*Tennessee Woman*, Vanguard 6528.
*Memphis Charlie*, Arhoolie 303.
*Mylon*, Cotillion 9026.
*Takin' My Time*, Arhoolie 1056.
*Goin' Back Down South*, Arhoolie 1074.
*Leave the Blues to Us*, Capitol 11450.
*Light of Your Shadow*, Sussex 7001.
*Times Gettin' Tougher Than Tough*, Crystal Clear 005.
*Harmonica According to Charlie*, Kicking Mule 305.
*Curtain Call*, Red Lightnin' 044.
*Memphis Tennessee*, Mobile Fidelity, MFCD-775.
*Tell Me Where All the Good Times Have Gone?*, Blue'it 103.
*Mellow-Dee*, Crosscut 11013.
*Ace of Harps*, Alligator AL 4781.
*Signature*, Alligator AL 4801.
*In My Time*, Alligator AL 4818.
*Takin' Care of Business*, Kent 8001.
*Rough News*, Virgin 42856.
*Curtain Call Cocktails*, West Side 819.

*Continental Drifter*, Virgin 47130B.
*Takin' My Time Going Back Down South*, Arhoolie 203.

---

# BILLY BRANCH

## *Harp Attack*

The harmonica was considered a minor instrument at the turn of the century; then practitioners like John Lee "Sonny Boy" Williamson I, Sonny Boy Williamson II, and Little Walter showed the world the beautiful textured harmonies that the instrument could produce. Undoubtedly it was in Chicago that the harmonica became a dominant blues instrument. One of the best second-generation Chicago harp players, who has carried on the tradition established by the aforementioned harmonica geniuses, has given the world a harp attack. His name is Billy Branch.

Billy Branch was born on October 3, 1951, in Chicago, Illinois, but grew up in Los Angeles. It was in the Golden State that he first picked up the harmonica at the age of ten. He immediately began to make up simple tunes and carried his new best friend around with him everywhere he went. By his middle teens the harmonica was no longer a novelty attraction; it had become part of his identity. He dreamed of someday playing before large audiences.

At the age of eighteen Branch returned to the Windy City and enrolled in the University of Chicago. He graduated four years later with a degree in political science, but his heart did not belong to the world of academia; by then, he was a full-fledged musician. During his years as a student, Branch had been struck hard by blues fever and it had a permanent impact on the rest of his life. He immersed himself in the local blues scene, frequenting Rosa's, Queen Bee's, and Theresa's Lounge—all mainstays of the Chicago blues club circuit. He studied and learned much from the masters who ruled the Chicago harmonica scene of the time, including Big Walter Horton, James Cotton, Junior Wells, and Carey Bell.

Branch paid his dues for the next couple of years and in 1975 his hard work finally began to pay off. After winning a harmonica battle at a local club, he gained the attention of record executives from Barrelhouse Records and cut his first songs. While nothing positive came from this first recording venture, all was not lost; he had also caught the eye of blues bass legend Willie Dixon. Branch secured a steady gig in Dixon's band for the next six years.

Although he was busy touring with Dixon's Chicago All-Stars, Branch found time to form the Sons of Blues. The band consisted of Branch, guitarist Lurrie Bell (the son of Carey Bell), bass player Freddie Dixon (son of Willie Dixon), and Garland Whiteside. Perhaps it was the impressive pedigree that the group boasted, or maybe it was the intensity of four young, talented, hungry musicians; but the band cooked from the minute it came together. They toured Europe and turned the Berlin Jazz Festival on its ear in 1981.

Upon their return home they were invited to participate in Alligator's *Living Chicago Blues, Volume 3*, sessions, which showcased some of the new blues singers destined to make a mark on the music. The Sons of Blues, A. C. Reed, Lovie Lee, and Lacy Gibson were all featured on the album. Although it was a big break for the Sons of Blues, it was an even bigger break for Branch. He was soon hired as a session player, and has appeared on over sixty albums for the Alligator label. A partial list of the Alligator artists whose albums he has played on includes Koko Taylor, Johnny Winter, Willie Dixon, Son Seals, Lou Rawls, Kinsey Report, Lonnie Brooks, Oscar Brown, Jr., and Valerie Wellington.

Branch also found time to make a few solo recordings, such as the vibrant *The Blues Keep Following Me Around*. Included on the CD was a rousing rendition of Sonny Boy Williamson II's "Bring It on Home," a good-time version of Willie Dixon's "Flamin' Mamie," and the song "Evil," cut in the style of Howlin' Wolf as a tribute to the growling legend. The last song on the CD was taken from his Sons of Blues projects. The tune, "Where's My Money?," was a perfect example of the dynamic tension between Branch's expert harmonica playing and Carl Weathersby's (who joined the group in 1984) burning guitar work.

One of Branch's more interesting projects was *Harp Attack!* in 1990, with Carey Bell, James Cotton, and Junior Wells. All three were long-time mentors of Branch so it was a thrill for him to record with them; it also served to enhance his burgeoning reputation. All four harpists shared the spotlight, with Branch taking lead vocals on Little Walter's "Who" and "New Kid on the Block." An incredible harp supersession, it was guaranteed to make harmonica fans froth at the mouth with excitement. The CD, which also included the instrumental proficiency of Lucky Peterson, won a W. C. Handy award.

Branch continues to record and perform.

Billy Branch is a one of the leading harmonica players of the modern blues era. His slick Chicago-style licks have put him in the forefront of the blues scene. Branch's popularity in the blues community is a result of his major contributions as a musician and as a human being. He has been involved in several positive projects; for example, he appeared on *Heavy Harp*, a benefit album for the Sonny Boy Williamson II Blues Museum.

Although Branch has been strongly influenced by the mainstays of the Chicago blues scene, he has developed his own unique sound. A capable soloist, Branch is not interested in overwhelming his audience with a flurry of cascading notes that assault one's senses. Instead, he seduces the listener with a delicate touch, letting each note melt in the air. Although he will occasionally fire up the crowd with lightning-fast runs, he is more concerned with the emotional depth his music has to offer.

Branch has recorded with several legends during his long, illustrious career, including Muddy Waters, Big Walter Horton, Son Seals, Lonnie Brooks, Koko Taylor, Johnny Winter, and Albert King. Since Waters, Horton, Dixon, and King have passed on, it must have been a special thrill to play with those blues stars. The treasure that is the Chicago blues has been passed on to young men like Branch. To his great credit, Branch has been a proud torch bearer, and the memory of all the great Chicago bluesmen he played with burns fiercely in his heart.

Branch has also appeared at the Chicago Blues Festival many times alongside contemporary Chicago-style blues singers like Son Seals, Melvin Taylor, Lil' Ed Williams and the Imperials, Charlie Musselwhite, and Joanna Connor. In a list of today's Who's Who of Chicago blues artists, Billy Branch is at the forefront, and is one of the better-known blues singers on the circuit.

Perhaps Branch's biggest contribution to the blues, beyond his studio and live work, is his creation of and involvement in the Blues in the Schools program. This requires Branch to visit area middle schools and show the kids from tough backgrounds that there is a better choice in life than gangs, drugs, and violence. The way is paved with music (the blues) and a more positive, nonviolent means of self-expression. The children receive an education on the history of the blues and different blues styles, plus a chance to write, sing, and perform the blues. A graduation ceremony at the end of the workshops showcases how well the students have absorbed the blues. The program, which was initially the brainchild of Branch and his mates in Sons of the Blues, has spread to other parts of the United States, including South Carolina and Wisconsin.

Branch has gained considerable attention as one of the best harmonica blues players of the modern era. Some of his awards include the Most Outstanding Blues Harp Player in 1982 and 1983 by the Living Blues Awards. He won W. C. Handy awards for "Keeping the Blues Alive in Education" in 1990 and 1993. He won an Emmy Award for "Precious

Memories," a tribute to 47th Street. Perhaps his most satisfying award has been his role in the Blues in the Schools Project. Branch is one bluesman who gives back to his community.

In an effort to expand his popularity—and spread his message—Branch has turned to different media outlets. He has made several television and film appearances that include a couple of stints on the *Today Show* in 1994 and 1995. In 1993, he was a guest on *The Bryant Gumbel Show*. In 1992, he spoke with Charles Kuralt on the *Sunday Morning* show. His film career includes three full-length productions: *Next of Kin*, *Adventures in Babysitting*, and the TV feature film *Precious Memories—Tribute to 47th Street*. Branch has also been linked to several blues documentaries. It is rare for a blues singer to gain such wide coverage in the television and film industry. Branch has taken advantage of every opportunity presented to him and opened doors for himself and his music with his good sense of humor, alertness, huge heart, and musical ability.

Branch is a true globetrotter. In 1992, he took his funky harmonica sounds to China as part of the George Gruntz Big Jazz Band Tour. In 1994, he toured Japan as part of the American Cultural Festival. He has also been on many tours sponsored by the United States Information Agency. The exotic locations to which he has taken his infectious harmonica blues include Nicaragua, Bolivia, Haiti, Chile, Spain, Italy, Belgium and Barbados. Many of these countries are rarely treated to a live appearance by a true American bluesman. He has also toured Europe a number of times, building a large fan base across the Atlantic.

Billy Branch is one of the leading lights of the modern Chicago-style blues. Along with Lurrie Bell, Son Seals, Melvin Taylor, and Ed Williams, Branch has kept an African American presence in the Chicago blues. He has inherited the blues throne once occupied by Little Walter, Big Walter Horton, and Sonny Boy Williamson II. It is Branch who will lead the Chicago harmonica school into the next decade with his harp attack.

## Discography

*Where's My Money?* Red Beans RB 004.
*Mississippi Flashback*, GBW.
*The Blues Keep Following Me Around*, Verve 31452768.
*Satisfy Me*, House of Blues 1459.
*Live '82*, Evidence 26049.
*Romancing the Blue Stone*, Black and Blue

# LURRIE BELL

## *Living Chicago Blues*

The Chicago blues, steeped in tradition and history as it is, remains a viable form to this day. The influx of a new generation of blues singers ensures that the genre enjoys success with a contemporary audience. Some of the best Chicago blues artists today can claim impressive pedigrees. One of the leading voices in contemporary Chicago blues is someone who has been living the Chicago blues ever since he was a little boy. His name is Lurrie Bell.

Lurrie Bell was born on December 13, 1958, in Chicago, Illinois, and from the very beginning he was surrounded by the blues. His impressive family background included his father, Carey Bell, a noted Chicago harmonica player who had occupied the chair in Muddy Waters's band; his cousin, Eddie Clearwater; and his grandfather, Lovie Lee. He picked up the guitar at an early age and appeared on stage with his father's band when he was eight, delighting the crowd with his promise and ability.

The living room of the Bell household was a central station for Chicago blues singers and Lurrie knew all of the musicians on a first-name basis. Many of them—Big Walter Horton, Pinetop Perkins, and Eddie Taylor, for example—encouraged his ambition to become a noted blues artist. Lurrie made his recording debut on Edward C. Campell's *King of the Jungle* album while still in his teens.

At the age of fifteen Lurrie, already an experienced bluesman, became the guitar player in Koko Taylor's band. He toured with Taylor throughout the United States and Europe, carving out a name for himself. He joined the Sons of Blues in the early 1980s, which also featured Billy Branch and Freddie Dixon (son of bass legend Willie Dixon). A rather loose outfit that toured sporadically, they also recorded songs for two Alligator Records anthologies, *Living Chicago Blues, Vol. 3*, and *The New Youngbloods*.

Bell spent most of the 1980s as a hired gun. He recorded the album *Son of a Gun* with his father. He toured with Koko Taylor. He appeared at numerous blues festivals throughout the country and the world, playing his crisp Chicago blues lines with solid precision. Although he seemed to be on top of the world, however, all was not well with Bell.

He suffered from health problems that limited his ability and desire to play music. An extremely talented guitarist with the ability to create pure blues magic, Bell would often disappear for days, leaving no clue to his whereabouts. He would resurface unannounced, ready to entertain with his smoking guitar. This instability hurt the advancement of his career.

In 1990, Bell released his long-awaited debut album, *Everybody Wants to Win*, on the JSP label. It was a strong record that demonstrated his unique capabilities as both a singer and a guitar player. After a bleak period, Bell recorded his follow-up album, *Mercurial Son*, for Delmark Records. It was an engaging effort that offered a variety of musical forms, which gave the record a charming or a fragmented quality, depending on one's point of view. On this record Bell expanded the parameters of his Chicago-style blues to include rock and roll, rhythm and blues, funky boogie, and ballads. He even sang one song a cappella.

For the first time in his career, Bell seemed to enjoy a period of consistency. He followed *Mercurial Son* with *700 Blues*. His third solo album was more of a traditional blues recording, with Bell replicating the delicate touch of B. B. King. Bell's solos clearly demonstrated that he was a first-rate talent who could hold his own in any cutting contest on any stage in the world. His powerful guitar work breathed life into the title cut "700 Blues" as well as "I've Got Papers on You Baby," "Honey Bee," "You Got Me Dizzy," and "I'll Be Your 44." His playing throughout the record was energized and focused.

His fourth solo album, *Kiss of Sweet Blues*, was also a commercial and critical success. It featured the clean, emotional fingerpicking guitar work that Bell had become known for in the recording studio as well as in live appearances. Some of the highlights of the CD included "Wicked Hearted Woman," "Bad Dog," and two distinct guitar tracks, "Lurrie's Boogie Guitar" and "Lurrie's Funky Groove Thang." With this release Bell established himself as a dynamic Chicago-style blues guitarist who delivered music that burned with a fiery intensity reminiscent of Otis Rush.

His fifth solo endeavor, *The Blues Had a Baby*, strengthened his reputation as one of the most powerful blues singers on the circuit. The material on this CD consisted of more traditional material such as "Who Do You Love?," "Rollin' and Tumblin'," "Mean Black Spider," "Mean Old Frisco," and "Five Long Years." It was a rocking album that showed Bell's ability to churn it up with the best of them. But more importantly the album left no doubt that Bell had stabilized his career and personal life and was ready to assume the throne as the premier guitarist in the talent rich Chicago blues family.

He continues to record and perform, most often with his group, the Vampin' Blues Band.

Lurrie Bell is one of the prime practitioners of the contemporary

Chicago blues style. A gifted guitar player with a gritty voice tailor-made to sing the nasty, amplified, urban Chicago blues, Bell has not really attained his true potential. Although his recording output has been consistent over the past ten years, he has yet to gain the lofty position that was predicted for him in his youth.

He is a central figure among the small army of younger-generation African American performers intent on keeping the blues legacy alive. His guitar playing is clear and precise, without the use of distortion. There is an outpouring of emotion in his playing, a dynamic sound that creates interesting and dangerous dimensions. Bell has consolidated all the various influences he heard as a young boy listening to his father's band rehearsals, and channeled them into his own playing.

His gravelly voice is just another of his many weapons. To sing the Chicago blues properly, one must reach deep within one's soul and growl like a grizzly bear that has been gargling with sharp knives. Bell drops words like bombs that explode with a sheer power that complements his heavy string-bending on the guitar. Bell has melded the straight stomping Chicago blues he learned as a child with a more contemporary sound that includes elements of soul, funk, pop, and rock.

The two biggest influences on Bell, outside of those that were central to his very early development, were Hubert Sumlin and Jimi Hendrix. Sumlin, a legendary Chicago blues figure, was an integral part of the Howlin' Wolf Band. A guitar player who never received his fair share of acclaim, Sumlin was able to add another dimension to the Wolf's growling voice. His guitar solos were unpredictable runs of squealing notes that gave the listener chills. He was in many ways a progressive guitar player ahead of his time.

Jimi Hendrix was a blues painter who used different musical shades—jazz, rock, the blues, funk, soul, and psychedelic molten metal—to create his modern blues sound. It was from Hendrix that Bell learned how to incorporate these shades into a cohesive picture of sounds. Although he doesn't share Hendrix's affection for distortion, Bell is a major fan of Jimi's skillful and expert use of color tones.

Bell has played countless concerts and headlined the 1996 Chicago Blues Festival, drawing rave reviews. In 1999, he toured Italy and Switzerland, adding these two countries to the extensive list of places he has conquered with his stunning guitar work and stinging kingbee vocals. He is a frequent performer at Rosa's lounge, one of the most popular clubs in Chicago. Lurrie has also played guitar on a number of his father's recordings, including *Carey Bell's Blues Harp*, *Brought Up the Hard Way*, *Heartaches and Pain*, *Son of a Gun*, *Dynasty*, *Deep Down*, *Harpmaster*, and *Goin' on Main Street*.

Despite possessing an assortment of weapons in his musical arsenal, Bell remains a puzzling blues figure. One day he is dazzling a crowd with his breathtaking guitar work and vocal prowess; the next day he fails to show up for a performance. Although in the past ten years he has stabilized his career, his true potential remains untapped. Whatever his shortcomings, however, there is no question that Lurrie Bell remains one of the bright lights of the contemporary Chicago blues scene. He is a genuine example of someone who is living the Chicago blues.

## Discography

*Everybody Wants to Win*, JSP 227.
*Mercurial Son*, Delmark 679.
*700 Blues*, Delmark 700.
*Kiss of Sweet Blues*, Delmark 724.
*The Blues Had a Baby*, Delmark 736.
*Young Man's Blues: The Best of the JSP Sessions (1989–1990)*, JSP 2102.

With Carey Bell:

*Son of a Gun*, Rooster Blues 2617.
*Carey Bell's Blues Harp*, Delmark 622.
*Heartaches and Pain*, Delmark 666.
*Carey and Lurrie Bell, Dynasty!* JSP 222.
*Goin' on Main Street*, Evidence 26055.
*Harpmaster*, JSP 250.
*Deep Down*, Alligator AL 4828.
*Brought Up the Hard Way*, JSP 802.

# LIL' ED WILLIAMS

## *Imperial Blues*

The thick, electric Chicago blues style is now two generations old, yet many of the qualities that first brought the genre attention in the 1950s are still in place. The amplified, slashing slide guitar, the beefy wailing solos, the gut-wrenching harmonica wailings, the heavy, evil vocals, and the solid drop beat are so well known that they have become standard additions to every blues musician's vocabulary. One of the new practitioners of the dynamic Chicago blues sound is the man responsible for the Imperial blues. His name is Lil' Ed Williams.

Ed Williams was born on April 8, 1955, in Chicago, Illinois, into a musical family. Williams's uncle was the legendary J. B. Hutto, a well-known Chicago slide guitarist who was tutored by the one and only Elmore James. While Williams was growing up, Hutto would often arrive with his houserocking band and entertain the entire neighborhood during family barbecues. Hutto, a seasoned performer, was able to hypnotize the crowds at these gatherings and left a deep impression on young Edward.

In fact, there was an instant bond between Williams and his uncle, as they both shared a love of music and performing. Soon Williams was playing the drums, dreaming of the day when he would be in his own band in front of a live crowd like his Uncle J. B. Eventually Williams switched over to the guitar and concentrated on mastering the slide technique. By his late teens Williams was a remarkable broomduster, with the genuine touch of someone who had listened to a lot of blues while growing up.

When he was seventeen, Williams joined a soul group. Although it was a good experience and helped his musical maturation, Ed knew that he wanted to front his own band. Two years later he did just that. He knew what he wanted his group to sound like and chose his bandmates very carefully. He wanted musicians who not only were proficient on their respective instruments but also could create a song by starting with a single note, an idea, a bass line.

Williams recruited Dave Weld to play rhythm guitar and Kelly Littleton on drums. He added his brother James "Pookie" Williams on bass, and rounded out the group with his own searing slide guitar and strong blues voice. They became Lil' Ed Williams and the Blue Imperials and began to tour the Chicago blues clubs, delivering some of the wildest, hottest blues heard in the city. They built up an enthusiastic following around the Chicago area and waited to be discovered. The major goal of the band was to transfer the dynamic energy of their live show onto a record and release it to the buying public.

When Bruce Iglauer, owner of Alligator Records, was searching for local talent to put together another of his anthologies featuring Chicago's best new acts, he was given the name of Lil' Ed Williams and the Blue Imperials. Iglauer, an intelligent and knowledgeable man always on top of the blues scene in Chicago, was vaguely familiar with the band. So he invited them down to the Alligator studios to cut a couple of songs for the New Bluebloods project.

Lil' Ed Williams and the Blue Imperials walked into the studio with mixed feelings. They had never been inside a recording studio before and were a little nervous, but at the same time they were confident of their abilities. What was supposed to be a quick two-song set turned into a miracle for the band. The staff at Alligator were so enamored with the band that they recorded enough songs to fill three albums. Not long after this, the band's first record, *Roughhousin'*, was released.

The record took the blues world by storm, and the critics could not find enough superlatives to express their pleasure. Roughhousin' was a genuine Chicago-style blues album featuring the dynamic slide work of Williams, who immediately drew comparisons to Elmore James, Hound Dog Taylor, and J. B. Hutto. Some of the outstanding tracks on the album included "Old Oak Tree," "You Done Me Wrong for the Last Time," "Everything I Do Brings Me Closer to the Blues," "Mean Old Frisco," "Car Wash Blues," "Midnight Rider," and "Pride and Joy." Alligator and Williams and his Blues Imperials could not have asked for a stronger debut record.

The band broke out of the small West Side blues clubs they had been confined to and toured the country, appearing at the Long Beach Blues Festival, the San Francisco Blues Festival, and the New Orleans Jazz & Heritage Festival. They worked the crowd into a frenzy with their high-energy boogie-blues material. As a result of their newfound success, they embarked on a European tour as soon as they had fulfilled their commitments in the United States.

In 1989, *Chicken, Gravy & Biscuits*, containing songs left over from their miracle session of a year before, was released. A howling good time, their second disc earned them an even wider fan base. As in the first effort, the energetic, raw slide-guitar work of Williams was at the forefront. A few of the highlights included "Master Charge," "Can't Let These Blues Go," "Blues for Jeanette," "Chicken, Gravy & Biscuits," "20% Alcohol," and "Face Like a Fish." Williams and the Blues Imperials made the blues a fun adventure.

In 1992, the CD *What You See Is What You Get* added to their burgeoning popularity. By this time Williams had established himself as one of the best slide guitarists on the scene. He coupled his electric playing with hard-boiled vocals, and with quality material. "Life Is Like Gambling," "Travelin' Life," "Packin'," "Find My Baby," and "What Am I Gonna Do?" made the disc a must-have for all blues fans of genuine house-rocking music.

The band at this point included Lil' Ed on guitar and vocals, Mike

Garrett on second guitar, Eddie McKinley on tenor saxophone, James "Pookie" Young on bass, and Kelly Littleton on drums. They were a tight unit and spent a great deal of time on the road together, including tours of Australia and Europe.

In 1992, Alligator Records, which Bruce Iglauer had founded in the early 1970s for the express purpose of recording his favorite blues singer Hound Dog Taylor (or so the rumor persists), celebrated its twentieth anniversary with a concert. Lil' Ed Williams and the Blue Imperials, despite sharing the stage with such blues talent as Koko Taylor, Elvin Bishop, Lonnie Brooks, Katie Webster, Lucky Peterson, Billy Branch, Lurrie Bell, Dave Hole, and other Alligator artists, stole the show. That concert was the highlight of the group's career up to that point.

By the end of 1992, Lil' Ed Williams and the Imperials had been on the road constantly for five years. They had been barraged by interviews from a press wanting to share in their success. The immense pressures finally took their toll on Williams, who broke up the Blue Imperials and went into seclusion for a couple of years. He emerged from his "retreat" in 1996 to record two albums. The first was with his old friend Dave Weld, the first guitar player of the Blue Imperials; the second collaboration was with Willie Kent.

The two adventures were successful enough to spark Williams out of "retirement." He re-formed the Blue Imperials and recorded the album *Get Wild!* Williams wrote twelve of the fourteen tracks on the album, including "You Got to Stop," "Standing on the Corner," "Compact Man," "Cannonball," and "Get Out." The album also included two J. B. Hutto songs, "Too Late" and "Pet Cream Man." More importantly, Ed Williams, with the stinging slide guitar and street-tough vocals, was back stronger than ever. His new band included Kelly Littleton on drums, James "Pookie" Young on bass, and, of course, Lil' Ed Williams on slide guitar and lead vocals. The comeback was a complete success when Lil' Ed and the new version of the Blue Imperials played at the prestigious Chicago Blues Festival.

Lil' Ed and the Blue Imperials continue to record and tour.

Lil' Ed Williams is a blues treasure. Ever since Bruce Iglauer gave him his big break over a decade ago, Ed and his band have thrilled millions of fans throughout the United States and around the world. He is one of the most exciting Chicago blues acts on the scene today. He has been able to harness his incredible talent and channel it into a successful career.

Williams may very well be the best slide-guitar player today. He is certainly in the upper echelon of "sliders." His searing guitar licks are expressive, fresh, and dripping with blues flavor. He can kick out the hard-driving Chicago blues shuffles with a precise and concentrated attack. There is very little that Williams cannot do on the guitar.

He is also a real treat to watch in concert. His wild guitar antics—the duck walk, the playing behind his back and between his legs—are all part of the package. He can perform all those tricks without missing a note. He has taken a page from the Charley Patton, T-Bone Walker, Chuck Berry, and Jimi Hendrix books on how to entertain a crowd.

He plays every concert as if it were his last one. In many ways, Lil' Ed and the Blue Imperials have taken over where the J. Geils Band left off. Although Williams and his band are more blues-oriented than the rock-and-roll J. Geils Band, both groups were favorite live draws because they played genuine houserocking music.

Lil' Ed Williams and the Blue Imperials occupy a special place in the current Chicago blues scene. They are a known commodity and one of the most popular groups on the circuit. Williams and his band of house-rocking rebels have not only revved the Chicago blues motor up a couple of notches, they have also maintained an African American presence on the scene. Their butt-rocking blues boogie continues the tradition of Elmore James, the Howlin' Wolf Band, J. B. Hutto, Earl Hooker, and other wild Chicago blues acts.

Williams is a superb bandleader, able to direct his group with class and distinction. He allows the members of the band to explore their own territory and spreads the fame around. He does not bark orders like some grizzled old war general, but leads by example. His ability to unite the various talents of the members of his band into one potent force only emphasizes his leadership qualities.

Although he suffered some personal problems, Williams was able to rebound and climb back to the top of the Chicago blues heap with enthusiasm and fire. In many ways he has taken over the role of his uncle J. B. Hutto and Hound Dog Taylor by delivering his infectious brand of house-rocking music to the masses. Lil' Ed's future appears to be bright, and one hopes he can handle the pressures that go along with being somebody who is totally entertaining with his imperial blues.

## Discography

*Roughhousin'*, Alligator AL 4749.
*Chicken, Gravy & Biscuits*, Alligator AL 4772.
*What You See Is What You Get*, Alligator AL 4808.
*Get Wild!* Alligator 4868.

With Dave Weld:
*Lil' Ed and Dave Weld*, Earwig 4936.
*Who's Been Talkin'*, Blind Pig 4941.

---

# MELVIN TAYLOR

## *Blues on the Run*

The contemporary Chicago blues scene includes a variety of artists of both the traditional and the experimental nature. By expanding the parameters of the genre, the modern blues singers have kept the style fresh. There are many different artists, all playing their own brands of music, under the umbrella that is the Chicago blues. One of these artists is as diverse as any of the modern Chicago blues singers and has given the world his blues on the run. His name is Melvin Taylor.

Melvin Taylor was born on March 13, 1959, in Jackson, Mississippi. Although he boasts an authentic Mississippi birth certificate, Taylor was reared in Chicago from the age of three. He developed an interest in music as a youngster and first tried his hand on the drums and the bass before making the guitar his instrument of choice. Taylor blossomed quickly on the guitar, and joined the group the Transistors as a teenager. He remained in the band until the group split up in the early 1980s.

Although the Transistors were a rhythm-and-blues quartet, Taylor enjoyed many different kinds of music. His two prime musical heroes were Muddy Waters and Jimi Hendrix. The gritty Chicago blues of Waters and the rock-drenched blues of Hendrix helped shape Taylor's overall guitar sound. He also listened to jazz, particularly the incredible Wes Montgomery.

After the Transistors disbanded Taylor joined the Legendary Blues Band, which included Pinetop Perkins, who had at one time backed up Taylor's idol Muddy Waters. It was a fantastic opportunity for Taylor, as the band toured the West Coast and Europe during his tenure. While many bluesmen had made strong impressions on European audiences in the past, Taylor hit a particular nerve that endeared him to fans across the Atlantic; his fan pool had grown tenfold. Taylor has been a regular performer throughout Europe ever since.

Taylor recorded two albums in France in the early 1980s. The first, *Blues on the Run*, was a stunning debut that showcased his incredible virtuoso talent. Taylor, who had grown up listening to the hard-rock blues of Jimi Hendrix, the jazz stylings of George Benson, and the deep blues of Muddy Waters, had taken the best of all three styles and welded them together to create his own sound. Taylor shone on songs like "Tremblin' Man," "Low Down Dirty Shame," "Cold, Cold Feet," and "Chitlins con Carne." Thanks to Taylor's sharp guitar skills, an album that might have sounded disjointed was a piece of pure blues magic.

A couple of years later he recorded *Melvin Taylor Plays the Blues for You*, which featured Lucky Peterson on piano. The dynamic dueling between Taylor's searing guitar work and Peterson's rocking piano rhythms created a tense, razor sharp sound. The conversation between the two instruments propelled the album to dizzying heights. Taylor had finally found someone who could match his musical abilities. There were many interesting songs on the album, including "Talking to Anna Mae, Pt. 1," "Talking to Anna Mae, Pt. 2," "I'll Play the Blues for You," "Tribute to Wes," "Voodoo Daddy," and the original composition "Groovin' in Paris."

Although he was a star in European blues circles, Taylor had a difficult time getting his career started in the United States. Eventually he found work at Rosa's Lounge, one of the better-known blues clubs in the Windy City, which he adopted as his permanent base. The arrangement between Taylor and Rosa's provided Melvin with financial security and the club with a first-rate blues star. But just as his live act was flourishing, his studio career—despite two previously recorded albums—had fallen silent.

It wasn't until 1995, eleven years after his last recording, that Taylor entered the studio again with the Slack Band backing him up. The subsequent release, *Melvin Taylor and the Slack Band*, once again was a vehicle for Taylor's axe workouts. It seemed that he was paying homage to all the guitar players who had inspired him over the years. Taylor covered the Hendrix classic "Voodoo Chile (Slight Return)" as a show of respect for the Seattle guitar master. He also covered "All Your Love (I Miss Loving)," the Otis Rush standard, as well as "Don't Throw Your Love on Me So Strong," the Albert King chestnut. While the album did not propel him to stardom, it did serve notice that Taylor was one of the brightest and best guitar players on the blues scene.

His follow-up *Dirty Pool* was once again a blues-guitar fan's delight. He covered three Stevie Ray Vaughan songs, "Too Sorry," "Telephone Song," and "Dirty Pool," the last of which gave the album its title. The classics "Floodin' in California," "Right Place, Wrong Time," "I Ain't Superstitious," and "Kansas City" were also included on the album. The rhythm section of Steve Pott on drums and Willie "Big Eyes" Smith on bass provided Taylor with a smooth pad to take off from and land on.

His next release, *Bang That Bell*, once again demonstrated Taylor's love for exploring different venues, including blues, rock, and jazz. The album kicked off with the title cut "Bang That Bell," and flowed into "Love Is a Gamble." Taylor's highly energized guitar playing turned simple songs like "Another Bad Day " into masterpieces of modern blues. He added two old blues standards, "Trick Bag" and "If You're Going to the City." Without a doubt, the strangest song on the album was "Even Trolls Love Rock & Roll." An interesting collection that gathered little interest from blues purists, it was a hit with blues fans who preferred their guitar heroes with the ability to blend different elements into something special.

Taylor, who can usually be found at Rosa's Lounge on many nights, also travels to Europe on a regular basis in order to retain his strong fan base there. Now that he seems to have the recording side of his career on track, Taylor may soon gain the respect that he is due here, as well.

Melvin Taylor is a perfect example of the modern blues guitarist. He has used the blues as the foundation of his overall sound, but has explored different avenues of music that interest him. Because he is such an incredible guitar player, he is able to shape the different musical forms to create a cohesive, even effort.

In some ways, Taylor has followed in the footsteps of Jimi Hendrix. Just prior to his death Hendrix had begun expanding his own blues-rock foundation to explore the areas of jazz and soul. Much of the material that was released after Hendrix's death was divided into jazz, rock, blues, and soul categories. Taylor, instead of recording material that can be separated into different categories, simply unites all of the styles under one umbrella. Also like Hendrix, Taylor caught his first big break in Europe.

Taylor is able to match guitar pyrotechnics with any axe man on the circuit today. He can unleash a blistering attack of notes that sting like a thousand wasps. He can also play it smooth and mellow, like another of his guitar heroes, George Benson. His chameleon-like talents on the guitar are reminiscent of Buddy Guy.

In the blues everything is connected; no artist is an island no matter how unique their individual sound. Taylor, who has borrowed from many legends including Hendrix, George Benson, and Chicago blues hero Buddy Guy, now finds himself influencing younger artists on the scene. Certainly Kenny Wayne Shepherd and Jonny Lang have benefited from copying Taylor's ability to create modern blues from a number of different musical elements.

Perhaps the only weak point in Taylor's armor as a blues artist is his voice. He does not possess an overly powerful voice and it is often lost amid his strong guitar chops. Taylor's voice cannot erupt with the same intensity that his playing can. This, however, is hardly a major drawback. Many of the greatest guitar players, including Hendrix, did not boast magnificent singing voices.

In the roster of Chicago blues guitarists Taylor occupies a special place. He is not a traditional slide player in the mold of an Earl Hooker, Elmore James, or Ed Williams. He is not strictly a rhythm player, like Jimmy Rogers, either. He can play blistering Chicago blues like Son Seals, but has many different sides to his guitar persona. Taylor's fondness for different shades of blues is an acquired taste for traditional fans of Chicago blues guitar.

Nevertheless, there are few guitar players today who can match Taylor's ability on the instrument. He has proven that the modern blues sound, though based on the blues, is a melting pot of different musical styles. His guitar virtuosity has drawn comparisons to some of the greatest players in history including Jimi Hendrix, Stevie Ray Vaughan, Muddy Waters, Buddy Guy, Wes Montgomery, and George Benson. Whatever style of blues he is playing, there is no doubt that Taylor will always keep the listener alert with his blues on the run.

## Discography

*Blues on the Run*, Evidence ECD-26041-2.
*Melvin Taylor Plays the Blues for You*, Evidence ECD-26029-2.
*Melvin Taylor and the Slack Band*, Evidence 26073.
*Dirty Pool*, Evidence 26088.
*Bang That Bell*, Evidence 26107.

# PART THREE

# Modern American Electric Blues

In the 1940s and 1950s the amplified blues was in its infancy as pioneers like T-Bone Walker and Lonnie Johnson broke new ground with their innovative electric styles. While some blues singers remained dedicated to the acoustic form, others like B. B. King, Albert King, Freddie King, Johnny "Guitar" Watson, Johnny Copeland, Muddy Waters, Elmore James, John Lee Hooker, and Albert Collins plugged in. The first generation of electric blues warriors established the format that future guitar heroes would eagerly follow and expand on.

These pioneers of the modern electric blues realized the fruits of their labors in the 1960s with the explosive marriage of the blues and rock. This was the era that produced Jimi Hendrix, Jeff Beck, Johnny Winter, Jimmy Page, Eric Clapton, Alvin Lee, Mike Bloomfield, and Rory Gallagher. But by the late 1970s and early 80s the blues-rock era had given way to the modern electric blues.

The modern electric blues blended classic electrified Chicago and Texas blues riffs with the hard-edged rock sound. Although the style had not changed much from the blues-rock format, there was a freshness to it. The movement was spearheaded by Stevie Ray Vaughan and a host of others, including Rod Piazza, Jimmie Vaughan, Joe Louis Walker, Robert Cray, William Clarke, Tinsley Ellis, Kim Wilson, Anson Funderburgh, Little Charlie & the Nightcats, Delbert McClinton, Kenny Neal, and Fenton Robinson.

In the 1990s—the post–Stevie Ray Vaughan era—the modern electric blues continued to thrive, with acts such as Kenny Wayne Shepherd, Chris Duarte, Jonny Lang, Lil' Ed Williams, Melvin Taylor, Lurrie Bell, Larry McCray, and Monster Mike Welsh taking up the mantle of past proponents of the genre. The American electric blues continues to fuel the imagination of blues artists around the world. Although it is not a pure strain, the American electric blues is the most popular form at this moment.

The performers spotlighted in this section are a fair representation of the electric blues genre in the past thirty years. They include artists from all over the continental United States, indicating how far the electric blues have spread throughout the country, especially since the end of the first golden age of rock and roll.

Jimi Hendrix is the most spectacular electric guitarist the world has ever known. Often categorized as rock guitar, the Hendrix sound was firmly rooted in the blues. It was Hendrix who provided the portal through which other American electric blues musicians could pass to find their own styles.

Johnny Winter is a Texas bluesman who has expanded the parameters first established by T-Bone Walker to include rock. One of the hardest of the blues rockers, he has always had one foot firmly planted in the blues and the other in rock. He is a student of the Jimi Hendrix school of guitar playing.

Rod Piazza is a West Coast jump blues enthusiast who took the best elements of the expatriates and blended it with a healthy dose of jazz and pop to create his contemporary rollicking blues style.

Joe Louis Walker is a modern electric blues guitarist who has consolidated the styles of his favorite Chicago guitarists—Buddy Guy, Otis Rush, and Magic Sam—and blended the result with his unique vision to create his own sound.

Robert Cray is the epitome of the contemporary electric blues guitarist. He has combined his love of the blues with large chunks of soul to create a truly modern style.

William Clarke was an excellent harmonica player, and, along with Kim Wilson and Rod Piazza, was the best of the modern electric blues set. His untimely death left a hole in the electric harmonica world that has never been filled.

Jimmie Vaughan is a third-generation Texas blues guitarist who has never forgotten his Texas blues legacy, but has forged ahead with a more contemporary sound. He was part of one of the most popular bands—The Fabulous Thunderbirds—to play smoking electric blues music.

Stevie Ray Vaughan was the most spectacular guitarist to appear on the electric blues scene since Jimi Hendrix. Vaughan revived the blues when the genre had lost much of its popularity with older blues fans.

Tinsley Ellis is a fiery blues guitarist in the mold of Jimi Hendrix and Johnny Winter. His Georgia roots, which include Blind Willie McTell and the Allman Brothers Band, shine through his music.

Kenny Neal is another modern blues singer who can boast of an authentic blues pedigree. His father, Raful Neal, is an important Louisiana blues artist. Kenny Neal has carried on the Louisiana blues tradition with style and grace.

Larry McCray is a national blues act whose driving guitar riffs owe as much to Jimi Hendrix as they do to his Detroit rhythm-and-blues roots. He is the leading blues singer in a thriving Detroit blues scene.

Lucky Peterson is an East Coast musical prodigy who has been a fixture on the blues scene for many years. He has managed to carry on and expand on the piano tradition first established by Leroy Carr, Jimmy Yancey, and others, by playing the Hammond organ.

Kenny Wayne Shepherd is the wave of the future. A serious challenger for the electric blues guitar throne, he has followed in the footsteps of Stevie Ray Vaughan while managing to carve out his own niche.

Jonny Lang is another blues hope for the future. He has been able to mix his many influences to create a modern sound that has gained a whole new generation of blues fans.

# JIMI HENDRIX

## *Red House Blues*

In 1948, when Muddy Waters cut his first two songs for the Aristocrat label, he ushered in the electric blues era. For the next twelve years Waters played straight, electric blues that changed the face of popular music forever. In the 1960s, the course of music began to shift again. The folk boom of the early 1960s, the soul movement, the pop movement, and the British Invasion all borrowed heavily from the blues; however, it was the marriage between the blues and rock and roll that brought about the modern electric blues era. Although the blues-rock genre boasted many fine guitarists, a new hero was needed, one who would consolidate all styles into one cohesive sound. He arrived like a warm summer breeze with his Red House Blues and proceeded to turn the music world on its ear. His name was Jimi Hendrix.

Jimi Hendrix was born Johnny Allen Hendrix on November 27, 1942, in Seattle, Washington, part of the wartime baby boom. Since little Johnny's mother was sickly, he was shuffled around from one relative to another. When his father returned from overseas he reclaimed his son, changing the boy's name to James Marshall Hendrix.

Little Jimi grew up in abject poverty in Seattle's ghetto district. Al Hendrix and his son moved around often, usually just ahead of the child-welfare people. The elder Hendrix, who had trouble finding work, had his son and Jimi's brother Leon to worry about. Jimi Hendrix faced a grim future until one day when he was nine years old he discovered what would become his lifelong best friend: the guitar.

The secrets it possessed and the magic it could produce held Hendrix spellbound. A gifted musician, he developed quickly and by the time he was in his early teens he was the best guitar player in all of Seattle. In high school Hendrix joined his first professional band, called the Rocking Kings. Even back in those early days it was clear that Hendrix was going to be something very special; he outshone all the others in the band.

Hendrix quit school at sixteen and enlisted in the army. Since he was in top physical shape he was able to choose which branch of the army he wanted to join and decided on the paratroopers division. He yearned for a Screaming Eagle badge; Hendrix had no fear of jumping out of planes. He was stationed in Fort Campbell, Kentucky, in the Deep South, and it was here that he began to closely study the rural blues.

There was an elementary essence to the country-blues that all guitar players who dreamed of fusing the blues with other musical forms had to completely understand. Hendrix, already a serious student of the blues, dug deep within his soul to learn the intricacies of the down-home blues. This deliberate course of action at this stage of his development was crucial to his ability to mesh the old blues with a wider range of styles.

Not long after earning his Screaming Eagle's badge, Hendrix was released from the army because of a back injury he had sustained during one of his jumps. But before he left he met a fellow soldier named Billy Cox. The two jammed together and formed a band that played on the army bases. Hendrix and Cox moved to Nashville after their release from the army, but found little work there.

Hendrix made his way back west to Vancouver and found a steady gig there until Little Richard swept through the Canadian city and took Jimi with him. Little Richard—the self-proclaimed "King of Rock and Roll"—had hit the big time while washing dishes in a restaurant in 1955. For two years he produced some of the craziest, wildest rock-and-roll hits, which borrowed deeply from the blues. He quit at the height of his fame after the jealous remarks of some rival and turned to religion. Little Richard, who strongly believed that the musical winds would change in his favor, continued to play the thumping rock and roll that had made him famous.

As a sideman in Little Richard's band, Hendrix earned very little and traveled by bus with the rest of the back-up group as they roamed the country playing in large cities and small towns. It was here that Hendrix developed his road stamina and showbiz pyrotechnics that would serve him well later on. After a year in Little Richard's band, Hendrix jumped ship and joined an R&B tour that included the Supremes, Ike and Tina Turner, Jackie Wilson and others, playing the rhythm chords that he knew with his eyes closed. When the tour ended, Hendrix, ever the nomad, drifted to New York City. He arrived in Harlem, which seemed a universe away from his hometown of Seattle. It was while living in Harlem that Hendrix joined the Isley Brothers, and King Curtis and the Knights, for brief periods. Despite the sea of black faces, Harlem seemed confining to Hendrix; he soon moved to Greenwich Village.

Hendrix was enchanted with Greenwich Village; it boasted an interesting history; it was a haven for bohemians, artists, and struggling musicians; he fit right in. Imaginary musical lines that featured folk, blues, pop, rock, jazz, or rhythm & blues divided the Village. After playing in a number of different bands, Hendrix felt it was time to lead his own group. He settled down right away and put together a band called Jimmy James and the Blue Flames (taken from an old Junior Parker band name) that included Randy California. The band played at the Café Wha? an odd little club that was darker than midnight in Persia and was at the low end of all the places in the Village. But it was a perfect place for Hendrix to forge his new sound: at the Café Wha? he could work on things without getting booed off the stage.

For the next year Jimi Hendrix paid his blues dues with a vengeance. He was often seen around the Village carrying his guitar case, which contained all of his worldly possessions; he slept in doorways, in the park, and in the ruins of burnt-out buildings. It was a frustrating time for Hendrix, a brilliant virtuoso who was considered just another guitar player in the Village. Although he did find some respite in playing with John Hammond, Jr., for a few gigs, Hendrix remained in obscurity.

Then, one magical summer night, Chas Chandler, on the advice of those who knew Hendrix was special, ventured into the darkness of the Café Wha? and saw Jimi perform. Chandler, the ex-bass player of the Animals, one of the premier R&B groups of the early sixties, offered to take Hendrix to England and become his manager. Hendrix, a true rolling stone, agreed, on the condition that he would meet Eric Clapton.

It was in England that Hendrix formed his band The Jimi Hendrix Experience, with Noel Redding on bass and Mitch Mitchell on drums. The power trio created a wall of sound that astonished the usually placid British crowd. Through Chandler's contacts and The Jimi Hendrix

Experience taking whatever gig that came their way, the band developed a devoted following and became one of the top groups in England.

In 1967, after the success of a few singles ("Hey Joe," "Purple Haze," "The Wind Cries Mary"), the band's first album, *Are You Experienced?* was released. On that first record Hendrix managed to synthesize all of the various musical styles into one cohesive sound. Anyone who wanted an idea of what direction the blues were heading needed only to listen to this album; it was ripe with blues classics. "Manic Depression" was a waltz turned into a modern blues song that sounded like Charley Patton on acid. "Foxy Lady" was a masher, a monster song of molten metal that dripped like heavy drops of blues fire. The song "Fire," more of a rocker than a blues tune, featured a burning solo, a blues run akin to Blind Willie McTell, only sped up. The title song "Are You Experienced?" was a simple love song with chunks of blues rhythm chords and lead runs that turned it into something special; a song Muddy Waters would have recorded if he had been a rocker. The blues showpiece of the album was "Red House." Hendrix took the standard twelve-bar blues and turned it inside out with his unmatched virtuosity.

Although he and the band were stars in England, Hendrix was unknown in his native America. That all changed at the Monterey Pop Festival in June of 1967, when The Jimi Hendrix Experience left the crowd dumbfounded with his powerful technique and modern blues vision. They played blues classics like "Killing Floor," and blues ballads like "Hey Joe." Hendrix performed a version of "Like a Rolling Stone," an intelligent choice considering the immense popularity of Bob Dylan at the time. Hendrix made the song his own. He included "Wild Thing," making it sound like a blues rag gone the way of soul, and finished his set with "Fire," setting his guitar on fire. Instantly, Hendrix was catapulted to superstar status.

The Jimi Hendrix Experience was soon one of the most sought-after bands to appear live in the world, topping even the Beatles and the Rolling Stones. No one had heard anything quite like Hendrix and his band. After a short stint as the opening act for the Monkees, Hendrix toured the United States and Europe as a headliner, since after his appearance at the Monterey Pop Festival no one dared follow him on stage.

Despite his stature as the most electrifying guitar player, the pressure of stardom began to rear its ugly head. In Gothenburg, Sweden, Hendrix destroyed a hotel room, landing in jail for a night courtesy of Gothenburg's finest. It was, however, a minor incident that only aided in furthering his rebel-hero status in the eyes of young people throughout the world.

The band's second album, *Axis: Bold as Love*, was built around a theme that Hendrix had studied for some time. The axis of the world exercised its power over all human life and the rest of creation. Once again it was a pure example of the modern blues that Hendrix had created through his vast imagination, his incomparable musical knowledge, and undeniable talent. The song "If 6 Were 9" was a funky blues number. "Little Wing" was a beautiful, haunting blues ballad, while "Spanish Magic Castle" contained a harsher blues edge. The title song, "Axis: Bold as Love," was a spattering of blues tonalities and emotions that was a perfect example of how Hendrix was expanding the parameters of the traditional electric blues to incorporate universal dimensions of every conceivable sound known to humankind.

Without a doubt the benchmark of Hendrix's brief but very powerful recording career was the album *Electric Ladyland*. The opening chords splashed blues colors and set the tone for the remainder of the album. All of Hendrix's musical ideas incorporating his expansion of blues parameters were present on this album. The song "Crosstown Traffic" was a boogie/rock-and-roll number with elements of jazz; but its foundation was blues. He covered the Guitar Slim hit "The Things I Used to Do," a solid rhythm and blues number. "Gypsy Eyes," a song that never garnered enough attention, was a cousin to such Delta tunes as "Rollin' and Tumblin'," "If I Had Possession Over Judgment Day," and "Louisiana Blues," recorded by Muddy Waters.

Hendrix, who had been a Bob Dylan fan from the very beginning, eventually recorded several of Dylan's songs, including "Drifter's Escape," "Like a Rolling Stone," "Can You Please Crawl Out Your Window?" and the genuine treasure "All Along the Watchtower." Hendrix took "All Along the Watchtower" to its outer limits, reconstructing the song with a blues intro reminiscent of that low-down Delta sound. The middle section of the classic, one of Hendrix's most brilliant solos, was a blues slide arrangement of a flurry of notes that paid tribute to Buddy Guy, Magic Sam, and Otis Rush.

But the blues showpieces of the album were "Voodoo Chile" and "Voodoo Chile (Slight Return)." In "Voodoo Chile" Hendrix freed the twelve-bar blues structure much in the same way that practitioners of free verse rescued poetry from confining rhyme schemes. Although some of the verses of the song rhymed, they did so with an elasticity that fit the stretched-out musical structure that Hendrix built. The song "Voodoo Chile (Slight Return)" was more of a hambone, a down-home gritty song with stark rhythm patterns infiltrated with deep blues guitar runs.

From this point on the career of Jimi Hendrix began to plunge into chaos. He broke up his band and brought in Billy Cox, his old army buddy, and Buddy Miles, the burly drummer who had played with a variety of rhythm-and-blues groups. The Band of Gypsies recorded one album, a live show at the Fillmore on New Year's Eve in 1969. A powerful trio that was short-lived, the band broke up soon after and Mitch Mitchell was brought back into the fold.

Although Hendrix immortalized the "Star Spangled Banner" at Woodstock in one of the most magical moments in the history of modern music, he was still plagued by personal problems. He was arrested for transporting drugs through Canadian customs. Although he faced stiff jail time at the height of his career, the charges were eventually dropped, but the residue of the incident remained.

Hendrix played a messy set at the Isle of Wight Festival in September of 1970. Two weeks later, Jimi Hendrix, the most spectacular electric bluesman in history, was found dead in a London flat. Hendrix, who died on September 18, was twenty-seven years old.

Jimi Hendrix was a modern blues superstar. He was the greatest exponent of modern electric blues guitar the world has ever seen. He ushered in the post-modern blues era with his guitar pyrotechnics, his expansive vision of the contemporary blues, and his underrated songwriting ability. There are no modern blues guitar players to emerge in the past thirty years who have not been touched by Hendrix in one way or another.

The foundation of the Hendrix sound was the rural blues of the Mississippi Delta. But Hendrix wasn't about to interpret the blues to try to sound like a Robert Johnson or a Charley Patton. Hendrix made the blues his own by stretching the style—and the sound—to its breaking point, but never beyond. Hendrix's understanding of blues tones and textures was second to none.

Though he was not the first to incorporate different elements into his blues-based style to create something new and exciting, Hendrix did it better than anyone else before him or since. He expanded the parameters of the blues and updated them to fit into the many forms of music that had been derived from the original Mississippi Delta blues. He blazed a trail that was followed by Stevie Ray Vaughan, Robin Trower, Frank Marino, Ed Williams, Melvin Taylor, Jimmie Vaughan, Eric Clapton, Robert Cray, Mike Bloomfield, Johnny Winter, Rory Gallagher, Dave Hole, Javier Vargas, Yuri Naumov, Kenny Wayne Shepherd, Duke Robillard, Ronnie Earle, and Sven Zetterberg.

In concert, he covered many blues songs beyond his own compositions, including "Hootchie Cootchie Man," "Spoonful," "Catfish Blues," "Two Trains Running," and "Killing Floor." Hendrix took the song "Killing Floor," revved it up to an insane speed and delivered the definitive rendition. He made "Killing Floor" into a burning blues-rocker that none of Howlin' Wolf's guitarists, despite their sound talent, could have conceived of. His genius shone through most strongly when he was updating blues classics to fit his modern blues tastes.

Of all the guitarists who swept through after the passing of Hendrix, none came closer to capturing the same spirit and energy than Stevie Ray Vaughan. Vaughan is one of the very few guitarists who could take a Hendrix song and mold it into something fresh and exciting without sounding like a mere imitator. Vaughan delivered versions of "Little Wing" and "Voodoo Chile (Slight Return)" that left fans begging for more. It took courage, talent, and a genuine blues soul to attempt a Hendrix song; Stevie Ray Vaughan was the only guitar player to accept and deliver on that challenge.

In many ways Hendrix was a link in the chain that began with Charley Patton and included T-Bone Walker. Like Patton and Walker, Hendrix was a showman who played guitar with his teeth, behind his back, between his legs. He would get down on his knees and wiggle his tongue in time with the flurry of notes that his lightning quick fingers could create like a furious rainstorm. He also cut a dashing figure on stage; he always wore colorful clothing: red velour pants, yellow frilly shirts, scarves, a gangster hat or a red bandana.

The Jimi Hendrix guitar style has been talked about since he first blew everyone's mind back in the fall of 1966, and it is still a source of discussion to this day. There are some answers to the question of what made it so special, but there remains some mystery. He made extensive use of volume; Hendrix was without a doubt the loudest guitar player in the world. He was a left-handed guitarist who played the instrument upside down and restrung. This unusual approach put the control knobs on the top instead of the bottom, allowing him to adjust them quickly with a slight touch. Hendrix often rewired his guitars so that he could control the sound by slightly touching the toggle switch. He employed a wah-wah pedal, reverb, distortion, the tremolo arm, a fuzz box, a uni-vibe, and an octavia with the touch of a supreme sorcerer.

Although he is associated primarily with the Fender Stratocaster, Hendrix used a variety of guitars, including the Gibson Flying V as a tribute to one of his mentors (Albert King). He also played a Gibson "Les Paul," a Fender Jazzmaster, a Zamaitis (a twelve-string acoustic), an Epiphone, a Washburn, and the Italian-made Goya. He became universally known as the Marshall masher for his extensive use of Marshall amplifiers. But he also used Sunn, Fender Twin Reverbs, Burns, and Silvertone amplifiers.

His guitar technique included the finger tremolo, the distinctive shaking of one's fingers on the fretted strings. He was also a monster string bender in the mold of Albert King. Hendrix was capable of playing rhythm structures and lead runs simultaneously. He was a masterful slide guitarist who never used a regular bottleneck, but, instead, rings that he would slide along the strings to create his blues guitar magic. He was also a master of feedback. Hendrix knew instinctively which note would produce feedback with a simple touch.

Another guitar effect that Hendrix used was his tuning. He always tuned down a half-step to enable him to bend the strings more easily. (Many guitar players, including Stevie Ray Vaughan, followed suit and tuned their guitars that way too.) While studying the rural country bluesmen, he had discovered that they tuned their guitars differently for almost every song. Robert Johnson never recorded a song in standard tuning. Skip James was also known for his strange minor chord tunings.

Jimi Hendrix is the most important electric blues guitarist in the history of modern music. He used the blues as a springboard to explore every musical spectrum possible. He recorded only three proper studio albums in his professional career, which lasted only five years. The Hendrix legacy has been shrouded in controversy because of the circumstances of his death, and the many swindlers and vultures that appeared after his death to cash in on his name.

Although he was with us for only a short time, there is no denying Hendrix's ability on the electric guitar, as a songwriter, and as a leader of the modern blues movement. The reverberations of his dramatic, fast-paced career are still felt today. He is the most important guitar player who ever lived, because with his Red House Blues, he changed the way the instrument would be played forever. Hendrix will never be replaced.

**Discography** (Those marked with * were released during his lifetime.)

*Are You Experienced?* Reprise RS6261.
*Axis: Bold as Love*, Reprise RS 6281.
*Electric Ladyland*, Reprise 2RS 6307.
*Smash Hits*, MSK 2276.
The Cry of Love, MS 2034.
Rainbow Bridge, MS 2040.
Hendrix in the West, MS 2049.
War Heroes, MS 2103.
Crash Landing, MS 2204.
Midnight Lightning, MS 2209.
The Essential Jimi Hendrix Vol. 1, Reprise RS 2245.

*The Essential Jimi Hendrix Vol. II*, Reprise RS 2293.
*\*Band of Gypsies*, Capitol STAO 472.

━━━━━━━━━

# JOHNNY WINTER

## *Albino Bluesman*

The Texas blues tradition boasts a long line of independent individuals who, though proud of the Lone Star blues legacy, were also interested in establishing their own styles. Blind Lemon Jefferson, Sam Lightnin' Hopkins, T-Bone Walker, Clarence "Gatemouth" Brown, Johnny Clyde Copeland, Freddie King, and Albert Collins were all premier guitar stylists. The new generation of Texas blues guitar players have also asserted their independence. Billy Gibbons of ZZ Top has his own distinct touch, as does Jimmie Vaughan, and, of course, Stevie Ray Vaughan. In the late 1960s, a new Texas blues guitar slinger arrived on the scene and immediately began to carve out his own identity as the so-called Albino bluesman. His name was Johnny Winter.

Johnny Winter was born February 23, 1944, in Beaumont, Texas. An albino in a world where different often meant trouble, Winter turned to music to find solace. He discovered the guitar, which became his best friend, and was influenced by the African American blues grooves he heard on the late-night radio stations. At the age of fourteen he formed his first band with his younger brother Edgar, also an albino. But Johnny moved beyond garage bands in a hurry. While still in his teens he was cutting singles that gained regional attention and playing in blues bars, holding his own against older, more experienced axe men. Even as a kid, Johnny could uncork a blistering run of notes that would shake the roof off any juke joint.

The Texas roadhouse blues bar scene is an excruciating grind. Many of the bands never make it past that level, but Winter possessed a special talent. His big break came when a *Rolling Stone* article sang his praises. Soon he was playing in some of the best rock/blues clubs in the country, including the Fillmore, The Scene, and the Avalon Ballroom in San Francisco. His fierce guitar attack and razor-edged vocals eventually earned him a recording contract with Columbia, the legendary label that boasted

Bob Dylan and, later on, another young Texas guitar wizard named Stevie Ray Vaughan.

Winter's first album, simply entitled *Johnny Winter*, struck a major chord with the blues-rock audience of the day. He was immediately compared to Jimi Hendrix, Jeff Beck, Duane Allman and other leading guitar players of the era. The album was packed with blues treats, including "Mean Mistreater," "I'm Yours, and I'm Hers," "Leland Mississippi Blues," "When You Got a Good Friend," and "Be Careful with a Fool." The album also boasted appearances by blues legends Willie Dixon and Big Walter Horton.

*Second Winter*, his next album, contained more hot blues, but had a harder rock edge. It was another winner, and, with the release of *Johnny Winter and ... Live*, in just two quick years he had become one of the hottest acts on the blues-rock circuit. However, the pressures of his newfound stardom began to take their toll. Winter was seduced into the tangled web of hard drugs and became a heroin addict. Heroin had claimed the life of Janis Joplin only a few short months before, and it was also about this time that Eric Clapton was slipping into the black darkness. Winter's promising career came to a screeching halt as he dealt with the addiction that threatened to end his life.

It took a couple of years before Winter overcame his addiction; the album *Still Alive and Well* was his triumphant return as it served notice that the Albino bluesman was back in fine style. The pile-driving rocking blues on this album were some of his best work and proved that he had survived the heroin scare as he worked diligently to put his career back in complete order.

The next few years were productive ones as he played a full concert schedule and recorded on a regular basis. However, he had left much of his blues roots behind to concentrate on rock and roll material. In 1977 that all changed when he began an association with Muddy Waters, who had seen his career decline in the past ten years.

The teaming of Waters and Winter was a winning combination. The *Nothin' but the Blues* album helped Winter regain the blues fans he had lost over the past few years. Winter, who considered Waters to be like a second father, even produced Waters's comeback albums in the late 1970s that included *Hard Again*, *I'm Ready*, *Muddy "Mississippi" Waters Live* and *King Bee*. They toured together and their musical partnership lasted for a few short but very productive years.

Throughout the 1980s Winter continued to record albums that had a heavier rock-and-roll side than a blues personality. In concert he unleashed his bottleneck riffs and stinging solos with a fervent passion. Although he never really benefited from the blues revival of the decade, he was not hurt by it either, as he continued to roll along, building on the reputation he had established in the late 1960s and early 1970s. In the 1980s, a new generation discovered Johnny Winter and his delicious slice of hard blues-rock.

The presence of Winter in the blues is a given. Throughout the 1990s he went about playing his venues and releasing good albums to the public. He did not attract attention by running afoul of the law or making a spectacle of himself just to keep his name in the news. Although he doesn't make a large splash or hog the news headlines, Winter is not a forgotten man. He remains one of the best blues-rock guitarists on the tour circuit today.

Johnny Winter is a blues survivor. He has overcome many obstacles in order to continue to play the searing lead guitar that has earned him his reputation as one of the most imaginative and fiery musicians in the last half-century. He is a unique performer who thrives on the blues-rock synthesis that he loves so much. Although he can not be credited with inventing the hybrid, he remains one of its best exponents.

In many ways Winter has been an example for other acts to emulate. Some of the most popular guitarists who have followed in his footsteps include Joe Satriani, Dave Hole, George Thorogood, Ronnie Earle, Tinsley Ellis, Melvin Taylor, Kenny Wayne Shepherd, Stevie Ray Vaughan, and Jonny Lang. He has been an inspiration to those individuals who were different and not afraid to take a stand. Winter has always let his chiseled guitar work do his talking for him.

The Johnny and Edgar Winter sibling relationship has been an interesting one. Both have forged respectable careers for themselves, following their own paths, while also appearing on each other's albums and sharing the stage at different times. The albums *Together—Live!* and *Hey, Where's Your Brother?* are good examples of the two just having fun and playing the music they grew up listening to. The Winter brothers served as a blueprint for a later sibling blues act, the Vaughan Brothers: while both Stevie Ray and Jimmie Vaughan carved out their own individual careers, when their paths crossed it was often a special moment.

The Johnny Winter guitar style is a hybrid of Texas/Chicago blues and hard-driving rock and roll. He learned from such Texas blues legends as Albert Collins and even T-Bone Walker, incorporating a tinge of jazz runs in his high-energy solos. He also followed a more modern blues sound that included blues with a harder edge. Muddy Waters, Howlin' Wolf, and Jimmy Reed were all important contributors to his style. The slide-guitar work of Elmore James was another vital lesson that Winter picked up and never forgot. He took the best parts of all of these elements to create his Albino blues.

Winter has a grizzly voice that was tailor-made for the kind of harsh blues he wanted to build his career on. Although his voice does not have a wide range, it assaults the listener like a missile, combining in harmony with his powerful guitar work. The perfect balance between the two indicates Winter at his very best. His unique style—the hammer-down guitar chords, the rapid-fire solos and incredible slide breaks, in tune with his rough-edged voice—is instantly recognizable to all blues fans. There is no one else in the world with a sound quite like that; Winter can cut through a brick wall with his dynamic sound.

Johnny Winter has kept the blues-rock flame alive for many years, long after it had almost been extinguished. Winter, a genuine musician, never tried to be something he wasn't. He was a blues-rocker and that is the image he projected on all of his albums and in concert. Although he could also play the slow blues with the best of them, Winter never tried to play a style of music that didn't feel right to him.

With a long, colorful discography and a record for smashing stages all over the world as long as anyone else's, Johnny Winter was able to escape the Texas blues-bar scene to go on and create a long and interesting career. Although he has never received the true credit he was due, Winter has always delivered with a feverish intensity his special brand of blues that has made him a legend in blues-rock circles.

## Discography

*Johnny Winter*, Columbia CK-9826.
*Second Winter*, Columbia CK- 9947.
*Johnny Winter and ...*, Columbia CK-3022.
*Johnny Winter and ... Live*, Columbia CK-30475.
*Austin Texas*, United Artists 139.
*Still Alive and Well*, Columbia CK-32188.
*Saints and Sinners*, Columbia 66240.
*John Dawson Winter III*, Blue Sky PZQ-33292.
*Captured Live!* Blue Sky ZK-34033.
*Nothin' but the Blues*, Blue Sky ZK-34813.
*White Hot & Blue*, Blue Sky 33475.
*Raisin' Cain*, Blue Sky 36343.
*Guitar Slinger*, Alligator AL-4735.
*Serious Business*, Alligator AL-4742.
*Third Degree*, Alligator AL-4748.
*And/Alive*, Columbia CGT 33651.
*The Winter of '88*, MCA 3436.
*Birds Can't Row Boats*, Relix RRCD-2034.
*Let Me In*, Pointblank 91744-2.

*Scorchin' Blues*, Epic 52446.
*Together—Live!* Blue Sky PZT-34033.
*Hey, Where's Your Brother?* Pointblank 86812-2.
*Live in Houston, Busted in Austin,* Magnum 100
*Blues to the Bone*, Relix 2054.
*Rock & Roll People*, Sony 20319.
*Jack Daniels Kind of Day*, Thunderbolt 142.
*White Lightnin'*, Thunderbolt 149.
*Livin' in the Blues*, Sundazed 6070.
*Ease My Pain*, Sundazed 6071.
*School Boy Blues*, Collectables 672.
*Sidemen*, Collectables 673.
*Electric Blues Man*, Thunderbolt 509.
*Liberty Hall Sessions (Live)*, Magnum 82.
*White Hot Blues*, Sony 65213.
*White Heat*, M.I.L. Multimedia 3031.
*Live in NYC '97*, Virgin 45527.
*Livin' in the Blues*, Delta 21241.
*Suicide Won't Satisfy*, Thunderbolt 192.
*Black Cat Bone*, Thunderbolt 193.
*Walkin' by Myself*, Relix RRCD-2048.

# ROD PIAZZA

## *Jumpin' Blues*

Blues influences are as varied as blues styles. All of the old blues masters have touched one or more individuals of the new generation of blues singers. Although George "Harmonica" Smith never attained the same popularity as Little Walter, Sonny Boy Williamson II, Junior Wells, John Lee "Sonny Boy" Williamson I, and Big Walter Horton, he was a mentor to two very important modern harmonica players. One of these blues artists made wise use of Smith's teachings to forge a successful career with his swinging, jumpin' blues. His name is Rod Piazza.

Rod Piazza was born on December 18, 1947, in Riverside, California. He grew up on the West Coast listening to many different kinds of music, including the rock-and-roll explosion of the 1950s, rhythm and blues, jazz, and the good-time surf/pop music of the Beach Boys. But it was the blues, particularly the harmonica workouts of the Mississippi Saxophone, Little Walter, and the hard-edged riffs of George "Harmonica" Smith, that pointed him toward his musical destiny. He settled on the harmonica as his instrument of choice in his early teens, and practiced incessantly with aspirations of some day playing with his two idols.

When he turned eighteen, Piazza formed the Dirty Blues band. They released two albums on the ABC/Bluesway label. The first, in 1967, was self-titled, and the second, *Stone Dirt*, was issued in 1969; both featured the tough vocals and sharp playing of Piazza. He disbanded the group after the second album to form a band with one of his boyhood idols, George "Harmonica" Smith.

George "Harmonica" Smith was born on April 22, 1924, in Helena, Arkansas. He fell in love with the blues at an early age, and, having honed his harmonica skills to the point where he could make a decent living, he roamed the South looking for work. Like many other bluesmen from the South, Smith moved to Chicago in the early 1950s and eventually gained the coveted harmonica chair in the Muddy Waters band. Although his stint with Waters wasn't a long one (he left after one year), Smith picked up valuable performing tips from Muddy. He relocated to the West Coast, where he found steady work and became a respected member of the West Coast blues community, performing with a variety of bluesmen. He returned occasionally to the Windy City to perform and often shared the stage with Otis Spann and Otis Rush.

It was upon one of Smith's returns to Los Angeles from Chicago that he and Piazza began to work together. They formed the band Bacon Fat and proceeded to tear up stages with their electrifying one-two harmonica punch. Piazza, ever the alert student, was eager to learn all the performing tricks that Smith was willing to teach him. Bacon Fat released two albums, *Grease One for Me*, in 1970, and *Tough Dude*, in 1971. They also toured extensively, backing such blues legends as Big Mama Thornton, T-Bone Walker, and Big Joe Turner. Piazza also found time to release a couple of solo albums, *Bluesman* and *Chicago Flying Saucer Band*, neither of which did much to boost his career.

In 1973, Piazza met keyboardist, and his future wife, Honey Alexander. They played together off and on for a couple of years and then formed the Rod Piazza Blues Band. In 1980, Piazza, along with Miss Honey and longtime bass player Bill Stuve, officially became Rod Piazza and the Mighty Flyers. They had already built a strong reputation in the California blues community as a band that delivered hard-rocking, Chicago-influenced, smoking blues. Despite receiving recognition as a top-notch live attraction, they were unable to secure a recording contract from a major label in the 1980s. Between 1981 and 1985, the Mighty Flyers released three albums: *Radioactive Material* (1981), *Filo Under Rock* (1984), and *From the Start to the Finish* (1985). All three records were an honest testimony to the band's genuine character. Although ignored by all the major labels, the band would not be denied, and continued to play every concert with the same ferocity as if they were an internationally rated band with a major recording contract. In 1989, Rod and Honey were married.

On October 2, 1983, George "Harmonica" Smith died. His death was a severe blow to Piazza, who had learned much from his mentor and had covered some of the elder bluesman's songs, including "California Blues." On the *Blues in the Dark* album, Piazza and the band paid tribute to Smith the best way they knew—through their music. The song "4811 Wadsworth (Blues for George)" was a heartfelt number that showed Piazza's respect for the deceased bluesman. Beyond that, though Smith has long passed away, his spirit lives on in Piazza with every note he plays on stage and in the studio.

At the beginning of the 1990s, the Mighty Flyers' fortunes began to change. Their first record for Black Top was *Blues in the Dark*, in 1991. It featured the same formula that had been captivating audiences for a decade: Piazza with his fierce harmonica chops wailing over a heavy wall of sound. The success of *Blues in the Dark* enabled the band to headline at major concert venues throughout the country and abroad. Although they wouldn't record another album until 1997, Rod Piazza and the Mighty Flyers were accepted as a major blues act throughout the blues community.

In 1997, *Tough & Tender*, the band's first true studio album in five years, was released on the Tone-Cool label. Ten of the songs on the album were penned by the husband-wife team of Rod and Honey Piazza, with guitarist Rick "L.A. Holmes" Holmstrom writing the other. While the songs did not contain the subtlest of lyrics, the harmonies and tones compensated for that lack of depth; the playing was outstanding throughout the work. With such groove tunes as "Power of the Blues," "Tough and Tender," "Sea of Fools," "The Teaser," "Blues and Trouble," and "Hang Ten Boogie," the band demonstrated that they were a premier West Coast blues-jazz quintet capable of rocking with the best of them.

Not only were Rod Piazza and the Mighty Flyers finally achieving the kind of recognition they deserved for their studio work, they also were honored by the blues community. They captured the W. C. Handy award for Band of the Year in both 1999 and 2000. Piazza received a W. C. Handy award as Instrumentalist of the Year in 1998. With the talented lineup in the Mighty Flyers, it is only a matter of time before the adulation spreads throughout the entire band.

The *Here and Now* CD, released in 1999, was a critical and financial success. A powerful, swinging album, it was a modern jumpin' blues effort that would have made T-Bone Walker, PeeWee Crayton, and all of the West Coast stylists smile in appreciation. The band really cooked on such rocking jump-blues numbers as "Chicken Shack Boogie," "Bad, Bad Boy," "Low Down Dog," and "Deep Fried." Everyone shone on the album and served notice that Piazza was not the only one with talent in the band.

Rod Piazza and the Mighty Flyers continue to record and perform.

Rod Piazza is a blues gem. His career has been the model of consistency since the mid 1970s, as he has, with his infectious harmonica playing and the help of his talented band, carved out his own niche in the blues world. Rod Piazza and the Mighty Flyers are one of the most exciting and spectacular live attractions on the tour circuit today. He is a respected artist in the blues community and is a prime exemplar of the West Coast jump blues.

The Piazza harmonica style owes a great deal to a variety of influences. There is, of course, the aforementioned George "Harmonica" Smith. Piazza learned three important lessons from Smith: how to excite and work an audience; how to survive life on the road; and how to appreciate the precious gift that is the blues. The mentor-student relationship between Smith and Piazza is reminiscent of other such partnerships in modern blues history. Certainly the musical friendship between Son House and John Mooney comes immediately to mind. The close connections that both Rory Block and Bonnie Raitt had with some of the old country-blues masters, including House, Mississippi John Hurt, Fred McDowell, Skip James, and Bukka White, are other beautiful examples.

Piazza also learned much from Little Walter, who had a major impact on Rod's early development. Although they did not enjoy the same kind of close working relationship that Piazza had with Smith, he picked up some important technical tips from Little Walter. More than any other stylist it was Little Walter who showed Piazza the wide range and possibilities of the harmonica. Like Little Walter, Piazza learned how to "swing" on his blues harp.

Other important influences were the jazzy West Coast horn styles of various players. Like many other blues harmonica stylists, Piazza thinks of his instrument as a horn and plays it as if it were one. His ability to add textures to a song like those of the horns in a jazz combo is one of the essential elements of his overall style.

Piazza is as much a link to the past as he is to the future. He has taken the sharp-edged Chicago blues teachings of George "Harmonica" Smith and turned them into a modern sound that is appreciated by today's blues fans. Despite his close association with Smith and his close study of Little Walter and the West Coast jazz horns, Piazza has never been an imitator. He has always strived to break new ground as a harmonica player, leaning toward innovative sounds rather than recycling old material.

Rod Piazza is one of the most important of the modern harmonica players who are furthering the traditions established by pre-war harpists like Sonny Boy Williamson I and post-war harmonica players like Little Walter, James Cotton, Big Walter Horton and Junior Wells. Piazza can play it smooth and slow, grooving in the pocket, or burn it up with a furious intensity that is pure overdrive. His wide range of abilities enables him to deliver a mosaic of harmonica sounds.

Rod Piazza is also a splendid bandleader, capable of expertly uniting the different personalities and their respective talents into a cohesive whole. In concert, a group dynamic flows among all band members, as Piazza never dominates the spotlight and allows everyone in the group an equal chance to shine. They are truly among the elite of the modern electric blues groups, and their brand of infectious jumpin' blues is always guaranteed to bring the house down. Any duet between Honey Piazza and Steve Mugalian is a showstopper.

There is no doubt that the members of the Mighty Flyers have played a major role in Piazza's rise to the top, despite the occasional lineup changes. In 1995, when long-time guitarist Alex Schultz left the band, Piazza was able to recruit Rick "L.A. Holmes" Holmstrom. Holmstrom, with his hot, jazzy guitar licks, added a new and exciting dimension to the band's musical dynamics. The departure of Jimi Bott initiated a search for a drummer, and the winning candidate was Steve Mugalian, who provided a different texture to the band's overall sound.

The two longest-serving members of the band, Bill Stuve and Honey Piazza, have been with Piazza for over twenty years. Stuve, who has also released a couple of solo albums, is a steady rolling man who has always laid down a solid bass. The solid playing of Miss Honey on keyboards provides a launching pad for Piazza's solo explosions. She is also a prolific songwriter who contributes a good batch of songs for every studio album. Her easy-on-the-eyes presence in concert adds to the band's distinct personality. Rod and Honey are one of the few husband-and-wife blues teams on the circuit today; they evoke memories of another partnership that thrilled blues fans long ago, Ma and Pa Rainey.

After the sad passing of William Clarke, Piazza was thrust to the forefront of the West Coast jumpin' blues harmonica style. His band is now one of the best and brightest West Coast blues stylists around, as only Little Charlie and the Nightcats can be said to be in the same class. There will always be a place for a band like Rod Piazza and the Mighty Flyers with their unique West Coast jumpin' blues.

## Discography

*Bluesman*, LMI 1005.
*Chicago Flying Saucer Band*, Gangster.
*Harpburn*, Black Top 1087.
*So Glad to Have the Blues*, Murray Bros 1009.
*Blues in the Dark*, Black Top 1062.
*Live at B. B. King's Blues Club*, Big Mo 1026.
*California Blues*, Black Top 1062.
*Tough & Tender*, Tone-Cool 1165.
*Vintage—Live 1975*, Tone-Cool 116.
*Here and Now*, Tone-Cool 471170.
*The Essential Collection*, Hightone 8041.
*Mighty Flyers*, Right Hemisphere 101.
*Robot Woman II*, Shanghai 100.
*Alphabet Blues*, Black Top 1076.

With Dirty Blues Band:

*Dirty Blues Band*, Bluesway BLS-6010.
*Stone Dirt*, Bluesway BLS-6020.

With Bacon Fat:

*Bacon Fat*, Blue Horizon [1969].
*Grease One for Me*, Blue Horizon 4807.
*Tough Dude*, Blue Horizon 2431001.

With the Mighty Flyers:

*Radioactive Material.*
*File Under Rock*, Takoma 7108.
*From the Start to the Finish*, Pausa 72011.

# JOE LOUIS WALKER

## *A Blues Soul*

At the turn of the century blues singers were considered by "respectable folks" to be incarnations of the devil on earth. Today blues singers are seen in a more favorable light, as they win prestigious awards, rub elbows with high-ranking public officials, appear in the best venues throughout the world, and gain respect and recognition for their contributions to global music. Ironically, blues singers today are no different in spirit than the blues singers of yesteryear. One of the modern electric blues artists who is a true blues soul is a sound example. His name is Joe Louis Walker.

Joe Louis Walker was born on December 25, 1949, in San Francisco, California. He discovered the guitar at fourteen and taught himself the basics of the blues. But Walker was not limited in his musical tastes; he also dabbled in rock. One of the most important influences in his early development as a musician was Mike Bloomfield. The two were roommates, and Walker picked up some valuable tips from Bloomfield. Bloomfield expanded Walker's musical horizons by introducing him to the music of Jimi Hendrix and The Grateful Dead. At the strong urging of his friend, Walker made a special trip to Chicago to get closer to the modern urban blues scene, which proved to be a valuable experience later on in Walker's career.

After a decade of trying to make a name on the blues scene without much success, Walker turned to gospel music. He joined the Spiritual Corinthians and stayed with the group for ten years. The blues seemed like a part of his distant past until he rediscovered the music at the New Orleans Jazz & Heritage Festival in 1985. Walker immediately left the world of gospel music and re-embraced the blues. He formed a band called the Boss Talkers and recorded the album *Cold Is the Night* on the High-tone label. The batch of songs included on the album were all original compositions written by Walker, except for "Ten More Shows to Play," which he co-wrote with Lowell Fulson.

The band's touring schedule filled up with dates and they returned to the studio brimming with confidence to record their follow-up album, *The Gift*. The Boss Talkers provided a fine set of musicians for Walker to work with and the addition of the Memphis Horns only enhanced the product. The lineup of the Boss Talkers changed over the years, but one of the constants was Henry Oden on bass. He also served as arranger on occasion.

*Blue Soul,* their third album released on the Hightone label, featured hard blues and folk blues with elements of gospel music thrown in for good measure. Walker was quickly carving a strong reputation in the blues business. While his studio work had garnered some favorable attention, however, his live act was virtually ignored; that is, until his 1988 appearances at Slim's in San Francisco.

Two albums of live material were released on the Hightone label, both recorded at Slim's club. They included some memorable tunes, including "Hot Tamale Baby," a tribute to Clifton Chenier, the Zydeco king; "Little by Little," the old Junior Wells song; and a duet with Angela Strehli, "Don't Mess Up a Good Thing." Huey Lewis played harmonica on both volumes one and two.

Walker left Hightone and signed with Verve Records in 1993. His releases on Verve demonstrated a definite maturity in his playing, his singing, and his songwriting. The more polished studio work on *Blues Survivor, Blues of the Month Club,* and *Hello Everybody* established him as one of the leaders in contemporary blues. By the middle of the 1990s Walker was being favorably compared to Robert Cray: both were capable of delivering innovative guitar licks, smooth vocals, accessible songs, and stately concert performances. Each artist boasted a strong fan base, with each camp claiming their candidate as the leader of contemporary blues.

Walker's next effort, *Preacher & the President,* was a textbook example of how a modern blues record should sound. It contained fresh, imaginative songs that worked together like a series of stories in a book. The playing was sharp and crisp, demonstrating a high level of musicianship, and the record was not overproduced. Walker and the Boss Talkers decided the direction of the album would be a melting pot of musical styles tied together by a fine blues string.

Their follow-up album, *Silvertone Blues,* was a back-to-the-roots album featuring a raw collection of mostly acoustic blues that drew rave reviews from the purists and that included interesting duets with James Cotton and Alvin Youngblood Hart. The barrelhouse, boogie-woogie piano of Kenny Wayne added an exciting texture to the entire production, while the rhythm section of Joe Thomas on bass and Chris Sandoval on drums added another dimension to the CD.

The album indicated the wide range of Walker's style and musical gifts; without a doubt it was the best album he ever recorded. From the opening cut, "Runnin' from the Devil," to the Robert Nighthawk classic "Crying Won't Help You," the album cooked. The Sunnyland Slim standard "It's You Baby" was a standout. The driving boogie numbers "Kenny's Barrelhouse" and "Silvertone Blues" firmly established the intensity of classic down-home blues at its finest, as Walker left no stone unturned with this bountiful collection of blues and blues-shaded treasures.

He continues to record and perform.

Joe Louis Walker is a solid blues fixture. He has been on the scene for well over a decade and has shone with his display of talent, wit, and blues sense. Although not as well known as he should be, Walker has earned the respect of his fellow musicians throughout the blues community. He has covered much territory in his career and his standing as blues journeyman is just part of his story.

He is a natural guitar player who rolls out funky rhythms and smooth solos with an ease that doesn't justify his current level of recognition. Walker appears to be hardly playing a lick when in fact he is churning out chunks of burning notes that give the listener chills. He is capable of playing slow country-blues with as much feeling as a roomful of guitarists, hard-edged Chicago stomp and romp, stylish jazz runs, and beautifully crafted gospel passages. He is a guitar player's guitarist, an excellent example for any blossoming musician to study and learn from.

His soul-soaked voice is an extension of his guitar playing. His ten years as a gospel singer taught him control and tone. He sings with intense emotion and is able to vary his delivery to fit the style of music that emerges from his singing guitar. He possesses one of the best contemporary blues voices in the business and is underrated as a singer.

Walker, along with Robert Cray, has helped to maintain a relatively young African American presence in the electric blues. Although he turned to gospel and made an impact in that genre for a decade, his true calling is the electric blues. He is an immensely talented individual and a true inspiration for all aspiring African American musicians unsure of what musical path to follow.

Walker has injected respectability and class into the blues in the same way that T-Bone Walker did in his era. Although it is unfair to compare someone still building his career, like Walker, to a legend like T-Bone, there are many similarities. Joe Louis definitely took a page from T-Bone's book of blues playing and behavior. Like T-Bone, Walker injects his blues with large chunks of jazz and soul. Joe Louis projects smoothness, gentleness, and a sophistication that reminds one of T-Bone. Despite sharing the same surname, they are not related; yet, when one compares their singing and playing it makes one wonder if they are not intertwined more closely than just as blues singers.

Another major influence on Walker was Buddy Guy, the current king of Chicago blues, who is a genuine blues chameleon with the ability to mimic any performer in blues history. Although Walker has not followed the same path as Guy, they share some common characteristics in their ability to create special blues worlds with their finely honed skills.

Joe Louis Walker, a product of the West Coast blues scene, has carried on the tradition established by T-Bone Walker, Amos Milburn, Lowell Fulson, Pee Wee Crayton, Percy Mayfield, and Charles Brown. He possesses the same cool vocals and the same stinging yet controlled guitar attack, and is able to handle a wide range of material. The West Coast blues, that primarily jazzy, piano-driven music of expatriates, is alive and well in the capable hands of Joe Louis Walker.

He is also an excellent bandleader who has guided various aggregations of the Boss Talkers throughout his career. His ability to unite all elements and personalities is one of his strongest assets. In addition to the Boss Talkers, Walker has worked with a veritable who's-who of blues musicians, including James Cotton, Alvin Youngblood Hart, Angela Strehli, and Lucky Peterson, to name just a few.

Joe Louis Walker has never been accorded superstar status simply because he has never delivered a sensational album. Although his recorded efforts have been solid and very good, the one smash hit that would define his career and earn him the true respect he deserves has so far eluded him. Nevertheless Walker, a tremendously talented individual, has proven that he is a genuine blues soul.

## Discography

*Cold Is the Night*, Hightone 8006.
*The Gift*, Hightone 8012
*Blue Soul*, Hightone 8019.
*Live at Slim's*, Hightone 8015.
*Live at Slim's*, Vol. 1, Hightone 8025.
*Live at Slim's*, Vol. 2, Hightone 8036.
*Blues Survivor*, Verve 314-519063-2.
*JLW*, Polygram 523118.
*Blues of the Month Club*, Verve 527999.
*Hello Everybody*, Verve 7999.
*Preacher & the President*, Polygram 533476.
*Silvertone Blues*, Polygram 547721.
*Great Guitars*, Polygram.

# ROBERT CRAY

## *The Contemporary Bluesman*

The essential sound of the blues is derived from its African roots, the chants of the field hollers, church and gospel music, and black entertainment at the turn of the twentieth century. But in the past hundred years the infiltration of other styles of music, including soul, gospel, rhythm and blues, rock and roll, and pop, has expanded the rigid parameters of the blues. Today the blues embrace a healthy mixture of a variety of musical ideas. One of the most important artists to stretch the boundaries of the standard blues forms to give his music a more modern appeal is known as the contemporary bluesman. His name is Robert Cray.

Robert Cray was born on August 1, 1953, in Columbus, Georgia. Since his father was in the military, young Robert was able to call many places home, including Atlanta, Virginia, California, and Germany. It was in Germany that he began his musical career by learning to play the piano. By the time the family had settled in Tacoma, Washington, Robert was playing the guitar, trying to imitate his rock-and-roll heroes Keith Richards, Eric Clapton, Jeff Beck, and Jimmy Page.

Cray was an eager student of music and listened to rock, pop, rhythm and blues, soul, and country while growing up. Sam Cooke and Ray Charles were important early singing influences, but it wasn't until 1969, when he attended an Albert Collins concert, that Cray was properly introduced to the blues. From that point on Cray directed his energies toward building a blues career, jamming with an untold number of budding musicians in the Tacoma area. In 1974 he formed the Robert Cray band with bassist Richard Cousins. They hooked up with Cray's idol, Albert Collins, and served as his back-up unit for some time before breaking out on their own.

Through extensive touring they built a devoted following around Seattle and surrounding areas. In 1980, Cray's first album, *Who's Been Talkin'?* was released on Tomato Records. It contained "Who's Been Talkin'," a Willie Dixon composition, as well as O. V. Wright's "I'm Gonna Forget About You" and the Freddie King classic "The Welfare (Turns Its Back on You)." There were also a couple of Cray's own tunes, the best being "Nice as a Fool Can Be" and "That's What I'll Do." Although a solid effort that in retrospect features all the Cray trademarks—the imaginative guitar playing, the husky, soulful voice, the careful choice of material—the record did not break him out as a national blues act.

The quality of the next two albums, *Bad Influence* and *False Accusations*, demonstrated a definite maturity on Cray's part; however, despite the fact that both were legitimate efforts from a major-league blues artist, again neither did much to increase his popularity. Each album was made up of a handful of what are now Cray classics.

On *Bad Influence*, the originals "Phone Booth," "Bad Influence," "So Many Women, So Little Time" were complemented by two superb covers: "Don't Touch Me," an old Johnny "Guitar" Watson staple, and Eddie Floyd's "Got to Make a Comeback." The power of the album proved that Cray was ready to step forward and assume the title of major blues act; however, he still wasn't given his proper due. *False Accusations* was also a fine contemporary blues record but without the same power as its predecessor. However, it did include the memorable "Playin' in the Dirt," the title cut "False Accusations," and "I've Slipped Her Mind."

In 1985, Cray teamed up again with his idol Albert Collins and with the Fire Maker, Johnny Copeland, to record *Showdown!* Seemingly overnight, the respect that Cray had been seeking for so long arrived in a gift-wrapped box. The landmark recording won Cray his first of many Grammy awards; it was the kind of album every artist dreams of putting together. Cray's name became synonymous with modern blues guitar.

The breakthrough album opened many doors for Cray. He became a headliner and played concerts all over the United States, Canada, Europe and the Far East. His follow-up album, *Strong Persuader*, won him another Grammy. He made an appearance with Chuck Berry and Keith Richards in the movie *Hail Hail Rock 'n' Roll*. He was invited to perform with Eric Clapton on *24 Nights*, a live album recorded at the Albert Hall that also featured the fine guitar work of Jimmie Vaughan, Albert Collins, and Buddy Guy, and the rollicking piano of Johnnie Johnson.

Cray's sixth album, *Don't Be Afraid of the Dark*, was also a million seller and won him another Grammy. Once again, Cray wrote or had a hand in writing nearly all the songs on the record. There is no doubt that *Don't Be Afraid of the Dark* was a wonderful modern blues collection, but the power of *Strong Persuader* was a hard act to follow. Despite some weak tracks, however, blues fans snapped it up, enhancing Cray's reputation as the consummate contemporary blues artist.

His follow-up *Midnight Stroll* was also another winner and proved that Cray had the magic touch. While he had not forsaken his blues roots, there was more of a soul feeling to *Midnight Stroll* than any previous effort. Cray, who possesses a deep, rich voice, was able to achieve the perfect blend of the Albert Collins blues and Otis Redding soul that he had been seeking since his first release. It all came together nicely on the song "The Forecast (Calls for Pain)."

Despite his very hectic touring schedule, Cray continued to pump out blues-soul-flavored records that won him a Grammy or a W. C. Handy award—or sometimes both. Although *I Was Warned* did not win him any prizes, it was still a powerful effort that featured strong tracks, including the title cut as well as "Just a Loser," "I'm a Good Man," "Picture of a Broken Heart," and "Price I Pay." This record was a clear example of Cray's Southern-fried soul-blues music. *I Was Warned* also featured the composition skills of Steve Cropper (Cray and Cropper co-wrote "On the Road Down"). Boz Scaggs also contributed a song he co-wrote with producer Dennis Walker, "Picture of a Broken Heart."

By the early 1990s Cray could do very little wrong. *His Shame + A Sin* record, a return to a more pronounced blues sound, was another hit. The album was important for a few reasons, perhaps the biggest one being the departure of Richard Cousins, who had been with Cray for almost twenty years; Karl Sevareid replaced Cousins on bass. The Albert King gem, "You're Gonna Need Me," was the highlight of the album, which featured many wonderful moments, including "1040 Blues," "I Shiver," "Some Pain, Some Gain," "Leave Well Enough Alone," and "I'm Just Lucky That Way."

Cray continued to deliver solid blues records with seemingly little effort. *Some Rainy Morning* exemplified the work of a professional modern bluesman earning his pay, with Cray's excellent guitar playing and instantly recognizable vocals the two engines that drove the album along. There was the usual array of self-penned Cray classics like "Moan," "Never Mattered Much," "Little Boy Big," as well as Syl Johnson's "Steppin' Out" and Wilson Pickett's "Jealous Love," two cover songs that burned with unusual intensity.

Cray's eleventh album, *Sweet Potato Pie*, was released in 1997. It was recorded in Memphis, which guaranteed his usual soulful feel. The funky horns and driving rhythms underline one of the best efforts of his career. Cray wrote seven of the songs on the CD, including "Do That for Me," "Back Home," "Little Birds," "Not Bad for Love," and "I Can't Quit." There was also an excellent rendition of the Redding song "Trick or Treat." With this album Cray left no doubt that he was the best exponent of the post-modern blues-soul sound anywhere.

The culmination of Cray's interest in blending blues and soul together was achieved in *Take Your Shoes Off*. It burned with a Memphis soul groove and the material was outstanding, with soul-drenched tracks like "24-7 Man," Solomon Burke's "Won't You Give Him (One More Chance)," and "Love Gone to Waste." The inclusion of Willie Dixon's "Tollin' Bells" ensured that the album wasn't a pure soul effort.

Cray continues to record and perform.

Robert Cray is a modern superstar of the blues. He owns a bag full of Grammy Awards; his albums have sold millions of units; his name is popular in many corners of the globe, even where the blues have not yet caught on with genuine intensity; and he has the admiration and respect of his peers. The name Robert Cray elicits nods of familiarity, clenched fists, and knowing grins throughout blues circles everywhere. More than anything Cray has managed to combine his deep interests in soul and blues to create his own distinctive sound.

If he had not chosen a blues path in music, Cray would have made a large impact on soul music. His smooth-as-a-jewel voice sets him apart from other blues singers who shout the lyrics for emphasis. Cray's deep vocalizing carries the listener to a world of rainy nights spent in dimly lit, smoke-filled nightclubs, full of mystery and intrigue. His rich, soothing vocals are as much an asset to him as are his distinctive abilities on the guitar.

Perhaps the best word to describe Cray's guitar playing is accessible. It does not offend or insult the listener; it creates a world of comfort with few unexpected directions. Every note chosen fits snuggly with the previous one played and the one to follow. Although his solos are calculated, precise, and true exercises of guitar mastery, however, they still leave something to the imagination. Cray has a master's touch on the guitar and his knowledge of the fret board is impeccable.

But Robert Cray is more than just another bluesman with a good voice and impressive guitar chops; he is a visionary. Cray realized a long time ago that to survive as a modern blues singer he needed to expand the parameters of the genre in order not to sound like an imitator. Although many modern blues artists incorporate different styles into their blues, none have quite the same touch as Robert Cray. He is unique, untouchable, and undaunted.

Robert Cray, along with Stevie Ray Vaughan, Albert Collins, and Johnny Copeland, was largely responsible for the great blues revival that occurred in the 1980s. And he was one of the main architects of the popularity the blues enjoy today. It is more than a decade since *Showdown!* was released, but it still is coveted by blues fans and continues to sell impressive quantities every year. It remains one of the best blues albums of the past twenty years.

Robert Cray has carried on where Albert Collins left off. Collins—the single most important influence on Cray—built his career on pure blues. Although Cray has laced his blues sound with large chunks of soul, pop, rhythm and blues and rock, he has never completely strayed from the blues foundation. Collins made his mark as an individual bluesman because of his stark, individual guitar playing, and Cray has done the same. But Cray has been able to surpass the popularity of his mentor because of his vocal gifts.

Other important influences on Cray were B. B. King, Jimi Hendrix, Albert King, and Otis Redding, as well as the second generation of guitar players from the West Side, Buddy Guy, Magic Sam, and Otis Rush. He can roll out smooth, controlled solos like those of B. B. King. He has united several musical tastes into his own personal sound the way Jimi Hendrix did. He can bend strings in the same vein as Albert King. He has taken a page from the "Clown Prince of Soul," Otis Redding, in the way he entertains the crowd. He has taken the urban, amplified Chicago blues of Magic Sam, Buddy Guy, and Otis Rush, and incorporated it seamlessly with his other musical flavors.

After more than a decade at the top of the business, Cray has become the blues singer newcomers admire and look to imitate. One of the best examples is Dave Hole, the Australian blues guitarist with the heavy slide sound. Although Cray is not known for his slide-guitar abilities, his intelligent approach to the music has obviously rubbed off on Hole. But Hole isn't the only blues singer to be profoundly influenced by Cray; Javier Vargas, with his smooth guitar lines and his ability to create his Spanish blues by combining different musical concepts, owes a great debt to Cray. Kenny Wayne Shepherd and Jonny Lang are two others who have benefited greatly by listening to the records of Cray. Both Shepherd and Lang are modern guitar slingers who have forged their own sound instead of imitating the old blues masters, in much the same way that Cray did more than twenty years ago.

Cray is one of the most celebrated and honored of the modern American electric bluesman; his many Grammy and W. C. Handy awards are solid proof. He has won the Grammy for Best Contemporary Album on five different occasions: in 1999, *Take Your Shoes Off* was his fifth. He shared a Grammy with Jimmie Vaughan, Eric Clapton, Bonnie Raitt, B. B. King, Buddy Guy, Dr. John, and Art Neville for *SRV Shuffle*, a tribute to the late Stevie Ray Vaughan. He has also scored a few W. C. Handy awards: Vocalist of the Year in 1986-87; Band of the Year in 1987; Contemporary Album of the Year for *Bad Influence* in 1984; and for *Showdown!* in 1986. Every year from 1984 to 1987, Cray was nominated as the Contemporary Male Artist of the Year. He won on three different occasions for Single of the Year: in 1984 for "Phone Booth," in 1986 for "Changed Heart," and in 1987 for "Smoking Gun." He won for Song of the Year in 1986 for "False Accusations."

There is one more credit that must be attributed to Cray. Although his musical canon is loaded with classics, it is the song "Smoking Gun" that is regarded as the definitive example of the Robert Cray sound. The pure-as-spring-water vocals, the inventive guitar licks, the multi-flavored textures of musical styles are fused together perfectly. Many blues singers with an incredible amount of talent go through their entire careers without being able to say they have given the blues one major classic; not Cray. "Smoking Gun" is one song that many aspiring blues guitarists practice until they know it note for note.

When the question arises about the current state of the blues and its impending future, Robert Cray is always mentioned. As long as he continues to roll out his fine guitar lines combined with his suave and eloquent vocals, the future of the blues will burn brightly. Trust in the contemporary bluesman.

## Discography

*Who's Been Talkin'?* Tomato 269653.
*Bad Influence*, Hightone 8001.
*False Accusations*, Hightone 8005.
*Showdown!* Alligator 4743.
*Strong Persuader*, Mercury 830 568-1.
*Don't Be Afraid of the Dark*, Mercury 834 923-1.
*Midnight Stroll*, Mercury 846 652.
*I Was Warned*, Mercury 314 512 721-2.
*Shame + A Sin*, Mercury 314-518237-2.
*Some Rainy Morning*, Mercury 526867-2.
*Sweet Potato Pie*, Mercury 534483.
*Take Your Shoes Off*, Rykodisc 10479.
*Too Many Cooks*, Tomato R2-70381.

# WILLIAM CLARKE

## *Electric Harp Blues*

The West Coast blues style has a long history, dating back to the 1930s and 1940s, that includes such blues greats as T-Bone Walker, Pee Wee Crayton, Charles Brown, Lowell Fulson, and Percy Mayfield. More piano-based and jazz influenced than other styles of blues, the West Coast genre continues to entertain audiences today, thanks to a dedicated group of young blues singers. One of these modern warriors stunned the world with his electric harp blues in the 1980s and 1990s. His name was William Clarke.

William Clarke was born on March 29, 1951, in Inglewood, California. Although he was surrounded by a variety of music in his own backyard, including the show-biz tunes of Hollywood, first-rate West Coast jazz, and the good-time surfing music of the Beach Boys, Clarke was more interested in the British Invasion groups. He listened intently to the Rolling Stones and developed a taste for their brand of blues. When he was sixteen, he tried guitar and drums before eventually settling on the harmonica as his instrument of choice.

By his late teens he had decided to pursue a serious career as a blues singer and began to frequent the clubs around his neighborhood. In his travels he met and befriended T-Bone Walker, Eddie "Cleanhead" Vinson, Big Joe Turner, Pee Wee Crayton, Lowell Fulson, Big Mama Thornton, Shakey Jake Harris, Ironing Board Sam, R. S. Rankin, Smokey Wilson, and his greatest influence, George "Harmonica" Smith. They all encouraged the young Clarke toward a path as a blues musician as he developed his own distinct style.

His friendship and professional ties with George "Harmonica" Smith accelerated Clarke's evolution as a first-rate harpist. Smith's impressive résumé included a stint in the legendary Muddy Waters band of the 1950s. When George talked, young harmonica players like Clarke were eager to listen. His pearls of wisdom were exactly what a young, inexperienced blues harpist like Clarke needed.

Before he ever entered a recording studio, Clarke played hundreds of gigs all over the West Coast backing up his heroes and often sharing the stage with Smith. When he was unable to secure a recording contract from a major label, Clarke opted to record and release the albums himself. It was a painstaking process, but it taught him the ropes of record producing, specifically the amount of energy, dedication, and patience it takes to make a good blues record.

His first five albums hinted at the true genius that was William Clarke; but they were very rough and uneven compared to the polished records he would cut later on for Alligator. *Hittin' Heavy*, his first recording, was released on the Good Time label with Hollywood Fats backing him on guitar. Blues from Los Angeles featured his mentor George "Harmonica" Smith. *Can't You Hear Me Calling?* was an excellent foreshadowing of future projects that would prove to be more commercially and critically successful. *Tip of the Top* was dedicated to George "Harmonica" Smith, who had died the year before; now Clarke was on his own. *Rockin' the Boat* was a live recording that caught the attention of Bruce Iglauer, the president of Alligator Records.

While he was cutting obscure records for small labels, Clarke was touring California, the West Coast, and other nearby states playing hundreds of gigs and planting seeds through word of mouth that he was the next big name in electric harmonica blues. Those seeds would take time to sprout and ripen, but when they did, William Clarke would be reaping a bumper crop. Clarke, who also was a family man, worked as a machinist to support his family. He was biding his time and quietly paying his blues dues.

It all paid off handsomely when Bruce Iglauer stepped in and signed Clarke to a recording contract. It was time to reap the harvest of the seeds that he had planted with the sweat of his brow. His debut for Alligator Records, *Blowin' Like Hell*, caught the attention of the entire blues community. It was a dynamic effort that featured the jazzy, swinging West Coast blues sound; Clarke's harmonica drove the entire production along like a finely tuned engine humming with immense power. Some of the highlights of the album included "Lollipop Mama," "Gambling for My Bread," and "Lonesome Bedroom Blues."

There wasn't a weak track on the album as it burned with a funky groove. As in a fairy-tale Hollywood script, Clarke was catapulted to national attention seemingly overnight. Once, he had scrambled to scrape together gigs to keep his band on the road, but suddenly his was one of the most in-demand blues bands on the planet. In 1991, Clarke played over 250 concerts all over the United States and Europe and capped the year off with a W. C. Handy award for best blues song, "Must Be Jelly."

Clarke maintained the momentum with his second Alligator release, *Serious Intentions*. One of the best contemporary blues sets of the past decade, *Serious Intentions* clearly announced that William Clarke was a harmonica genius to all those who hadn't caught on yet. Some of the highlights included "Pawnshop Bound," a humorous look back at his leaner days when he was hustling to keep body and soul together. "Educated Fool," "Feel Like Jumping," and "Work Song" were all destined to become classics, the very songs that inspire young harmonica players to practice hard day and night.

By now William Clarke was as well established as any blues artist on the scene. He worked a heavy tour schedule all over the United States, Europe, and Canada, appearing at major blues festivals and in the top clubs. He had two excellent CDs on the market and his reputation had grown wider than the fat notes he played that never failed to stun audiences. He was the best harmonica player in the world, ahead of such stalwarts as Kim Wilson, Rod Piazza, and Charlie Musselwhite.

The aptly titled *Groove Time*, Clarke's third record on Alligator, summed up his music. When he took the stage, whether it was in a tiny, dimly lit smoke-filled club or a prestigious arena with thousands of screaming fans, it was time to groove; and no one could groove like William Clarke. It was on *Groove Time* that Clarke was able to make the happy marriage between the romp-and-stomp Chicago style and the jumping, jazz-oriented West Coast swing. "Daddy Pinnochio," "Saint or Sinner," and "Watch Dog" were some of the standouts on the CD. If anyone was looking for some harmonica-driven, foot-tapping, swinging blues, then they didn't have to look further than *Groove Time*.

Clarke's fourth project on Alligator, *The Hard Way*, showed him at the pinnacle of his blues career. It was a first-rate CD from a world-class harmonica player and singer. Clarke shone throughout the album, blowing his harp like a man possessed and singing with a matching ferocity. For his efforts Clarke won the 1996 W. C. Handy awards for Album of the Year, Song of the Year ("Fishing Blues"), and as Instrumentalist of the Year. The future seemed bright for the world's greatest exponent of the electric harmonica blues.

William Clarke played as hard as he worked. He lived for the blues and poured every ounce of energy into every single note he played. His concerts were legendary performances and his success was well earned; Clarke had taken the hard way his whole career. Along his travels, he had developed an alcohol dependency that had begun to affect his playing. Like Stevie Ray Vaughan before him, Clarke had faced and conquered his demons. He successfully remained sober, but the damage to his body had already been done. On November 2, 1996, the harmonica blues giant died of a bleeding ulcer in a Los Angeles hospital. He was forty-five years old.

William Clarke was a blues original. He was able to absorb the lessons that the old blues masters (particularly his mentor George "Harmonica" Smith) had shared with him and turn them into blues gold. He was, at the time of his death, regarded by many as the greatest electric harmonica player in the world. Even his detractors would be hard-pressed to admit that he wasn't one of the top two or three harp instrumentalists on the planet.

The secret of Clarke's harmonica appeal can be traced to two important factors. One, he was technically one of the soundest harpists in the history of the blues; he was a master of both the cross and chromatic harps. Two, he exuded the self-confidence of a Little Walter and explored musical dimensions that other harmonica players dared not enter.

Clarke developed his unique harmonica playing by taking a very scholarly approach. He studied various types of music, including jazz organists such as Jack McDuff, Jimmy McGriff, Shirley Scott, and

Richard "Groove" Holmes. He also listened intently to the sweet saxophone sounds of Eddie Lockjaw Davis, Gene Ammons, Lyne Hope, and Willis Jackson. The West Coast rhythms of these saxophone-organ swing bands were ingrained in Clarke's musical subconscious. He added the influences of Little Walter, Sonny Boy Williamson II, Junior Wells, and James Cotton—the premier Chicago harmonica players of the 1960s—to the teachings of George "Harmonica" Smith, who played the same brand of blues. The final ingredient was Clarke's own brilliant invention.

But Clarke was more than just a great harmonica player. He was also a crafty lyricist whose point of view centered on his working-class background. Many of his songs rang true with the working people living on the edge, just one bill away from financial ruin, one step ahead of the landlord and the repo man. "Pawnshop Bound" is an obvious song of despair and tough times, as is "Gambling for My Bread." There is an authenticity to many of Clarke's songs of hard times; he was not a casual observer, but lived the life.

Because his harmonica prowess gained so much attention, his vocal talents were sometimes overlooked. His voice was tailor-made for the swinging, jumping, rollicking blues style he played so effectively. He was a more than passable vocalist and never received the proper credit for his thick, hard vocals.

Along with Paul Butterfield, Clarke was one of the best harmonica stylists of the modern electric blues. His quick, precise choice of notes was derived from a pure instinct that he had built up during the lean days when he was paying his dues hanging out in the South Los Angeles ghettos. Although he had been influenced by a large and diverse group of musicians, Clarke was able to create his own individual style of blues that also incorporated large chunks of jazz, soul, and rock. There was never a doubt that Clarke knew how to rock the house; he had an uncanny sense of timing and rhythm.

The death of William Clarke was a major blow to the blues community and the music world at large. Just when it seemed that he had caught his second wind after having conquered his demons, he was cut down. He was heading toward new territory with his last album for Alligator and there is no telling what heights he would have scaled had he lived. However, despite a career that was cut off so abruptly, Clarke left us with a healthy catalog of his electric harp blues and many great memories.

## Discography

*Hittin' Heavy*, Good Times 1003.
*Blues from Los Angeles*, Hittin' Heavy 1002.

*Can't You Hear Me Calling?* Rivera 502.
*Tip of the Top*, Snatch 1002.
*Rockin' the Boat*, Rivera 503.
*Blues Harmonica*, Watch Dog 1005.
*Blowin' Like Hell*, Alligator AL 4788.
*Serious Intentions*, Alligator AL 4806.
*Groove Time*, Alligator AL 4827.
*The Hard Way*, Alligator AL 4842.
*Deluxe Edition*, Alligator AL.

# JIMMIE VAUGHAN

## *Thunderbird Blues*

The Texas blues tradition is filled with intense, independent characters who have made an important impact on the genre as a whole as well as on the Texas strain with their driving rhythms, hard-rocking guitar licks, and ingenious lyrics. The list includes the Father of the Texas Blues, Blind Lemon Jefferson, and incorrigible rebels like Sam Lightnin' Hopkins, T-Bone Walker, and Clarence "Gatemouth" Brown. And then there are Albert Collins, Freddie King, Johnny "Guitar" Watson, and Johnny Copeland. The modern electric blues movement is speckled with Texas bluesmen: Anson Funderburgh, Johnny Winter, Smokin' Joe Kubek, Stevie Ray Vaughan, and Billy Gibson, not to mention the man responsible for the thunderbird blues. His name is Jimmie Vaughan.

Jimmie Vaughan was born on March 20, 1951, in Dallas, Texas. He started playing guitar at an early age and displayed a facility that earned him the admiration of other musicians around the neighborhood, especially his little brother, Stevie Ray. While a youngster, Jimmie Vaughan discovered the blues of Muddy Waters, Buddy Guy, and B. B. King, and was hooked forever. But it was the Texas blues guitarists—Blind Lemon Jefferson, T-Bone Walker, Albert Collins, Oscar and Johnny Moore—who had the major impact on the impressionable young Vaughan.

He formed a band, the Swinging Pendulums, with his brother Stevie when he was thirteen. But his big break came when he joined the Chessmen, a local Dallas band led by Doyle Bramhall, who was a major influence on both Vaughan brothers. By the time he was fifteen, Jimmie Vaughan was a local rock star and had decided that he wanted to play music for a living. He realized that his opportunities in Dallas were limited, but Austin offered better possibilities.

At the age of sixteen he moved to Austin and for the next several years paid his musical dues. He played in a variety of bands, all with stars in their eyes chasing fame that never materialized. But in 1974 Jimmie Vaughan moved a little closer to his dream when he met a harmonica player from Minnesota. His name was Kim Wilson.

Kim Wilson was born in Detroit, Michigan, on January 6, 1951. He moved to California, but eventually settled in Minnesota. While most young boys who were interested in music picked up a guitar, Wilson took up the harmonica and by his late teens was a very good harmonica player. His biggest influences were Little Walter, George "Harmonica" Smith, Lazy Lester and James Cotton. Minnesota, not exactly a hot spot for blues singers back in the mid-sixties, provided Wilson with the place and space to get his chops down right. The first time he visited Austin, he made a favorable impression on all the local musicians including Jimmie and Stevie Ray Vaughan. A year later, Jimmie Vaughan decided to put a band together and called on Wilson. Wilson moved to Austin and the Fabulous Thunderbirds were born.

Despite the dynamic duo of Vaughan and Wilson, who sounded like the second coming of Muddy Waters and Little Walter, it was not instant success for the pair. The band, rounded out by Keith Ferguson on bass and Mike Buck on drums, often played Antone's, the newly opened bar/club in Austin that was a hangout for local musicians. The T-Birds developed a reputation as a thrilling live act but it wasn't until 1979, four years after the formation of the band, that they were able to secure a recording contract with a major label.

The band's first release on the Tacoma label, entitled The Fabulous Thunderbirds, did not make them overnight stars; it was tough going for a few more years. The band switched to Chrysalis Records and recorded three albums: *What's the Word?*, *Butt Rockin'* and *T-Bird Rhythm*. Despite lineup changes (Fran Christina had replaced Mike Buck) the Thunderbirds continued to churn out hard-driving, rocking blues that never failed to entertain a live crowd; but they were unable to capture the electricity of their live shows in the studio.

That all changed with the band's 1986 effort, *Tuff Enuff*. They had finally managed to deliver the same energy they created in front of an audience on record. They were instantly catapulted into the national blues spotlight. The title song was a top-ten hit and the album itself made it into the top twenty. Besides the outstanding title track, other highlights included "Wrap It Up," "Tell Me," "True Love," "Amnesia," and "Down at Antone's." Overnight, people discovered the hypnotic, boogie-woogie blues-rock that the band's most fervent followers had been enjoying for over a decade.

The band followed up their big hit with *Hot Number* and *Powerful Stuff*. Although both releases featured the same no-nonsense approach to blues-rock as the immensely successful *Tuff Enuff*, neither of the two latter albums provided the band with the same commercial and critical power. Nevertheless, they retained their position as one of the elite rocking blues band on a national and international level.

In 1989, after fifteen years as a Fabulous Thunderbird, Vaughan left the band to pursue a solo career. His first project was with his little brother Stevie Ray. The collaboration between the two Vaughan Brothers produced the acclaimed *Family Style, the Vaughan Brothers*. It was an album blues fans had anticipated for years. Unfortunately, any further future projects were eliminated by the tragic death of Stevie Ray in 1990.

Jimmie Vaughan, decimated by his brother's death, retired from the music business for a couple of years to grieve and decide his next move. By 1993 he was playing the occasional concert; in 1994 he returned with his first solo album, *Strange Pleasures*, which received good reviews and sold respectably well. It was a solid album with many highlights, including "Boom-Bapa-Boom," that had a driving Texas boogie beat. Other songs like "Tilt a Whirl," "Six Strings Down," "(Everybody's Got) Sweet Soul Vibe," and the title track "Strange Pleasures," all featured Vaughan's fat, sinister guitar lines. It was a hearty return to the blues world by Vaughan, considering the personal tragedy he had suffered. He supported *Strange Pleasures* with a national tour.

In 1998, he released his second solo album, *Out There*. The album showed Vaughan at his blues best with a collection of songs that ran together with frightening power. He used his greatest attributes—his guitar mastery and charisma—to create a product that entertained fans of all ages, whether they were hard-core blues fans demanding authenticity or newcomers to the blues looking for a path to follow. It was a true blues album created by a Texas bluesman who, after thirty years in the music business, knew what an audience liked and delivered just that. The rocking tunes "Like a King," "Out There," and "Motor Head Baby" were balanced with a slow, mouthwatering, "Can't Say No." Vaughan, one of the best blues guitarists in the last thirty years, let his instrument do the talking on "The Ironic Twist" and "Little Son, Big Son." *Out There* was a first-rate contemporary album by one of the best modern American electric guitar players.

He continues to record and perform.

Jimmie Vaughan is a quiet superstar. He remains one of the best-kept secrets in the blues, but at the same time his name is instantly recognized by any avid blues fan. Vaughan is one of the premier guitar stylists of the last twenty years. His incredible tone, his tasty guitar licks, and his stage persona have inspired a whole new generation of blues hopefuls. With the death of his younger brother Stevie Ray, a succession of axe warriors have all laid claim to a vacant throne. Jimmie Vaughan, who could easily occupy that royal position out of respect for his brother, has chosen to remain quiet.

Jimmie Vaughan was instrumental in putting the fledgling Austin music scene on the musical map. His hard-driving riffs and inspired solos were the cornerstones of what became known as the Austin sound. He was present from the beginning and helped shaped the style, the music, and the feeling of that era as much as anyone else.

Vaughan is an underrated guitarist because of his approach to playing the instrument. Instead of note-infested solos he produces a sparser quantity of licks with more feeling and intensity than a roomful of guitar players. While he looks as if he were hardly playing, the musical wall he builds is thick and real. Vaughan's playing has always been genuine and pure; there are no flashy tricks or gimmicks in his music.

He occupies a special place in the hierarchy of Texas blues guitarists. While he is of the later generation that includes his brother Stevie, Johnny Winter, Billy Gibbons, Delbert McClinton, and Smokin' Joe Kubek, he has also been inspired by the legion of Texas guitarists who came before him. Any avid blues fan can draw a straight line from Johnny "Guitar" Watson to Jimmie Vaughan. However, despite drawing upon the deep Texas source that includes T-Bone Walker, Sam Lightnin' Hopkins, Albert Collins, Blind Lemon Jefferson, Johnny "Guitar" Watson, and Johnny Clyde Copeland, Vaughan forged his own individual sound by melding the old with the new.

Vaughan is one of the most important contemporary blues guitarists in the world. Although he has not done very much since leaving the Fabulous Thunderbirds, his credentials remain solid. He was at the forefront of the blues revival of the 1980s; the Fabulous Thunderbirds blazed a trail that many bands have followed. Vaughan has been an important influence on Mike Morgan, Jeff Healey, Colin James, Chris Duarte, Amos Garrett, Kenny Wayne Shepherd, Jonny Lang, and Monster Mike Welch.

However, the greatest influence that Vaughan had on any modern guitar player was on his brother, Stevie Ray. While they were growing up, Jimmie was always a step ahead of his little brother and proved to be a major inspiration. Stevie Ray often claimed that his big brother was the greatest of the contemporary players. Whether he was being kind or truly speaking from the heart, few ever bothered to argue with such an authority as Stevie Ray.

Jimmie Vaughan has earned his rightful place in the hall of modern American electric bluesmen because of his vast contributions to the genre. After thirty years on the musical scene, he has survived and remains one of the most respected guitarists in the world. There is no doubt that he can still shake an audience with his greasy, high-flying thunderbird blues.

## Discography

*Strange Pleasures*, Epic 57202.
*Out There*, Epic 67653.

With The Fabulous Thunderbirds:

*The Fabulous Thunderbirds*, Chrysalis F2-21250.
*What's the Word?* Chrysalis F2-21287.
*Butt Rockin'*, Chrysalis F20-21319.
*T-Bird Rhythm*, Chrysalis F2-21395.
*Tuff Enuff*, Epic 40304.
*Hot Number*, Epic 40818.
*Powerful Stuff*, Epic 45094.

# STEVIE RAY VAUGHAN

## *Texas Flood*

When the marriage between the blues and rock and roll began to dissolve in the middle of the 1970s, the popularity of the blues had to be reinvented. While disco and punk rock garnered most of the musical headlines in the late 1970s and early 1980s, the blues were quietly rebuilding into a force to be reckoned with. It wasn't until 1983, however, that the blues resurgence occurred, when the music world was swept away by a Texas flood. The man who spearheaded the blues revival possessed a genuine blues soul, an individualistic spirit, and a distinctive virtuosity. His name was Stevie Ray Vaughan.

Stevie Ray Vaughan was born on December 21, 1954, in Dallas, Texas.

Although he idolized many blues greats, especially Albert King, the most important influence on Stevie was his older brother Jimmie. When his brother wasn't around, Stevie would unofficially borrow his guitar and marvel at unlocking the secrets that the instrument held. Eventually, he acquired his own proper guitar and quickly developed his own guitar skills. By the age of eleven he had already figured out "Jeff's Boogie," note for note. Anyone with a keen perception and appreciation for the musically gifted knew Stevie Ray was already something special on the guitar. But in order to turn his immense potential into concrete stardom, he first had to pay his dues.

He played in many local pickup bands from the tender age of twelve, in places that he wasn't legally old enough to be in. He jammed with the members of ZZ Top long before they were international stars. From the moment he had picked up his brother's guitar he had known that he wanted to be a low-down, six-string gunslinger. He developed an excellent guitar sensitivity to go with his oversized forearms and his large hands; he possessed many of the physical and mental tools to go far in the music business. Eager to pursue his love of music, he dropped out of high school a few months before graduation and headed to Austin.

After stints in the groups Blackbird, the Nightcrawlers, and Krackerjack, Stevie Ray joined his first professional band, called the Cobras. With a lead guitarist who attacked the guitar fretboard with blazing speed and heart-stopping precision, the name Cobras was perfect. Despite the band's promise, however, the group fell apart and Stevie Ray was forced to pick up the pieces and start all over again.

His next musical project was the Triple Threat Revue, with a lineup that consisted of W. C. Clarke on bass, Mike Kindred on keyboards, Freddie Pharoah on drums, Lou Ann Barton on lead vocals, and Stevie Ray on guitar. All possessed interesting musical résumés, having played all over Austin, the state of Texas, and the country. Although an odd mixture of musical personalities, the band could really tear it up. Despite the individual talent and the unlimited potential of the group as a whole, it, too, fell apart about a year later. Vaughan pared down the group to a power trio and named it Double Trouble, from the title of an old Otis Rush song.

Stevie Ray Vaughan and Double Trouble went through a few personnel changes until a set lineup of Chris Layton on drums, Tommy Shannon on bass, and Stevie Ray on guitar was settled on. It was this new version of his band that Vaughan took to the Montreux Jazz Festival—the first unrecorded band to ever play that prestigious event. The stage was left in smoldering ashes after their appearance. His performance at the festival aroused interest from an unlikely source: David Bowie invited Vaughan to play on the *Let's Dance* CD. It was a good warm-up experience for Stevie Ray, for not long after that he went into the studio with Double Trouble to record *Texas Flood*.

*Texas Flood* was the breakthrough album that Stevie Ray Vaughan had waited his entire career to record. Not only did the album catapult him to fame, it also officially ushered in the blues revival of the 1980s. Vaughan had reinvented the blues in a way that no one had heard since Jimi Hendrix came blasting through a stack of Marshall amplifiers some fifteen years before. Stevie Ray sparked a fire that drew new blues fans into the fold and provided a genuine guitar hero for older blues fans to cheer.

Every cut on the album was a classic. "Pride and Joy," "Texas Flood," "Rude Mood," all featured his undeniable guitar wizardry, his deep passion, his strong Texas blues roots, and his ability to boogie like a man possessed. It was a prime audio-bible for every aspiring blues and rock guitar player on the planet. Seemingly overnight, the band's tour schedule overflowed with requests.

To prove that *Texas Flood* was not a one-shot fluke, Vaughan followed up his stunning debut with the standout *Couldn't Stand the Weather*. It was on this album that Vaughan ventured into taboo territory, by a guitar player's standards, when he dared to include the previously uncovered Jimi Hendrix anthem "Voodoo Chile (Slight Return)." It was both a tribute to Hendrix and a statement by Vaughan that although the Seattle guitarist's material was sacred, it was not untouchable.

As he rapidly approached superstardom, Vaughan was beginning to experience personal problems. His marriage to his wife Lenny had failed. A legendary party animal who had indulged in drugs and alcoholic excess for years, he was starting to show the effects of his hard-living ways. His third album, *Soul to Soul*, suffered from a lack of direction despite the addition of Reese Wynans on keyboards. Later that year, when he passed out at a concert, it was clear that Vaughan needed help to overcome his substance-abuse problems.

Despite initial denial, he eventually checked himself into a clinic and started to rebuild his personal life. Through his inner strength and the help from family and friends, Vaughan managed to rehabilitate himself so he could continue his career. The album *In Step* was his triumphant return. From the opening song, "The House Is a Rockin'," to "Let Me Love You Baby" and the very personal "Wall of Denial," Vaughan clearly demonstrated that he was back.

While at one time he had craved drugs and alcohol, he now preached restraint and a healthier lifestyle to his friends, in concert, and to anyone else who cared to listen. Vaughan had worked out the demons that had haunted him for so many years and was on the fast track to a career revival.

One of the important events that was to be part of his comeback was a 1990 concert in Wisconsin, where he shared the stage with Eric Clapton, Robert Cray, Buddy Guy, and his brother Jimmie. The open-air concert was a celebration and Stevie Ray Vaughan had not sounded better in years.

Once the concert had ended, Stevie Ray, eager to return to Chicago, bargained for a seat on a helicopter that had been specifically assigned to carry the musicians to and from the concert. It was a cloudy night with dense fog. Stevie Ray, who had played one of the best concerts of his life, outshining such great guitarists as Clapton, Cray, Guy, and his brother Jimmie, never made it to Chicago. The helicopter crashed and Stevie Ray Vaughan died on August 27, 1990. He was thirty-five years old.

Stevie Ray Vaughan was a blues phenomenon, and one of the greatest guitar players of the twentieth century. His incomparable dexterity, his whiskey-drenched vocals, and his warm Texas spirit made him a legend. Stevie Ray Vaughan had shot across the musical sky like a meteor and captured everyone's attention for a brief moment.

The Stevie Ray Vaughan guitar style can be traced to four very important influences. The first is the Texas blues tradition. Vaughan was a monster player, in the same vein as Freddie King, Jimmie Vaughan, and Albert Collins. He was a pure Texan and possessed the individualistic spirit that all the Lone Star State blues axe men inherit. His tones, his tasty choice of notes, and his hard-driving rhythms were all traits of his playing.

Perhaps the biggest influence on Stevie Ray was his brother Jimmie, who was three years older than he. Jimmie Vaughan blazed the trail and opened up doors for his little brother. Stevie Ray was always proud of his older brother and wanted to be just like him, but Jimmie Vaughan, no slouch as a guitar player, never had a direct influence on Stevie Ray's playing. They might have traded some licks while growing up, but their friendly rivalry, contrasting personalities, and age difference always relegated Stevie Ray to second place. But Jimmie Vaughan taught his brother how to teach himself, and that was the most important lesson the older brother could have bestowed on the younger.

While B. B. King, Freddie King, Muddy Waters, Lonnie Mack, and dozens of other famous guitarists touched Stevie Ray in a special way, it was the large, left-handed Albert King who stood above the others. From a very early age Stevie Ray focused his attention on the Albert King style and eventually had the tone down cold. Years later, at Antone's one night, Stevie Ray was able to sit in with his legendary hero, who was astonished at the young Texan's mastery of the Albert King style. Vaughan had gained the respect of his idol.

The fourth greatest influence—and perhaps the most important—on Vaughan was Jimi Hendrix. Both were from lower-class families; both discovered the guitar at an early age; both had a deep, instinctive understanding of the rural blues. And they both had only a handful of years in the public spotlight, but made more of an impact than other blues singers with much longer careers. Both astonished listeners with their skills; both incorporated large chunks of rock and soul into their blues foundation. Both cut dashing figures on stage: Stevie Ray Vaughan wore a bad black hat perched on his head just so, colorful clothing, and cowboy boots.

They both rose quickly to superstardom after one incredible concert, Hendrix at the Monterey Pop Festival and Vaughan at the Montreux Jazz Festival. Both experienced personal problems as their careers went crashing out of control; both were haunted by many demons, experimenting with drugs and alcohol. They both played Fender Stratocasters and used Marshall amplifiers almost exclusively. The comparisons between Hendrix and Vaughan are as eerie as the circumstances surrounding their deaths.

Vaughan sparked the blues revival that still continues to this day. A decade later, his music sounds as fresh as when it was first recorded. Dozens of guitarists have emerged from the concert stage to challenge for the super-chops throne left vacant by his tragic death, but none have been able to fill Vaughan's impossibly large Texas blues shoes.

After his death, tributes poured forth from the many lives that he had touched. The community of musicians was in mourning: not only had they lost one of the true greats; they had also lost a brother, a comrade, a dear friend, and a special human being. In 1992, Buddy Guy finally received a Grammy for best contemporary blues album—*Damn Right, I've Got the Blues*. It included an instrumental entitled "Remembering Stevie." Both Bonnie Raitt and John Lee Hooker dedicated albums to the memory of Vaughan.

Unlike what happened after the death of Jimi Hendrix, however, the memory of Stevie Ray Vaughan has not been desecrated. Only three posthumous albums have been released—*Family Style, The Vaughan Brothers*; *The Sky Is Crying*; and *In the Beginning*. The album with his brother had been recorded before Stevie Ray's death. Ten years after his tragic death the album *In the Beginning*, recorded with the late Albert King, won a W. C. Handy award for Album of the Year and Contemporary Album of the Year. The power of Stevie Ray Vaughan reigns on.

Aside from his own mostly excellent material, Vaughan was a guest performer on a number of other works. He appeared on three different

Lonnie Mack releases, on Marcia Ball's *Soulful Dress*, on James Brown's *Gravity*, on Johnny Copeland's *Texas Twister*, and on Bob Dylan's *Under the Red Sky*, to name a few. He also added the soundtracks of the movies *Bull Durham* and *Rocky IV*, among others, to his distinguished résumé.

Stevie Ray Vaughan's professional career was brief but potent; his few years in the limelight only intensified his accomplishments. He was a nice kid from Texas who possessed a talent that could not be duplicated and he passed through like a warm Texas summer breeze. He pushed himself to his outer limits and beyond, giving the world his precious Texas Flood blues. There certainly will never be another like him.

**Discography**

*Texas Flood*, Epic 38734.
*Couldn't Stand the Weather*, Epic 39304.
*Soul to Soul*, Epic 40036.
*In Step*, Epic 45024.
*The Sky Is Crying*, Epic 47390.
*In the Beginning*, Epic 53168.
*Family Style, The Vaughan Brothers*, Epic 46225.

# TINSLEY ELLIS

## *The Georgia Flame Thrower*

There is in every musician's journey a turning point, a defining moment. For one fifteen-year-old aspiring blues guitarist, it was the night he was handed a broken string from the guitar of the legendary B. B. King. From that night on, this individual was determined to become an important blues singer, and he did, earning the nickname the Georgia Flame Thrower. His name is Tinsley Ellis.

Tinsley Ellis was born on June 4, 1957, in Atlanta, Georgia. He was reared in southern Florida and discovered the guitar at an early age. He became inseparable from his newly found friend and practiced hard to hone his skills. Like other modern musicians, Ellis listened to a wide variety of music and borrowed elements from each form to incorporate into his own developing style.

At seventeen he returned to his native Atlanta and teamed up with Preston Hubbard (who would later join The Fabulous Thunderbirds). The two renegade blues rockers played the club scene, paying their dues. In 1981, along with "Chicago" Bob Nelson, a well-seasoned harpist, they formed the Heartfixers. They took the name from one of Albert King's songs, "Heart Fixin' Business." The band quickly raced to the top of the Atlanta bar circuit, and, following a string of spectacular heart-stopping performances, decided their act was polished enough to allow them to record. Over time they recorded four albums.

Ellis also appeared on the Nappy Brown studio recording *Tore Up*, after which he felt it was time to establish a solo career. Despite his well-earned reputation as one of the hottest blues rockers in the business, it took courage to head out on his own. When Bruce Iglauer signed Ellis to Alligator Records, a promising partnership was established.

Ellis's first effort for his new label was *Georgia Blue*, released in 1988. Any doubters and detractors were quickly silenced. The disc burned with an unusual intensity on songs like "Can't You Lie," "Free Man," and "Double Eyed Whammy." The record helped put the name Tinsley Ellis on the tongues of new fans in cities throughout the country. Tinsley Ellis, genuine guitar hero, had arrived.

Although it had not been overnight success for Ellis, it now seemed that he was unstoppable. He expanded his burgeoning fame with his next release, *Fanning the Flames*, a logical extension of his previous effort. Another album that combined his volcanic rock eruptions with his urban blues sensibility, its highlights included the burning "Leavin' Here," "Pawnbroker," "Born in Georgia," and "Must Be the Devil." *Fanning the Flames* catapulted Ellis to the forefront of the blues-rock movement.

By 1992 Ellis had established himself as one of the most exciting live acts around, and his studio material only enhanced his guitar-hero status. The release of his third CD, *Trouble Time*, revealed a mature, confident Ellis in his playing and in his songwriting abilities. The tracks "Highwayman," "Sign of the Blues," and "What Have I Done?" emphasized his bountiful talent. The addition of Peter Buck and Chuck Leavell only helped to strengthen an already powerful effort.

If the three previous recordings had established and expanded his reputation, Ellis's fourth release, *Storm Warning*, truly solidified his position as one of the most riveting blues artists in the world. The 1994 album featured Ellis with his smoking road band comprising James Ferguson on bass, Stuart Grimes on drums, Chuck Leavell on organ, Derek Trucks on slide guitar, Alley Scholl on harmonica, and Count M' Butu on percussion for one track. Just two of the many standouts included "Wanted Man" and "To the Devil for a Dime." This collection of songs enabled Ellis to claim the title of Atlanta's most daring and dangerous blues guitarist.

His next CD, *Fire It Up*, repeated the success of *Storm Warning*. A true gunslinger's collection, it features such red-hot blues songs as "Diggin' My Own Grave," "Just Dropped In," "I Walk Alone," and "If That's the Way He Loves You." Ellis now occupied a very lofty plateau that had once belonged to guitar heroes like Jeff Beck, Eric Clapton, Jimmy Page, Duane Allman, Johnny Winter, Jimmie Vaughan, Buddy Guy, and Robin Trower. An appearance on NBC Sports during the Olympic Games in 1996 helped spread his name even further.

By this time Ellis had not only conquered the recording industry but had also been a consistent concert performer for over a decade. He was a glorious road warrior, performing at least 200 concerts a year throughout the United States, Canada, Australia, Europe, and South America. A traveling bluesman with his axe sharpened to a fine humming tone, he also had developed crowd-pleasing theatrics. He had shared the stage with many famous blues contemporaries, including Robert Cray, the legendary Koko Taylor, and the revitalized Allman Brothers.

He had also been a favorite of the critics for years, receiving encouraging reviews in leading magazines and newspapers across the country. Critics and fans seemed unable to get enough of his raw, energized blues with the hard-edged rock sound. Tinsley, who came from a long line of Atlanta attorneys, had broken that particular tradition; but he had continued the high standards of Atlanta blues first established by Blind Willie McTell, Buddy Moss, and Curly Weaver. Not since McTell had Atlanta been so proud of a native-son musician.

In 1999, Alligator Records reissued *Cool on It*, which Tinsley had recorded with the Heartfixers at the beginning of his career. It was another exciting set of hard-edged boogie tunes and somber blues ballads. The burning pyrotechnic guitar abilities, the powerful material, and the unmistakable voice were present in songs like "Time to Quit" and "Sailor's Grave on the Prairie." There was no doubting Ellis's talent; he had come a long way from this first obscure effort to his current status as one of the true kings of contemporary blues.

For his next effort, *Kingpin*, Ellis switched over to Capricorn Records without missing a beat. The album was a mixture of Ellis originals and cover songs. Each track was fueled by his incredible guitar work, as was apparent on "Heart Fixing Business," "Dyin' to Do Wrong," "I'll Be Loving You," "Other Side of Town," and "Slingshots and Boomerangs." Reese

Wynans made a guest appearance playing the organ, piano, keyboards, and electric piano. It was a well-received set that enhanced Ellis's reputation as a consistent deliverer of top-notch albums.

He continues to record and perform with his band the Heartfixers.

Tinsley Ellis is a true star of contemporary blues. He has recorded one hot CD after another and his concert appearances have drawn rave reviews. He is one of the new breed of modern electric blues guitar warriors who have carried on the tradition established by Jimi Hendrix and Stevie Ray Vaughan. What separates Ellis from the rest of the pack are his talent, his heart, his dedication, and his intensity. Although Ellis is best known as a rocker who plays blues-drenched music, he also blends New Orleans funk and rhythm and blues with his blues-rock foundation to create an original, vibrant sound.

His voice supports his hard-rocking guitar skills, but contains different elements. There is a soul dimension to his vocals that adds great depth and balance to his overall sound. Although he doesn't possess the greatest range, Ellis gets the job done with intelligence and pure emotion.

Ellis can claim a long list of influences, including Elmore James, Clarence "Gatemouth" Brown, Freddie King, and B. B. King. Other past legends who have shaped the Ellis style are the Chicago blues fixtures Otis Rush, Magic Sam, Buddy Guy, Howlin' Wolf, Willie Dixon, Muddy Waters, John Lee Hooker, and the rock and roll of Bo Diddley and Chuck Berry. Another key element in Ellis's musical foundation is the rhythm and blues of the early British R&B bands—the Yardbirds, the Rolling Stones, and the Animals. A serious student of the guitar, Ellis has absorbed the lessons of past masters and incorporated everything he learned into his own ingenious playing.

While he has gained considerable attention for his guitar skills, Ellis has not received proper credit for his songwriting ability. He writes most of his material by drawing from experiences on the road, an excellent source for songs. Themes of lost love, loneliness, homelessness, are scattered throughout his music catalog. Not above covering songs from other blues artists, Ellis has recorded Freddie King's "Side Trained" and Junior Wells's "Early in the Morning," among others.

Ellis also is a proficient acoustic guitarist, a side of this performer that shows up in his live shows. His ability to deliver his special brand of hot blues in either acoustic or electric form underlines another dimension to his versatility. In 1996, Ellis turned heads when he opened up for Robert Cray, playing a well-received acoustic set.

He is also a guitar aficionado, with a varied collection that includes a 1966 Gibson ES 345, a custom shop Stratocaster, and a variety of acoustic instruments that can be hooked up to a PA system. Like other guitar collectors, Ellis is keen on preserving the classic instruments of yesteryear for their beauty and originality. The same care that goes into the selection of his guitars for different songs goes into all other aspects of his musical career. It is one of the reasons he has attained such success.

Now a senior spokesman for the blues, Ellis is an important influence on the new generation of blues-rock guitarists. One of these new artists, Jonny Lang, opened up for Ellis at Buddy Guy's Legend and Manny's Car Wash in New York City. Lang even recorded one of Ellis's songs, "A Quitter Never Wins."

A regular fixture at many festivals, Ellis knows how to work a sizable crowd as well as or better than many other acts on the blues concert circuit. In 1998, Ellis and his band appeared at a number of festivals, including the Tampa Bay Blues Festival and the Punta Gorda Blues Festival in Florida; the Music Midtown Blues Festival in Atlanta; Toledo Blues and Rock festival; Riverhead Festival in Chattanooga; the W. C. Handy Blues Festival in Hudson, Kentucky; Albany, New York's Capital City Blues Festival; and the Kalamazoo Blues Festival in Michigan. His ability to perform with equal brilliance in clubs, outdoor festivals, and more intense settings is an important reason that his career has been so successful. After he destroys the stage with his smoldering guitar work, it is very intimidating for the next performer to climb up there after him.

Wherever in the world he performs, Ellis is continuing the tradition of the Atlanta blues that was first established by Blind Willie McTell and his running buddies Curly Weaver and Buddy Moss. In many ways Ellis has also picked up where Duane Allman left off. Although not quite the monster slide player that the late Allman was, Ellis can hold his own. The Allman Brothers, not original Atlanta natives, nevertheless made the Peach State their home base during the late 1960s and early 1970s. When Ellis plays on stage—no matter the location or venue—he invokes the spirits of past Atlanta guitar players. He has also shared the spotlight with a number of other blues artists, including Albert Collins, Buddy Guy, Robert Cray, Otis Rush, and James Cotton during his twenty-plus-year career.

Ellis's guitar work sounds like a hurricane blowing trees down, lifting the roofs off houses, and tearing down solid structures. It is the sound of the sea on an angry night, but the power is beautiful because there is an inner coherence to its motion. It has been a long journey from the night he received a broken guitar string from B. B. King to his current position as one of the best modern American electric bluesmen. Those who are aware of his music are glad the Georgia Flame Thrower made the trip.

**Discography**

*Georgia Blue*, Alligator AL 4765.
*Storm Warning*, Alligator AL 4823.
*Trouble Time*, Alligator AL 4805.
*Fire It Up*, Alligator AL 4852.
*Fanning the Flames*, Alligator AL 4778.
*Kingpin*, Capricorn 2021.

As a Heartfixer:

*Live at the Moonshadow*, Landslide 1007.
*Cool on It*, Alligator AL 3905.

# KENNY NEAL

## *Louisiana Bayou Blues*

The regional down-home blues of the Southern states have always been built on a mixture of ideas and tastes that reflected their particular region. The Louisiana style, a laid-back, percussive, gloomy approach to the blues, favorably complemented the rural surroundings. Lazy Lester, Slim Harpo, Lightnin' Slim, Silas Hogan, and Lonesome Sundown are just some of the fathers of the Louisiana blues school. Today the regional blues tradition of Creole country is in the very capable hands of the Louisiana Bayou bluesman. His name is Kenny Neal.

Kenny Neal was born on October 14, 1957, in Baton Rouge, Louisiana. His bayou blues roots are deep and rich. His father, singer and harmonica player Raful Neal, a longtime exponent of the Louisiana blues, was a major influence on Kenny, as were the other Louisiana blues singers who frequented the Neal household. Lazy Lester, Buddy Guy, and Slim Harpo were just some of the musicians who put an early and permanent stamp on little Kenny's future direction. The young Neal wanted to lead his own band, but before he matured into the role he had to pay his blues dues. Kenny, one of ten children, would call on the friendship of his brothers in later years to achieve his goal.

His first instrument was the harmonica, but he quickly added bass, piano, trumpet, and guitar to his musical abilities. Neal cut his performing teeth at the tender age of six when he appeared with his father, playing the piano. By the time he was thirteen, Neal was a full-fledged musician in his father's band. When he turned seventeen he became the bass player in Buddy Guy's band and his development as a musician was greatly accelerated. Guy, who had benefited from the generosity of Raful Neal in the early days of his blues career in Louisiana, was only returning the favor. In four years with Guy, Neal honed his guitar skills and proved that he was ready to spread his wings.

He moved to Toronto where he formed the Neal Brothers Blues Band with some of his siblings Raful Jr., Noel, Larry, and Ronnie. Kenny also spent time fronting the Downchild Blues Band, one of Canada's longest-lived and most successful blues bands. But the irresistible, hypnotic rhythms of his native Louisiana landscape were calling him; it was time to go home.

Upon his return to Baton Rouge, Kenny quickly put his band together again. Handling the guitar and harmonica chores himself, he rounded out his ensemble with a family rhythm section that included Frederick on keyboards, Darnell on bass, and Graylon on drums. The group caught fire quickly and toured extensively around the Baton Rouge/Louisiana area, building an appreciative audience. The Neal name, legendary in Louisiana blues circles, certainly enhanced the band's rapid rise in popularity.

It was clear from the very start that the years spent away from home had allowed Kenny to develop as a musician and mature as a person. His confidence and ability to work a crowd were evident in the first concerts the band performed. His three-prong attack—stirring guitar work, chilling harmonica playing and stage presence—combined to capture the imagination of his audiences.

In 1986, Neal recorded his first album, *Bio on the Bayou*, released on the King Snake label. The record, which was later released on Alligator Records under the title *Big News from Baton Rouge*, contained some of the most explosive and definitive Louisiana swamp blues. Three of the songs were co-written by Neal and Bob Greenlee, the owner of the King Snake label. Greenlee also played bass on the album. Neal personally wrote three of the songs, including "Bio on the Bayou," "Early One Morning," and a traditional arrangement of an old Louisiana blues tune called "Evalina." The last song on the album featured an acoustic version of "Early One Morning," and displayed Neal's country-blues side. The album also featured Darnell Neal playing bass on some songs, as well as the King Snake Horns.

Neal began to attract some well-deserved attention as a live performer. His first tour of England drew rave reviews and left everyone begging for more. In his native country he became a fixture on the blues concert and festival circuit. Despite a heavy schedule of touring all over the country and across the Atlantic, Neal still found time to write and record songs for his next album.

The CD *Devil Child* was released on Alligator Records and increased his surging popularity. Many critics and blues fans began comparing Neal to Robert Cray, a wonderful compliment for any blues singer. The album *Devil Child* contained many highlights, including the title cut "Devil Child," "Any Fool Will Do," "Bad Check," and the crowd-pleasing "Yack Yack Yack." Once again Bob Greenlee played bass on the album and co-wrote many of the songs with Neal. As a special tribute to the large influence his father had on him as a musician and a human being, Neal recorded one of his father's songs, "Change My Way of Livin'."

The next album, *Walking on Fire*, showed Neal at his leanest and meanest. A delightful mixture of Louisiana swamp blues, hard R&B, and an acoustic side, the effort provided clear evidence that Kenny Neal was one of the leading young blues lights in America and the world. Once again, the constants that had made the two previous albums a success were evident on *Walking on Fire*. The prolific writing team of Neal and Greenlee was responsible for a majority of the songs. The album also featured the Silent Partners rhythm team, and the Horny Horns from the James Brown Orchestra, as well as Lucky Peterson, fellow label mate, on keyboards. While the album contained some fiery tunes like "Look But Don't Touch," "Bad Luck Card," and "My Only Good Thing," it was the song "Blues Stew" that summed up *Walking on Fire*, and, in a sense, Neal's entire musical career. Many ingredients had been blended together to create the tasty Kenny Neal blues sound. He was a young man with many musical facets and the talent to utilize each one like a master chef, mixing ingredients and adding a special spice to make a harmonious dish.

Despite a hectic recording and tour schedule, Neal found time to act in *Mule Bone*, a play written by Langston Hughes and Zora Neale Hurston. It was an all-blues affair with music written by Taj Mahal. Neal included two of Hughes's poems on the album *Walking on Fire*, "Morning After," and "Bad Luck Card." For his efforts, Neal won the Theater World award for "The Most Outstanding New Talent On and Off Broadway."

He continued his relentless touring of the U.S. and Canada, appearing at such national blues events as the Chicago Blues Festival, the King Biscuit Festival, the Motor City Blues Festival, the Beale Street Festival, the River Walk Festival, and, of course, the hometown New Orleans Jazz & Heritage Festival. On his tours of Europe he appeared on German television and headlined the Amsterdam Blues Festival.

The release of his fourth album, *Bayou Blood*, clearly demonstrated that Neal had not lost any of his hard-boiled Louisiana edge. *Bayou Blood* included the standout tracks "Howling at the Moon," "Gonna Put You Out of My Misery," "Lightning's Gonna Strike," the title track, "Bayou Blood," and ten other songs. *Bayou Blood* featured a stripped-down production from previous albums. Gone were the Silent Partners and the Horny Horns. Instead the album spotlighted Neal on guitar, harmonica, and vocals, Lucky Peterson on keyboards, either brother Noel or Darnell on bass, and Ken Johnson on drums. The blues stew still contained all the necessary fixings to make the record a smash hit, but it was a less complicated, less ambitious undertaking.

In 1993, Neal, a well-seasoned traveler, added Africa and the Dominican Republic to his list of tour conquests, as a guest of the United States Information Agency. The list of African countries included Uganda, Rwanda, Burundi, Tanzania, Madagascar, Kenya and Ethiopia. Neal acquired a whole new legion of fans in these blues-starved countries and converted many devotees to his brand of hot, sweaty, Louisiana swamp blues. In 1994 Neal added Japan to his travel list, opening for B. B. King.

Also in 1994, Neal managed to find time to put together his fifth album, *Hoodoo Moon*. The album contained twelve songs, including "I'm a Blues Man," "Just One Step," "The Real Thing," "Carrying the Torch," and "Don't Fix Our Love." It featured the return of the Horny Horns and once again spotlighted Neal's tremendous versatility on harmonica, guitar and vocals. As on his previous studio effort Kenny was backed by Lucky Peterson, Noel Neal, and Ken Johnson.

Neal continued to tour throughout the United States and the world, converting the skeptics into firm disciples of his soul-stirring Louisiana blues style. In 1997, *Deluxe Edition*, a compilation of Neal's first five albums, was released on Alligator Records. Some of the tracks featured on *Deluxe Edition* included "Caught in the Jaws of a Vise," "Walking on Fire," "That Knife Don't Cut No More," "Hoodoo Moon," and twelve more of his best-known songs. Unfortunately, *Deluxe Edition* marked the end of his long-term business relationship with Alligator Records.

His next effort, *Blues Fallin' Down Like Rain*, appeared on the Telarc International label. It contained some reworks of such blues classics as the Jimmy Reed tune "Big Boss Man," and "My Babe," the song Little Walter made famous, as well as "The Things I Used to Do," the Guitar Slim classic. Original compositions included "Just a Matter of Time," "Shadow of the Moon," the title cut, "Blues Fallin' Down Like Rain," and "Full-Time Fool." For the song "The Things I Used to Do," Neal played the lap steel guitar.

He continues to record and perform.

Kenny Neal is one of the biggest stars of contemporary blues. He has managed to carve an impressive career both as a live performer and a recording artist. He has carried the Louisiana blues torch with great pride and deserves to be in the same company as Lazy Lester, Slim Harpo, Raful Neal, Lightnin' Slim and other denizens of the bayou country's blues pantheon. But more than just an imitator, Neal has managed to channel the lessons he learned as a youngster listening to these legends play and talk music in his very own living room into something modern without sacrificing the roots.

He is a two-instrumental artist, equally talented on the guitar and the harmonica. He is a gifted guitarist who can hold his own in any blues-cutting contest. His blistering guitar work has earned him comparisons with Buddy Guy and Robert Cray. His harmonica licks honor all the great harp players from Little Walter to Slim Harpo and his father, Raful Neal. His harmonica playing emphasizes his Louisiana blues roots more than his guitar chops do.

His soul-soaked vocals add a further dimension to his incredible musicianship. There is a balance between his scorching guitar work, his accessible harmonica riffs, and his slow, Louisiana singing. An intelligent musician, he has been able to blend all three together to create a unique sound. While his instrumental abilities have gained their fair share of recognition, his singing has been overlooked.

One of the most exciting blues singers on tour, Neal always leaves his fans screaming for multiple encores. He has worked with B. B. King, Bonnie Raitt, Muddy Waters, Aaron Neville, Buddy Guy, Steve Miller, and John Lee Hooker, among others. He uses a variety of instruments in concert, including a 1964 Stratocaster, a 1957 Stratocaster, and a 1952 Fender Lap Steel guitar. The 1957 Stratocaster has paper money lacquered into the finish. His versatility as a performer is highlighted during his live appearances, where he can show an exciting visual side that is not possible in his studio work.

Although he is perhaps the most famous blues musician in the Neal family, Kenny is certainly not the only one. Larry Neal is a drummer who plays in Kenny's band on occasion. Graylon is another drummer who also has played drums with Kenny, as well as with Fenton Robinson. Raful "Lil' Ray" Neal is a respected guitarist who fronts his own band and has worked with Bobby "Blue" Bland, Little Milton, Bobby Rush, and his father. Noel Neal is a bass player who has worked with Buddy Guy, James Cotton, Junior Wells, Johnny Winter, Koko Taylor, Lucky Peterson, Lonnie Brooks, Larry McCray and Sherman Robertson. Ronnie Neal, another drummer, has worked with various family members. Charlene and Darlene have appeared with various family members as singers. Jackie Neal has been both a solo artist and has appeared with family members. Darnell is a bass player and has worked with his brother for a long time. Some of Kenny's nephews have already showcased their inherited musical gifts: Tyree Neal, a multi-talented artist who plays the harmonica, guitar, bass, drums, and sings, has appeared at the Baton Rouge Festival. Joshua Neal is a bass player who has appeared on stage. Trellis Neal is a drummer following in the family footsteps quite nicely.

Like those of other contemporary artists, the blues sound of Kenny Neal is a mixture of different influences. He is able to meld the Louisiana swamp blues that he soaked up as a kid with a good dose of rock, soul and even funk. The funk adds muscle to his soulful side and creates a much-needed balance. His musical attack is like an alligator cruising the bayou for prey, biding his time until he is ready to unleash a ferocious attack on the unsuspecting victim.

Kenny Neal is one of the most important bluesmen of his generation. After a lifetime in music, Neal has established himself as a genuine and respected force. He is the caretaker of the Louisiana blues tradition and has assumed the reins from his father, Lazy Lester, Slim Harpo, and Lightnin' Slim. Undoubtedly, with his three-pronged attack of guitar, harmonica, and vocals, Neal will ensure that the Louisiana Bayou blues retains the respect and recognition it deserves well into the twenty-first century.

## Discography:

*Big News from Baton Rouge*, Alligator Records, AL 4764.
*Devil Child*, Alligator Records, AL 4774.
*Walking on Fire*, Alligator Records, AL 4795.
*Bayou Blood*, Alligator Records, AL 4809.
*Hoodoo Moon*, Alligator Records, AL 4825.
*Kenny Neal: Deluxe Edition*, Alligator Records, AL 5604.
*Blues Fallin' Down Like Rain*, Telarc International, 83435.
*What You Got*, Telarc 83467.

# LARRY MCCRAY

*Assembly-Line Blues*

The state of Michigan has a long and varied musical history. Its blues roots go back to the practitioners of the 1930s and 1940s, Baby Boy Warren, Bobo Jenkins, Eddie Burns, Eddie Kirkland, and its most famous blues son, the incomparable John Lee Hooker. But the Wolverine State is also known for its strong rock-and-roll heritage, as well as the Motown/soul sound and pop flavor. One Michigan artist has welded together equal parts of blues, rhythm and blues, rock and roll, boogie-woogie, and soul to create his modern electric assembly-line blues. His name is Larry McCray.

Larry McCray was born April 5, 1960, in Magnolia, Arkansas. His early life in Arkansas was one of poverty, hard work, and music. His father was a harmonica and guitar player who passed down his love of music to his nine children, including Clara, a guitarist, Carl, a bass player, and Steve, a drummer. Larry, the second youngest, received his first guitar from his sister Clara and immediately began to unlock the secrets of his prized possession. When he was a teenager, the McCrays left their small farm in the backwoods of Arkansas and settled in Saginaw, Michigan.

Larry eventually found work in a car factory on the assembly line. But like another famous Michigan musical hero, Barry Gordy, Larry possessed much more ambitious goals. While he toiled in the General Motors plant during the day, he could be found playing guitar around the various blues clubs at night. After a decade of paying his dues he finally caught his first real break.

He was spotted by a record executive from the Virgin label and signed to a contract. His first studio effort, *Ambition*, released on Pointblank Records, was successful enough to allow him to quit his factory job and concentrate solely on his blossoming musical career. The album, recorded under primitive conditions (it was cut in a friend's basement studio), hinted at all the qualities that would make McCray a national act. Already his smooth, rich soul voice, his refreshingly understated guitar style, his uncanny feel of timing and rhythm, and his masterful sense for instrumental arrangements were in place.

The wealth of material on the album showcased McCray's versatility and creative muscle. The song "Nobody Never Hurt Nobody with the Blues" demonstrated his approach to a hard blues-rock sound, while "Secret Lover" and "Me and My Baby" revealed his soul side, powered by the warmth of his husky vocals. The Albert King classic "The Sun Rises in the East" proved that McCray could burn a song into the minds of his listeners. With that first CD, McCray served notice that he had arrived and planned to stay for a very long time.

The album caught the eye and ears of many and, instead of returning to the grind of the small clubs scene, McCray was soon touring with the great Albert Collins. Collins, who had fashioned a beautiful musical career out of pure blues with his inventive approach to the electric guitar, was a mentor to the young McCray. The influence of Collins on McCray was evident on the latter's next release, *Delta Hurricane*.

*Delta Hurricane* was recorded under much different circumstances than his previous effort. For *Delta Hurricane*, McCray traveled with his band to Memphis, where they were backed by the Uptown Horns, giving the album more of a soul-soaked, tough rhythm-and-blues edge. McCray's excellent guitar work was not buried under an avalanche of other instruments or relegated to a secondary role, however. His growling guitar remained the prime driving force and stood boldly in line with the Uptown Horns to create a pile-driving, earth-shaking record.

McCray wrote or co-wrote only three of the eleven songs on the album: "Blue River," "Hole in My Heart," and "Blues in the City." The majority of the material was written by Dave Steen, including "Adding Up," "Last Four Nickels," "Witchin' Moon," and "Three Straight Days of Rain." The collection of tracks on the album was a fair representation of how a contemporary blues album should sound. A more ambitious project than his debut, *Delta Hurricane* was a foreshadowing of good things to come.

McCray's next project was a guest appearance on a tribute album to Sonny Terry and Brownie McGhee. *Climbin' Up* featured McCray's tasteful guitar work and was recorded shortly before Sonny Terry passed away. Like many other modern blues singers, McCray had not forgotten the pioneers who had broken down many barriers and opened many doors for the future generation.

McCray found time between session work and a heavy tour schedule to record another album in 1996. *Meet Me at the Lake* was a return to a blues-rock format that included the Bluegills, a band led by Charlie Walmsely. The combination of the Bluegills' musical competence and McCray's solid guitar and vocals created an enjoyable example of contemporary blues. All the cuts on the album were written by Walmsely except "Moon Is Full," an Albert Collins composition.

The album kicked off with a rousing Walmsely original, "Too Much Rooster," which set the tone for the rest of the set. *Meet Me at the Lake* was a perfect example of a group of talented musicians having fun playing the blues. The good-time atmosphere was reflected in some of the titles of the songs: "More Walk, Less Talk," "In a Funk in a Phone Booth," "Moon Is Full," and "Havoc." While the CD didn't win any major awards it provided the listener with forty-five minutes of happy blues.

McCray played at blues festivals all over the country, and especially around the Midwest, which had always been the foundation of his fan base. He was involved in the *Paint It Blue* project, a tribute disc to the music of the Rolling Stones. The sessions included Alvin Youngblood Hart, Taj Mahal, the Holmes Brothers, and Lucky Peterson. McCray rolled out a hard-driving blues version of "Midnight Rambler." He also helped out Clarence "Gatemouth" Brown on "Ventilator Blues," adding his distinct guitar lines and impressive dark voice. In the meantime, McCray was writing new songs for his next album.

The long-awaited *Born to Play the Blues* featured the trademark McCray hot guitar licks and soulful vocals along with a wealth of material not heard before on any of his CDs. McCray, who was able to weld different musical forms into his assembly-line blues, was also capable of uniting traditional blues with a fresh modern sound. His precise, smartly placed notes were like steel-driven rivets that joined, set, and cemented a sound blues structure. There were many fine moments on the album, including "I Feel So Damn Good (I'll Be Glad When I Got the Blues)," "Sunny Monday," and "Worried Down with the Blues." The album was a solid example of a professional blues musician maintaining his credibility while expanding his appeal. McCray had done it again.

Since then McCray has continued his hectic tour schedule, appearing at numerous blues festivals and in concerts all over the country and abroad. An exciting performer, he is able to squeeze notes from his guitar that are pure delight. His next recording promises to be an interesting project.

Larry McCray is a modern electric blues warrior. His guitar is his weapon and he is able to blast out rounds of bullet notes with the fluidity of a sharp marksman. His voice is a battle cry, an emotional display of deep blues feelings. His songs are a reflection of the everyday activity of human life. McCray has used all of his abilities to mold a fine blues career and establish himself as one of the best contemporary artists.

The McCray sound owes a debt to a variety of influences that include the usual blues giants: Albert King, B. B. King, Albert Collins, and Muddy Waters. But McCray has also been touched by the soulful Bobby "Blue" Bland. Bland's soul-blues material of the 1950s and 1960s helped usher in a new era and cleared a path for modern blues artists like McCray. Another important influence on McCray was midwestern modern bluesman Son Seals. At his best, Seals is able to conquer an audience with his heavy guitar sound and tough vocals; McCray and Seals are like two blues-soul brothers.

McCray has also delved deeply into the rich Michigan musical legacy. He has taken up the blues flag of the early pioneers on the Motor City blues scene—artists such as Baby Boy Warren, Bobo Jenkins, Eddie Burns, Eddie Kirkland, Alberta Adams, and John Lee Hooker—and carried it with pride, class, and distinction. But McCray has also inserted large chunks of the trademark hard, pile-driving rock-and-roll sounds of Ted Nugent, Bob Seger, Alice Cooper, Grand Funk Railroad, and other Michigan rock acts into his blues foundation.

McCray also incorporated the funky rhythm-and-blues sound of Motown into his own music. The strong bass lines, the expressive lyrics, the soulful vocals are all parts of the McCray identity that he shares with the Motown artists. His stage presence also owes a debt to the Motown style: McCray puts on a show that is more akin to the Temptations than the pyrotechnics of Charley Patton, T-Bone Walker, or Jimi Hendrix. His ability to fuse all of these elements into one workable sound is a credit to his ability and creative genius.

Larry McCray is perhaps the biggest star on the Detroit blues scene, but certainly not the only one. A partial list of Detroit blues artists includes Mud Puppy, Mystery Train, Thorneta Davis, The Alligators, Johnny Bassett, The Butler Twins, Alberta Adams, Motor City Josh, Big Dave and the Ultrasonics, Mimi Harris and the Snakes, the Howling Diablos, Nikki James and the Flamethrowers, Johnny "Yard Dog" Jones, Randy Volin and the Sonic Blues, and many others. They appear at the Ann Arbor Blues Festival, the Kalamazoo Blues Festival, the International Blues Festival, the Hart Plaza Blues Festival, and area clubs like the Magic Bag, Sisko's on the Boulevard, the Attic Bar, and Moby Dick's. One of the main driving forces behind the Detroit blues scene is Sweet Daddy Pasman, whose regular Sunday-night blues show on radio showcases many of Michigan's local blues acts as well as the entire history of the genre from the very beginning to the most modern artists.

When not on tour or in the studio assembling one of his standout contemporary blues albums, McCray can be found fishing on one of Michigan's beautiful lakes, rivers or bays. He lives in the state of Michigan, demonstrating a real commitment to the area. He is able to sing so convincingly of the hard-working, hard-playing people of the state and the Midwest because he lives the life. His songs are genuine and drawn from true experiences.

McCray has also added his talent to a number of recordings by other artists. His unique guitar work can be heard on the James Cotton release *Living the Blues*; on Lucky Peterson's *I'm Ready*; Derek Trucks's *Out of*

*Madness*, and John Primer's *Knockin' on Your Door*. He played the bass on Freddie Jackson's *Just Like the First Time*. He contributed the song "Miss You" on the album *Blues Power: The Songs of Eric Clapton*, as well as "All Along the Watchtower" on the *Tangled Up in Blues: The Songs of Bob Dylan* project.

Larry McCray is one of the most cherished national blues artists on the scene. He is a classic example of a modern electric blues singer doing what he does best. An American original, McCray, like some of the older bluesmen, moved from the South to the North to establish his career, but never severed the ties with the blues he learned as a child. He has thrilled millions with his assembly-line blues and will continue to do so in the future.

### Discography

*Ambition*, Pointblank 2-91388.
*Delta Hurricane*, Pointblank 87784.
*Meet Me at the Lake*, ATM 1124.
*Born to Play the Blues*, House of Blues 161404.

# LUCKY PETERSON

## *A Blues Prodigy*

The magnetism of the blues attracts different people at different ages. Some blues singers are captivated by blues fever in their early teens, and their musical maturation coincides with their growth into adulthood. There are, however, some individuals who are struck hard by the blues at a very early age. Yet it has been a firm belief on the blues scene for a hundred years that in order to understand the subtle nature and hidden dynamics of the music, one had to experience them. This meant that blues singers had to be older, wise in the ways of the world, having lived (or living) in misery. A well-seasoned blues singer was a person who had suffered through hard times and knew all about poverty and heartache. One young boy was a recent exception to this rule, as he became a blues prodigy by showing remarkable skill and talent long before he was old enough to acquire a driver's license. His name is Lucky Peterson.

Lucky Peterson was born Judge Kenneth Peterson on December 13, 1963, in Buffalo, New York, into a musical family. His father owned the Governor's Inn in Buffalo, which featured appearances by Albert King, Jimmy Reed, Howlin' Wolf, and Muddy Waters, as well as pianists Roosevelt Sykes and Otis Spann, among others. Peterson made an immediate connection with the music and at the tender age of five was playing the Hammond B-3 organ with remarkable aptitude.

He caught the attention of Willie Dixon, who ushered little Lucky into the studio, where the latter cut the pop song "1-2-3-4." It was an immediate hit and Peterson became a prodigy overnight. He came after Little Stevie Wonder and before Little Michael Jackson. The song earned him appearances on a few talk shows, including *The Tonight Show*, *What's My Line*, *The David Frost Show*, and the *Ed Sullivan Show*.

Although he released no other songs for the next few years, Peterson remained active in music and by his late teens had added the guitar to his impressive musical capabilities. He joined Little Milton's band for a three-year stint that saw him tour all over the country and Europe. The on the road adventures shaped Peterson's future outlook and gave him a better understanding of the trials and tribulations of a true professional musician.

After his stint with Little Milton, Peterson joined Bobby Blue Bland's band and remained there for the next three years. His years spent with Bland provided him with more invaluable life lessons for someone trying to make it big in the music world. Peterson learned much from Bland, the soul-blues man; however, while he had benefited from touring and playing in both Little Milton's and Bobby Blue Bland's respective groups, Peterson decided that it was time to begin his solo career.

His first solo record, *Ridin'*, initially released on the French label, Isabel, and featuring guitarist Melvin Taylor, was an excellent debut album. Peterson the child prodigy had matured into an exciting adult contemporary blues singer. The triple threat of guitar, keyboards, and voice were prominent on *Ridin'* from the very first song. Throughout the record, whether he was playing one of his own songs or performing a cover version of Willis Dixon's "Little Red Rooster," or Jimmy Reed's "You Don't Have to Go" and "Baby, What You Want Me to Do?" Peterson's musical precision was remarkable. He clearly demonstrated that the prodigy label he was tagged with years before had not been a mistake.

Peterson jumped to the Alligator label for his next two albums. *Lucky Strikes* was a first-class effort by a talented musician whose superior command of the guitar and keyboards provided the highlights of the album.

His sincere yet funky vocals were the remaining weapon in his three-prong attack. While *Ridin'* had demonstrated a certain maturity, *Lucky Strikes* was considered his debut as an adult musician. Some of the highlights of the album included "Over My Head," "Heart Attack," and "She Spread Her Wings."

The CD *Triple Play* only enhanced his already impressive credentials as one of the best blues singers around. It was recorded in the King Snake studios, where a special kind of magic existed between artist and facility. Everything just clicked and Peterson delivered one of the best albums of his solo career. The burning grooves on "Your Lies," "Six O'Clock Blues," "I'm Free," and "Don't Cloud Up on Me" proved his genuine blues mettle. However, the wonderful marriage between Peterson and Alligator Records ended and left him searching for a new label.

On his subsequent albums Peterson stretched out his sound, exploring a variety of other musical styles including rock and roll, country, soul, and pop. His first effort for Verve, *I'm Ready*, was a winner. Not only did he demonstrate his capability in handling and assimilating different musical elements, but he also displayed his incredible versatility as a musician. He worked the Hammond organ and the Wurlitzer electric piano into dimensions never heard before, the best example of this wizardry being the song "Junk Yard." Other highlights of the album included the Willie Dixon classics "I'm Ready," and "You Shook Me." He also slipped in the Howlin' Wolf chestnut "Who's Been Talking?" With Larry McCray handling the guitar chores, Peterson delivered a solid contemporary blues record to the masses. But he was just getting started.

The album *Beyond Cool* was an avatar of Peterson's musical abilities. He effortlessly pumped out expert and controlled musical passages, layers of harmony, and funky rhythms. While the material was somewhat disjointed Peterson held it all together with his beyond cool musicianship. A little-known Hendrix composition, "Up from the Skies," was preceded by the Bo Diddley song "Compared to What?" On this effort more than any other, Peterson broke out of the blues/pop mold that he had been known for and explored his rock-and-roll side.

While the critics were not enthusiastic about *Beyond Cool*, Peterson rebounded with his next and last record on the Verve label, *Lifetime*. It was on this album, a modern collection of contemporary blues numbers that hinted at exciting and different possibilities, that Peterson truly demonstrated his varied musical abilities. Peterson played the guitar, piano, organ, electric piano, and Clavinet, and was responsible for the horn and vocal arrangements. He also sang lead and background vocals. There were more original compositions on this record than on previous efforts, including the title cut, "Lifetime," "Ecstasy," and "Wash My Back."

He also co-wrote five other songs, including "Time," "Bad Condition," and "The Last Thing I Need." But *Lifetime* was not without its cover versions, as Sting's "We'll Be Together" and the Sam Cooke classic "Change Is Gonna Come" were part of the eleven-song set.

By this time Peterson was a concert favorite, touring all over the United States, Europe, and Canada. His outstanding command of a variety of instruments enabled him to put a different spin on any song no matter the style. His live shows were a guided tour of modern music history. Peterson was able to duplicate the magic of his live shows in the studio. His recordings also reflected his sheer brilliance in combining different musical ideas and working them out on a number of instruments, which gave his work a special flavor. There were precious few blues singers who had the range and artistic flair of Lucky Peterson.

His next album, *Move*, had a bluesier feel to it. The mixture of originals and covers, including Prince's "Purple Rain," the Isley Brother's "It's Your Thing," and Robert Cray's "Don't You Even Care?" made for an interesting record. The song "Pickin'," was an instrumental tribute to Albert Collins. The tune "You're the One for Me" had an Albert King–style guitar solo. Although the material covered a wide range of styles, Peterson pulled the entire project off with his tasteful display on the guitar and the Hammond organ.

The next album, *Lucky Peterson*, was another intriguing collection. There was a soul number, "Shake" (featuring the Late Night Horns), a Willie Nelson country tune, "Funny How Time Slips Away" (including a duet with Joe Louis Walker), and the pop classic "Ode to Billie Joe." The rest of the album covered blues territory, specifically on "Deal with It," "Seduction," and "Tribute to Luther Allison," an original Peterson tune.

Lucky Peterson continues to astound all with his new material and his frenzied live shows.

Lucky Peterson is a rare blues bird. Although he has been criticized for his experimentation, Peterson is too musically gifted to stick to the limited, traditional form of the twelve-bar blues. He is a highly creative artist who must explore the limits of his enormous talents. He has been a model of consistency, churning out fascinating contemporary blues albums and keeping his name fresh on the concert circuit. He is a dynamic performer who attacks crowds with his triple threat of guitar/keyboards/vocals as well as with his gift of making the modern blues he plays fun.

He has been performing in front of live audiences for more than thirty years. Thirty years is longer than the *lives* of such blues legends as Robert Johnson, Charley Patton, Bessie Smith, Magic Sam, Elmore James, Magic Slim, Jimi Hendrix, and Janis Joplin, to name just a few.

Many prodigies strike the musical world like a lightning bolt only to fizzle out by their early teens and eventually fade from the scene. Peterson managed to avoid this particular land mine.

There is no denying Peterson's ability on the keyboards, be it the Hammond B-3 organ, piano, Clavinet, or electric piano. He is adept at each one and can rock the house with the best of them. In many ways Peterson has continued the legacy that began with such great pianists as Leroy Carr, Jimmy Yancey, Roosevelt Sykes, Sunnyland Slim, and others. The claim that the piano blues have dried up in the last thirty years is false. Peterson has taken the keyboard sound of the early barrelhouse piano players and given it a modern touch. Peterson is capable of playing barrelhouse blues, West Coast jazz styles, and the hard stomp of the Chicago blues, all delivered with a modern taste. His versatility in all forms is one of the secrets to his longevity.

He has also developed into a unique talent on the guitar. A true modern blues guitarist, Peterson was influenced by a number of contemporary artists. He possesses the distinct touch of a Buddy Guy, Albert King, or Albert Collins. He is also able to unleash a hard-edged blues barrage in the style of Jimi Hendrix. Few blues singers have managed to develop their musical skills to the point where they are more than proficient on the guitar *and* the piano, the two prime instruments in blues music.

One of the strongest influences on Peterson's musical vision was Bill Doggett. Doggett was more of a jazz, rhythm-and-blues artist than a pure bluesman; he spent time in Louis Jordan's band in the late 1940s and early 1950s. He was an extremely talented organist/pianist whose biggest hit was "Honky Tonk" in the 1950s, during the height of the first rock-and-roll craze. He worked with Ella Fitzgerald, Eddie "Lockjaw" Davis, Johnny Otis, and Illinois Jacquet. The impact he had on Peterson is immeasurable.

Peterson himself has made a huge impact on a number of modern blues singers, including Robert Cray, Kenny Wayne Shepherd, and Jonny Lang. Cray studied Peterson's cool approach to the blues and incorporated that essential element into his own style. Lang and Shepherd, both blues prodigies, look to Peterson for guidance in a business that burns out prodigies with a deadly regularity.

There is no doubt that Peterson's greatest contribution to the blues has been his musical versatility; this has not gone unnoticed by his fellow modern blues mates. Peterson has added his incredible talent to the works of Carey Bell, James Cotton, Etta James, Jimmy Johnson, Little Milton, Lazy Lester, Kenny Neal, Raful Neal, Otis Rush, Lonnie Shields, Melvin Taylor, Joe Louis Walker, Rufus Thomas, and Junior Wells, to name a few. His many-faceted abilities are always in demand.

During a career that spans almost forty years, he has built up a steady following of devoted fans. Although some might argue that he never fulfilled the promise he showed as a youngster, Peterson has earned the respect of many of his contemporaries. His career has been one long, pleasant journey from the moment he was tagged as a blues prodigy.

## Discography

*Ridin'*, Evidence 26033.
*Lucky Strikes*, Alligator AL 4770.
*Triple Play*, Alligator AL 4789.
*I'm Ready*, Verve 517513-2.
*Beyond Cool*, Verve 314521147.
*Lifetime*, Verve 531202.
*Move*, Polygram 537897.
*Lucky Peterson*, Polygram 547433.

# KENNY WAYNE SHEPHERD

## *Young Man's Blues*

Today's blues artists have the luxury of eighty years of recorded blues music from which to draw inspiration. It is inevitable that their individual sounds reflect the masters of the past. Yet, despite the many influences, all young blues artists are keen on developing their own blues voices. One of the young guitar slingers has added the grit of Muddy Waters, the touch of Albert King, the savvy of B. B. King, the sheer power of Jimi Hendrix, and the ferocity of Stevie Ray Vaughan to his own sound to create his own young man's blues. His name is Kenny Wayne Shepherd.

Kenny Wayne Shepherd was born on June 12, 1977, in Shreveport, Louisiana. He lived a normal childhood until he was seven years old, when his father, who worked in radio, took him along to a Stevie Ray Vaughan concert. That night, like most nights, Vaughan connected with his audience in a primal, ceremonial way. And, while Vaughan's virtuosity hypnotized everyone in the crowd that night, none was more swept away than little Kenny Wayne Shepherd.

Shepherd soon started badgering his father for an electric guitar. A few months later his wish was granted and young Kenny immediately began to teach himself the rudiments of blues guitar by listening to his father's old Muddy Waters records. Much like his idol Stevie Ray Vaughan, Shepherd had an inborn ability to play guitar. His long hours of practice and intense study of the blues would eventually pay off handsomely.

By the time he was thirteen there was no doubt that Shepherd was a special talent. He was the best undiscovered blues guitarist in the country and probably the world. However, there still remained hurdles to overcome. He had never played in public, and, like most entertainers, he had butterflies floating around in his stomach—butterflies so strong, they felt like bald eagles.

One night, while in New Orleans on a family trip, Shepherd overcame his stage fright when he sat in with Brian Lee, a local blues guitar wizard. Shepherd impressed the crowd and won over Brian Lee. Once he had cleared the hurdle of playing in front of a live audience, Shepherd was destined to be a blues star.

Through the careful guidance of his father, Ken Shepherd, Sr., Kenny began to climb the ladder of success. It was his father's ability to land his son a recording contract with Giant Records that triggered Kenny Wayne Shepherd mania. His first album, *Ledbetter Heights*, showed the promise, the genius, and the industriousness of the young bluesman with the hot guitar licks. Shepherd wrote and co-wrote more than half of the songs on the album. While the songwriting proved that he possessed a maturity beyond his years, it was the playing that really shone. Kenny had formed his own band, featuring Corey Sterling on vocals, Will Ainsworth on bass, and Jimmy Wallace on keyboards, to back him up. The album also featured the contributions of Brian Lee and the expert drumming of Chris Layton, from Stevie Ray Vaughan's band Double Trouble.

The album captured Shepherd and his band in a state of rabid concert heat. They played as if they had a wild, enthusiastic crowd cheering them on instead of being in a cold, lonely recording studio. Shepherd bared his soul on numbers like "Riverside" and "While We Cry." Ever since the spectacular debut of Jimi Hendrix had forever changed the way the world viewed nascent guitar heroes, anyone who could play riveting blues-rock garnered immediate fan support. Shepherd was no exception.

Shepherd went on tour to promote the album and opened up for B. B. King, one of his biggest idols. The exposure he received helped boost record sales. *Ledbetter Heights* sold in excess of half a million copies, an astounding number considering it was a blues record and one by a relatively unknown artist still in his teens. But Shepherd had managed to capture the imagination of blues-rock fans.

His second album, *Trouble Is*, promised more of the same rocking blues as on *Ledbetter Heights*, which had gained considerable airplay. The Kenny Wayne Shepherd mania machine was in full motion. He reminded longtime blues fans of Jimi Hendrix, and newer blues fans of Stevie Ray Vaughan, who had passed through not so long ago. Shepherd even included the Hendrix classic "I Don't Live Today" on *Trouble Is*. Shepherd's bold confidence was reminiscent of the spirit displayed by Stevie Ray Vaughan a decade earlier.

Shepherd released his third CD, *Live On*, in 1998; it was also a monster seller. His concerts were sold-out shows and he sent people home talking about the beautiful power of the blues. He was designated as one of the great blues hopes of the twenty-first century. Kenny Wayne Shepherd, now in his early twenties, has taken the blues world by storm and continues to thrill audiences all over the United States and abroad. There is great expectation for his next album.

Kenny Wayne Shepherd is a blues phenomenon. He had achieved more by his late teens then most veteran bluesmen have in their entire careers. Although his discography is relatively thin—which is understandable considering his youth—he has already created an impressive sound catalog of music. There is something special about Kenny Wayne that goes beyond his playing. He has an aura about him, a magnetism that makes people stop talking when he enters a room.

Shepherd is a guitar virtuoso of the highest order. He has the distinctive ability to play rhythm and lead simultaneously. He has an uncanny sense of rhythm and timing. His attack is clear and precise. He dazzles with technique, passion, and a style that sends many writers scrambling for their thesauruses. In just five short years he has shot across the blues sky like a brilliant meteor, forcing everyone to take notice. His maturity as a guitarist is evident when one listens to his albums in chronological order. Although a prize blues prodigy when his first album hit the airwaves, his style has shed some of the influences and evolved into one with more individuality.

The greatest inspiration for Kenny Wayne Shepherd was the late, great Stevie Ray Vaughan. The two have many things in common. They are both from the same area; both play a distinctive Texas blues–drenched guitar; both listened to Albert King, Muddy Waters, Freddie King, and B. B. King when growing up. They both burst upon the music scene as relative unknowns and immediately made a huge impact; they both cherish and cover Jimi Hendrix songs.

Despite an almost endless list of similar traits, it is unkind and unfair to label Shepherd with the tag of "heir apparent to the Stevie Ray Vaughan guitar throne" as so many writers have done. Although he has definitely borrowed a page or two from the Vaughan guitar vocabulary, Shepherd is his own person. The same unjust pressure was placed upon Vaughan when he first broke onto the scene as he was compared, both favorably and negatively, to Hendrix.

Along with Jonny Lang, Chris Duarte, and Monster Mike Welch, Shepherd holds the future of the blues in his large, talented guitar playing hands. He has learned his lessons well from past masters and has been able to assert himself in order to climb to the top of the blues mountain. His undeniable talent, his tasty choice of material for albums, and his meteoric rise are all part of the Kenny Wayne Shepherd mystique.

He is wise beyond his years in his ability to reach mass audiences with the media tools available to him. His commercial for Gap Jeans, for example, sparked a furor as Shepherd blasted his way through a danceable Texas boogie shuffle that teased the audience. He fully understands the task at hand and realizes he possesses many advantages, as well as the knowledge to use them to further his career.

With three strong albums and a string of memorable performances to his credit, Shepherd has proven himself time and again. He is the real thing. It is a pleasure for all the blues fans who missed out on Jimi Hendrix and Stevie Ray Vaughan to be able to follow the career of Kenny Wayne Shepherd. He has delighted and surprised everyone with his young man's blues and will continue to do so for years to come.

## Discography

*Ledbetter Heights*, Giant 24621.
*Trouble Is*, Warner Brothers 24689.
*Live On*, Warner Brothers 24729.

# JONNY LANG

### Blues from the Badlands

When one thinks of blues scenes, Chicago, Memphis, New Orleans, Atlanta, Austin, Houston, Dallas, and Detroit immediately come to mind.

But North Dakota? Nevertheless, thanks to the widespread appeal of the blues throughout the continental United States in the past forty years, artists have emerged from every corner of the country, including the western portion. One guitar prodigy, with his blues from the badlands, has proven that geography is no barrier to the development of a blues singer. His name is Jonny Lang.

Jonny Lang was born Jon Langseth on January 29, 1981, in Fargo, North Dakota. Lang was reared in a small town in North Dakota and lived the anonymous life of any farm kid. He developed an interest in music at an early age, however; his first instrument was the saxophone but he switched to guitar in his early teens. After only one intense year of practice, the kid from the badlands was ready to conquer the world with his incredible talent.

He joined his first professional band, the Bad Medicine Blues Band, at the age of twelve, and after assuming full leadership of the group renamed it Jonny Lang and the Big Bang. They performed anywhere they could find work, eventually moving to Minneapolis in 1994 because it offered more opportunities for young aspiring blues musicians than the wheat fields of North Dakota. Three years later Jonny Lang and the Big Bang recorded their first album, *Smokin'*, which received rave reviews and attracted the attention of some of the major labels, including A&M. Two years later, his first effort, *Lie to Me*, for his new label catapulted Lang into the blues spotlight.

It was a daring album for a sixteen-year-old to make. The CD, released in 1997, showcased not only Lang's incredible guitar playing but also his vocal prowess, which astonished many: The kid sounded like a grizzled blues veteran straight from the Mississippi Delta rather than a teenager from North Dakota. The album contained some original Lang material as well as carefully chosen cover versions of Sonny Boy Williamson I's "Good Morning Little School Girl," and Big Joe Turner's "Matchbox." Despite the musical show of power that Lang displayed on the album, however, it was clear that he had some maturing to do as a musician and as a person.

Lang toured extensively to promote *Lie to Me* and astonished fans everywhere he performed with his masterful virtuosity and his veteran blues voice. He opened up for bands like the Rolling Stones, Aerosmith, Blues Traveler, and his idol, B. B. King. Lang also showed his maturity as a performer when he headlined some of the dates during his world tour. In the meantime he was working on material for his next release.

The 1998 release, *Wander This World*, demonstrated a definite maturity in all aspects of his playing. It was a first-rate album from a true rising star of the blues. Lang used his blues-based licks as the launching pad for the exploration of other styles, including soul, funk, and rock. There were recognized blues influences like Albert Collins, B. B. King, and Luther Allison; but there were also touches of Otis Redding, Eric Clapton, Stevie Wonder, and the artist formerly known as Prince. (David Z, the engineer/producer behind some of Prince's best work, was also the guiding light behind *Wander This World*.)

Lang covered the traditional twelve-bar blues format with "Angel of Mercy" and "Cherry Red Wine"; he made the latter song, a Luther Allison chestnut, melt in one's mouth. He rocked the house with "The Levee" and "Still Raining," and satisfied the soul pundits with the songs "Walking Away" and "Second Guessing." The album was also a family affair, as Lang's mother and sister added some backing vocals. In all, the CD was a major-league effort by a major-league blues talent despite his tender age of seventeen.

The release of *Wander This World* wiped away all doubters about Jonny Lang. He combined the power of his vocals, the tastiness of his playing, and the musical diversity of a veteran artist to create something truly wonderful. It gained Lang recognition from a variety of sources, a rarity for someone so young.

He continues to record and perform.

Jonny Lang was a blues phenomenon in the 1990s. He emerged as a peach-fuzzed teen and stunned the world with his dazzling musical ability. His guitar work is stunning, his vocals harsh: Lang does not pamper or whine the lyrics; he sings them like a man. His emergence was a reflection of the modern electric blues movement, which had garnered considerable attention ever since the arrival of Stevie Ray Vaughan.

Lang's style is a work in progress as he continues to grow as an artist. His influences are clearly detectable and include the single-line smoothness of B. B. King. But Lang has taken the B. B. King style and added Stevie Ray Vaughan's speed and power. Lang has also added the soul of both King and Albert Collins. There is also a touch of Albert King's incredible note bending in Lang's style. The hard Chicago sound of Luther Allison is another element in Lang's guitar vocabulary.

Although his guitar work has garnered tremendous attention, it is his voice that strikes people the hardest. His voice is experienced; not only does he have good pipes but he has a singer's vision. Lang sings as if he had spent years on the road, chain-smoking menthol cigarettes and gargling razor blades for breakfast.

Lang is a good example of the new breed of blues artist. He is relatively young, has concentrated on one style of the blues, and has toured as much as he has recorded. He has also united the traditional blues with his ultramodern vision. He does not play pure blues but uses the blues as a base from which to explore different avenues, including rock, soul, funk, and jazz.

Since the arrival of Jimi Hendrix on the blues scene, the virtuoso guitar player has garnered most of the spotlight. Lang is another power guitarist in the long list that included Hendrix, Johnny Winter, Eric Clapton, Robin Trower, Ronnie Earl, Duke Robillard, Stevie Ray Vaughan, Jimmie Vaughan, Robert Cray, Tinsley Ellis, Son Seals, Kenny Wayne Shepherd, and many others. Like the others in this list, he has taken the lessons of the first generation of blues singers and molded his own style from their bountiful gifts. But Lang also has respect for the past masters.

Lang—along with Kenny Wayne Shepherd, Corey Harris, Ben Harper, Susan Tedeschi, Deborah Coleman, Chris Duarte, and Monster Mike Welch—is one of the bright lights of the future of the blues. He is a serious contender for the super chops throne, having to fight other blues prodigies like Shepherd for the title. A pure blues rocker who can drop liquid blues notes, Lang's future direction remains a question mark. How far will he stretch his blues base? Will he abandon the blues for a different musical direction? Whatever path he takes, there is no doubt that as an immensely talented individual he will make it exciting.

Despite his short time in the spotlight, Lang has already covered much territory. With each concert performance under his belt, with each new album, he continues to set standards that will be difficult to match. Already, with his blues from the badlands, Lang has proven that one can be a blues wonder at any age.

## Discography

Kid Jonny Lang and the Big Bang:
*Smokin'*, Oarfin 9523.

Jonny Lang:
*Lie to Me*, A&M 540640.
*Wander This World*, A&M 540984.

# PART FOUR

# Contemporary Blues Women

The classic female blues singers of the 1920s continue to influence today's singers. The music of Bessie Smith, Ida Cox, Ma Rainey, Sippie Wallace, Victoria Spivey, Trixie Smith, Mamie Smith, Clara Smith, Lucille Hegamin, Alberta Hunter, Ruth Brown, Lucille Bogan, and Sara Martin can still be heard in the sound of the contemporary blues women. From the 1930s through the late 1960s the music of Big Mama Willie Mae Thornton, Alberta Adams, Billie Holiday, Big Maybelle, Ruth Brown, Sarah Vaughan, Etta James, and Koko Taylor carried on the tradition of female blues. Today's blues women have, like their male counterparts, nevertheless been able to forge something new using elements of the past.

One of the primary new elements that the contemporary female blues singers have introduced is their instrumental gifts. Although a handful of the classic female artists played the piano and guitar, most were singers. Today, many of the blues women are highly proficient musicians. Marcia Ball is a rock solid piano player; Bonnie Raitt, Rory Block, Joanna Connor, Sue Foley, Deborah Coleman, Susan Tedeschi, and Debra Davies are all fabulous guitarists, genuine virtuosos who have expanded the parameters of blues guitar in new and interesting ways.

The artists in this section are a fair representation of the current group of female blues singers on the circuit. At the same time, the work of Deborah Coleman, Debra Davies, Ann Peebles, Saffire—Uppity Blues Women, Shamekia Copeland, Dana Gillespie, Denise LaSalle, Ellen McIlwaine, Tracy Nelson, Valerie Wellington, Zora Young, and Susan Tedeschi should not be ignored; they are all important contributors to the blues. After eighty years of making records and a longer history as performers, the women of the blues have played an integral part in the birth, growth, and popularity that the genre currently enjoys.

Janis Joplin was the premier blues-rock queen of the 1960s. She was one of the bridges between the female rhythm-and-blues singers of the 1950s and the modern movement.

Like Sippie Wallace and Victoria Spivey, Angela Strehli is a Texas blues singer who was instrumental in the blues revival of the 1980s. She is a fixture on the Austin blues scene.

Rory Block is one of the leading exponents of the acoustic blues style. She has maintained an interest in the genre and has provided a fresh female point of view.

Marcia Ball, another Texas blues singer, is cut from the same mold as Sippie Wallace. Her rollicking piano playing and strong voice have been entertaining crowds for years.

Bonnie Raitt is an excellent slide guitarist and one of the most popular blues singers on the contemporary scene. She has extended the sound of her blues to include rhythm and blues, pop, and rock, giving her important crossover success. However, Raitt has never strayed far from her roots despite her flair for experimentation.

Lou Ann Barton is the queen of the Texas roadhouse blues scene. She was instrumental in the blues revival of the 1980s. Her raunchy, controlled blues voice is reminiscent of Janis Joplin's.

Joanna Connor is a slide-guitar player whose style derives more from the Mississippi Delta bluesmen than from the classic female blues singers. Her driving rhythms and riffs have earned praise for her talent on the six-string instrument.

Sue Foley is a Canadian blues singer who has made a home in Austin, Texas. Her guitar playing and singing make her a perfect example of the new generation of female blues singers.

# JANIS JOPLIN

## *Pearl's Blues*

The marriage between the blues and rock and roll in the 1960s produced some of the most memorable characters in recent musical history. More than anything else, it seemed that unknowns were enthusiastically embraced overnight and hailed as superstars. Perhaps one of the best examples of this instant-stardom phenomenon, who melded blues and rock with pure expertise, was the singer who gave us her Pearl's Blues. Her name was Janis Joplin.

Janis Lyn Joplin was born on January 19th, 1943, in Port Arthur, Texas. Port Arthur is an oil-industry town that lies in the southwestern corner of the Lone Star State. A small town can be stifling and Joplin, an inventive, creative child, felt the need to escape from the claustrophobic conditions through her imagination. A serious student of the arts, Joplin was a talented artist, writer, and singer; but it was in music that she would leave her mark. Even as a youngster she showed a deep interest in the blues, listening to old Huddie "Leadbelly" Ledbetter and Bessie Smith records until the needle wore through the grooves.

But before launching her blues career, Joplin turned her attention to folk music. Her interest in folk music eventually took her to California in 1962, where she stayed for a few months before returning to Port Arthur. The next time she landed in San Francisco it would be in an entirely different set of circumstances. She drifted for a few years, searching for something meaningful to do with her life. An intelligent person, she enrolled in the University of Texas in Austin, but never completed her degree. She moved across the country but returned to Port Arthur. She lived in Houston and Austin for short stretches but eventually returned home. When she received a letter from a friend saying that she was needed in San Francisco, she immediately moved out there. This time she was there to stay.

Big Brother and the Holding Company was a blues/rock/psychedelic band that had a permanent residency at Chet Helms's Avalon Ballroom. They were a good band, but one of many trying to become big stars in a very crowded market. When they added Joplin, however, they became something special. By this time Joplin had decided to sing the blues, and with her raucous, big-as-Texas voice, the audience was riveted by her sound. In a few months the band became one of the main attractions in the San Francisco area.

The band's big break came at the Monterey Pop Festival in 1967, during the summer of love. With Sam Andrews and Jim Gurley on guitar, Dave Getz on drums and Peter Albin on bass, and Joplin on lead vocals, the group electrified the audience at the festival. Joplin cut through the hot California air with her blues-drenched voice that evoked the ghost of Bessie Smith and comparisons to Big Mama Willie Mae Thornton. By the time she had finished her set, Joplin was well on her way to stardom.

The band was signed to a contract by Columbia and released its first album, *Cheap Thrills*, shortly after the appearance at Monterey. It was an instant hit and the song "Piece of My Heart" raced up the charts. Suddenly Joplin wasn't some unknown Texas folkie with a penchant for singing the blues, but had been crowned the Hippie Queen of the blues-rock set. The immense pressure this recognition instantly put on her shoulders would prove too much to bear.

As a result of their electrifying appearance at Monterey, the band was immediately barraged with tour dates all over the country. Despite their success, Joplin left Big Brother and the Holding Company at the end of 1967, citing musical differences. It was a bitter breakup and the members of Big Brother and the Holding Company—without Joplin as their center-point—drifted into obscurity.

Joplin's next project was the Kozmic Blues band. A loose aggregation of musicians that included Richard Kimode on piano, Sam Andrews, and Snooky Flower, as well as a horn section, the group dulled the sharp, primitive sound of Big Brother. But Joplin forged on and continued to drive audiences crazy with her wild, sexually charged performances of old blues chestnuts like "Summertime" and "Ball and Chain." She managed to release an album, *I Got Dem Ol' Kozmic Blues Again Mama!* The most noteworthy song from this era was "Try (Just a Little Bit Harder)." Although the album received favorable reviews and did well on the charts, the band was doomed from the very beginning. Joplin soon disbanded the Kozmic Blues project and moved on to her next group.

The Full Tilt Boogie Band was better organized and included John Till on guitar, Brad Campbell on bass, Ken Pearson on organ, Richard Bell on piano, and Clark Pierson on drums. Together, they recorded *Pearl*, an affectionate nickname bestowed upon Joplin by her close friends. It was a masterpiece, a bare-bones album that focused on her powerful, emotional voice. It is this album that is responsible for keeping her name somewhat fresh in music circles. It included the Kris Kristofferson composition "Me and Bobby McGee," which went to number one. The comical "Mercedes Benz," a Joplin original, was also a hit. "Cry Baby" revealed her blues-rock side. The album also contained "Buried Alive in the Blues," "Tell Mama," and "Move Over."

Unfortunately, on October 4, 1970, before the album was completed, Janis Joplin died of a heroin overdose. She was 27 years old.

Not only because of her tragically short career, Janis Joplin was the most important white female blues singer of her generation, who inspired a legion of others. She was a complex character who was as much a product of the turbulent sixties as were Jimi Hendrix and Jim Morrison. She attained the same level of superstardom as they did, and wrote a very special chapter in the history of contemporary blues. Arguably her rise to fame was too quick; she was apparently unable to handle the extreme pressures that accompany the bestowal of such high praise.

Janis Joplin was nevertheless one of the most fascinating blues artists in the history of the genre. She could be as tough as nails, use shocking language, and behave outrageously. She could be pleasant, sweet, and funny. She could also appear needy, confused, and vulnerable. Which one was the true Janis Joplin? Probably all of them. There were numerous facets to her personality that she flashed with uncontrolled quickness One was never sure which side of her would emerge, especially when she was on stage.

She thrilled her audiences with the multiple roles she played; she could appear fresh and strong one minute, then old and used the next. She poured everything she had into each performance; she lived and died for her art. Although she played guitar at one time, she was never known as an instrumentalist. Her voice—molded in the tradition of Bessie Smith and Big Mama Thornton—was her blues calling card. It had a rough-edged, coarse, untrained element that was counterbalanced by her blues sensibility. Although she did not possess the most original blues voice, the passion she displayed in every note and song made up for any short-comings as a vocalist.

She also lived a fast-paced lifestyle that inevitably ended her existence. There were plenty of drugs; she was rarely seen without a bottle of Southern Comfort or Jack Daniels. She was sexually experimental and lurid tales of her tastes continue to abound to this day. The one positive constant in her life was the blues, but it was never enough to make her happy.

Janis Joplin was a true rebel. She was constantly opposed to any type of conformity. As a youngster growing up in the constraining environment of Port Arthur, she was always interested in doing whatever it took to spice things up. She had her brushes with the law. She was charged with using profanity onstage during her brief career. There was no way of knowing which direction she would take when confronted with an obstacle.

Janis Joplin was one of the first modern divas. The divas that dominate today's music scene owe a considerable debt of gratitude to Joplin. She opened the door for such acts as Madonna, Britney Spears, Melissa Etheridge, Alannah Myles, Bonnie Tyler, Cindy Bullens, Kim Carnes, Courtney Love, Ashley Cleveland, Marylin Scott, Kim Lembo, and Joan Osborne, to name a few. She was also instrumental in raising the status of the blues singer, and her efforts made it somewhat easier for Bonnie Raitt, Rory Block, Lou Ann Barton, Marcia Ball, Angela Strehli, Joanna Connor, and Sue Foley to attain the success they now enjoy.

In many ways Janis Joplin created the blueprint for the modern female blues singer. She was able to reach back fifty years and make the old songs she covered sound fresh and exciting. She was the starting point from which many first-time blues listeners dug deeper and discovered the wonders of Bessie Smith, as well as the entire list of classic female blues singers of the 1920s.

Her particular brand of blues was not pure, however. It included elements of rock, jazz, folk, soul, and funk. The incredible depth and grit of her voice enabled her to sing all kinds of material with equal fervor. This ability to incorporate other styles into her blues foundation blazed a path for all the female blues singers who came after her.

There have been many books written about Janis Joplin. They include *Buried Alive* by Myra Friedman, who was Albert Grossman's secretary and knew Joplin personally. Her in-depth account sheds great light on the real Janis Joplin during her three turbulent years in the international spotlight. Other books have not been so favorable. *Going Down with Janis*, by Peggy Caserta, is a more sordid account that focuses on the substance abuse, alcoholism, failed relationships both male and female, outrageous, childish behavior, and disillusionment and loneliness. Other books about Joplin include *Janis Joplin: Her Life and Times*, by Deborah Landau, and *Piece of My Heart: A Portrait of Janis Joplin*, by David Dalton.

There have also been a number of greatest-hits packages, all released after her death in an effort to cash in on her lasting popularity. As in the caser of Jimi Hendrix, many of the greatest-hit collections are repetitions of earlier releases. Some of the posthumous records are of poor quality and the best examples of her work remain the albums that were released during her lifetime. The sole exception is *Pearl*, which was released a few months after her tragic death.

Whatever her shortcomings, Janis Joplin was an incredible blues singer. She possessed magic and a power in her voice that has never been duplicated by any other female rock-blues singer. She remains vivid in the memories of a generation that saw her pass through much too quickly. As her music and her life are discovered by each new generation, it is genuine proof that Pearl's blues have survived the test of time. There will certainly never be another one quite like her.

## Discography

*I Got Dem Ol' Kozmic Blues Again Mama!* Columbia CS-9913.
*Pearl*, Columbia 5341.
*Janis Joplin's Greatest Hits*, Columbia 32168.

### With Big Brother and the Holding Company:

*Cheap Thrills*, Columbia CK-9700.
*Big Brother and the Holding Company*, Mainstream 56099.

# ANGELA STREHLI

*Soul-Shake Blues*

There are many ways to measure a successful blues career. One criterion is longevity, though it is not always the best barometer. Robert Johnson, Jimi Hendrix, Janis Joplin, Bessie Smith, and Blind Lemon Jefferson were all important blues artists whose time in the sun was over too quickly. Another way to measure success is the impact that one blues singer has had on succeeding generations, which is sometimes difficult to assess. Was Muddy Waters more important than T-Bone Walker? Did B. B. King have a bigger influence in shaping modern guitar styles than Albert King? Importance is often a matter of perception; and, while the female blues artist who created soul-shake blues may not have received as much publicity as other singers, she has played a vital part in contemporary blues history. Her name is Angela Strehli.

Angela Strehli was born on November 22, 1945, in Lubbock, Texas, into a musical family. Her brother, Al Strehli, eventually became a folk songwriter of some note. Angela grew up listening to the blues, country, Latin, rock and roll, and jazz that she heard on the powerful Texas radio stations in the early 1960s. Before focusing on a career as a singer, she learned to play the harmonica and the bass guitar. Like other Texas blues women before her—Big Mama Willie Mae Thornton, Victoria Spivey, and Sippie Wallace, for example—Strehli paid her dues by playing in every dive, gin mill, club, and roadhouse in the great state of Texas. An intelligent woman, she learned the ropes of the music business quickly and stored the information for later use.

She eventually left Texas and spent some time on the South Side of Chicago, where she sang with Muddy Waters, Howlin' Wolf, Willie Dixon, Buddy Guy, Otis Rush, and Magic Sam. She incorporated some of the gritty Chicago blues sound into her own developing style and moved on, landing in Southern California in the late 1960s. She spent 1967—the summer of love—in San Francisco hanging out with Janis Joplin, who was soon to be the reigning queen of the blues-rock scene.

There is an old adage in Texas that everyone who leaves eventually returns to the Lone Star State. In 1970, tired of the California scene, Strehli returned to her state of birth and settled in Austin. At the time Austin's major claim to fame was as the state capital; the important music scenes were in Dallas and Houston. But a new blues empire was brewing in Austin that would put the city with a bohemian reputation on the musical map.

Clifton Antone was of Lebanese descent and hailed from Port Arthur, Texas, the home of blues queen Janis Joplin. He worked in the family grocery store, learning the value of a dollar, but in the back of his mind he knew there was more to life than selling sandwiches, milk, and eggs. Once he had developed a love for the blues, he wanted to honor all the great musicians who had given so much to the world. The obvious answer was to open a blues club and book all the old bluesmen who were still alive and physically capable of entertaining an audience.

In midsummer 1975, Antone's opened for business. Antone, an intelligent businessman, hired Strehli to run the club. She was the perfect manager because she was older and wiser than all the younger musicians— the Vaughan Brothers, Doyle Bramhall, and Lou Ann Barton—who were then part of the Austin blues scene.

Under her expert guidance Antone's became a top-notch club. Albert King, Muddy Waters, Buddy Guy, and Otis Rush all stopped in to jam. They were backed by the best local blues acts Austin had to offer, including Strehli herself. Unaware that she was writing a page in blues history, Strehli became a mainstay and an integral part of the early Austin blues scene. Although she was instrumental in helping Antone's become one of the best-known blues clubs in America and the world, her own career suffered.

In 1982, however, she revived her career by forming her own band and beginning to tour around Texas on a regular basis. A gifted vocalist with all the class and sophistication of an opera singer, Strehli showed that she had not lost her touch. In 1986, she recorded an EP, *Stranger Blues*, that became the first release on the Antone record label.

In 1987, she released *Soul Shake* and things were never the same after that. Her first solo album, *Soul Shake* brought her the recognition as a female blues artist that she had long sought. It was a powerful collection of songs featuring her strongest performance, as the material and the band were first rate. Strehli covered an impressive array of material that included a Motown song, "Back in My Arms Again," and the blues classic "Wang Dang Doodle."

Her next project was the 1990 collaboration with longtime friends Lou Ann Barton and Marcia Ball on *Dreams Come True*. It was an excellent album that united the three greatest living exponents of the Texas roadhouse tradition. They all had their time to shine in the limelight and the album was an evenly produced and well-crafted collection.

In 1994, Strehli's second solo album, *Blonde and Blue*, was released on the Rounder label. Once again it featured an eclectic mix of songs that were all tied neatly together by Strehli's strong Texas roadhouse voice. Although it did not make the same impact as *Soul Shake*, *Blond and Blue* was a positive step forward in her career. The legendary Steve Cropper— of Booker T and the MGs fame and a long list of other credits—played guitar on a few cuts, which reflected the deep respect that Strehli commanded in the music community.

There was a good balance of blues and soul material on the album. The songs "Never Like This Before" and "Um, Um, Um, Um, Um, Um (Curious Mind)" were remakes of old soul numbers that were given Strehli's blues slant. She poked fun at her Texas roots with "Two Bit Texas Town." The track "Going to That City" was a reference to the trek she made between her two unofficial homes, Austin and San Francisco. All the songs on the album exuded a quiet confidence, a sureness that was classic Strehli.

After a four-year hiatus, Strehli returned with her third solo album, *Deja Blue*. A true modern blues album, it featured a mixture of styles tied together by her gritty, incendiary voice. The set kicked off with a powerful "Cut You Loose" that hummed along with a genuine Texas blues shuffle. But Strehli did more than blues on this work as she extended her range to include soul-drenched numbers like "A Man I Can Love" and "Give Me Love." She shook things up with "Boogie Like You Wanna" and "Hey Miss Tonya." The title track, "Deja Blue," was a pure Texan tune that Strehli handled with relative ease.

Strehli, who now resides in San Francisco, has not severed her Texas roots. She continues to tour regularly throughout the United States, Europe, and Canada with her band that includes Denny Freeman on guitar, Mark Kazanoff on saxophone and harmonica, Pat Whitefield on bass, and George Ralns on drums. They are well-seasoned veterans of the Texas/Austin blues scene. Her next studio work is greatly anticipated.

Angela Strehli is a matriarch of the blues. In a career that spans more than thirty years, she has been present for the launching of many blues careers, including those of Stevie Ray Vaughan, The Fabulous Thunderbirds, Janis Joplin, Sue Foley, Lou Ann Barton, and many others. She is a classy woman who has earned the respect of everyone she has worked and performed with. She is a perennial favorite at the Austin Music City awards and has won other honors. One could argue that she has been under-recorded, but her slim discography is nevertheless an interesting one.

Strehli possesses a blues voice with enough range to allow her to venture into pop, soul, and rhythm-and-blues territory with an easiness and smoothness. She can wrap her voice around any type of song and make it her own. There is a reassuring quality to her voice, a soothing element that relaxes the listener.

Her voice is unique in the contemporary female blues lineup because of this liquid quality. She does not possess the rough-cut edge of Lou Ann Barton's vocals, or the raunchiness of Marcia Ball's Texas/Louisiana energized shout. Strehli is closer to Bonnie Raitt in style, but there is that special individual element that separates her voice from those of her peers; Strehli's voice occupies a unique place in the contemporary female blues pantheon.

Although she boasts a long list of inspirations, the two main modern influences on Strehli were Etta James and Tina Turner. From Etta James, the gutsy rhythm-and-blues singer whose career stretches over forty years, Strehli acquired a musical toughness, the confidence to explore different venues, and a touch of class. From Tina Turner, whose lengthy career in show business rivals that of Etta James, Strehli learned how to control an audience with a certain note, a seductive pose, and impeccable timing.

Strehli is also an important link in the Texas female blues tradition. She is of the third generation of blues singers to carry on the legacy established by Victoria Spivey and Sippie Wallace in the early 1920s, and Big Mama Willie Mae Thornton after World War II. She is the bridge between Janis Joplin and latter-day Texas belters like Lou Ann Barton, Marcia Ball, and Sue Foley.

Perhaps Strehli's biggest contribution to the Texas blues scene—aside from her concert appearances and record catalog—is as a key figure in the development of the Austin blues scene. It was Strehli who commanded the respect of the Vaughan Brothers, Kim Wilson, Doug Sahn, Doyle Bramhall, Denny Freeman, and Lou Ann Barton. She gained the respect of Clifford Antone, who knew that Strehli and only Strehli could deal with the array of zany musical characters in Austin who were hanging around waiting for their big break.

Along with Marcia Ball, Lou Ann Barton, Rory Block, Janis Joplin, and Bonnie Raitt, Angela Strehli is one of the most important contemporary blues singers. She was instrumental in bringing recognition to the female blues scene with her intelligence and charm. Perhaps because of her slim recording catalog, she has not received the same attention as Bonnie Raitt, Rory Block, and Marcia Ball; she has certainly never had to endure the pressures of instant stardom that Janis Joplin suffered through.

Nonetheless, she has performed songs from a variety of sources that demonstrate her versatility as an artist. She has covered tunes written by her female contemporaries Marcia Ball, Sister Sarah Brown, and Tina Turner, to name a few. But her range is much wider than this. She has included soul numbers from the talented pens of Curtis Mayfield, Bobby Robinson, Booker T. James, David Porter, and Isaac Hayes. She has also performed songs from the Chicago-style blues catalog of Little Walter, Muddy Waters, Buddy Guy, and Willie Dixon. She has gone back to the old blues of the first generation of Chicago bluesmen that includes Tampa Red. Her repertoire also includes some of the Jimmy Reed/Eddie Taylor sweet blues of the late 1950s and early 1960s.

She has shared the stage with a host of Austin blues regulars, including Jimmie Vaughan, Denny Freeman, Reese Wymans, Clifford Antone, Kim Wilson, and Sue Foley. She has worked with such legends as Matt "Guitar" Murphy, James Cotton, Muddy Waters, Buddy Guy, and Otis Rush. She has also shared the stage with fellow contemporaries Marcia Ball and Lou Ann Barton.

While her own discography is thin, she has appeared on a variety of releases by other blues singers, including Denny Freeman's *Out of the Blue*; Doug Sahn's *Juke Box Music*; Marcia Ball's *Gatorhythms*; Matt "Guitar" Murphy's *Way Down South*; and Joe Louis Walker's *Live at Slim's, Vol. 1*, among others. She has also served as a producer on Antone's *10th Anniversary Anthology*, and on Memphis Slim's *Together Again One More Time/Still Blues Across the U.S.A.*

Strehli is an important modern blues singer not just because of her wonderful voice, but also because of her longevity and experience. She serves as a role model for younger blues singers like Sue Foley, Susan Tedeschi, and Deborah Coleman. She is a class act, a true Texas spirit, and a genuinely great singer. It is unfortunate that we have not been able to hear more examples of her soul-shake blues.

**Discography**

*Soul Shake*, Antone's ANT-0006-2.
*Dreams Come True*, Antone's ANT-0014.
*Blonde and Blue*, Rounder 3127.
*Deja Blue*, A & M 161399.

# RORY BLOCK

## *High-Heeled Blues*

The evolution of the female blues story is one of the most fascinating chapters in the blues genre. From the humble beginnings of Ma Rainey to the contemporary sound of today's performers, women have always been pillars of the blues community. The modern female blues singers are a varied group that includes Bonnie Raitt, Marcia Ball, Angela Strehli, Lou Ann Barton, Joanna Connor, Sue Foley—and the woman best known for her high-heeled blues. Her name is Rory Block.

Rory Block was born Aurora Block on November 6, 1949, in Princeton, New Jersey, but later moved to Greenwich Village, New York. Although her father played the classical violin, at the age of ten Rory was more interested in the burgeoning folk music scene. She picked up the guitar and began to teach herself the country-blues. Her father, who was a retailer, owned a small shop in Greenwich Village that was frequented by folk singers Tim Hardin, Bob Dylan, Joan Baez, Pete Seeger, John Sebastian, Ramblin' Jack Elliott, Dave Van Ronk, and a host of others. The thrill of meeting these individuals only fueled Block's musical ambitions and her taste for folk music.

As a teenager hers was a typical face in the Village crowd, blending in with the locals and tourists with her acoustic guitar slung over her shoulder. She was a serious student of the folk/blues idiom and was determined to become a big star. Block, who possessed a natural curiosity and a charming personality, was able to strike up conversations with some of the blues singers passing through the Village. She met and received important lessons from Son House, Mississippi John Hurt, Mississippi Fred McDowell, Bukka White, Skip James, and the Rev. Gary Davis.

But she formed her closest ties with Stefan Grossman, a white intellectual blues scholar, who shared the same passion as Block did for the old masters and their deep, soulful music. At fifteen, Block left New York behind and traveled with Grossman to California. Their adventures on the road provided interesting material for a blues diary. Upon her return to New York, Block and Grossman recorded an instructional album, *How to Play Blues Guitar*, for Kicking Mule Records. She played coffeehouses and clubs, entertaining audiences with her country-influenced brand of blues. Although she was a promising guitar player and vocalist, Block "retired" from the music business in the early 1970s to raise a family.

After a brief hiatus, Block returned to the music business with a renewed spirit. Unfortunately times had changed and the country-blues had fallen out of favor with audiences. She recorded three albums with RCA and Chrysalis, though none of the efforts was a reflection of her musical vision. Block, who was meant to play and sing the country-blues of the Delta/Piedmont legends, put out albums that lacked artistic direction.

In 1981, she connected with Rounder Records and the two formed a winning combination. Rounder executives encouraged Block to play the country-blues she loved so much and the result was *High Heeled Blues*. The dues she had paid from the age of ten when she first picked up the guitar to the moment *High Heeled Blues* was released had been worthwhile. The record was a financial and critical success.

*High Heeled Blues* featured songs by Robert Johnson, Skip James and some Block originals. The album, produced by long-time friend John Sebastian (who played harmonica and electric baritone guitar on the album), displayed a heartfelt simplicity. Block's renditions of the classic songs she covered were full of emotion and executed with precision and dedication. Block had found a formula that worked; and she built her career on it.

She followed *High Heeled Blues* with *Blue Horizon*—a logical extension that helped widen her fan base. Once again there was a good balance between old country-blues favorites and Block originals. There was an authentic feel to the album, in the guitar work, in the vocals, and in the production. At a time when the country-blues torch had faded into near obscurity, Block was rekindling the flame from a fresh female point of view. Of note on the album was Block's stretching out musically to play piano and synthesizer in addition to her usual brilliant acoustic guitar work.

Block grew as an artist with each successive album. *Rhinestones & Steel Strings* saw her playing pedal steel guitar. Her next release, *I've Got a Rock in My Sock*, included the traditional blues and folk numbers with more pop-oriented material. It also boasted guest appearances by the great Taj Mahal and the incomparable Stevie Wonder. Without a doubt, Block was gaining respect throughout the musical community.

Her next effort, *Houses of Hearts*, released in 1987, was a special one for a very important reason. Rory's eldest son, Thiele Davin Biehusen, had died in 1986, shortly before his twentieth birthday. He was a fine young man who had filled his mother's heart with pride, and the loss encouraged Block to dig to the very depths of her soul as a blues artist. The result was this album dedicated to her son. Many of the songs dealt with her tragic loss, including the title cut "House of Hearts," "Farewell Young Man," "Heavenly Bird," "Morning Bells," and "Gentle Kindness."

Block rebounded from her son's death in fine fashion with the CD *Mama's Blues*. It earned wide critical acclaim for its spark, originality, and deep blues tone. From the Robert Johnson classic "Terraplane Blues" to the burning title track that featured Jorma Kaukonen's distinctive electric guitar, and the last song, an original gospel, "Sing Good News," the CD was a genuine jewel. It showcased a very talented blues artist at the height of her creative powers.

If *Mama's Blues* boldly announced that Block was the single most important female blues singer on the circuit, then her next CD, *Ain't I a Woman*, cemented that title for her. *Ain't I a Woman* was regarded by many devoted fans as her best CD, which was debatable considering the strength of many of her previous recordings. *Ain't I a Woman* roared with poetic lyrics, perfect musical execution, and the incredible guitar talent of Mark Knopfler. More than in any previous work, Block was able to capture the past with a strong pulse of the contemporary. She wove the eleven cuts into a magical journey that took one from Jerusalem to Mexico and into the personal life of Maggie Campbell. The CD also included the Robert Johnson classic, "Come On in My Kitchen."

Block's next release, *Angel of Mercy*, was another winner. It demonstrated a new maturity in Block's songwriting as she explored themes that depicted genuine characters struggling with the difficult decisions and ordeals of everyday life. The emotional impact of the song "A Father and Two Sons" was used by the American Bible Society in a video. Block was stretching and reaching new heights with her musical ability.

Her next collection of songs, *When a Woman Gets the Blues*, followed the formula of *High Heeled Blues* and *Mama's Blues*: the CD was a hand-picked collection of country-blues classics. Her definitive acoustic style and plaintive voice evoked the spirits of past legends as she updated the classics "Preaching Blues," "Joliet Bound," "Tallahatchie Blues," "Hellhound on My Trail," and "Tain't Long for Day" to a modern sound. With this CD there was no doubting her supreme position on the modern acoustic blues throne.

The CD *Tornado* contained mostly Block originals as well as a resounding cover of "The Last Leviathan." It was a CD—complete with Rory's soulful vocals and inspired playing—that had something for everyone, from polished pop songs to traditional and contemporary blues, country twang to a tinge of soul music. Block, well respected in the musical community, was pleased to have Mary Chapin Carpenter, Stuart Duncan, Will Lee and Paul Shaffer (from the *Late Night with David Letterman* band), David Lindley and Jerry Marotta guest on the album. The song "Mississippi Bottom Blues" summed up Block's career in a nutshell. The Mississippi part was a reflection of the Delta/acoustic style she practices so well; the Bottom was a clear reference to the way the music emerged from the very depths of her soul; and the Blues part was self-explanatory.

With her thirteenth album on Rounder Records, *Confessions of a Blues Singer*, Block proved that one could never hear enough of a good thing. Block took the listener on a journey through the Mississippi Delta and the down-home regional blues of Atlanta, Florida, the Carolinas, Texas, and Louisiana. Two songs stand out on the CD, both Robert Johnson's songs: "Ramblin' on My Mind" and "If I Had Possession Over Judgment Day." The CD also includes a traditional and inspired reprise of the Blind Willie McTell classic, "Statesboro Blues."

Rory Block continues to perform and record

Rory Block is contemporary female blues star, one of the foremost practitioners of traditional country-blues style. She is a masterful guitar player and a strong singer with a voice that elicits the entire spectrum of human emotions. She is an incredible performer and a prolific recording artist. There are many, many facets to the appeal of the Block sound.

Although her roots are in the Delta style, Block has developed her own unique sound. Her approach is to channel the emotions and energy that exist in her heart through her playing. Often, her aggressive guitar playing costs her a fingernail or two: She has sliced her finger and splattered blood all over the place on many concert nights. Because she plays with such ferocity and is a throwback to the days before guitarists used picks, Block pays a heavy—and painful—price to maintain her slamming, percussive style.

Although she has gained considerable attention for the strong consistency of her recorded songs, Block has always balanced her studio work with life on the road. A true road warrior, Block plays one hundred to three hundred concerts a year, including blues festivals in the United States and Europe. At this point in her career, Block does not have to do three hundred shows a year to sell her music. Yet she still brings her music to the people, proving she is more interested in the music itself than the scent of money.

In concert, Block is a genuine treat. With her vast repertoire to choose from, no two shows are alike. There is spontaneity to her music that creates an air of suspense and tension. Like all good performers, Block feeds off the mood of her audience, and if her first song doesn't get them, the second one does. Block takes her audience on a spiritual journey to the lost days when the Mississippi Delta singers ruled the musical world. But she delivers the memories through a contemporary sound that links the past with the present, creating her own special world and in the process taking the audience with her.

Block, like all country-blues artists, was inspired by the original acoustic performers: Charlie Patton, Son House, Robert Johnson, Skip James, Rev. Gary Davis, Bukka White, Mississippi Fred McDowell, Tommy Johnson, Willie Brown. She has also always adored the classic female blues singers like Ma Rainey, Bessie Smith, and Memphis Minnie. Despite a very successful career as a modern blues artist, she has never forgotten the roots of the music or the singers that were responsible for the creation of the genre.

But Block's sources go even deeper. There is a soul/Motown element in her music, a reflection of the strong respect she has for Aretha Franklin, Curtis Mayfield, Wilson Pickett, Gladys Knight, James Brown, Otis Redding, Marvin Gaye, and Fontella Bass. This rhythm-and-blues, funky sound can be found scattered throughout her recorded catalog.

Certain country singers, like Roscoe Holcomb, as well as the great bluegrass stylists like David Grisman, Frank Wakefield, Jodie Stecker, John Herald, Roger Sprung, and Eric Weissberg, also had a special impact on Block. She has incorporated the skill and dexterity of country pickers like Allison Krauss and Ricky Skaggs, who also have a genuine affection for the early roots of country music. Block, an intelligent woman, has always understood the hypnotic attraction of all kinds of music and the power it holds over people. This special insight is one of the key elements in her rise to the top of the music world.

Yet other influences that are traceable in Block's music are the simple rock-and-roll flavor of the Beatles, the Rolling Stones, Herman's Hermits, and Gerry and the Pacemakers. The polished studio productions of their sessions go a long way toward explaining the smoothness in Block's own albums. The music of John Sebastian, Maria Muldaur, Stefan Grossman, Marc Silber, and Jack Baker also had an impact on her musical outlook. The acoustic blues-based music of Taj Mahal is yet another major influence on Block's development. Block has always been receptive to the music around her, and in creating her own distinct style has left no stone unturned.

One of Block's strongest assets as a blues artist is her polished songwriting ability. The themes of her songs go beyond the traditional blues fare; she writes about such unpopular subjects as death, alcoholism, violence against women, and alienation in society. She is more than capable of dealing with these uncomfortable topics in a mature, artistic manner that doesn't cost her any credibility. Her penetrating insight into the human condition separates her from other contemporary female blues artists.

Over the years Block has graduated from a Galiano, her first guitar, to the coveted Martin. She has played several other types, including a Schoenberg, a Yamaha, a Gibson, an Alvarez, a Tokai, and others. In concert, she can usually be seen playing her favorite Martin acoustic guitar, but she has quite a collection to choose from. Her mood and the set list dictate the type of guitar she will use in concert on a particular night.

There is no denying that Block is a rare talent with an incomparable spirit and dedication, but until recently she had been shut out on the awards front. Nevertheless, she has won four W. C. Handy Awards: one for Acoustic Album of the Year in 1996 for *When a Woman Gets the Blues*, and again in 1999 for *Confessions of a Blues Singer*. Her third and fourth

W. C. Handy awards were for Traditional Female Artist of the Year in 1997 and 1998, respectively. She has won two NAIRD/INDIE Awards, as well as "Blues Guitarist of the Year" in France.

One of the most meaningful aspects of Block's career has been her opportunity to work with her son Jordan. They have recorded together (the song "Walk in Jerusalem" is a classic example), and share a life on the road. The experience of seeing mother and son together on stage is a rare treat in the blues since there are relatively few mother-and-son acts on the circuit. Block's son seems destined to follow in his famous mother's footsteps; but, like his mother, he is independent and will carve his own niche in the music world.

From day one, Rory Block was determined to build a career on the acoustic blues. When she started out, the crowds were small and the record sales were slow. After all, the country-blues flame had been turned down to a mere flicker. But two decades later the country-blues have made a strong comeback and Rory Block, with her high-heeled blues, is one of the artists responsible for keeping the tradition alive during the leaner years. Rory Block is a blues jewel; she should continue to shine for a long, long time.

## Discography

*How to Play Blues Guitar*, Kicking Mule 150.
*Rory Block (I'm in Love)*, Blue Goose BG-2022.
*Intoxication So Bitter Sweet*, Chrysalis CHR-1157.
*You're the One*, Chrysalis CHR-1233.
*High Heeled Blues*, Rounder 3061.
*Blue Horizon*, Rounder 3073.
*Rhinestones & Steel Strings*, Rounder 3085.
*I've Got a Rock in My Sock*, Rounder 3097.
*House of Hearts*, Rounder 3104.
*Mama's Blues*, Rounder 3117.
*Best Blues and Originals*, Rounder 11525.
*Ain't I a Woman*, Rounder 3120.
*Angel of Mercy*, Rounder 1994.
*When a Woman Gets the Blues*, Rounder 3139.
*Tornado*, Rounder 3140.
*Gone Woman Blues: The Country Blues Collection*, Rounder 11575.
*Confessions of a Blues Singer*, Rounder 3154.

# MARCIA BALL

## *Hot Tamale Baby*

In the 1920s, Victoria Spivey and Sippie Wallace put the Texas female blues tradition on the blues map. In the 1940s and 1950s, Big Mama Willie Mae Thornton carried on where Spivey and Wallace had left off. In the 1960s, Janis Joplin was the champion of Texas female blues. In the 1970s, a new sound emerged from Austin that featured some of the best female blues talent in the world. The Austin sound was built on a mixture of rhythm and blues, country, soul, Cajun, and jazz; it was a reflection of the varied artists who made Austin an important venue for music. One of the major contributors to the Austin sound was the fiery blues pianist nicknamed Hot Tamale Baby. Her name is Marcia Ball.

Marcia Ball was born on March 20, 1949, in Orange, Texas, but grew up in Vinton, Louisiana, just east of the Texas line. Such musical luminaries as Clarence "Gatemouth" Brown, Clifton Chenier (the king of zydeco blues), and Johnny Clyde Copeland, among others, built the blues legacy of that area. It was long a hotbed of country, blues, gospel, Cajun, zydeco, rockabilly, and swamp rhythms, which were all important influences on young Ball. She absorbed these different styles as she developed into a first-rate pianist. Any possibility of becoming a classical pianist was squashed by her love of the swinging blues rhythms that seemingly ran through her veins.

While attending Louisiana State University in Baton Rouge, Ball played in the blues-based rock band Gum. Although the band never gained any national attention, it was a good training ground for the young pianist/vocalist. After graduation she moved to Austin in the late 1970s, just as the blues scene was really getting its act together. The Vaughan Brothers, Angela Strehli, Lou Ann Barton, and dozens of minor acts were ready and able to help put Austin on the music map.

Upon arriving in Austin, Ball didn't waste much time. She formed the band Freda and the Firedogs, a rollicking, barrelhouse boogie band that became a crowd favorite on the Austin club circuit. Despite their popularity, Ball left Freda and the Firedogs to sign as a solo artist for Capitol Records. Her first release, *Circuit Queen*, was a creditable effort but didn't win her very many new fans. Ball, who had always been a quick study from the minute she placed her hands on a piano keyboard, had to teach herself the process of making albums.

She moved to Rounder Records, and her mix of Texas boogie with

New Orleans rollicking rhythm and blues began to pay off. She started to tour extensively and built a strong reputation as one of the wildest acts on the circuit. Her first release on Rounder, *Soulful Dress*, a smash hit, struck a particular chord with the blues crowd because it was the kind of record a person could stomp, dance, or play air piano along to; it was fun blues. Ball smartly mixed her remarkable originals with classics like "I'd Rather Go Blind" and "Jailbird." She was able to get Stevie Ray Vaughan to make a guest appearance at a time (1984) when Vaughan's popularity was soaring.

She recorded two more albums in the same vein. *Hot Tamale Baby* featured Ball's hard-driving piano thrills with more commercial arrangements such as "That's Enough of That Stuff," which became the new Mardi Gras theme song. The title song, "Hot Tamale Baby," an original Clifton Chenier composition, reminded listeners of Ball's roots. That New Orleans party music had always been a crowd favorite and in many ways Ball picked up where Professor Longhair had left off. Ball made her mixture of New Orleans swamp boogie and Texas roadhouse blues accessible.

Her next release, *Gatorhythms*, was another huge financial and critical success. This effort showcased Ball's polished songwriting abilities, whereas in the past she had leaned more heavily on cover songs. Her mixture of pounding Texas boogie piano and Louisiana soul was a winning formula and Ball, an intelligent woman, knew a good thing when she heard it. With the song "Mama's Cooking" it all came together quite nicely. The CD was also interesting for another reason: Lou Ann Barton was a guest vocalist, a foreshadowing of future events.

*Dreams Come True*, one of those events, combined three of the best female blues singers of the modern era. Lou Ann Barton, the Texas roadhouse queen, Angela Strehli, the queen of the Austin scene, and Long Tall Marcia Ball, the queen of Louisiana gator rhythms and Texas swing, poured their souls into the recordings. Each had a chance to showcase her particular talents. A decade later, *Dreams Come True* remains a favorite, and the fact that a second joint project never materialized was a disappointment to blues fans everywhere.

In 1994, *Blue House* was released—her first solo work in five years. Once again Ball pounded out expert Louisiana/Delta roadhouse blues. Her voice, an extension of her excellent piano virtuosity, proved that Ball was still at the top of her game. The inclusion of "Fingernails," a Delbert McClinton original, drew comparisons between Ball and her powerful fellow Texan. Ball, who had raised eyebrows with her previous releases, struck a deeper chord with *Blue House*. She was highly touted as one of the best blues artists on the circuit, with the chops to back up the proclamation.

Despite a heavy tour schedule Ball managed to put out *Let Me Play with Your Poodle* in 1997. Two of the cover songs on the album gave it another dimension. The title track was an old Tampa Red song and "Crawfishin'" was a New Orleans standard that Professor Longhair had made famous. She balanced these two songs with her crafty compositions "American Dream" and "Why Women Cry." While she had always shown that she could rock the house away, Ball also demonstrated here that she could deliver tender ballads with meaningful lyrics that focused on the struggles of daily life.

The success of *Dreams Come True* spurred Ball to make another collaboration record, this time with Irma Thomas and Tracy Nelson, called *Sing It*. The three women combined their wealth of musical experiences to create a truly great record. The fusion of rhythm and blues, country, and New Orleans second-line party music was a runaway hit. There were equal solo spotlights and three-part harmonies with songs from a host of talented writers, including David Egan, Dan Penn, Sarah Campbell, Sarah Brown, Gary Nicholson, and Steve Cropper. The accompanying band was an all-star aggregation of Memphis and New Orleans players, including guitarist Michael Toles and keyboardist David Torkanowsky.

Ball continues to record and perform.

Marcia Ball is a blues queen. She has been rocking audiences with her mixture of Texas roadhouse stomp and Louisiana boogie rhythms for two decades. Her consistent release of excellent albums has greatly enhanced her popularity. She is without a doubt one of the premier female blues singers on the circuit and her success can be attributed to the fact that Marcia Ball is a complete package.

She is a masterful piano player with a subtle dexterity that enables her to play straight-ahead rhythm and blues, driving riffs, slow ballads with notes falling like raindrops, and everything in between. She is the all-important modern link in the piano blues style, one she inherited from such greats as Leroy Carr, Sunnyland Slim, Big Maceo Merriweather, Roosevelt Sykes, Albert Ammons, Pete Johnson, Meade "Lux" Lewis, Otis Spann, Fats Domino, Allan Toussaint, and her cherished idol, Professor Longhair.

She has a clear, uncluttered voice that pumps life into any song whether it be an original composition or a cover version. That voice has become synonymous with the New Orleans blues style and she is a favorite draw at Mardi Gras. With a voice that was tailor-made for her brand of Gulf Coast boogie blues, Ball's excellent vocals make her style of blues a thoroughly enjoyable experience.

Ball is an accomplished songwriter in the same vein as the classic female blues singers of the 1920s, Ida Cox, Victoria Spivey, and Sippie

Wallace. With her keen business sense, she has always skillfully guided her career with one foot on the performance side of the blues and the other foot firmly planted on the business side of popular music.

She knows her way around a recording studio and the technical touches on every one of her releases bear her seal of excellence. One of the secrets of her success as a recording artist is that Ball never considers recording an album until she has a wealth of first-class material written. Because of this brilliant strategy, it is rare to find a weak track on any of her works. She also must have a perfect handle on a cover song before she decides to include it with her own excellent tunes.

Ball is a road warrior, performing hundreds of dates a year in the United States, Canada, and Europe. A hometown favorite on the Texas/ Louisiana club circuit, Ball has used her popularity as a springboard to national and international recognition. She has played at hundreds of festivals and is a perennial performer at the New Orleans Heritage Festival.

Another party that would not be complete without Ball is New Orleans' annual Mardi Gras event. In 1996, Ball ventured into a different branch of the music business with a video called *Big Shots, Stew Pots & Zulu Kings*, from Rounder records. The slick production celebrates the New Orleans Cajun culture that is an integral part of Ball's live show and song catalog.

Over the years Ball has worked with a great number of musicians, including a steady back-up band that has accompanied her in the studio and on the road. A partial list of those who have played an integral part in the Marcia Ball story includes: Mark Kazanoff, Derek O'Brien, Don Bennett, Stuart Sullivan, Doyle Bramhall, Jon Blondell, Gary Schlecta, Keith Winking, George Rains, Rodney Craig, David Murray, Randy Zimmerman, Steve Williams, John Treanor, John Reed, Red Rails, and Riley Osbourne.

Ball has had an illustrious blues career spanning more than thirty years. Along with Bonnie Raitt and Rory Block, she is one of the leading artists on the contemporary female blues scene. Whether live or in a studio setting, she is always fired up. She has received glowing reviews from music critics in several countries, has been the subject of favorable television documentaries, and continues to thrill her large base of devoted fans. There is no doubt that Long Tall Marcia Ball has written her own page in blues history with her rollicking, touching, hot tamale baby blues.

## Discography

*Circuit Queen*, Capitol 11752.
*Soulful Dress*, Rounder 3078.

*Hot Tamale Baby*, Rounder 3095.
*Gatorhythms*, Rounder 3101.
*Dreams Come True*, Antone's, ANT-0014.
*Blue House*, Rounder 3131.
*Let Me Play with Your Poodle*, Rounder 3151.

As Freda and the Firedogs:
*Freda and the Firedogs Live*, Big Wheel 10876.

On Video:
*Big Shots, Stew Pots, & Zulu Kings*, Rounder 1.

# BONNIE RAITT

## *A Blues Angel*

The legion of slide guitarists that includes Son House, Robert Johnson, Muddy Waters, Earl Hooker, Robert Nighthawk, Elmore James, Duane Allman, and Johnny Winter has been primarily a male domain. But in modern times, as women have asserted their independence and explored different avenues previously closed to them, a fresh sound in the blues has emerged. In the late 1960s, a young Californian came out sliding and grinding like an old Mississippi Delta bluesman, and used her distinctive skills to spread her wings, becoming not only one of the most popular blues performers in the world, but a true blues angel. Her name is Bonnie Raitt.

Bonnie Raitt was born on November 8, 1949, in Burbank, California. Her father was a Broadway star and her mother an accomplished pianist; show business was in her blood. At the age of eight she received an acoustic guitar—a Stella—which opened up a whole new universe to her. The guitar became her best friend and Raitt developed her skills quickly. Upon hearing the country-blues she was swept away by the broomdusters' ability to make a guitar moan and cry by sliding a glass or metal tube along the metal strings. She dreamed of playing slide on a par with the greats like Robert Johnson, Son House and Muddy Waters.

In 1967 she moved to Boston to attend Radcliffe College. In her spare time she continued to play and sing, building a small but enthusiastic following in the coffeehouses and clubs around the campus. After two years of college she quit to pursue a career in music, and it was about this time that she caught the attention of Dick Waterman. Waterman, one of the white students who had spent time searching for old, forgotten blues artists during the folk/blues craze in the early 1960s, was managing some of the legendary musicians. Through Waterman's connections, Raitt shared the stage with Howlin' Wolf, Mississippi Fred McDowell, and one of her true idols, Sippie Wallace.

Raitt had blossomed into a solid slide guitarist by this time, but the invaluable experience of firsthand instruction from Mississippi Fred McDowell, Son House, Mississippi John Hurt, and Sleepy John Estes helped her hone her technique. She performed regularly and enlarged her fan base throughout the East Coast. At the tender age of twenty-one, she signed a recording contract with Warner Brothers—one of the major labels.

Early the following year she began work on her first album with a top-notch lineup of musical friends that included Junior Wells, A. C. Reed, and a back-up band called the Bumblebees. Raitt played acoustic and slide guitar as well as piano. Standout selections on the album included Robert Johnson's "Walking Blues," Stephen Stills' "Bluebird," and the traditional "Since I Fell for You," which was given a distinctive Raitt treatment. There were also two covers, "Women Be Wise" and "Mighty Tight Woman," from the song catalog of her idol, Sippie Wallace.

That first record, simply entitled *Bonnie Raitt*, served as a blueprint for her next few releases. These efforts contained a mixture of blues, rock, and rhythm-and-blues material; the sources of the songs were usually unknown songwriters; and her powerful guitar work was the center of focus. Without a doubt, Raitt was ready to take the music world by storm.

Each successive album generated its own highlights and boasted a couple of classics to add to the Raitt canon. *Give It Up*, her second release, was a landmark album for different reasons. It contained three Raitt originals, "Give It Up or Let Me Go," "Nothing Seems to Matter," and "You Told Me Baby." There was a Sippie Wallace composition, "You Got to Know How," as well as "Under the Falling Sky," the first of many Jackson Browne tunes that would find their way onto Raitt's albums in the future. Raitt was supported by a group of Woodstock musicians, including Erik Kaz, Marty Grebb, Terry Eaton, and John Payne. *Give It Up* also boasted appearances by Paul Butterfield and members of his newly formed band, Better Days. Raitt dedicated the album to the people of North Vietnam and to the memory of one of her mentors, Mississippi Fred McDowell.

The album *Takin' My Time*, Raitt's third in three years, was another solid collection with particular highlights. It featured a wealth of eclectic material that ranged from the pure blues of Fred McDowell to the genius of the then-unknown Randy Newman. There was a Jackson Browne song, "I Thought I Was a Child," and a Mose Allison song, "Everybody's Cryin' Mercy." Musically, the talented Taj Mahal and the members of Little Feat, including the incredible Lowell George, supplemented Raitt's usual excellent guitar work. Interestingly, there were no Bonnie Raitt originals on this album.

While her recording career was going strong, the touring side of her career was equally active. She played coffeehouses, college campuses, and smaller venues where she was backed up by many of the people who played on her albums, including Erik Kaz and longtime Raitt bass player Freebo. Even with three strong albums under her belt, however, Raitt was still not a major attraction; but this lack of recognition only encouraged her to forge on with her genuine blues spirit.

Her fourth album in four years, *Streetlights*, was another exceptional effort. Once again Raitt covered a variety of material, including Joni Mitchell's "That Song About the Midway," James Taylor's "Rainy Day Man," and "Success," by Allan Toussaint. No one at the time was assembling blues records with such a variety of musical flavors and diverse musicians with greater success than Raitt. Despite the different elements, the entire production contained a sharpness that was pure Bonnie Raitt.

*Homeplate* was Raitt's most ambitious project to date and involved a large contingent of musicians, including horns. The material was first-rate and spotlighted songs from Allan Toussaint, Delbert McClinton, Bill Payne, and Erik Kaz. Jackson Browne, Tom Waits, and J. D. Souther provided background vocals. Raitt played electric slide guitar on "Sugar Mama," and sounded like a direct descendant of Delta standout Son House. The energy she poured into these complex productions was truly incredible.

*Sweet Forgiveness*, Raitt's sixth album, was a major breakthrough effort for one of the best female blues artists on the contemporary scene. It featured the monster hit "Runaway," made famous by Del Shannon. But Raitt recorded the song in her own style, complete with slide guitar. The record also featured Jackson Browne's "My Opening Farewell," Eric Kaz's "Gamblin' Man," Mark Jordan's "Two Lives," and "Takin' My Time" by Bill Payne, a member of Little Feat. This was her second consecutive album produced by the legendary Paul Rothchild, famous as the guiding hand behind the Doors, the Paul Butterfield Band, and Janis Joplin. The effort placed Raitt among the top blues stylists.

Raitt's last album of the 1970s, *The Glow*, was interesting for different reasons. The number of backing musicians had been scaled down from previous efforts, but the quality was world-class. Danny Kortchmar and Waddy Wachtel played guitar, Bob Glaub played bass, Bill Payne contributed keyboards, and Rick Marotta provided drums and other percussion instruments. There were also noted guests like Paul Butterfield blowing harp and Don Gralnick on piano. Raitt played both electric and slide steel guitar like a champion. The wealth of material featured ten songs, including the Raitt original "Standin' by the Same Old Love," the Bobby Troup classic "The Boy Can't Help It," Jackson Browne's "Sleep's Dark and Silent Gate," a pair of soul classics from Isaac Hayes—"I Thank You" and "Your Good Thing (Is About to End)"—and Robert Palmer's "You're Gonna Get What's Coming."

The first Raitt offering of the 1980s, *Green Light*, was a return to basics for Raitt. The slick production of *The Glow* had been replaced with a more roots-oriented approach. It featured an eclectic mixture of material from a variety of sources, including Bob Dylan's "Let's Keep It Between Us," and Eric Kaz's "River of Tears" (dedicated to the memory of Lowell George, the leader and found of Little Feat who had passed away). Other powerful tracks included "Green Light," "Me and the Boys," "Willya Wontcha," and "I Can't Help Myself." Ian MacLagan, Jackson Browne, and Johnny Lee Schell provided Raitt with more-than-adequate support. On this album, more than on any of the previous few releases, Raitt's excellent guitar work stands out.

*Nine Lives*, her ninth and last album on the Warner Brothers label, was a major disappointment. For once, Raitt was unable to unite the myriad musicians, styles, and ideas together into one cohesive, working unit. It was a disjointed album that nevertheless featured some good songs such as "Angel," "No Way to Treat a Lady," "Crime of Passion," and "Runnin' Back to Me." Once the album was finished, Warner Brothers unceremoniously dropped Raitt from their stable of artists.

Raitt's fall from grace can be traced to this point. She had no recording contract, her tour had been cancelled, and she was fighting substance-abuse problems. She needed a change and to regain control of her life. At this point many critics had written her off, and long-standing fans clung to her first few albums as reminders of her better days.

In 1986, Raitt signed with Capitol Records and released *Nick of Time*. The material had a funkier, bouncier sound; she had crossed over to a more pop-oriented style. Raitt had discovered how to retain her blues identity while attracting an entire section of the music-buying public that had previously ignored her. She played more guitar on this album and the material was first-rate. The title cut, "Nick of Time," was a Raitt composition, as was "The Road's My Middle Name." The rest of the material came from outside sources, including Bonnie Hayes, John Hart, and Jerry L. Williams. The record propelled Raitt back into the spotlight.

*Luck of the Draw* followed and only enhanced Raitt's newfound appeal. Raitt became one of the most popular performers in the country and her records sold in large quantities. The album yielded two hits, "Something to Talk About" and "I Can't Make You Love Me." In a span of four years Raitt had turned a stagnant career back into a vibrant, healthy one. She was the darling of the press and performed in front of the largest audiences of her career. Raitt dedicated *Luck of the Draw* to Stevie Ray Vaughan, the late, great Texas bluesman.

Her third release for Capitol Records, *Longing in Their Hearts*, endeared her to a still greater legion of fans. It contained five original Raitt compositions, the most of any of her past efforts. She had conquered her demons, had married Michael O'Keefe (since divorced), and her life never seemed better. Her relaxed state apparently enabled her to pour all her energies into the album. The songs "Love Sneakin' Up on You," "Circle Dance," "Feeling of Falling," "Steal Your Heart Away," "Storm Warning," and "Hell to Pay" anchored the record.

Although Raitt had been a true road warrior since the beginning of her career, often spending up to eight months of the year on tour, she had never delivered a live album. So it was only fitting that she release *Road Tested*, a double set that was recorded in Portland, Oregon, and Oakland, California. The album featured the two sides of Raitt's career: her early penchant for folk/blues material, and her later, more commercial pop/rock, rhythm-and-blues sound. Some of the highlights of the live disc included "Thing Called Love," "Something to Talk About," "The Kokomo Medley," "Burning Down the House," and "I Can't Make You Love Me." Bryan Adams, Kim Wilson, and Bruce Hornsby joined Raitt on stage in addition to her usual back-up band.

*Fundamental*, her fourteenth major release, was another ambitious project that included guest appearances by Sheryl Crow, Elvis Costello, and Los Lobos. Once again the focal point of the entire band was Raitt's tasty slide guitar work. There was a mixture of blues, reggae, rock, and soul—a true contemporary blues album. "Lover's Will," "Fearless Love," "Spit of Love," "Round and Round," "Meet Me Halfway," and "I'm on Your Side" were a few of the record's strong points. She immediately went on tour to support her latest creative achievement and was well received. Her days of coffeehouses and small, intimate settings had been replaced by bigger venues to accommodate her ever-growing fan base.

Raitt continues to record and perform.

Bonnie Raitt is a blues sweetheart. With fifteen albums to her credit and a bevy of awards, she is firmly established as one of the most popular and important female blues singers on the circuit. A pretty woman with reddish locks that tumble down past her shoulders and an engaging smile, Raitt has always been closely connected to her fans. The mere mention of her name evokes nods of recognition throughout the country and the world. In many blues corners she is considered today's finest exponent of the slide guitar tradition.

Although she has garnered a reputation as an imaginative, sincere songwriter, with an uncanny ability to make the ordinary appealing in a fresh new way, Raitt has also recorded numerous songs from other artists throughout her career. Jackson Browne has supplied Raitt with a number of his compositions scattered throughout her fifteen recorded albums. She has also covered the tunes of Eric Kaz, Bryan Adams, Jimmie Vaughan, Allen Toussaint, Del Shannon, Bonnie Hayes, and many others. More than just an imitator, Raitt has taken the gems written by those artists and put her personal stamp on each one.

While Raitt is recognized as a multi-talented artist, it is her guitar work that first earned her the public's attention and is the foundation of her sound. Raitt, a first-rate slide guitar player, is a master on the steel guitar and National steel guitar, as well as electric and acoustic. She plays a searing slide style that is a cross between the Mississippi Delta stalwarts like Son House and Robert Johnson and the more modern sound of Duane Allman and Delbert McClinton.

Her inspirations are wide ranging. They include such Delta stars as the aforementioned House, as well as Mississippi John Hurt, Mississippi Fred McDowell, and the boogie master John Lee Hooker. But there is also a noticeable hint of Chicago blues in her sound that can be directly traced to Otis Rush, Buddy Guy, and Muddy Waters. The greatest female blues singer to have an impact on Raitt was Sippie Wallace, the Texas-born singer/piano player who blazed the trail for artists like Raitt, Marcia Ball, Lou Ann Barton, and many others. It was Bonnie's lifelong dream and extreme pleasure to work with Wallace in the late 1960s and early 1970s. Raitt's dedication and devotion to the old blues masters have always been among her most endearing qualities.

The fact that Raitt grew up in the early 1960s listening to Bob Dylan is reflected in her strong folk/pop side. Dylan, who made a serious impact on a wealth of musicians of different branches of the musical tree, can claim Raitt as a direct disciple. She was also influenced by the soft acoustic rock that emerged from her native Southern California in the late 1960s and early 1970s. James Taylor, Joni Mitchell, and Carly Simon are a few of the artists she emulated.

Raitt also developed an affinity for the heavy rhythm and blues of the early Rolling Stones records, as well as the modern pop sound of Randy Newman and the traditional down-home folk/blues/rock of The Band. In turn, Raitt has her own coterie of direct and indirect disciples. Raitt, who established the boundaries for women guitar players, has had a tremendous impact on Joanna Connor and Sue Foley, two of the best instrumentalists on the planet. She has also had an impact on the careers of pop divas Melissa Ethridge and Alanis Morissette.

While Raitt truly idolized Sippie Wallace, she also admired Ida Cox and Victoria Spivey, for different reasons. Both Cox and Spivey had been astute businesswomen. Raitt, following in their path, has always been in control of her career choices. While a staff helps her manage her complex and hectic career, Raitt is her own boss. Her understanding of the business side of the recording industry is an important lesson that all aspiring blues singers should study and adapt to their own situations.

Raitt is a champion of the blues and is a strong believer in important causes. She has worked tirelessly to ensure that acoustic blues artists such as Mississippi John Hurt, Mississippi Fred McDowell, Skip James, Son House, and Big Joe Williams are not forgotten. She has played numerous charity concerts in support of the Rhythm and Blues Foundation, and is a co-founder of MUSE (Musicians United for Safe Energy). Despite her pronounced success, Raitt has never turned her back on the importance of supporting blues causes, as well as other viable important humanitarian issues.

Raitt is a perennial Grammy favorite and has won a roomful of the coveted musical awards. Her 1989 hit, *Nick of Time*, won four awards, including Album of the Year. Her 1994 effort, *Longing in Their Hearts*, won her another golden prize. She has shared awards with Delbert McClinton and John Lee Hooker. She was also presented with a Grammy for her part in the Stevie Ray Vaughan tribute album that she shared with Jimmie Vaughan, Eric Clapton, Robert Cray, B. B. King, Buddy Guy, Dr. John, and Art Neville.

The Bonnie Raitt story is a heartwarming tale of a young girl who became enchanted with the country-blues she heard on the radio and turned her dream into a reality. Her blend of blues, pop, rock, and country music has allowed her to attain a large audience and to explore different musical paths despite some criticism she has received because of it. Although she might not now play as much slide guitar as she did when she first appeared on the scene, and although she has adopted a more commercial musical front on her last few albums, she will always remain a blues angel.

## Discography

*Bonnie Raitt*, Warner Brothers 1953.
*Give It Up*, Warner Brothers 2643.
*Takin' My Time*, Warner Brothers 2729.

*Streetlights*, Warner Brothers 2818.
*Homeplate*, Warner Brothers 2864.
*Sweet Forgiveness*, Warner Brothers 2990.
*The Glow*, Warner Brothers 3369.
*Green Light*, Warner Brothers 3630.
*Nine Lives*, Warner Brothers 25486.
*Nick of Time*, Capitol 91268.
*Luck of the Draw*, Capitol 96111.
*Longing in Their Hearts*, Capitol 81427.
*Road Tested*, Capitol 53705.
*Fundamental*, Capitol 56397.
*Someone to Talk*, Capitol 15736

# LOU ANN BARTON

## *Texas Roadhouse Queen*

The Austin blues scene that began to take shape in the early 1970s attracted singers from all over Texas. Marcia Ball came from Louisiana via Orange, Texas; Angela Strehli hailed from Lubbock; the Vaughan Brothers, Jimmie and Stevie Ray, hailed originally from the Dallas suburb of Oak Cliff. One of the other major contributors to the Austin blues sound initially called Forth Worth her home. Today she is known as the Texas Roadhouse Queen. Her name is Lou Ann Barton.

Lou Ann Barton was born on February 17, 1954, in Fort Worth, Texas. She grew up in a middle-class family with a father who was a truck driver and mother who ran a bookstore. Since music was all around her, it was only natural that Barton should show more than a passing interest. Like all good Texans she listened to rhythm and blues, rock and roll, blues, country, bluegrass, Texas swing, and Mexican music. During her teenage years, fellow–Texan Janis Joplin ruled as the dominant blues queen and Barton was greatly influenced by the blues-rock belter. Barton also developed a particular taste for the tough sounds of both Irma Thomas and Wanda Jackson. By her mid-teens, Barton had already begun to sing in dark venues that fifteen year olds didn't really belong in. But then, Barton was no ordinary fifteen year old.

Tired of the relatively stifling musical scene in Fort Worth, she decided to try her luck in Austin, the state capital. Barton, who had already paid her dues singing all over the Lone Star State with an incredibly long list of bar bands, found a home in Austin. Something big was happening and she fit right in with the likes of Jimmie Vaughan, Angela Strehli, Stevie Ray Vaughan, Doyle Bramhall, Denny Freeman, Tommy Shannon, and the rest of the Austin blues crowd.

Barton found work in Austin sitting in with early versions of the various bands that the Vaughan brothers assembled. Barton is the only person who can claim that she took part in early formations of both The Fabulous Thunderbirds and Stevie Ray Vaughan and Double Trouble. She also appeared with the Robert Ealey Band and Marc Benno's group. Although her tenure in The Fabulous Thunderbirds was short-lived, she had a longer stay in Stevie Ray's Triple Threat Revue.

The Triple Threat Revue featured Stevie Ray Vaughan as lead guitarist, W. C. Clark on bass, Freddie Pharoah on drums, Mike Kindred on keyboards, and Barton as the main vocalist. It was a dream band, with all the pieces forming a strong synthesis. However, after barely a year together, the band started to fall apart; Clark was the first to leave, then Pharoah departed. Barton remained with Stevie Ray through the name change from Triple Threat Revue to Double Trouble. But in late 1979 she, too, finally quit the band.

Barton then joined Roomful of Blues, an East Coast band that had been formed in 1967 by guitar wizard Duke Robillard and Al Copley. The group enjoyed limited success during its first few years, but after securing a recording contract in 1977, saw better times ahead. In 1979, Robillard left the band and was replaced by Ronnie Earle. With the addition of Earle and with Barton, Roomful widened its fan base and made several important gains. But in 1981 Barton left Roomful of Blues to pursue a solo career.

While a member of Double Trouble, Barton had caught the eye of Jerry Wexler, the legendary producer/talent scout. He teamed up with Glenn Frey (of Eagles fame) to secure Barton a deal with Asylum Records. The resulting effort, *Old Enough*, was a stunning debut. Backed by the famous Muscle Shoals Horns, Barton received favorable reviews from the critics but the album was a commercial failure.

Barton drifted along for the next few years, singing whenever she could with pick-up bands all over Texas. Although Austin was her home base, she was no stranger to the clubs in Houston, Dallas, San Antonio, and every other town that boasted a blues venue. She rebounded somewhat in 1986 with another solo album.

*Forbidden Times* was recorded on the small Spindletop label. Once again it featured Barton's tough-as-Texas-moonshine vocals, but the record soon disappeared without a trace. Despite the failure of the album, Barton still ruled the Texas roadhouse scene. No one could growl louder, sound more dangerous, and capture the audience's attention more completely than Barton.

Perhaps the adage that three times is the charm is true. In 1989, Barton recorded her third solo album, *Read My Lips*, on the Antone label. The album included guest appearances by Kim Wilson of The Fabulous Thunderbirds, David "Fathead" Newman on saxophone, and Jimmie Vaughan. (Vaughan has played on at least one cut on all of Barton's solo albums.) *Read My Lips* was a huge success. It catapulted Barton from her place as an obscure Texas barrelhouse wailer to the more prominent position that she had sought for the past decade.

On *Read My Lips*, Barton performed songs by Hank Ballard and Slim Harpo, and also covered other R&B chestnuts. The highlights of the album included "Sexy Ways," "Shake Your Hips," "You Can Have My Husband," "Rocket in My Pocket," "You'll Lose a Good Thing," and "Mean, Mean Man." *Read My Lips* was a real cooker; it burned with the intensity of a Dallas sidewalk on a blistering summer day.

She repeated the success of *Read My Lips* on *Dreams Come True*, the collaboration with fellow contemporary female blues singers Marcia Ball and Angela Strehli for Antone's. The three angels of fire combined to deliver a first-rate product. There was a natural chemistry among the artists that was captured on record. The material was a mixture of Ike Turner classics, Marcia Ball compositions, and other rhythm-and-blues favorites. What made the CD so special was the blending of the three different personalities. Strehli sang in clear audible tones, Ball whooped it up, and Barton added a sultry touch.

From powerful numbers like "Fool in Love" to "Snake Dance" with its Louisiana voodoo vibes, the record served notice that the Texas blues scene was alive and well. Although the venture proved a success, however, Barton did not benefit as much as did Strehli and Ball, whose careers continued strong. In fact, from this point on Barton's career sagged badly. The promise of a second album with Ball and Strehli fell through and left Barton roaming the Texas club circuit in search of work.

In 1998, eight years after *Dreams Come True*, Barton finally recorded another album, *Sugar Coated Love*. It was another power-packed catalog of songs that included "Someday," "I Feel Like Breaking Up Somebody's Home," "Rock 'n' Roll 800," "Not Even Me," and "Te Ni Nee Ni Nu," parts one and two. It was well received, but, like her other projects, it failed to bring Barton the national attention she has sought so long.

Barton continues to tour and record sporadically.

Lou Ann Barton is a blues treasure. She is a talented chanteuse with a vocal range that can render a tearful country song into a torrential downpour, a soul number into an incendiary incident, and a blues tune into a dark tapestry of carefully woven human emotions. But her voice is only part of the complete Lou Ann Barton package.

She is an incredible live performer. On stage, Barton is like a tigress that has just escaped from her cage. She pounces on her audience with her trademark caterwaul that shatters the world into a million fragments. Her sassy, hands-on-hips bravado is a crowd pleaser that never fails to hit the mark. She is an incurable tease, with her pouty lips and suggestive gestures.

Her manipulative use of the microphone adds another dimension to her stage persona. She uses it as an effective tool to seduce and elate the audience, and to emphasize a particular word. A twenty-year veteran of the stage, Barton knows how to hypnotize a crowd, how to hold their attention with a mixed bag of tricks. Her looks, her stage dress, her mannerisms, even her habit of flicking cigarettes into the crowd, are all part of the live Barton legend.

Along with Marcia Ball, Rory Block, and Bonnie Raitt, she is one of the true forces in contemporary female blues. She has been voted as the "Best Female Vocalist" in the *Austin Chronicle* Reader's Poll on three different occasions, in 1984, 1986, and 1987. Although her recorded output is not as extensive as that of other female blues singers on the scene, she has gained the respect of many in the music field. Barton appeared on Marcia Ball's *Gatorhythms*, Sister Sarah Brown's *Sayin' What I'm Thinkin'*, Robert Ealey's *I Like Music When I Party*, Angela Strehli's *Deja Blues*, and Jimmie Vaughan's *Strange Pleasure* CDs.

Perhaps most important, Barton was one of the prime architects of the Austin blues sound. Her tenure in The Fabulous Thunderbirds, in Stevie Ray Vaughan's groups Triple Threat Revue and Double Trouble, as well as stints in Roomful of Blues and the Robert Ealy band are legendary. She has worked with the cream of the Austin blues scene, including Jimmie Vaughan, Stevie Ray Vaughan, Angela Strehli, Reese Wynans, Sister Sarah Brown, David "Fathead" Newman, Mark Kazanoff, and many others.

Barton is a true Texas blues queen. She is a strong link in the chain that started with Victoria Spivey and Sippie Wallace and includes Big Mama Willie Mae Thornton, Janis Joplin, Marcia Ball, Angela Strehli, and Sue Foley. The Texas spirit, the fierce independence that all blues singers from the Lone Star State seem to have in abundance, runs strong and deep through Barton. In Texas, she is the undisputed queen of the roadhouse bar scene; it is most unfortunate that she has never gained national recognition.

In many ways she is the female counterpart of Delbert McClinton. McClinton, a Texas fireballer with powerful and interesting guitar licks, has never received his fair due. He continues to sing the blues, however: it is what he loves best. McClinton's recording career is a little more consistent than Barton's and he, too, covers songs from past Texas blues heroes. A collaboration between McClinton and Barton would be very interesting.

Barton's diverse song selections reflect her roots. Janis Joplin was an important figure in her development, as was Big Maybelle and the effervescent Etta James. Blues great Irma Thomas also had a profound influence on Barton. Another important singer in Barton's musical background was Patsy Cline, the country singer whose ability to wrap herself around a song left her audience in stunned appreciation. Another singer Barton has tried to emulate is the great Wanda Jackson.

Like some of her musical heroes, Barton has a darker, less glamorous side. She has an abrasive personality; she is a hard partier with a foul mouth, and the ability to offend with her raucous behavior. She has never been able to maintain a consistent recording career, because of some bad judgments, tough breaks, and probably because of her reputation as someone who can be difficult to deal with.

However, Barton's recorded output does not reflect her true abilities. Despite being under-recorded, Barton remains a strong presence in blues circles. She retains her fire and passion for the blues and her live shows are well worth the price of admission. Although she might not possess a mountain of trophies or gold albums, Barton remains the undisputed queen of the Texas roadhouse scene.

## Discography

*Old Enough*, Discovery Ant 021.
*Forbidden Times*, Spindletop SPT-107.
*Read My Lips*, Antone's Ant 0009
*Dreams Come True*, Antone's ANT-0014.
*Sugar Coated Love*, M.I.L. Multimedia 3043.

# JOANNA CONNOR

## *Big Girl Blues*

The female presence in the blues has a long, fascinating history that is as old as the genre itself. From the classic period of the 1920s, throughout the next seven decades, hundreds of blues singers, each with her own unique style, have contributed to the female blues sound. Today, the blues world sparkles with a galaxy of female artists who sell millions of records, tour constantly throughout the world, and win prestigious awards. Among them is the contemporary female blues singer who has given the world her big girl blues. Her name is Joanna Connor.

Joanna Connor was born September 13, 1962, in Brooklyn, New York. She was reared in Massachusetts and developed an interest in the blues at an early age, thanks to her mother's large record collection. Mrs. Connor also took her daughter to see modern blues singers like Taj Mahal, Bonnie Raitt, Ry Cooder, and Buddy Guy. Joanna acquired her first guitar at the age of seven and it became her best friend. By her mid-teens she had developed sufficient chops to be part of various garage bands around her neighborhood.

Connor moved to Chicago when she was twenty-two to try her luck in the Windy City. She eventually found work in the clubs, sharing the stage with Buddy Guy, James Cotton, A. C. Reed, and Junior Wells. After a quick stint in Johnny Littlejohn's group, she joined the 43rd Street Blues Band, led by Dion Payton. Payton and his band were constantly touring in and around the Chicago area, as well as out of state. The highlight of her time in Payton's band was an appearance at the 1987 Chicago Blues Festival.

Although Connor enjoyed traveling and playing in Payton's hardworking band, she had matured to the point where she was ready to establish her solo career. In 1988 she quit Payton's band and formed her own group.

She continued to work the bar circuit with her new band and the following year recorded her first album. Her debut, *Believe It!* released on the Blind Pig label, was rough around the edges but contained a heavy dose of pure passion for the blues-rock she had fallen in love with as a young girl. For years, Connor had played the bar-band blues but had never had any success with the style. Her first CD changed all that. *Believe It!* kicked off with "Texas Flyer" and kept on rocking with "Doctor Feelgood," "I'm Satisfied," "Pack It Up," "Soul's on Fire," and "Good Rockin'

Daddy." In all, the record shone the spotlight on a blossoming artist; she might not yet have reached her full maturity as a musician, songwriter, and singer, but it was very clear from the first ringing notes that Joanna Connor was an exceptional blues talent.

After the release of *Believe It!* the Joanna Connor band broke out of the Chicago blues-bar circuit and performed throughout the United States, Canada, and Europe. The heavy electric sound of Connor's stinging slide guitar made a huge impact on fans throughout her concert rounds. Since few women could muster such a greasy sound with the same force as Connor, she became a novelty act in blues circles. Connor was blazing her own trail.

Her next album on Blind Pig Records, *Fight*, was another winner. Connor had matured as a singer, musician, and songwriter. Her voice was powerful and her guitar work was dazzling, especially on her reworking of Robert Johnson's "Walking Blues" and Luther Allison's "Fight." Her previous effort for Blind Pig had featured only one original Connor composition. *Fight* included eight of Connor's own songs, including "Living on the Road," "Texas," "Your Love Was Never Mine," "Child of Two Worlds," and "No Good for Me."

Her career was gaining momentum. Her next album, *Living on the Road*, for Inak, was a logical follow-up to *Fight*, although she took a different approach with this record. Here, Connor was solo, just a blues girl, her guitar and her voice. One of the highlights of the album was "The Sky Is Crying," the old Elmore James chestnut that Stevie Ray Vaughan covered with such brilliance. Connor's version of that song enhanced her reputation as one of the best blues guitarists on the circuit. There were other hard-driving blues rockers on the album as well, including "Good Woman Gone Bad," "Jalapeno Mama," "Midnight Sunrise," "Wildfire Woman," and "Boogie Woogie Nighthawk."

By this time Connor had proven that she ranked among the best slide-guitar players in the world. Her affection for the heavy, bar-band rocking blues had not subsided and she delivered it with as much spirit as anyone else. She was the female answer to George Thorogood, the Delaware Destroyer.

*Rock & Roll Gypsy* showed Connor at her leanest and meanest. On this album of interpretations of blues-rock classics, Connor covered a lot of territory, from Luther Allison's "Slipping Away" to Delbert McClinton's "Never Been Rocked Enough," as well as the seminal classic, "Driving Wheel." She also had the audacity to cover the Hendrix classic, "Fire," in a rendition that burned with incredible brilliance.

Her next album, *Big Girl Blues*, encouraged comparisons between Connor and Bonnie Raitt, one of the most celebrated female blues singer.

Although they both played masterful slide guitar, Connor rocked harder than Raitt, who was exploring different avenues. The first song and title cut, "Big Girl Blues," immediately powered the album into high gear and was followed by "43rd Street," a touching reminder of her days in Dion Payton's band. Other standouts on her landmark album where Fly Away, "Sister Spirit," "Meditations," "Heart of the Blues," and "Smoke It Up." This was her most even album, with no weak tracks; every song rocked. *Big Girl Blues* placed Connor at the top of the contemporary female blues heap.

Her fourth album, *Slidetime*, on Blind Pig, demonstrated a noted maturity in her songwriting, playing, and singing. Connor wrote nine of the eleven songs on the album and co-wrote the other two with members of her band. Her searing slide work was most prevalent on "My Man" and "Free Free Woman." Connor, a true believer in the two-guitar, bass, and drum format, kept it intact for *Slidetime*. This is simply one of the hardest blues-rock records released in the past decade.

Connor continues to record and perform.

Joanna Connor is a slice of blues sunshine and one of the premier female blues artists on the contemporary scene. There is a distinct originality in her playing, her songwriting, and her singing. She has delivered a succession of albums that rock with a strong blues fever, and has asserted herself as one of the true talents on today's tour circuit. The freshness she brings to the blues makes her music accessible and a fan favorite for those who enjoy a direct approach to their blues-rock.

Along with Bonnie Raitt, Rory Block, Sue Foley, Deborah Coleman, and Debbie Davies, Connor is a leading exponent of the female blues guitar tradition. But, she plays with more power than any of her peers and with a harder rock edge. She is a diversified artist with a nonetheless clear idea of what kind of music she likes to play, and she executes her vision with a decided precision.

Connor is simply one of the best guitar players in the business. Her burning slide work is tremendous; perhaps only Bonnie Raitt can be said to match her in this area. She is a dedicated artist who has honed her slide-guitar technique until she can hold her own among the heaviest players. She displays a muscular sound that reminds one of monster players like Freddie King, Albert King, Rory Gallagher, Duane Allman, Johnny Winter, Jimi Hendrix, Jimmie Vaughan, and Stevie Ray Vaughan.

Her voice is husky, perfectly suited to the blues-rock style that she excels in. Although her vocal range is limited, she can more than handle the heavy blues-rock songs that make up her repertoire. The balance between her stinging guitar work and roadhouse voice is delivered in a carefully calculated two-pronged attack. With years of bar-band experience in her résumé, Connor is able to push a song through a beer-filled, rowdy crowd. In fact, the rowdier the patrons the harder she drives to capture their imagination. Her sultry vocals can charm even the toughest of crowds.

Perhaps Connor's only weak spot as a performing and recording artist is her songwriting. Although she has a creditable list of albums under her belt, they feature few memorable songs that she penned herself. Her songs are all written and recorded in the bar-band vein, her marked territory, and after a while they tend to sound the same. Connor has not yet written a song that is associated solely with her name, one that makes people stop in their tracks in true admiration of her songwriting talent.

Nevertheless, Connor is a versatile artist who is comfortable blasting gritty, urban blues Chicago-style, pounding out Texas shuffle with ease and the right amount of verve, or wrecking the place with her hard-edge rock. Although she is included in the contemporary female blues section of this book, she could easily qualify in the American electric blues section, or in the Contemporary Chicago Style category. To understand Connor's varied ability, one need only trace her roots and influences.

One of the most important blues guitarists to have a profound effect on Connor was Luther Allison. Allison was born August 17, 1939, in Mayflower, Arkansas, and moved to Chicago when he was eighteen. While he absorbed the music of Muddy Waters, Howlin' Wolf, Elmore James, Freddie King, and B. B. King, Allison had a hard rock edge to his sound. His use of a wah-wah pedal separated him from other Chicago blues–style guitar players. His synthesis of blues and rock is a sound that Connor has incorporated in her own playing. Allison wasn't afraid to experiment, and it was he who widened the parameters of traditional blues to include a rock element.

Another important influence on Connor was Jimi Hendrix, the guitar wizard who used the blues as his musical foundation to explore other styles, including rock, funk, jazz, pop, and soul. It was Hendrix who boldly stated with his guitar pyrotechnics that a guitarist should follow his heart and play the music he wanted to play, not what everyone else wanted him to play. Connor, who has been criticized for sticking to the blues-bar mold, has managed to build a successful career playing the music that is closest to her heart, proving all detractors wrong.

Perhaps one of the greatest influences on Connor is the Delaware Destroyer, George Thorogood. Thorogood, with his finely chiseled, heavy slide attack, also broke out of the bar-band circuit to record and perform in large venues. Despite his marked success, Thorogood never strayed from the riveting blues-bar music that he enjoyed the most. It was Thorogood who proved that the thrilling bar blues were an acceptable form; Connor has simply reconfirmed what Lonesome George knew all along.

Joanna Connor is a blues fireball who plays a brand of music that will always be popular. Although she might never achieve superstar status, that doesn't seem to bother this fine young blues woman. She is content to play hard blues with the occasional rock and rhythm-and-blues tune thrown in for variety. A pure artist like Connor is a rarity and we hope she never outgrows her big girl blues.

## Discography

*Believe It!* Blind Pig BP 3289.
*Fight*, Blind Pig BP 5002.
*Living on the Road*, Inak 1727.
*Rock & Roll Gypsy*, Ruf, 1003
*Big Girl Blues*, Ruf 5037
*Slidetime*, Blind Pig BP 5047.

# SUE FOLEY

## *Young Girl Blues*

In the 1970s and 1980s, one of the most dominant musical blues scenes on the planet, and one that featured a strong female blues presence, was Austin, Texas. Austin was the base for Texans Lou Ann Barton, Marcia Ball, and Angela Strehli. In the early 1990s, another female blues singer began to make a solid contribution to the Austin blues tradition, although she could not claim an authentic Texas birth certificate. She was a transplanted Canadian, and she stunned everyone with her young girl blues. Her name is Sue Foley.

Sue Foley was born on March 29, 1968, in Ottawa, Ontario. As a young girl she was first introduced to the blues through the music of the Rolling Stones, Led Zeppelin, Foghat, and other blues-rock groups of the 1970s. But her first live blues experience (a James Cotton concert), when she was fifteen years old, convinced her to pursue a blues career. Although James Cotton is a renowned harmonica player, Foley selected the electric guitar as her instrument of choice. She gained valuable experience jamming with local Ottawa bar bands, but in the mid-1980s, feeling a desire for a change, Foley moved to Vancouver and formed her first group.

For the next few years Foley toured all over her country and the United States with her group. While her opportunities in Vancouver were solid, Foley felt that her career was not moving along quickly enough. An enterprising young woman, she sent a demo tape to Antone's Records in 1990. By this time Foley had matured as a guitarist and vocalist; she played a wicked lead guitar.

Clifford Antone was impressed with the talented young blues singer and arranged for Foley to travel down to Austin for an audition. Foley, feeling that this was her big break, did not disappoint as she stunned Antone during the audition, which resulted in a recording contract with the famous label. In 1992 her debut album, *Young Girl Blues*, was released. More than a decade of sweat and paying dues went into the making of that album; it won rave reviews among critics and fans alike.

The opening cut, "Queen Bee," set the mood for the entire album; there was a cool balance, a mixture of slow, painful blues and real rock-drenched numbers. She delivered fresh versions of Ike Turner's "Cuban Getaway," Tampa Red's "But I Forgive You," and Earl Hooker's "Off the Hook." Foley played with expert control as her trademark pink paisley Telecaster roared like a lioness on a hunting expedition. She received more than adequate support from Derek O'Brien, Denny Freeman, Kim Wilson (of Fabulous Thunderbirds fame), and the legendary Pinetop Perkins. The album also featured a duet with the queen of the Austin blues scene, Angela Strehli.

If *Young Girl Blues* served notice to the blues community and the entire music world that Sue Foley had arrived, then her subsequent release, *Without a Warning*, only enhanced that reputation. On this CD Foley didn't fool around. She blasted through any misconceptions that she was a flash in the pan with a display of raw, hard-driving guitar blues that left most listeners agape. She wrote eight of the thirteen gems on the album and was truly fired up. Her cover versions of Magic Sam's "Come Into My Arms" and "Give Me Time" drew parallels between Foley and the legendary Chicago bluesman. Her own compositions, "Without a Warning," "Put Your Money Where Your Mouth Is," and "Annie's Driftin' Hearts," rounded out the power-packed collection. The success of *Without a Warning* opened doors to Foley that had been closed to her just a few months before.

She began to tour throughout the United States and went over to Europe, where she caused a sensation with her fiery brand of blues with an attitude. It all came together nicely in Paris, where the crowd adulation hinted that she was something special. If the attention overseas didn't impress anyone, then the stir she was causing back home was worth a second look. She was nominated for a Juno Award in her native Canada and knew she was making huge strides when she beat out W. C. Clark, a favorite in Austin, at the awards show. Foley won the "Best Blues Band" award as well, another feather in her cap.

Her third album, a pivotal work in any young blues artist's career, was special for many reasons. Foley wanted desperately to build on her recent success and keep the momentum going. The power trio format that evoked memories of other great blues-based bands such as Cream, the Jimi Hendrix Experience, ZZ Top, Stevie Ray Vaughan, and Double Trouble worked best for Foley. She had finally found two musicians who could keep up with her on stage and on the road (she toured nonstop), Jon Penner and Freddie Walden. The ultimate result was *Big City Blues*.

*Big City Blues* combined four Foley originals with seven cover songs that ranged from the grit and groan of Howlin' Wolf's "Howlin' for My Darlin'" to the muscle of Buddy Guy's "One Hundred Dollar Bill" and the brilliance of Willie Dixon's "As Long as I Have You" and "My Baby's Sweeter." There was also the sheer poetry of Bob Dylan's "To Be Alone with You" and "If You Gotta Go." Foley melded all of her biggest musical influences—Delta, Texas, Chicago—with her bar-band experience to create a contemporary blues album that ranked right up there. She had managed to consolidate all of her talent, strength, and maturity in the making of *Big City Blues*.

Foley had toured Japan, Norway, Denmark, France, and Germany as part of a low-budget working bar band. On her return to these countries to promote *Big City Blues*, she and her band rode in luxury. It was definitely a sign that Foley had earned respect and perks for all the dues she had paid. The road, never an easy part of any artist's career, became much friendlier to Foley.

Foley's fourth release, *Walk in the Sun*, was her first album to contain no cover versions, thus demonstrating her profound maturity as an artist. The evolution of Foley's sound was refreshing; she had traveled a long road from the girl who used to hang out in Ottawa pubs to one of the most highly respected female blues artists on the circuit. Her straight-ahead approach to guitar playing—with her signature pink paisley Telecaster—shone brightly on this album. With *Walk in the Sun*, she was no longer being compared to other female blues singers; they were being compared to her.

It was also this album that saw her expand the parameters of her traditional blues sound to include different styles. The fusion of her blues with elements of rock, soul, and pop were scattered throughout the songs, which included "Try to Understand," "Walk in the Sun," "Wayward Girl," "Train to Memphis," "Love Sick Child," and "Long Distance Lover." Despite the near-schizophrenic musical requirements, Foley managed to pull it all off with her excellent guitar work.

By this time, Foley was one very busy woman. She was constantly touring throughout the world and playing in Austin when she was on infrequent breaks. She was also working up songs for her fifth album. *Ten Days in November* once again consisted of all Foley originals. She belted out each song with a hearty roar that matched her fluid guitar lines. Some of the highlights included "Baltimore Skyline," "Long Way to Go," "Give My Love to You," "Winds of Change," and "New Roads."

Her follow-up *Love Comin' Down* saw Foley return to the more typical formula of original songs combined with cover versions. The wide range of styles, all done with a blues slant, included a roof-raising R&B chestnut, "Be Next to You," a Freddie King tune, "You're Barking Up the Wrong Tree," and a country instrumental, "Mediterranean Breakfast." But the album was held together by the true blues songs "The Same Thing," "Let My Tears Fall Down," and the powerful "How Strong." Foley's ability to record such diverse material and bring it all together proved again her strength as a blues artist. The contributions of Lucinda Williams and fellow Canadian blues singer Colin Linden were nice touches.

She continues to record and perform.

Sue Foley is a blues star. She is a legitimate concert draw and her albums sell massive quantities. One of the busiest blues singers on the circuit, Foley and her career are going full steam. She has earned a well-deserved reputation as a serious hard-driving blues guitarist with her hot, wild licks. She has added a new dimension to the female blues content.

Foley's drawing card is her incredible guitar playing. Her fluid guitar lines are as right as rain, and as sure as death and taxes. She can let fly a barrage of notes that run together with the power of a speeding meteor. Her smoking guitar work leaves many listeners numb with surprise, as much for her technical ability and pure emotion as for the fact that she is a woman.

Foley is a genuine beauty who could easily entice the audience with her sultry looks; yet, she relies more on her guitar expertise than her appearance to excite her fans. A burning opening riff promises to take the audience on a special journey. The attractive strawberry blonde sends out the message loud and clear that she is an outstanding guitarist whose scorching licks can burn a hole in one's soul.

One of Foley's greatest influences has been Bonnie Raitt. By the time Foley cut her first album (1992), Raitt was a long-established blues star who had won several Grammy awards and the respect of critics, peers, and fans worldwide. In a few short years, Foley has taken her place along-side Raitt in female blues circles. Many blues critics and fans believe that Foley is a better guitarist than Raitt and that she has eclipsed her role model.

Another major influence on Foley was Elmore James, the slide-guitar master of the postwar Chicago blues school who also had a profound effect on Duane Allman, Rory Gallagher, and many other modern blues slide guitarists. Like James, Foley plays a driving brand of hard blues with a rock edge. It is this harsher sound that has also drawn comparisons between Foley and the likes of Jimi Hendrix, Stevie Ray Vaughan, and Johnny Winter.

Sue Foley has carved an impressive place for herself in blues circles. The little girl with the pink paisley Telecaster is for real; she needs no smoke and mirrors to create her signature guitar licks. Foley is in the prime of her career and promises to deliver with intense passion her distinct brand of young girl blues to adoring fans all over the globe for many years.

## Discography

*Young Girl Blues*, Antone's AN0019.
*Without a Warning*, Antone's 25.
*Big City Blues*, Antone's 37.
*Walk in the Sun*, Discovery 74701.
*Ten Days in November*, Shanachie 8031.
*Love Comin' Down*, Shanachie 8036.

---

# PART FIVE

# Blues Around the World

In 1951, when Big Bill Broonzy took his sorrowful, acoustic blues to Europe, he changed the course of popular music forever. Blues fever spread like a contagion throughout the ancient, overcrowded cities across the Atlantic and around the globe. The dark musical vibes that had stirred deep emotions in the old masters were the same fiery excitement that seduced blues enthusiasts all over the world.

The first country to reflect the jungle rhythms of the legendary American bluesmen was England. British blues paid strict adherence to blues genres, to the point of precise replication. Alexis Korner, Graham Bond, Cyril Davies, John Mayall, the Rolling Stones, the Animals, and the Yardbirds were some of the earliest English bands keen on reproducing exactly the sounds they heard from old records they had managed to acquire. Later on, Cream, The Jeff Beck Group, Led Zeppelin, and Ten Years After continued where the first generation of British blues makers had stopped. It is important to note that many people, in America as well as in England, discovered the blues for the first time through the music of the Rolling Stones, Led Zeppelin, the Jeff Beck Group, Cream, the Yardbirds, the Animals, and other British blues bands.

The influence of the blues exploded throughout the world in the 1960s, for two main reasons. By this time American blues singers were acquiring a well-deserved reputation as globetrotters; and the marriage between the blues and rock and roll opened up venues that had remained closed to the originators, giving the genre a wider commercial appeal.

The blues artists in this category cover four continents: Asia, Europe, Australia, and North America; and twelve different countries. Although they might never attain the same international success as B. B. King, Sonny Terry, Buddy Guy, Muddy Waters, Little Walter, and other blues legends, many of the artists in this section are considered to be the "fathers of the blues" in their respective countries.

Today, the blues are a dominant force in world music. The music has come a long way from the gritty, plaintive, primitive sound that emerged from the poverty-stricken Mississippi Delta a hundred years ago. But no matter what changes have taken place, it is still the same blues fire that Charley Patton sparked so long ago.

Eric Clapton is one of the most famous blues singers in the history of the music. He has been a tireless champion of the blues and continues a brilliant career that has seen its share of triumphs and tragedies.

Rory Gallagher, an Irish blues rocker in the late 1960s and throughout much of the 1970s, was one of the first foreign blues stars to gain international acceptance.

Donnie Walsh is the leader and founder of Canada's best-known blues band, the Downchild Blues Band. He has been playing the blues for more than thirty years.

Hans Theessink is a blues singer from Holland who has defied all odds to become one of the most spectacular performers on the European and international circuits.

Dave Hole is a slide guitarist from Australia. Although he is not the only blues singer plying his trade in the Land Down Under, he is one of the finest.

J. J. Milteau is a blues harmonica player from France. His blues loops and wailings are reminiscent of Little Walter, Sonny Terry, Sonny Boy Williamson II, and Charlie McKoy.

Sven Zetterberg is a Swedish blues singer who has gained an international reputation as a solid performer.

Zucchero is an Italian blues singer who has single-handedly put Italy on the blues map. As his reputation continues to grow, so do the fortunes of the Italian blues scene.

Javier Vargas is a Spanish blues hero whose searing guitar work is well respected throughout the musical community. He has brought immense respect and credit to the Spanish blues.

Yuri Naumov is the "Father of Russian Blues" who defied the KGB in order to spread the gospel of the blues. His legend continues to grow in his native country.

Shun Kikuta is the finest exponent of Japanese blues. He is a prime example of the serious impact American blues has made on world music.

Silvan Zing is a Swiss piano player whose imagination has been captured by the romp and stomp of the boogie-woogie piano players of the late 1930s and 1940s, and who has proven that a good thing never goes stale.

# ERIC CLAPTON

*Stones in My Pathway*

There is a terrible price to pay for the mastery of the blues. To unlock the secrets of the hypnotic, secret rhythms of ancient sacred ceremonies is to disturb unforgiving powers. These powers are forbidden treasures, and anything that is forbidden is that much more attractive. To pursue the obsession of mastering the intricate, subtle systematic language of the blues is to suffer many obstacles and setbacks along the way. However, one guitarist has managed to overcome the stones in his pathway in order to become one of the greatest blues singers in history. His name is Eric Clapton.

Eric Clapton was born Eric Patrick Clapp on March 30, 1945, in Surrey, England. The product of a love affair between his teenaged mother and a Canadian soldier, Clapton was sent to live with his maternal grandparents from the time he was an infant; he later adopted his grandfather's surname, Clapton. He lived the quiet life of an English schoolboy until the blues came calling; from the first note he was hooked forever. He immediately devoted his entire existence to the long pursuit of mastering the seemingly diabolical powers that held such a magical spell over him.

At the age of seventeen he acquired his first guitar and, within a year, after an intense period of self-education from listening to the records of Big Bill Broonzy, Muddy Waters, and Robert Johnson, Clapton was ready to make his mark on the world. His first group, the Roosters, were a rhythm-and-blues outfit that provided a hint of the direction that Clapton's early career would take.

Upon leaving the Roosters in 1963, Clapton joined the Yardbirds—the top R&B band in Britain at the time. The band, consisting of Paul Samwell-Smith, Jim McCarty, Chris Dreja, and Keith Reif, jammed on the entire Chess catalog. Their interpretations of the songs of Willie Dixon, Muddy Waters, Howlin' Wolf, Little Walter, Sonny Boy Williamson II, and others made them legends. In 1965, the release of the single "For Your Love" marked the end of Clapton's tenure with the band: Clapton, ever the blues purist, considered "For Your Love" too commercial.

Not wanting to take on the burden of fronting his own band, Clapton joined John Mayall's Bluesbreakers. It was at this point that his status as Britain's premier guitar hero began to take shape. Mayall was one of the first Englishmen to show a deep interest in the blues, along with

Alexis Korner and Cyril Davies. Although his stay with Mayall was short (one year) Clapton made an impact and his work on the seminal classic, *Bluesbreakers*, is still revered today. But other interesting projects loomed on the horizon for Clapton.

In 1966 he formed Cream with Jack Bruce and Peter "Ginger" Baker. The psychedelic, improvised blues jams that Cream made famous greatly enhanced Clapton's reputation in his native country and, for the first time, across the Atlantic. It was Cream that became a prototype band for the Jeff Beck Group, The Jimi Hendrix Experience, Ten Years After, Led Zeppelin, The Allman Brothers, and dozens of other blues-based rock bands. The Cream repertoire included distorted yet interesting takes on such blues classics as "Sitting on Top of the World," "Born Under a Bad Sign," "Crossroads," "Spoonful," and "I'm So Glad." In the two years that the band was together, Clapton enjoyed the most successful commercial period of his career to that point. The demise of Cream was a sad day in blues-rock circles.

Clapton's next project was the short lived but influential Blind Faith. The group consisted of Clapton, Ginger Baker, Stevie Winwood, and Rick Grech. During their short time together they released one album with a controversial cover (the picture of a naked little girl holding an airplane), undertook one major tour, and then disbanded. The promise and potential of Blind Faith was never realized, but their first and only studio project contained two songs that became classics: Windwood's "I Can't Find My Way Home" and Clapton's "Presence of the Lord."

Clapton became a hired gun for the next year, playing with Delaney and Bonnie and backing John Lennon on the ex–Beatle's return to the stage. The Plastic Ono Band played a concert in Toronto with Clapton trying to avoid the spotlight. The shy guitarist with the burning licks who was hailed as a hero throughout the blues-rock world released his first solo album, simply entitled *Eric Clapton*, around this time. Ironically, while he was about to embark on what many consider to be his finest hour, he was also approaching one of his most arduous personal times.

The band Derek and the Dominos consisted of Clapton, Carl Radle, Jim Gordon and Bobby Whitlock. Their album, *Layla and Other Assorted Love Songs*, also featured Duane Allman extensively on slide guitar; the one-two guitar punch of Allman and Clapton created special magic. The title song, "Layla," inspired by Clapton's obsession for Patty Boyd, then married to ex–Beatle George Harrison, revolved around one of the oldest themes in the blues: the love of an unattainable woman. The album was also filled with blues covers and originals, including "Bell Bottom Blues" and "Have You Ever Loved a Woman" (a song first done by Freddie King). It also contained an excellent cover version of Jimi Hendrix's

"Little Wing," one that the Seattle guitar master would never hear because of his tragic death before the album's release.

It was at this point that the stones rolled into Clapton's pathway. Despite one of the greatest periods in his long, illustrious musical career, the album by Derek and the Dominos did not receive the praise that it would later garner. Clapton's despondency was increased further by the death of his close friend Duane Allman. Allman's contribution to Derek and the Dominos was one of the main driving forces behind the power, beauty, and soulful depth of their landmark record. Another source of personal turmoil was his inability to be with Patty Boyd, which only added to his depression. Clapton, frustrated and depressed over these three events in his life, sought refuge in drugs and alcohol.

The darkest period in Clapton's life and career followed. It is now public knowledge that a heroin habit almost destroyed him; he made no new recordings for two whole years. Eventually, after a few relapses, Clapton overcame his heroin addiction to concentrate on music once again. His comeback album, *461 Ocean Boulevard*, was a critical and financial success. Clapton had returned to the musical scene, but in the process had left the blues behind in favor of other musical styles, including pop, rock, country, reggae, and jazz. Although he would occasionally insert one or two blues songs in his recorded projects and live appearances during the 1970s, Clapton had strayed from the music he played so well.

Clapton entered the 1980s with a full head of steam. He was the great survivor of the seventies when others—Duane Allman, Barry Oakley, Keith Moon—had not been so lucky. But the stones were once again about to roll into his pathway. His struggle with alcohol took its toll in 1981, when Clapton collapsed on stage during a concert with vicious ulcers that almost ended his life. Clapton rebounded but spent much of the rest of the decade making passable albums that further estranged him from his blues roots.

In 1988, with Clapton facing an increasingly stagnant career, the four-side classic *Crossroads* was released. A compilation disc, it covered his entire career from the beginning through all of his musical journeys, including his solo career. Although it highlighted the many styles that he had experimented with, *Crossroads* made it very clear that Clapton was at his best playing the blues. The album catapulted Clapton back into the spotlight and foreshadowed the musical path he would take in the early 1990s.

The boxed set contained a number of classic blues and rock songs that were written or co-written by Clapton. There were also a good number of tunes that were the work of others. John Lee Hooker's "Boom Boom" was on the album, as was Big Bill Broonzy's "Key to the Highway," one of the highlights of the disc. The Robert Johnson compositions "Ramblin' on My Mind" and "Crossroads" were also part of the package. There were Otis Rush's "Double Trouble Blues," Willie Dixon's "All Your Love," and Freddie King's "Hideaway." The record demonstrated just how well Clapton had covered the great blues singers from the entire history of the genre.

On March 21, 1991, Clapton was faced with another stone in his pathway when his four-year-old son Connor died in a fall. The disheartening incident brought out the dark blues spirit in Clapton and sparked him to write the song "Tears in Heaven," a beautifully haunting ballad that became an international hit. The song reinforced his desire to play the blues, the music that had shaped his life so forcefully.

The resulting landmark album, *Unplugged*, generated renewed interest in the acoustic blues at a time when the genre was in severe decline. It was a masterful work and contained several classics, including "Before You Accuse Me," "Nobody Knows You When You're Down and Out," "Walkin' Blues," "Rollin' and Tumblin'," and "Malted Milk." But perhaps the most effective song of this modern acoustic blues collection was the reworked version of "Layla." The acoustic rendition of this song that had been associated so long with Clapton brought him to the musical forefront once again.

The comeback that had started with *Crossroads* was completed with the all-blues effort *From the Cradle*. It included such blues classics as "Blues Before Sunrise," "Hootchie Cootchie Man," "Five Long Years," "I'm Tore Down," "How Long Blues," "Blues Leave Me Alone," "Groaning the Blues," and "Standing Around Crying." A long awaited treat for diehard Clapton blues fans, the CD sold several million copies and proved once and for all that Eric "Slowhand" Clapton was a true blues master. In 1995, Clapton received a W. C. Handy special recognition award for *From the Cradle*.

After the release of *From the Cradle*, Clapton recorded a few CDs, though none hit the mark the way his blues gems of the early 1990s did. But in 2000 he has returned to the blues with a genuinely great album, *Riding with the King*. The twin masterful guitars of Clapton and B. B. King make this record a must for all casual and die-hard blues fans. Featuring remakes of twelve classics, including "Key to the Highway," which contains a sweet blues shuffle, the CD sounds like two old friends getting together for a late-night jam session. The grooves, the laid-back feeling, the undeniable musicianship, make *Riding with the King* a definite winner.

Clapton remains one of the most popular performers on the circuit and any new blues releases are always eagerly anticipated by his legion of fans.

Eric Clapton is a blues icon. He is arguably the single most important white influence on blues guitar in the past forty years. From the moment of his debut with the Yardbirds, Clapton has drawn attention to himself with his virtuosity. His name is synonymous with the blues and he has maintained interest in the genre with his brilliance, fire, and imagination, despite exploring different musical avenues.

The Eric Clapton style has been imitated but never duplicated. His laid-back, low-key approach to blues guitar has earned him the nickname "Slowhand." Clapton's ability to play sweet and low, rough and coarse, but with a delicately precise touch makes him the envy of every aspiring blues guitarist. He has been able to switch from electric to acoustic guitars without changing his style, evidence of the versatility that makes him one of the greatest guitarists of the past hundred years.

Clapton is also a champion of the blues. He has been able to bring attention to and revive the careers of forgotten bluesmen by including one of their songs on a CD, by having them open for him on concert tour, or by just mentioning their names in the press. No one has done more to elevate the blues in the eyes of mainstream fans than Clapton. Despite a wealth of original material spanning more than thirty years, some of Clapton's finest moments have been his personal renditions of a long list of blues classics.

It was Clapton who made sure that Skip James received the royalties he was due, when as a member of Cream he covered the song "I'm So Glad." It was Clapton who played with Freddie King on the latter's *Freddie King* (1934-1976) album that finally brought the large bluesman the recognition he deserved. Clapton has also brought other struggling artists to the international forefront, most notably Bob Marley. Clapton's version of Marley's "I Shot the Sheriff" brought the Jamaican singer the global adulation that had escaped him despite his incredible talent.

While he has made the songs of other people famous, Clapton is also a brilliant songwriter himself, providing the world with dozens of unforgettable classics. The songs "Presence of the Lord," "Let It Grow," "Wonderful Tonight," "Lay Down Sally," "I Can't Stand It," "Shape You're In," "Heaven Is One Step Away," "She's Waiting," and "Tears in Heaven" all flowed from Clapton's imaginative pen. His creative genius as a songwriter has often been underrated because some other artists composed so many of the songs he has been associated with during his career.

Clapton has written dozens of songs in collaboration with other artists. It was Jim Gordon of Derek and the Dominos who helped Clapton write "Layla." Jack Bruce and Felix Brown helped Clapton write some of Cream's biggest hits, including "Sunshine of Your Love." Robert Cray and Clapton together wrote "Old Love," which was included on the *Unplugged* album. Clapton has also written songs with Bobby Whitlock, Delaney Bramlett, and many others.

During his distinguished career Clapton has performed with many established blues stars, including Stevie Ray Vaughan, Robert Cray, Muddy Waters, Freddie King, Buddy Guy, B. B. King, John Lee Hooker, Albert King, Koko Taylor, Jimmie Vaughan, Rory Gallagher, and Zucchero. He has also shared the stage with rock artists Leon Russell, George Harrison, Stephen Stills, Rita Coolidge, Steve Winwood, and Dave Mason, to name but a few. But it is Clapton's appearance with the pioneers of the blues and folk genres that have often brought out the best in him. For example, during his one-and-only teaming with the legendary Pete Seeger, Clapton never played better. There is scarcely one important blues or rock artist of the past thirty years whom he has not performed with at some time in his career.

He has played many free concerts in honor of other musicians who have fallen on hard times, in order to preserve the blues, and to raise money for medical research. Perhaps one of his most interesting projects is his substance abuse treatment center located in Jamaica and called Crossroads. Clapton, having been able to exorcise the demons that have long haunted him, decided to provide other people with the same opportunity. It is another classic example of Clapton giving back to the community—to the world.

Throughout his career Clapton has been a doorway for the blues. He absorbed what the old masters had to teach him and brought their secrets to the international stage. He has delved deeply into the song catalogs of Robert Johnson, Muddy Waters, Elmore James, Freddie King, Albert King, B. B. King, and Big Bill Broonzy. He has also covered the songs of country/rocker J. J. Cale, most notably "Cocaine" and "After Midnight." Clapton has always demonstrated a deep and sincere respect for those who had a profound influence on him.

In turn, Clapton himself has inspired a whole new generation of guitar players, including Colin James, Eric Johnson, Joe Satriani, Coco Montoya, Eddie Van Halen, Stevie Ray Vaughan, Jimmie Vaughan, Ronnie Earle, Mark Knopfler, Pat Travers, Kenny Wayne Shepherd, and Jonny Lang. Clapton, as a non–American, has blazed the trail for aspiring blues artists all around the world. A partial list includes Hans Theessink, Dave Hole, Javier Vargas, Sven Zetterberg, Zucchero, Yuri Naumov, and Shun Kikuta. His "slowhand" style, the laid-back approach with the deft touch, is one that many guitarists have practiced in seclusion for years in order to master its intricacies.

Along with Jimi Hendrix, Jimmy Page, Jeff Beck, Duane Allman,

Rory Gallagher, Peter Green, Johnny Winter, and Mike Bloomfield, Clapton was a prime architect of the blues-rock marriage of the late 1960s. Although he has wavered from the blues since then, he has never really strayed far away. The magnetism of the blues has always pulled Clapton back into the fold.

Much has been written about Eric Clapton. There are a number of books (see bibliography at end of this book), as well as numerous articles in magazines and newspapers, some complimentary, some critical. But despite the negative reviews he has received and the stones that have blocked his pathway on many occasions, Clapton has always delivered and delighted us with his easy, controlled, and concise brand of "slow-hand" blues.

## Discography

*Eric Clapton*, Polydor 33329.
*Eric Clapton's Rainbow Concert*, Polydor 825 093.
*461 Ocean Boulevard*, Polydor 811 697.
*There's One in Every Crowd*, Polydor 829 649.
*E. C. Was Here*, Polydor 831 519.
*No Reason to Cry*, Polydor 813 582.
*Slowhand*, Polydor 823 276.
*Backless*, Polydor 813 581.
*Just One Night*, Polydor 800 093.
*Another Ticket*, Polydor 827 579.
*Money and Cigarettes*, Reprise 23773.
*Too Much Monkey Business*, Astro 20118.
*Behind the Sun*, Reprise 25166.
*Time Pieces, Vol. 2: Live in the '70's*, Polydor 811 835.
*August*, Reprise 2-25476.
*Big Boss Man*, Masters 12784.
*Crossroads*, Polydor 835 261.
*Journeyman*, Reprise 26074.
*24 Nights*, Reprise 2-26420.
*Unplugged*, Reprise 45024.
*The Magic of Eric Clapton*, Royal Collection 83107.
*From the Cradle*, Reprise 45735.
*Eric Clapton's Rainbow Concert*, Polydor 527472.
*Crossroads 2: Live in the '70's*, Polygram 527305.
*Live in Montreux*, ITM 960019.
*Pilgrim*, Warner Brothers 46377.
*Guitar Boogie*, RCA AYRI 3769.

*The History of Eric Clapton*, Atco SD-2-803.
*The Best of Eric Clapton*, Polydor 3503.
*Blues World of Eric Clapton*, Decca 387.
*U.K. Blues*, Beacon 51608.
*The Blues*, Polygram 547178.
*Blues Collection*, Polygram International 1676.
*Strictly the Blues*, Castle 103.

With John Mayall:

*Bluesbreakers—John Mayall with Eric Clapton*, London 800 086-2.

With Cream:

*Fresh Cream*, RSO 827 576-2.
*Disraeli Gears*, RSO 923 636-2.
*Wheels of Fire*, RSO 827 578-2.
*Goodbye*, Polygram 823 680-2-Y-1.

With Derek and the Dominos:

*Layla and Other Assorted Love Songs*, Polydor 847 090.

With B. B. King:

*Riding with the King*, Warner Brothers.

---

# RORY GALLAGHER

## *The Irish Mississippian*

The blues-rock marriage of the 1960s inspired many to take up the guitar and duplicate the sounds they heard. The fever swept across not only North America, but also the entire globe, in many areas that had never witnessed an authentic blues singer. Out in Ireland, a land known for its show bands, one young lad shunned the music of his native country in favor of American blues and became known as the Irish Mississippian. His name was Rory Gallagher.

Rory Gallagher was born in Ballyshannon, county of Donegal, in the Republic of Ireland on March 2, 1948. In the early 1950s, the Gallaghers moved to Cork, where young Rory first heard American blues on the radio. His life was changed forever. He bought his first instrument at the age of nine and taught himself the rudiments of blues guitar. Gallagher blossomed quickly; at eleven he was competing in local amateur shows, and at thirteen he was already leading his own band.

By then Rory had switched to an electric guitar. His first model was a cheap imitation of the classic American Stratocaster. But, when he was sixteen, he obtained a prized sunburst Fender Stratocaster model. The guitar and Rory were inseparable and he retained it for the rest of his life. He quit school at the age of fifteen to pursue his burning musical interests.

He joined the Fontana Show Band and toured Britain with the ensemble. At the time, Ireland was in love with the show band and the only way Gallagher could find work was to play in a group that contained ten or more musicians. Although it was not the type of music that he wanted to play, he was biding his time. The Fontana Show Band eventually evolved into a different version and renamed itself Impact. They toured different parts of Europe before the group broke up.

It was at this point that Gallagher formed the power trio Taste to play hard-driving heavy-riffed blues, the music he had fallen in love with as a young boy. The first version of the band Taste consisted of Gallagher on guitar, Eric Kitteringham on bass, and Norman Danery on drums. It was a short-lived aggregation, and Gallagher re-formed Taste with bassist Charlie McCracken and drummer John Wilson. They appeared frequently and built an enthusiastic following in their native Ireland.

This new version of Taste would prove to be a more successful one. The band moved to England in 1969, where they toured all over Great Britain and Germany. Later the following year, the group made their first visit to North America, playing in the United States and Canada in support of Blind Faith. Gallagher left his mark on every audience with his blistering bursts of bottleneck blues boogie.

Despite their heavy touring schedule the band found time to record their self-titled debut album. It contained burning blues riffs and stinging solos that became the band's trademarks. They recorded two more records, *On the Boards* and *Live Taste*, before the group broke up. Internal friction over Gallagher's popularity, which had far outdistanced the other members', fueled the disenchantment within the group. The band's final appearance was at the Isle of Wight Festival; it resulted in the live recording *Taste at the Isle of Wight*.

Gallagher then formed the Rory Gallagher Band with Gerry McAvoy on bass and Wilgar Campbell on drums. Throughout the years the band's lineup would change many times, with McAvoy being the most loyal to Gallagher. Whatever the lineup, the Rory Gallagher Band developed a reputation as one of the hardest blues-rock groups on the circuit. Their album *Live in Europe* earned them Musician of the Year honors in the Melody Maker's poll in 1974.

Throughout the 1970s, the Rory Gallagher band toured continuously all over Europe and the United States to arena-sized crowds. They also recorded regularly for the Polydor and Chrysalis labels. But as the marriage between blues and rock began to dissolve, Gallagher's popularity began to wane and, despite the blues revival of the 1980s, his fortunes did not improve.

By the end of the decade, however, after a long hiatus he returned to performing and recording. His 1987 record *Defender* revived his name in blues-rock circles. In 1991, he released *Fresh Evidence* on the Capo/I.R.S. label—Gallagher's very own record and publishing company. The album sparked a comeback for the Irish bluesman with the hot guitar licks. He toured the United States one more time and played to sizable, enthusiastic crowds.

He continued to make the rounds of Europe, but in 1994 he fell gravely ill while on tour. A few months later, on June 14, 1995, Rory Gallagher, the Irish Mississippian with the blazing bottleneck blues riffs, died at King's College Hospital in London from complications of a liver transplant. He was 46 years old.

Rory Gallagher was a blues cult hero worshipped by the fans who never lost their taste for blues-rock music. Although he never achieved great success, in his heyday Gallagher was a well-respected blues-rock guitarist. He was an original who always delivered the goods as a recording artist, and especially in front of a live audience.

At the heart of Gallagher's sound was his exceptional guitar playing. This combined power-packed riffs with a mean slide technique that was fueled by an incredible amount of genuine emotion. He often left audiences astonished after tearing apart another stage with his weatherworn but faithful Fender Stratocaster. His voice was harsh, like a Mississippi bullfrog with a sore throat.

Although he never wrote any truly memorable material, his cover versions of such standards as "Sugar Blue" and "Bullfrog Blues" are definitely classics. He was also a part of the legendary Muddy Waters London Sessions and even recorded a live album with Albert King.

Gallagher listened carefully to all the Kings—Albert, B. B., Freddie—and enhanced their popularity with his heavy, blues-drenched solos and hard crunching guitar style. He shares this trait with many of his contemporaries in the blues-rock fraternity of the 1960s and 1970s. Undoubtedly, Gallagher was as responsible for revealing the secrets of the blues to the international stage as any other late 1960s and early 1970s blues-rockers, including Jimi Hendrix, Jimmy Page, Eric Clapton, Jeff Beck, Robin Trower, Kim Simmonds, Johnny Winter, and Alvin Lee.

In many ways, Gallagher was Ireland's answer to Johnny Winter and Kim Simmonds of Savoy Brown. Like Winter and Simmonds, Gallagher had one foot firmly planted in the blues idiom and the other equally firmly planted in rock and roll. All three were monster guitar players who could drive a crowd into a frenzy when they uncorked their boundless energy in another searing solo. They also had a vast influence on the new generation of blues rockers of the 1980s and 1990s, including Stevie Ray Vaughan, Tinsley Ellis, Jimmie Vaughan, Kenny Wayne Shepherd, and Jonny Lang.

But Gallagher also had a profound influence on international music, thanks to his endless tours of blues-starved Europe and Asia. Foreign blues guitarists, such as Shun Kikuta, Javier Vargas, Sven Zetterberg, and Hans Theessink, were able to see Gallagher live and take a page from his book. Gallagher paved the way for European blues musicians who dreamed of acquiring the same fame that the American blues musicians enjoyed.

Gallagher cut a near-mythical figure with his rare sunburst Telecaster and his trademark attire of a working-class Irishman (faded blue jeans and lumberjack shirts). He was the people's guitarist and played as enthusiastically for an audience of one as he did for an audience of thousands. He always gave the crowd its money's worth.

Though he cut some interesting albums, Gallagher was best in front of a live crowd. In his native Ireland he was considered an icon, and deservedly so. Without a doubt, he is the father of Irish blues. He wrote blues songs that dealt with daily Irish life; songs of tedious chores, drinking at the local pub, and of good/hard times. The songs endeared him to his hometown fans. Upon his death, the people of Ireland lined the streets in one last show of respect for the man who had put the country on the world blues map.

Rory Gallagher is gone but not forgotten. He was a survivor who rode out the rise and fall of the blues-rock explosion. His dedication to the blues with a hard rock touch never wavered throughout his career, even during periods when he fell into near obscurity. Though he faded considerably in the latter part of his career, there is no denying his place among the most exciting, most highly skilled blues-rockers in history. Whatever his shortcomings, Rory Gallagher will always be remembered in the hearts of blues fans around the world who adored and cheered loudly for the Irish Mississippian.

## Discography

*Rory Gallagher*, Atlantic 33368.
*Deuce*, Atlantic 7004.
*Blueprint*, Polydor 5522.
*Tattoo*, Polydor 5539.
*Irish Tour '74*, Polygram PD 9501.
*Sinner and Saint*, Polydor 6510.
*Against the Grain*, Chrysalis 1098.
*Calling Card*, Chrysalis 1124.
*Photo Finish*, Chrysalis 1170.
*Top Priority*, Chrysalis 1235.
*Stage Struck*, Chrysalis 1280.
*Jinx*, Mercury 40571.
*Defender*, Demon 98.
*Fresh Evidence*, Capo/I.R.S. 1370.
*The Bullfrog Interlude*, Castle 187/3.
*Blue Day for the Blues*, IRS 35783.
*Live in Europe*, Castle ESM 377.

With Taste:

*Taste*, Atco 33296.
*On the Boards*, Atco 3322.
*Live Taste*, Polydor 2310082.
*Taste at the Isle of Wight*, Polydor 23831.

# DONNIE WALSH

## *Mr. Downchild*

Considering Canada's proximity to the United States, the original home of the blues, it was only a matter of time before citizens of the Great White North caught blues fever. The Canadian blues community has a long and deep history and boasts a fine lineup of practitioners. One of the pioneers of the country's blues scene for the past thirty years is known as Mr. Downchild. His name is Donnie Walsh.

   Donnie Walsh was born in March of 1947, in Toronto, Ontario. His first introduction to music was the jukebox that sat in the corner at his parents' resort in northern Ontario. It provided Walsh with a solid education of rhythm-and-blues and rock and roll songs. The resort also featured live bands that put stars in Walsh's eyes. An incessant fever burned inside him to emulate the songs he heard on the jukebox and from the bands that played at the resort. After receiving an acoustic guitar and a few lessons, however, Walsh grew impatient with the tedious hours of practice that mastering the guitar demanded, and abandoned his ambitions.

   The family moved back to Toronto when Walsh was in his teens. It was at this point that he rediscovered the magic of music through the blues. The hypnotic, sweet blues of Jimmy Reed rekindled the fire first lit so long ago. This time Walsh was more serious about his musical endeavors. The music of Reed eventually led him on a blues journey where he discovered the songs of Muddy Waters, B. B. King, Willie Dixon, Lowell Fulson, and a host of others.

   In the next few years Walsh paid his dues. While polishing his guitar skills, he worked a variety of jobs to make ends meet, including truck driver, short-order cook, cab driver, and as a sales clerk in the blues section of a record store. The golden opportunity to play any and all blues records gave him the chance to finish his musical "education." In 1969, he decided to form his own band with his good friend Gary Stodolok on second guitar, Jim Milne on bass, and Bob Fitzerald on drums. Donnie's brother, Richard "Hock" Walsh, was the band's vocalist. They called themselves the Downchild Blues Band.

   Once they had sharpened their act, they began to look for work and ended up playing their first professional gig at Grossman's in Toronto. Downchild soon became the house band and built an enthusiastic following despite numerous personnel changes. Cash Wall replaced Bob Fitzerald, and the hard-rocking tenor saxophones of Dave Woodward and Ron Jacobs were added to fill out the band's sound.

   When the lineup was settled on—at least for the time being—the band recorded its first album, under very primitive conditions. The "studio" was located in a basement parking garage and consisted of simple two-track recording equipment. The finished product, *Bootleg*, was—despite its shoestring budget and inauspicious birthplace—a solid work from a premier blues band. The album contained some imaginative originals from Walsh, including "Don't You Bother My Baby" and "Rockit," an instrumental. Bootleg opened many doors for the band, including an increased touring schedule that saw the band playing outside of Toronto for the first time. They performed in Winnipeg and Montreal. Their reputation as a fun, houserocking band enabled them to secure a contract with the label GRT.

Downchild's debut album on GRT, *Straight Up*, included "(I've Got Everything I Need) Almost," "Shotgun Blues," and their first big hit, "Flip, Flop, and Fly," the Big Joe Turner chestnut. The band, eager to cash in on their success with their studio recordings, toured heavily, sweeping across the vast Canadian landscape, and earned a respectable name for themselves in the United States at a host of festivals. But the link with the Blues Brothers—the *Saturday Night Live* contribution to the blues by Dan Aykroyd and John Belushi—really turned heads. The Blues Brothers' smash-hit album, *Briefcase Full of Blues*, included Walsh's "(I've Got Everything I Need) Almost," and "Shotgun Blues."

Downchild's frantic touring pace enabled the band members to meet many of the legends of the blues, including Buddy Guy, Robert Lockwood, Jr., Johnny Shines, Roosevelt Sykes, John Lee Hooker, Albert Collins, and Luther Allison. The band often opened up for major blues acts, such as B. B. King, Muddy Waters, Albert King, The Nighthawks, Johnny Winter, ZZ Top, Mike Bloomfield, Homesick James, Louisiana Red, Taj Mahal, Delbert McClinton, and Junior Wells. Their acceptance within the blues community indicated that they had arrived.

Despite a hectic list of concert dates, the band continued to record and release albums. The disc *Dancing* came out after *Straight Up* and was heartily accepted. While it contained some high-energy material like "Going Dancing," "Tell Your Mother," "Tell Me Baby," and "Must Have Been the Devil," it was not as commercially successful as their previous effort. Nevertheless, the band pushed on.

Although Downchild was enjoying its most successful period, there were still many lineup changes: Kenny Neal, the Louisiana Bayou boogie singer, left to pursue a solo career; Gene Taylor joined The Fabulous Thunderbirds; Dave Woodward eventually became a member of the Powder Blues Band.

The band's fourth album, *Ready to Go*, summed up the spirit of the group. With songs like "The Slide," "Do the Parrott," "Lazy Woman," "Caldonia," and "Heart Fixing Business," they proved that the party was still going on. The self-penned "Downchild Shuffle" alone made the record a worthwhile purchase. While they were not yet internationally known, they continued to deliver their jumping, swinging blues with the same amount of energy every night no matter the size of the crowd or the venue.

By the late 1970s, the Downchild Blues Band were one of the most recognized names in the business. Their brand of driving blues was linked to the Blues Brothers' good-time style, which helped Walsh and his mates widen their circle. The *So Far* album, a collection of their best up to that point, enabled the band to step back and catch their second wind.

In 1980, they returned with a vengeance, releasing two albums: *We Deliver* and *Road Fever*. *We Deliver* contained some genuine fiery blues tunes, including "It's a Matter of Time," "I Came for Your Daughter," "Tryin' to Keep Her 88's Straight," and "Summertime Blues." *Road Fever* was a smash, with songs like "Road Fever," "Stages of Love," "Money Trouble," "TV Mama," and "What You Gonna Do?" The band proved that they were back in fine form.

As the 1980s unrolled, Downchild plugged ahead with a heavy tour schedule. By this point in the band's career they were a well-known commodity and promoters could count on the band to fill the seats. Sadly, in 1982, Jane Vassey, after nine stellar years with the band, died of leukemia. Despite this severe blow the band kept churning out albums like *Blood Run Hot* and *But I'm on the Guest List*. Both records followed the formula of the previous releases and guaranteed fans a stomping good time.

In 1987, five years after their last release, the band resurfaced with *It's Been So Long*. It was one of the group's strongest efforts, anchored by songs like the title cut, "Bop 'Til I Drop," "My Baby She's Alright," "Bring It on Back," and "Not This Time." Mr. Downchild and his mates had proven that they had not lost their edge. The *Gone Fishing* set finished off the decade in fine form and opened the door for the band in the 1990s.

*Lucky 13*, Downchild's thirteenth studio release, clearly indicated that the group Walsh had created twenty years before had weathered all of the trends and fads to remain one of the most entertaining bands around. The record contained some of their best material, including "Dew Drop Inn," "Shoot That Moon," "Take Me Back Annie," "Changed My Ways," and "Lucky 13." It was a contemporary collection of blues-drenched material by a truly professional band.

Although the band has broken up at various times throughout its thirty-plus-year history, they have always managed to reunite to play more concerts and festivals and record more albums. Today the band, also known as Mr. Downchild, continues as the granddaddy of all Canadian blues bands. Their next release is always greatly anticipated and their next appearance is always just a few short hours away.

Donnie Walsh is a blues constant. He has been on the blues scene for thirty years and remains one of the dominant forces in the music business. He sports an impressive catalog and is the proud composer of over one hundred original songs. His instantly recognizable guitar and harmonica licks have pleased millions of fans throughout the world.

Walsh has been called the "father of Canadian blues," and with good reason. He is a blues pioneer on the Canadian scene. It was Walsh who paid the highest dues so later Canadian blues acts, such as the Jeff Healey Band, the Colin James Band, the Powder Blues, Sue Foley, the Sidemen, and the Highliners could also enjoy their success. The Canadian blues scene, which has blossomed nicely in the past few years, was relatively barren in the late 1960s when the Downchild Blues Band first started out. There were few blues clubs and the band had to play in rock-and-roll venues. Today, blues clubs can be found throughout Canada's major cities and large towns.

Because of their hard work the band has not been overlooked by the Canadian music industry. They have been nominated for numerous Juno awards, and have won Maple Leaf Blues Awards and Jazz Report Awards. Walsh was honored with the Great Canadian Blues Award in 1992 for his contribution to the Canadian blues scene. At the Maple Leaf Awards in 1999, Chuck Jackson won for Male Vocalist of the Year, Pat Carey won the best Horn Player of the Year award, and Gary Kendall won for Bass Player of the Year.

For years, Downchild has been a staple on Canadian radio and television. Their appearances range from a spotlight on the CBC to talk shows like *Open Mike* with Mike Bullard. Walsh, a relaxed individual, has always championed the blues and the Canadian blues scene in the interviews he has done. He has always spoken with honesty and sincerity of the music that he has made a living at for more than half of his life.

But beyond the awards, medals, and recognition, the true legacy of the band rests in their studio work and memorable live appearances. Throughout the band's long history, no matter who was in the band, the musicians were guaranteed to deliver a night of pile-driving blues that never failed to excite the crowd. The name Downchild garners appreciative nods from long-time blues fans and knowing grins from new blues fans who have just discovered the group.

There have been many changes in the band's lineup over the years, but today there is a set group that includes Chuck Jackson the singer (the group's fourth), who also plays harmonica. His battle of the harps with Walsh is one of their concert highlights. Jackson is also an active songwriter, contributing many classics on each album in the past ten years. Michael Fonfara is the keyboard virtuoso, who has played with Lou Reed and Solomon Burke among his long list of credits. Pat Carey adds his scholarly knowledge and distinct saxophone to Downchild's overall sound. Jim Casson, the drummer, and Gary Kendall provide a more than adequate rhythm section.

But the focus of the Downchild Blues Band has always been Donnie Walsh, who has overcome personal tragedy and other obstacles on his way to enjoying tremendous success. He has lost key band members through illness; his brother "Hock" died of cancer in 1997. He has also endured the defection of vital members who made major contributions to the band before their departures. But no matter the challenges that Walsh has faced, he has proven that the blues are in his heart and that his heart is in the blues.

### Discography

*Bootleg*, Special Records/BMG.
*Straight Up*, GRT.
*Dancing*, GRT.
*Ready to Go*, GRT.
*So Far: A Collection of Our Best*, Posterity.
*We Deliver*, Attic.
*Road Fever*, Attic 624637.
*Blood Run Hot*, Attic 1117.
*But I'm on the Guest List*, Attic 1151.
*It's Been So Long*, Stony Plain.
*Gone Fishing*, Stony Plain 1139.
*Good Times Guaranteed*, Downchild Music/Festival Distribution 126.
*Lucky 13*, Downchild Music/Festival Distribution 134.
*A Case of the Blues—The Best of Downchild*, Attic ACD1516.

# HANS THEESSINK

## *Blues from the Lowlands*

The widespread appeal of the blues has reached some interesting geographical areas that are known for other reasons throughout the world. Take Holland, for instance: The Netherlands is famous for its tulips, windmills, wooden shoes, and rich history. But in the past thirty years one individual has worked valiantly to put Holland on the blues map as well; arguably, with his blues from the Lowlands he has done just that. His name is Hans Theessink.

Hans Theessink was born on April 5, 1948, in Enschede, Netherlands. He spent his formative years living the typical life of a Dutch schoolboy until one day he heard Big Bill Broonzy and Huddie "Leadbelly" Ledbetter on a radio show. He was immediately captivated by the powerful, majestic sounds of the American bluesmen. Not long after that, he acquired his first guitar and began to reproduce the sounds that had stirred deep emotions inside him. Hans Theessink had caught blues fever.

By his late teens he was playing in clubs throughout Germany and the Netherlands. He had developed his own individual style based on the country-blues of Big Bill Broonzy, the Piedmont finger-picking of Brownie McGhee, and the folk music of his native Holland. He was also teaching himself to write songs; here, Leadbelly, the famous traveling songster, was an important inspiration.

In 1970, Theessink recorded his first album, *Next Morning at Sunrise*, on the Autogram label, a small independent European label. This record was not released in the United States. *Next Morning at Sunrise* contained the reworked classics "Death Letter Blues," and "Baby Please Don't Go." Already, with his first album, Theessink was proving that he was something special.

In between cutting albums, Theessink toured heavily throughout Europe and in his native Holland in an effort to establish his name; but stardom was not easy to come by. It would be another six years before he recorded another album, *Klasselotteriet*, for Rillerod Records, another small independent European company. The thirteen tracks, recorded in his native tongue, did little to advance his blues career beyond the borders of Holland.

On the other hand, *Slow and Easy*, Theessink's third album, was a rich blues effort. It showcased Theessink's versatility, and, more importantly, the songster persona that was becoming his main identity. The wide range of songs included "Cuckoo," "Shake Sugaree," "Chicago Blues," a gospel-influenced "Jesus on the Mainline," and a dynamite version of Robert Johnson's "Come on in My Kitchen." While the song "Come on in My Kitchen" had been covered to death, especially during the folk/blues explosion of a decade earlier, Theessink's version was unique. He put his personal stamp on that song and created a vision of the very Delta environment that Johnson composed the song in.

Like all foreign blues enthusiasts, Theessink dreamed of someday traveling to the United States to visit the original home of the blues. While many yearned to tour Chicago, the urban home of electric blues, others, like Theessink, wanted to head down to the Mississippi Delta where the story of the blues in America began. In 1979, Theessink fulfilled his ambition and arrived in the United States, where he met local blues singers and absorbed as much as he could before heading back to Holland. He returned to his country with a renewed spirit and wider vision.

His 1980 release, *Late Last Night*, reflected Theessink's time spent in the United States. There was a decidedly American flavor to the album in songs like "Money," "Gypsy Moth," "Late Last Night," "Drinking Problems," "All About My Loss," and the outstanding "Sweet Home Chicago." Without a doubt, Theessink had turned the corner and his career was truly beginning to gain serious momentum. He had also acquired a solid reputation as a first-class entertainer whose live show was a must-see.

He continued to perform, sometimes up to three hundred concerts a year, all over Europe, building upon his flourishing popularity with each performance and new release. The album *Cushioned for a Soft Ride Inside* (which featured Gerry Lockran) was a genuine collection and his best record up to that point. With definitive takes on such classics as "Midnight Special," "Going to Brownsville," "New Cocaine Blues," "Morning Train," "Come Back Baby," and "All the Good Times," Theessink had proven to the entire blues world that he was one of their best-kept secrets. The fluidity and authenticity of this record made many take notice of him outside of his established fan base.

He repeated his success with the *All Night Long* set. There wasn't a weak track on this album, from the revamped "Sweet Home Chicago," "Girl from the North Country," and "C. C. Rider," to the beautiful, haunting instrumentals "Walking the Boogie" and the folk/gospel favorite, "When the Saints Come Marching In." The album featured Peter Ratzenbeck, an old friend who would reappear over the years on other Theessink offerings. Theessink's virtuosity on a variety of guitars, bottleneck, and harp served notice that he was one of the most versatile blues performers anywhere in the world.

*Titanic* was a more ambitious project and reflected the musical path that Theessink would follow in the next few years. He was supported by a bevy of Dutch musicians, including Inrich Ciser on percussion and Mike Whellans on harmonica. But here was an odd assortment of instruments never seen before on a blues album. Iain Mackintosh played the concertina, John Ehde the cello, Finn Odderskov the baritone sax, Per Knudsen the bass and tuba, John Nargaard the accordion and jaw harp. In addition, Andrew John Huddleston and Lissa Ladefoged supplied backing vocals. Theessink himself sang, played a variety of guitars, the mandolin, the fiddle, and the dulcimer. This diverse blues "group" delivered an eclectic set of songs, including "Goodbye Monday Blues," "Mississippi You're on My Mind," "Titanic," "Shake Hands with the Sun," and "Play It Again Sam." It was a true modern blues album, recorded by one of the best contemporary artists on the scene.

In 1986, he returned to America and landed in New Orleans where he struck up a friendship with Jon Sass, a tuba player. Although the tuba was never a premier blues instrument, the combination of Theessink's well-honed guitar skills and Sass's mastery of the tuba created an interesting sound. Together they recorded *Baby Wants to Boogie*, with a little help from their friends Alex Munkas on drums, Christian Dozzler on harmonica, Flaco Jimenez on accordion, Nicola Parov on gadulka, and Pippa Armstrong and Dana Gillespie on backing vocals. Their reworking of "Stones in My Pathway," "Baby Wants to Boogie," "Nobody's Fault but Mine," and "When Things Go Wrong" put a new twist on each song. The rest of the album was composed of originals: "Slidin' Delta," "Darkest Hour," "Hunted Man," and "Went to the Doctor" shone every bit as brightly as the cover versions.

Theessink and Sass teamed up again to record *Johnny & the Devil* for the Flying Fish label based in Chicago. It was another collection of originals and covers that rang with an authentic feel thanks to Theessink's deep voice, his dexterity, and his expansive vision as a modern bluesman. All the songs had a funky, bouncy blues feel to them, including the title cut, "Johnny and the Devil," "Traveling Man," "Mississippi," "Flying Shoes," "Dough Roller Blues," and "False Accusations." Theessink stretched out musically on this work, playing acoustic, electric, and steel guitars, the dobro, the mandolin, the mandocello, the fiddle, the harmonica and the jaw harp, as well as handling the lead vocal chores. There were also more traditional blues instruments, such as drums played by Alex Munkar, with Carl Kaye on pedal steel guitar, Bummie Fian on trumpet, Christian Radovan on trombone, Christian Dozzier on harmonica, and Wolfgang Punchnig on alto sax. There were also Chris Haig on the fiddle, Geraint Watkins on accordion, and Jatinder Takur on tablas and sitar, which gave the album a world-music feel. Pippa Armstrong, Ali Thelfa, Doretta Carter, and Bobby Hammer provided backing vocals.

It was at this point in his career that Theessink began to carve a significant niche for himself in the American market, as each successive album helped him inch towards true international recognition. He was invited to play at the prestigious New Orleans Jazz & Heritage Festival, the Chicago Blues Festival, the Kerrville Folk Festival in Texas, the Toronto Blues Festival, and other such events all over North America. Without a doubt, he had become one of the better-known European blues singers.

The album *Call Me*, recorded in Munich, Hollywood, and Woodstock, featured the distinctive Theessink guitar touch and the usual array of support musicians. The addition of Jon Sass's strong tuba lines, and the contributions of Colin Linden, Maceo Parker, Bobby King, Pee Wee

Ellis, and Terry Evans, as well as two members of The Band, Rick Danko and Garth Hudson, ensured the project would be first-rate. Some of the highlights included "Lonely Days and Lonely Nights," "Call Me," "Rock the Boat," "New Orleans," and "Soul of Song." *Call Me* evoked comparisons between Theessink and Ry Cooder.

The *Hans Theessink & the Blue Groove—Live* session showcased him at his best in front of a live audience. An evening to remember, it was taken from a number of concerts and assembled to provide a solid presentation of what he could do in front of a live audience. The contributions of Sass, Ali Thelfa on drums, and Doreetta Carter on vocals only enhanced Theessink's imaginative acoustic blues. The live renditions of "Built for Comfort," "Jesus on the Mainline," "Rock the Boat," "Cocaine Blues," and "Shake Your Moneymaker" were excellent.

*Hard Road Blues* was a solo performance dedicated to the inspiration of Big Bill Broonzy. Theessink paid tribute to Broonzy with an acoustic set of deeply emotional and well played traditional songs. The masterpiece of the album, "Big Bill's Guitar," enabled Theessink to express the deep respect he had for Broonzy. Other special moments on the album were "Prison Blues," "Blind Willie," "Two Trains," "Vicksburg Is My Home," "Shotgun Blues," "Cypress Grove," and "Sitting on Top of the World." In some ways, the album conveyed the specific vision of what the rural blues were all about to those European fans who had missed the authentic performances of the early country-blues masters.

The album *Crazy Moon* was a perfect example of Theessink's ability to blend his distinct brand of acoustic blues with tasty flavorings of Cajun, Caribbean, Gospel, Texas, and even European classical traditions. Once again backed by Sass and Thelfa, Theessink scored with a winning formula. *Crazy Moon* also featured a guest appearance by Marcia Ball, who added her New Orleans gumbo/Texas roadhouse sound to the mix. There were also contributions from Terry Evans, a noted gospel singer from Los Angeles, a European collection of Celtic and Irish folk songs, and the Vienna addition of classical horns. It was an ambitious project that Theessink managed to pull off rather well. The highlights of the thirteen songs on the album included "Power of Love," "Homecookin'," and "Roll with the Punches."

Peter Patzak, an Austrian film director, used the music on the record as well as the album's title for a movie. *Crazy Moon* marked the acting debut of Theessink, who played a musician in the movie. Later, Theessink also starred in Thomas Roth's film, *The Lake*. While he made fine appearances in both productions, Theessink remained devoted to his musical career.

On his fiftieth birthday, Theessink celebrated by recording *Blue*

*Grooves from Vienna*, his fifteenth major release. The disc was a greatest-hit package, but also contained some rare recordings that covered a span of almost thirty years, more than half of Theessink's life. The album clearly demonstrated that Theessink was one of the premier European blues artist who deserved all the critical praise that had been heaped upon him in the last few years.

Theessink's next record, *Journey On*, once again united his European blues with other musical styles of gospel, soul, and folk to create something new and exciting. The album's tracks contained a mixture of seven originals and four cover songs, including "Feel Like Going Home" and "Bourgeois Blues." Other standouts on the disc were "Storm Warning," "29 Ways," "Louisiana Man," and "Set Me Free." The bouncy tuba lines of Jon Sass, the drums and tambourine of Ali Thelfa, the bass of Angus Thomas, the harmonica of Christian Dozzier, and the Wurlitzer piano of Richard Bell rounded out his band. Terry Evans added backing vocals.

One of his most interesting musical adventures was the album *Lifeline*, which was another large undertaking. A variety of musicians made important contributions, including the usual cast of Jon Sass and Ali Thelfa. Theessink also used the exclusive talents of the Holmes Brothers, Linda Tillery & the Cultural Heritage Choir, and Pee Wee Ellis on sax. There were two special guest appearances: Charles Brown—one of Theessink's most cherished blues heroes—added his smooth, rich vocals, and Insingizi Emnyama, a male choir from Zimbabwe, gave the record a totally different dimension. Theessink, focused on playing mainly different types of guitars, created a blues album with a genuine world flavor to it.

The thirteen tracks contained eleven originals and two covers, one by the Rev. Gary Davis and one by Blind Willie Johnson. With such a variety of musicians, many different styles were explored, including the pure blues of "Missing You" and "Soul of a Man," the jazzy flavor of "Love Sweet Love," and the country-speckled, self-penned "Ready for the Ride." The blending of such a collection of different voices came together beautifully on "Soul on Fire," "Six Strings Down," "Going Home," and "Missing You." The haunting "Mandolin Man" was a heartfelt tribute to Yank Rachell, the great blues mandolin player. Theessink, who had always admired Rachell, had desperately wanted to include him on *Lifeline* but the old blues master died before the album was made.

Today, Theessink is recognized as one of the best blues artists from anywhere around the world as he continues to add to his reputation with each new album release and concert performance.

Hans Theessink is a blues diamond. When he first began his career he was rough around the edges, an unknown blues traditionalist from Holland, a country not recognized as a blues hotbed. But fifteen albums and thousands of performances all over Europe, the United States, and other parts of the world later, he is a shiny gem whose music has pervaded the entire globe.

Theessink is a genuine bluesman of the world. His albums reflect a wide and deep vision that incorporates music from around the world. While he may be compared to Taj Mahal in his ability to blend his acoustic blues with all other types of music, he is more like Leadbelly, a songster with the unique gift of adapting to different styles. But despite his interest in other sounds, his heart has always belonged to the acoustic blues.

His guitar style is unique. A totally self-taught player, he never received any formal blues guitar lessons since there was no one in Holland to teach him. The result is an original style characterized by a particular groove and intuition. He is a laid back guitarist who allows the music to flow naturally from his heart and instincts to his fingers. Theessink, in an effort to help out aspiring bluesmen unable to benefit from a teacher, put together an instructional song book called *Fingerpicking & Bottleneck Favourites* for voice and guitar.

His various influences range from the Delta acoustic blues of Blind Willie Johnson, Big Bill Broonzy, and Robert Johnson to the folk music of his native Holland. The mandolin playing of Hank Rachell, the fingerpicking of Blind Willie McTell, and the golden voice of Charles Brown, all had a special effect on him. He also developed a taste for jazz, country music, reggae, and the roots music of the Caribbean and West Africa.

Theessink is a multi-instrumentalist, able to play a variety of guitars, the jaw-harp, the violin, the mandolin, the B-3 Hammond organ, and the harmonica. He has a precise, delicate touch and knows where to insert a strong tuba line, a run of mandolin notes, a harmonica break, or a violin passage in a song. His ability to mix the various dimensions of different instruments into one cohesive sound is one of his strongest musical assets. He ties everything together neatly with his intricate guitar skills.

Hans Theessink is the "father of the Holland blues." In the blues clubs in his native country he is a legend. He has put his country on the blues map with his spare, deeply felt Delta guitar sound and his rich vocals. He has blazed a path for the second generation of Holland blues singers to follow.

Theessink remains one of the best and most popular European blues singers on the international stage. He has managed to forge a career that is the envy of many blues singers. Although he has never received his proper due, Theessink has carried on with each inspired concert and new release. He has proven with his blues from the Lowlands that one need not be born in the Mississippi Delta or other parts of the American South to become a true blues singer.

## Discography

*Next Morning at Sunrise*, Autogram 130.
*Klasselotteriet*, Rillerod RLP-7601.
*Slow and Easy*, Autogram ALLP-230.
*Late Last Night*, Kettle Records KOP-7.
*Antoon Met 'n' Bok*, Jama 3.
*Cushioned for a Soft Ride Inside*, Autogram ALLP-271.
*Titanic*, Blue Groove BG-3020.
*All Night Long*, Extraplate EX-50.
*Baby Wants to Boogie*, Blue Groove BG-1020.
*Johnny & the Devil*, Blue Groove BG-2020; Flying Fish.
*Call Me*, Blue Groove BG-4020.
*Hank Theessink & the Blue Groove—Live*, Blue Groove BG-5020.
*Hard Road Blues*, Minor Music 801047.
*Crazy Moon*, RFR 1016.
*Blue Grooves from Vienna.*
*Journey On*, Minor Music 84172.
*Lifeline*, Blue Groove BG-9020.
*Fingerpicking & Bottleneck Favourites*, Doblinger 05 990.

# DAVE HOLE

## *Blues from Down Under*

Once the secrets of the blues was delivered to the international stage by the likes of Rory Gallagher and Hans Theessink, blues fever quickly spread to every corner of the globe. With the possible exception of Antarctica, the blues have touched every continent. While North America and Europe are famous blues centers, South America, Africa, Asia, and Australia are less well-known for producing famous blues singers. However, in Australia, a vibrant blues colony carries the blues torch with pride and distinction. One of the many Australian artists to achieve success has created his own world with his blues from Down Under. His name is Dave Hole.

Dave Hole was born on March 30, 1948, in Heswall, Cheshire, England. His family moved to Australia in the early 1950s, settling in Perth. Hole became interested in music at an early age, when his curiosity was piqued by the Hootchie-Cootchie-Man sounds of Muddy Waters. In his early teens, Hole acquired his first guitar and started trying to unlock the mysteries that intrigued him so much. By his late teens he had developed a more than passing interest in a career in music. Like most aspiring blues guitarists at the time, Hole paid close attention to Eric Clapton, Peter Green, and Brian Jones, as well as digging into the past and absorbing the classics of Elmore James, Mississippi Fred McDowell, and Robert Johnson.

After a two-year stint in England, Hole returned to Australia in 1974 to begin his blues career proper. He embarked on an exhaustive tour of clubs around Australia, earning a scant living as a live performer and paying his blues dues. In 1990, he recorded his first album but still didn't have a record deal. An engaging individual always willing to take a chance, Hole sent his new disc, *Short Fuse Blues*, to *Guitar Player* magazine. It created the big break he had been working for.

The album was given a strong review and was picked up by Alligator Records for distribution. One of Australia's best-kept blues secrets was about to invade the blues world. The album, *Short Fuse Blues*, recorded with his band Short Fuse, featured Hole's searing slide guitar work and powerful vocals. It was a guitar-player's album, and Hole drew immediate comparisons to Johnny Winter and Rory Gallagher. The band Short Fuse included Gary Peters on bass guitar, John Villani on keyboards, and Bob Patient on drums. Seven of the tracks were written by Hole, including "Keep Your Motor Running," "Short Fuse Blues," "Business Man," and "Take a Swing." It also featured the old Freddie King chestnut "I'm Tore Down," and the Hendrix classic, "Purple Haze."

It was a stunning debut album that served notice that Dave Hole had arrived and earned him praise from many critics and fellow blues musicians. His band's tour schedule took them all over Europe and North America; everywhere they played, Hole astounded the audience with his fiery brand of slide guitar.

His next album, *Working Overtime*, proved that his first effort was not a fluke. Hole delivered his sliding pyrotechnics with the precision and fury of a veteran blues axe slinger. The album included ten original Hole compositions, which served to strengthen his value as a songwriter, and the reworking of two blues classics, "Key to the Highway," the Big Bill

Broonzy signature tune, and "I Can't Be Satisfied," the old Muddy Waters chestnut. Among the highlights of the album were "Nobody Hears Me Crying," "Stormy Seas," "Twenty Years," and the title cut, "Working Overtime." The album drew rave reviews and firmly established Hole as one of the modern monster guitar players.

Hole and Short Fuse were very much in demand. Their tours of North America, Europe, and Australia earned the band a whole new legion of fans. In just two short years Hole had established himself as one of the prime blues acts on the circuit. He appeared at many festivals and left the stage smoldering with his scorching slide-guitar work. It was with great confidence that the band entered the studio to record their third album, *Steel on Steel*.

As in his first two releases, *Steel on Steel* featured Hole's trademark sizzling slide guitar work and his sharpened songwriting skills. It included twelve Hole originals and a cover version of "Going Down," which Freddie King had made famous. Other gems on the album were "Wildfire," "Quicksand," "Counting My Regrets," "Killing Bite," and "Take Me to Chicago." The record only enhanced Hole's already burgeoning reputation.

Hole changed strategies for his next album, *Ticket to Chicago*. He recorded the album with the cream of Chicago bluesmen, including Billy Branch on harp, Johnny B. Gayden on bass, pianist Tony Z, and Ray "Killer" Allison on drums. (Gayden played with Albert Collins, Tony Z was part of Buddy Guy's backup band as well as Larry McCray's band, and Allison had also spent some time in Buddy Guy's band.)

The opening track, "Out of Here," loudly announced that this was Hole's hardest rock-blues album as it roared down Michigan Avenue at the speed of a train dangerously out of control. Of the fourteen songs on the album, thirteen were written by Hole, including "My Bird Won't Sing," "Beyond Jupiter," "Wheeler Dealer," "Empty Train," and "Outlaw." The song "Bullfrog Blues" was dedicated to the recently deceased Irish blues-rocker Rory Gallagher. The album was a success and greatly enhanced Hole's strong foothold in the international blues scene.

In 1999, he recorded *Under the Spell*, once again backed by his Short Fuse band. The album featured many highlights, including "Short Memory," "Run with Me," "Blues Is the Truth," "Demolition Man," and "Cold Women with Warm Hearts." Unlike on his previous releases, all the songs on *Under the Spell* were written by Hole. Another power rock-blues effort, the album ensured Hole's reign as one of the best hard-driving guitarists into the next century.

He continues to record and perform.

Dave Hole is an international blues artist with a well-earned reputation as a monster guitar player. He has picked up where Rory Gallagher and Johnny Winter left off. In Australia, he has attained cult status. Hole has established his top-notch credentials with a succession of strong recording efforts, as well as solid live performances. He is a well-rounded artist who can deliver muscular blues with the best of them.

Hole has chiseled a solid position for himself among contemporary slide guitarists despite an unorthodox guitar technique. To compensate for an old soccer injury, Hole places the slide on his index finger and hangs his hand over the top of the neck. He uses a pick for a slide and is an adept fingerpicker. It is a unique style that enables Hole to deliver a totally different sound than blues fans are accustomed to. His burning licks and note-infested solos have layered textures and colored tones that produce a complete wall of sound.

He is a versatile performer who is capable of creating different moods with his spellbinding virtuosity. Hole can run and gun with the best of them, playing high-volume, energized rocking blues that leave the listener stunned. He can play it smooth and straight, demonstrating a subtle, sophisticated side. He can drop notes like rain, spooky and spinetingling. There is no limit to the worlds Hole can create with his diverse guitar abilities.

Dave Hole is a modern guitarist, influenced by the modern blues-rock guitarists who came before him, including Johnny Winter, Rory Gallagher, Eric Clapton, Stevie Ray Vaughan, and, of course, Jimi Hendrix. He shares Winter's dynamic slide ability, Gallagher's European guitar touch, Clapton's knack for covering old blues songs, Stevie Ray Vaughan's power, and the desire to let it all hang out like Hendrix.

Hole has been a special influence on Rob Tognoni, who hails from New Zealand. He has taken the young hotshot guitarist under his wing and nurtured his creativity. Hole, who learned from the great masters before him, is only repeating the gesture by helping out young Tognoni. It demonstrates a definite touch of class and professionalism on Hole's part.

Dave Hole is just one of many brilliant Australian blues musicians who include Kevin Borich, Phil Manning, Matt Taylor, the Rob Tognoni Band, Gwyn Ashton, Blue Heat, the Greg James Band, and dozens of others. The Australian blues family includes some of the most exciting performers in the world. Hole, who has been playing blues-rock as long as any of them, is also the leader of a core group of great blues artists who have yet to make their mark on the international scene.

Dave Hole has proven that with passion, developed talent, hard work, and a genuine sense of direction, a blues singer can gain international respect in blues circles no matter where he hails from. As he continues to entertain us with his blues from Down Under, Hole ensures that the blues-rock genre remains a vibrant form.

## Discography

*Short Fuse Blues*, Alligator AL 4807.
*Working Overtime*, Alligator AL 4814.
*Steel on Steel*, Alligator AL 4832.
*Ticket to Chicago*, Alligator AL 4847.
*Under the Spell*, Alligator AL 4865.

# J. J. MILTEAU

## *French Harp Blues*

The influence that the American blues have had on world music is truly immeasurable, transcending all lines of race, creed, color, nationality, and language. In France, the blues fever struck as hard as it did in other countries around the planet and the result was the creation of French blues. One of the best and longest-serving entertainers in France has thrilled his countrymen and fans throughout the world with his French harp blues. His name is J. J. Milteau.

J. J. Milteau was born on April 17, 1950, in Paris, France. Little is known of his early life, but by his teens he was listening to the imported records of Sonny Boy Williamson II, Sonny Terry, and Little Walter, which he was lucky enough to acquire. Inspired by his musical heroes, he took up the harmonica and dreamed of a career as a blues singer. As stardom was not easily forthcoming, and in order to pay the bills, he worked at a variety of jobs, including one as an employee in a record store, which gave him ample opportunity to seek out the recordings he coveted.

In his teens he traveled all over Europe, learning from other blues enthusiasts. Through his many on-the-road experiences, he collected the raw material that he would later use to create his cycle of imaginative, brilliant songs. He eventually made it to the United States and absorbed all that he could from the American bluesmen he met. Upon his return to France, he was determined to put his native country on the blues map with his swinging style of rocking harp blues.

Before he could fulfill these ambitions, however, the French army stationed him in Germany, where he began to really hone his harmonica skills. Upon returning to his native country, he played his harmonica all over Paris. The blues scene in France was made up of a small group of dedicated artists who traded blues riffs and swapped stories about the American blues legends they revered so much. Milteau might have been stuck playing his harmonica in small, dimly lit clubs for the rest of his life if it hadn't been for the French blues singer Eddie Mitchell.

Mitchell, one of the best-known French blues-rock singers at the time, had recently returned from America, where he had recorded with some premier American bluesmen, including Charlie McCoy on the harmonica. Searching for someone who could duplicate McCoy's driving harmonica riffs, Mitchell discovered Milteau, who sounded like the real McCoy. From that point on, Milteau made great strides in his career as he toured with Mitchell, gaining important exposure with French blues audiences. He also began to record with some of the best-known French pop and rock singers.

He developed quite a reputation throughout blues circles in France for his remarkable talents, wit, and energetic playing. He began to appear at the Utopia Club in Paris and it became his home base as well as the center of the burgeoning Parisian blues scene. With a versatile style derived from the harsh, Chicago sounds of Sonny Boy Williamson II, Little Walter, James Cotton, Big Walter Horton, and the country-blues wailings of Sonny Terry, Milteau impressed all with his fluidity and range. He rose through the ranks to eventually assume a leading position in the French blues community.

Milteau's solo recording career began in 1974 with the release of *33 Toures*. Some of the outstanding tracks were "Mama Blues," "Mountain Blues," "Jackson's Stomp," and "Rice Miller." An interesting debut album, it exhibited some of the characteristics that would appear in all of his future efforts. There was, of course, his enthusiastic harmonica playing, drenched with emotion; his clever selection of the right cover songs; the groove burned into his own compositions; and his sincerity. *33 Toures* was reissued as *The Harmonica* a few years later.

The *New Bluesgrass Collection* was released a year later and was a fine collection of songs that had inspired Milteau while growing up. The album kicked off with the rocking "King Charlie" and didn't let up. He explored many styles, including the country-inflected "It's Raining in Nashville," the Louisiana Boogie "Cajun Stomp," the chili-peppered "Maybe Mexico," and the title cut, "Bluesgrass." Milteau's ability to combine different styles into one cohesive package was quite remarkable. But he never tried to adapt his playing to any particular style of music, instead wrapping the songs around his style.

The next album, *Blues Harp*, demonstrated Milteau's chameleon-like abilities. He delivered electrified blues harp on "The Hook," which was reminiscent of the Chicago harp masters. But he also included a jazz number, "Woodbund," as well as a country-blues tune done in Rice Miller style. The song "Special 20" was a genuine rocker. He showed a skillful touch in his ability to synthesize his polished, distinctive blues sound with elements of jazz, rock, country, and soul.

The album *Explorer* was another example of Milteau fusing his blues vision with a variety of styles. His playing was exceptional throughout the album as he displayed a control and discipline on the instrument that was rather breathtaking, but he also made the album fun. The instrumental "Biscuit Boy" was a subtle tune that chugged along quietly, but Milteau managed to get his message across. "Down at Utopia" was a mood piece that evoked warm summer nights of hot music at the Utopia Club. The song "Fun Home" was a very technical piece that was a pure joy for harmonica experts and aspiring players. The Elmore James classic "I Can't Hold Out" was also part of the set. Milteau won a Victoire de la Musique (French Grammy) for *Explorer*.

A dynamic stage performer, Milteau recorded *Live* on Saphir Records after making a number of studio albums. It contained such classics as "Sweet Home Chicago," "Key to the Highway," and "Further on up the Road." All of these songs were more than mere imitations of the originals; Milteau delivered these classics with an unmatched energy, making the songs his own. The album also included "I Got to Go (Tribute to Sonny Boy Williamson II)" and "Robert Johnson," which again showed off his impeccable technique. There were elements of blues, jazz, soul, rock, and pop on this record. But perhaps the most interesting aspect of the album was Milteau's ability to unify the diverse musicians and their talents into one rocking, swinging outfit. He proved that he was a fantastic bandleader.

The album *Roads* repeated the patterns of many of his earlier recordings as it contained a healthy dose of blues, French pop, jazz, Celtic overtones, and rock. In an attempt to further extend his sound, Milteau included the complex rhythms of South Africa that had caught his imagination on his last world tour. The first song, "Blues Bop," established the feel of the entire collection. It was a jazzy, soul-shaking number driven by Milteau's brilliant harmonica playing. "Miss Boogie" was a true rocker. "Marcel and Marcella" was a pure example of the French popular waltz, pushed down interesting blues avenues by Milteau's ingenious playing.

Milteau tipped his hat (or you could say his harmonica) to Celtic music with the song "The Sailor and the Maid." The territory that Milteau covered on this album was simply phenomenal.

Milteau, never one to shy away from experimentation, recorded *Thanks for Coming*, honoring the Marine Band harmonica. He inserted himself in a group ensemble that featured many of France's best and most famous pop singers and made sure that the harp was part of the band but never at the forefront. Once again, Milteau covered a lot of musical territory. The song "Lonesome Crowd" was a hard rocker, while "When I Get Back Home in the Evening" had a slow, country-blues feel to it. The tune "Big Walter," a tribute to the late great harmonica player, featured the wide bends that had made him a legend in France and throughout the world. "Willie and Leadbelly" sounded like a 1930s Delta original instead of a song created halfway around the world in 1995.

Another experimental album was *Le Grand Blues Band & J. J. Milteau*. Milteau was always willing to take part in a jam session, and this album had a 1940s big-band feel to it. Among the highlights of the record was "Walking by Myself," a genuine rocker with Milteau blowing like a hurricane though he never went for the overkill. In "Fallin' Back in Love with You," Milteau helped the song shuffle along smoothly with his well-paced riffs. "Satisfy Susie," one of a few Lonnie Mack compositions covered on the album, had a modern swing feel guaranteed to please fans of both the blues and jazz.

*Bastille Blues*, Milteau's latest effort, is another mixture of several styles that include blues, rock, jazz, pop, and French folk music. Milteau sounds terrific on every cut, especially the title track. Without a doubt this album proves that Milteau should take his place among the best harmonica players in the world.

Today, Milteau continues to record and perform in his native country and all over the world.

J. J. Milteau is a blues breath of fresh air. In the past thirty years he has managed to put France on the blues map with his love of the blues, his genuine passion, and his incomparable skill. Milteau has raised eyebrows everywhere he has played and created a distinguished career with his noteworthy albums. With the appeal of the blues around the world, Milteau has assumed a leadership role in the French blues movement. Despite an impressive catalog and some memorable concert appearances, however, he remains one of the best-kept secrets in the blues.

Much of the Milteau mystique is based on his brilliant ability. He can blow crisp, hard Chicago blues riffs with the best of them or play it soft and mournful, creating the saddest of blues. He is comfortable in a big-band ensemble, a small combo, as part of a duo, or as a solo artist.

But most importantly, there is a genuine groove to Milteau's harmonica work. His music swings whether he is playing straight blues, rock, jazz, or some other blues-based music. His ability to play catchy riffs, sweet melodies, and rocking rhythm lines enables him to satisfy the tastes of all blues harmonica lovers.

Milteau plays a variety of Marine Band Hohner harmonicas almost exclusively, as did many of his heroes including Sonny Boy Williamson I and Sonny Terry. Each harmonica has a different tonality. The sounds he is able to draw from the instruments are incredible. In concert, he shakes the audience using a standard Shure Bêta 58 amplifier with a "Thierry Cardon" volume pot.

Milteau's influences run deep and wide. The efforts of Norton Buffalo, Bob Dylan, and the early records of the Rolling Stones touched him in a specific way. His study of the prominent 1960s jazz instrumentalists Miles Davis, Chet Baker, John Coltrane, and Sonny Rollins enabled him to reach greater dimensions with his sharp harmonica talents. He also developed a taste for the records of Stevie Wonder, George Benson, Billy Cobham, Stanley Clarke, and other musical personalities of the 1970s. Another 1970s power harp player that Milteau greatly admired was Magic Dick of the J. Geils Band.

But undoubtedly he was most strongly influenced by the great American harp players. Sonny Terry taught Milteau the importance of emotion, that even the greatest technical players are only as good as the passion they put into every note. Little Walter demonstrated the need for timing and the expert control of amplification.

Milteau is one of the best harmonica players in Europe and is a rival of the elite modern American blues harpists—Kim Wilson, Rod Piazza, William Clarke, Charlie Musselwhite, Billy Branch, and Paul Butterfield. Unfortunately, because he has not received the same exposure as the aforementioned harmonica players, Milteau remains undiscovered on a truly international level. However, it is only a matter of time until Milteau breaks through and is granted the true credit he deserves.

He has often been called the "father of French harmonica blues," and one need only listen to his recordings to understand why this statement is true. The first generation of French blues singers, like all other initiators of the blues in their respective countries, have blazed the path for others to follow. Milteau has been a special influence on Greg Szlapczynski: They have played many concerts together, and even co-wrote an instruction booklet called "The Complete Method of the Diatonic and Chromatic Harp."

Milteau is just one of a talented group of French blues singers that includes Vincent Bucher, Greg Szlapczynski, Paul Personne, Steve Verbeke, Benoit Blue Boy, Pascal Mikaelian, Laurent Cagnon, David Herzhaft, Xavier Laune, Michel Herblin, Sébastien Charlier, Nico Wayne Toussaint, Bruno Kowalczyk, Olivier Ker Ourio, and Thierry Crommen. The French blues scene is one of the most vibrant in the world. As one of the godfathers of French blues, Milteau remains one of the best spokesmen for the genre.

A list of the people Milteau has worked with would be a book unto itself, with many key players. Eddie Mitchell, the famous French blues/rock/pop singer, gave Milteau his first big break. Jean-Yves d'Angelo is a pianist who appears on many of Milteau's albums and has also served as a producer for a number of the great French harp player's efforts. While Milteau has recorded with many different guitarists, Mann Galvin has served as his main guitar player for a long time. In return, Milteau has played on albums recorded by Mitchell, d'Angelo, Galvin, the vocalist Michel Jonasz, and Nogaro, a French jazz singer, as well as many other members of the entertainment scene in France over the years.

As one of the brightest stars of the French blues movement, Milteau has also given back to the community in order to ensure that the flame of the French blues continues to burn. A perfect example is his album *Leo Discovers the Blues*, dedicated to helping young children discover the joy of the blues. An interesting story that deals with the history of the blues and the emotion needed to play this style of music, it is an excellent introduction for children who want to learn about the music. It is this type of effort that ensures that the next generation will grow up with a respect for the blues.

Like "foreign" blues artists Yuri Naumov, Shun Kikuta, Javier Vargas, Zucchero, Silvan Zingg, Rory Gallagher, Dave Hole, Sven Zetterberg, and Hans Theessink, Milteau has helped spread the popularity of the blues throughout his native country and the world. He has proven that the blues spirit lives on in many different forms.

Like Sonny Boy Williamson I, Milteau is a blues pioneer. In the Deep South, John Lee took the harmonica from its humble beginnings and made it an important element in a blues band. Milteau has introduced the blues harmonica in his country, ensuring its widespread acceptance throughout France and the rest of Europe. Milteau is also a starting point for French audiences who have gone on to discover old blues masters like Williamson.

The importance of blues singers like J. J. Milteau cannot be overstated. He has carried on where visiting bluesmen have left off. He has performed concerts all over Europe, as well as in blues-starved countries like Madagascar, Singapore, and China. A friendly man with a disarming charm, he visits and talks with local musicians, sharing his blues knowledge. The appearance of an authentic blues singer from some place other than the United States helps other aspiring blues musicians from poorer, underdeveloped nations believe there is a way out of their difficult situation.

With an interesting and varied discography, Milteau ranks as one of the most intriguing international blues singers today. His blues wailings are infectious and his deep emotion shines through his brilliant playing, leaving no doubt of his genuine love for the blues. Above all, Milteau has proven with his French harp blues that one does not have to be born in Chicago, the Delta, or some other part of the United States to make an impact on the music.

## Discography

*33 Toures*, Le Chant du Monde LDX 74524.
*L'Harmonica* (*The Harmonica*), Le Chant du Monde LDX 74524.
*New Bluesgrass Collection*, Le Chant du Monde LDX 74565.
*Blues Harp*, Le Chant du Monde LDX 74718.
*Explorer*, Saphir Records 192001.
*Live*, Saphir Records 192007.
*Routes* (*Roads*), EMI 8356392.
*Thanks for Coming.*
*Merci d'Etres Venus*, Odeon Records 8534322.
*Léo Découvrets le Blues* (*Leo Discovers the Blues*).
*Bastille Blues.*
*Le Grand Blues Band & J. J. Milteau.*

====

# SVEN ZETTERBERG

*Swedish Blues*

The blues-rock marriage of the 1960s inspired many young musicians not only in North America and Great Britain but the world over. Long after the divorce, many musicians continued to produce a fiery brand of blues-rock. In Sweden, a young guitar hero was keenly intent on keeping the blues-rock flame alive. His Swedish blues are a testimony to his determination and grit. His name is Sven Zetterberg.

Sven Zetterberg was born in 1952, in Skärblacka, Sweden. His musical awakening occurred when he was twelve years old and was introduced to the hard-driving harmonica riffs of Little Walter and Big Walter Horton. He became enchanted with the music and began to teach himself the harmonica. Later on, when he heard the ringing guitars of Eric Clapton, Jimi Hendrix, Jeff Beck, and Jimmy Page he switched over to the six-stringed instrument.

In his late teens he moved to Södertälje, near Stockholm, where he formed his first professional band, the Telge Bluesorkester. Like any other blues band just starting out trying to make a name in the music business, Telge Bluesorkester played every chance that came their way. They became one of the most popular bar bands on the Swedish club scene and Zetterberg's reputation as a blossoming guitar hero was established.

Telge Bluesorkester was a powerhouse band that included guitarist Big Texas Stoffe Sundlöf. Zetterberg and Sundlöf developed a strong friendship that has lasted thirty years. Together the two big Swedes have always been a dynamic package; they complement each other in a way few musicians do.

After the disbanding of Telge Bluesorkester, Sven formed Blue Fire, and, despite several personnel changes, carried on. Blue Fire eventually evolved into Chicago Express and the group recorded four albums. Though his duties with Chicago Express kept him extremely busy, Zetterberg also found time to participate in a Norwegian-Swedish blues and soul outfit called Four Roosters. The Four Roosters included Knut Reiersrud, a noted Norwegian blues-rock star on guitar.

Like every other blues singer born outside of America, Zetterberg's dream had always been to travel to the original home of the blues. In 1979, he finally got the chance to do just that. He was accompanied by four of his fellow countrymen and together they explored the Chicago blues scene. Zetterberg, who possesses an outgoing personality, was quick to make contacts with the bluesmen he deeply respected.

In 1983, Zetterberg returned to Chicago and had the opportunity to record an album with some of the city's finest bluesmen. The group, named Chicago Blues Meeting, consisted of a Scandinavian contingent that included Zetterberg, Slim Notini, Knut Reiersrud, and Torbjorn Sunde. The Chicago portion of the lineup included veterans S. P. Leary and Sunnyland Slim. The collection of songs was made up of Chicago blues standards and four Zetterberg compositions, including "Snake in My Room," which was the title of the record. An interesting concept, the effort underlined the vast differences between the Scandinavian blues musicians and the American-born bluesmen, creating a batch of unevenly performed songs.

Zetterberg also had the opportunity to show off his hot Swedish licks at Buddy Guy's birthday party, where his teaming with Junior Wells was one of the highlights of the evening. Once he had been fully accepted into the Chicago Blues singers' circle, he shared the stage with some of the biggest names, including Jimmy Rogers, Jimmy McCracklin, Lonesome Sundown, Louisiana Red, Sunnyland Slim, Eddie C. Campbell, Big Moose Walker, Luther Allison, and Eddie Boyd.

Zetterberg returned to Sweden and continued to tour and record with his band Chicago Express. After ten years of dominating the Swedish bar club scene as the number one attraction, the Chicago Express played one final concert and then disbanded. The performance was recorded and the album, *Steppin' Out—Alive!* contained some uptempo Chicago blues, a smattering of jazz, and pile-driving rock. With songs like "Tip on In," "All for Business," "Rambler's Blues," "The Groove," and "Don't Slow Me Down," it was easy to see why they were the top blues band in Sweden for over ten years.

Despite the breakup of the group, Sven remained visible in the music scene with a variety of projects, including his first solo album, *Blues from Within*. Again he mixed a variety of styles, including Chicago blues, Texas blues, soul, and rock, to create an exciting contemporary effort. Some of the highlights of *Blues from Within* included "People Don't Do Like They Used to Do," done in the style of the soul-blues of Bobby Blue Bland. "Plenty of Everything," a Zetterberg original, was a tribute to T-Bone Walker and his funky Texas blues shuffle. The song really rocked, reminding one of the rock-and-roll side of Stevie Ray Vaughan. Zetterberg displayed his deep roots with a period performance of "My Deepest Emotions," a homage to the driving, boogie-blues-rock of Fats Domino during his heyday. Zetterberg also paid tribute to B. B. King by doing a cover version of "You're Breaking My Heart."

Zetterberg was also able to balance his studio achievements with live performances. In 1993, he became one of the few European blues singers to appear in Africa. The eleven-day tour in Maputo, Mozambique, produced a genuine excitement and broke new ground for European blues groups. The blues that had originated from Africa had returned home through the efforts of Zetterberg and his bandmates.

Today, Zetterberg continues to tour with his own band, a quartet that consists of Kael Fahleryd on the upright bass, Bosse Skoglund on the drums, and Pelle Piano on keyboards. Never one to relax much, Zetterberg is involved in numerous other projects, including Knock Out Greg and Blue Weather, as well as taking part in the Southern soul band, Sweet Pain. He can often be found playing at the Rackis, one of Sweden's top blues bars, a stopping place for many blues greats including Junior Wells,

Luther Allison, Lazy Lester, Kenny Neal, Robert Cray, and Louisiana Red, among others.

Sven Zetterberg is a modern European blues artist. He is a master guitarist and harmonica player whose recording catalog has been inconsistent; but, no matter the project, Sven has always contributed wholeheartedly with his spirit and talent. Although he is a legend in his native Sweden and other parts of Europe, he has never made a large impact on the North American market. However, he has been instrumental in furthering the appeal of the blues on the international stage and has dedicated his career to playing uplifting, hard blues around the planet.

Zetterberg is a hard-crunching blues guitar player capable of intense dynamics. A large, hulking man, he injects every ounce of power into his playing. While his first blues sound was pure Chicago style, he has adopted the hard rock shades of many of the groups of the late 1960s and early 1970s eras. Led Zeppelin, Jimi Hendrix, Cream, The Jeff Beck Group, and Savoy Brown are just some of the bands that had a direct influence on the development of his guitar style.

But Zetterberg has stretched beyond the sometimes-narrow limits of blues-rock, extending his playing into the realm of jazz and soul. A musician with terrific intuition, his ability to jam on long instrumental breaks is just one of his many talents as a guitarist. He can hammer out hard-driving riffs or play it sweet and soft, melting the notes into beautiful pools of blues drops.

Zetterberg has kept two blues schools alive through his career. Although the blues-rock union faded many years ago, he has been able to maintain interest in the hybrid genre with his potent, fluid guitar chops. He is also one of the best Chicago-style guitarists playing outside the Windy City. He is capable of tearing out burning licks from his Stratocaster in the same vein as Otis Rush, Buddy Guy, and Magic Sam.

Not surprisingly, there is another interesting aspect to Zetterberg's music. Although he is best known as a solid blues rocker with a smattering of jazz and soul thrown in for good measure, he has never forgotten his roots. Traces of Swedish folk songs can be heard in his playing, which have brought him full circle. While bringing the blues from the outside world into Sweden, he has also brought the down-home music of Sweden to the outside world.

Zetterberg has earned the title of "godfather of Swedish blues" with good reason. He has blazed a trail for other Swedish blues bands to follow. Homesick Mack, The Blue Pearls, Bluesdogys, Jenny Behman, Brickyard, Tommy Cougar, The Instigators, Per and the Ouagadugu Boogie Oogie Band, and Wailler's Blues are just a few of the bands now touring the Swedish blues circuit. The blues scene in Sweden is as healthy as in any other part of Europe thanks in large part to the efforts of Sven Zetterberg.

Sven Zetterberg is like Old Man River as he just keeps rolling along, playing his venues and recording at every opportunity available to him. He has done much to put Sweden on the world blues map. The next step for Zetterberg is to break through to the North American market and gain the recognition his unique brand of Swedish blues deserves.

## Discography

*Blues from Within*, Amigo 2035.

With Chicago Express:
*Blues Around the Clock*, Pipaluck 3.
*The Blue Solution*, Amigo AMCD 2020.
*Watch Your Step!* Amigo AMCD 2026.
*Permanently Blue*, Amigo AMCD 2030.
*Steppin' Out—Alive!* Amigo 2033.

With Four Roosters:
*Rooster Blues*, Hot Club 2.

Chicago Blues Meeting:
*Snake in My Room*, Drive 3206.

---

# ZUCCHERO

## *Sweet Italian Blues*

The rich musical heritage of Italy is firmly imbedded in opera, and the country is famous for producing world-class opera singers. Italians are also famous for their traditional songs of *amore*, tender love ballads that make the heart swell with visions of passionate nights. In the past few years, however, the pulsating voice of the blues has gained a foothold in Italy's entertainment scene. The man most responsible for the upturn in blues fortunes is known for his sweet Italian blues. His name is Zucchero.

Zucchero was born Adelmo Fornaciari on September 25, 1955, in Roncocesi, Italy. He made his first musical connection through the church, singing in a choir and eventually learning to play the organ. He might have become a famous liturgical singer or perhaps an opera star had it not been for his discovery of the blues when he was thirteen. He immediately formed a garage band called New Lights, and, when that band folded, joined other groups of aspiring musicians from around the neighborhood. The bands usually played a mixture of rhythm and blues, the current pop hits of the day, and some good old-fashioned rock and roll. But the blues was Zucchero's first love.

After years of paying his blues dues traveling around Italy and other parts of Europe, Zucchero caught his first big break when he performed at the San Remo Festival in 1983, where he won the competition that paved the way for him to record his first album, *Un Po' di Zucchero*. Though it actually did little to advance his career, *Un Po' di Zucchero* introduced the combination of pop ballads and blues rhythms that would someday make him a household name throughout Europe.

Like many other international blues singers, Zucchero dreamed of going to America to study the blues firsthand. He eventually made the trip to the home of the blues and immediately hooked up with the Randy Jackson band. Jackson, a bass player with solid blues credentials, helped Zucchero gain a slight foothold in America. Their album, *Zucchero and the Randy Jackson Band*, contained the single, "Donne," which was Zucchero's first taste of success. It was a foreshadowing of future developments.

Usually it takes an artist some time to learn how to make albums that are both critical and commercial successes. However, with his very next release, *Rispetto*, Zucchero threatened to smash sales records in his native Italy. His folksy/Italian blues style struck a major chord with the record-buying public. Zucchero was the only Italian artist who was making blues-flavored down-home albums. The title track, "Rispetto," was one of the highlights of the album.

His next effort, *Blues*, catapulted Zucchero to superstar status as it became the best-selling album in Italy's history. It was his first taste of true success and it was very sweet. His reputation spread quickly throughout Europe. The songs on the record ran together like a smooth, fine Italian wine. The record began with "Blues Introduction," and segued nicely into "Con Le Mani." While most of the songs had Italian titles, the songs "Into the Groove" and "Hey Man" gave the album more of an international appeal. The instrumental "Dune Mosse" showed Zucchero at his best as he flashed his power, clearly demonstrating why he deserved the media attention that was about to fall down upon him.

The album *Oro Incenso & Birra* was another smash hit. It contained the single "Without a Woman," a duet with Paul Young that topped the charts in 1991. Zucchero became one of the biggest names in international blues. His blues-flavored material challenged the supreme reign that opera and pop had enjoyed on the Italian market for so long.

With his newfound power as one of the top-selling artists in the world confirmed, it was only a matter of time before people took notice. He appeared with Eric Clapton at the Royal Albert Hall, and a year later performed at the Freddie Mercury Tribute concert by special invitation of Brian May, Queen's underrated guitar player.

The album *Zucchero*, a greatest-hit package, featured "Diamante," one of his best-known songs, as well as "Wonderful Tonight," in collaboration with Eric Clapton. Zucchero had gained a tremendous amount of respect throughout the musical community. Other powerful songs on the record were "Dunes of Mercy," "You're Losing Me," "You've Chosen Me," and "Without a Woman." The mix of blues, pop, ballads, soul, and rock presented Zucchero as an international entertainer with a global appeal.

But perhaps his greatest triumph up to that point was his duet with Luciano Pavarotti, the world-famous Italian opera star, on the album *Misere*; this gained Zucchero widespread respect all over Italy. The two combined on the CD's title track, "Misere," and, as Pavarotti was the most popular entertainer in Italy, it was a brilliant strategic move for Zucchero. The songs "Brick," "Miss Mary," "The Promise," and "Gone Fishing" ensured that the CD would be another monster seller.

But the album was important for yet another reason, because it helped Zucchero prove that the blues was world music and belonged to everyone on the planet. He took his theory further by stating through the songs on the record that every strain of blues was the folk music of a particular group of people of a certain geographical area. Zucchero used every dimension of his talent to forge a very successful career singing blues music that touched everyone's life.

The album *Spirito DiVino* became a hit in Germany, Switzerland, Belgium, the Netherlands, and France, selling millions of copies. It featured a hypnotic groove in songs like "Voodoo, Voodoo," "No More Regrets," "Feels Like a Woman," "Come in Love," and "Diamante," despite the various musical styles. The theme of love—a universal one—was therefore appealing to a broad cross section of people all around the world. His ability to mix ballads, rhythm-and-blues fire, Italian folk music, pop, soul, and funk was a winning formula. The European tour he undertook to support the album was a celebration and earned him many accolades. Another major victory for Zucchero was his solo tour of North America in such cities as Los Angeles, New York, Chicago, San Francisco, Toronto, and Mexico City.

The next release, *The Best of Zucchero*, was another smash hit, selling several million copies and spawning another tour through Canada, the United States, and Latin America. Despite his vast fortune and incredible success, Zucchero still found time to play in a benefit for the Rain Forest Foundation in New York City. The concert helped the vital cause to save what is left of the world's tropical rain forest; it also shed a favorable light on Zucchero's personality that gained him a few more fans.

The next CD, *Overdose d'Amore*, was a compilation of his best ballads and demonstrated another side of this multi-talented individual. There was a blues shade to many of the songs on the record. His duet with Sheryl Crow on "Blue" dripped hot liquid blues. "Va Pensiero" had a strong contemporary rhythm-and-blues feel. "Mi Mucio Per Te," a duet with Sting, was a heavily polyrhythmic flavored number that borrowed interesting ideas from the West Indies. His smash duet with Pavarotti, "Misere," was also included on this album.

He continues to tour and record.

Zucchero is a blues superstar. He has sold countless albums across the world and has played thousands of concerts. He has created his own world of blues, one that is laced with blues, Italian folk ideas, pop, rhythm and blues, and soul. He is a passionate singer who is able to deliver blues songs like droplets of gold. There is something catchy about his songs. He has been able to assimilate a variety of musical styles into a very successful formula. Zucchero has developed a knack for writing blues songs that contain functional lyrics, inspired playing, and a polished appeal to a wide, global audience.

Besides Pavarotti, he has played with Miles Davis, Eric Clapton. Joe Cocker, Bono, Ray Charles, Sting, to name a few. The long list of illustrious names that Zucchero has been associated with is a good indication of the respect he has earned in the musical community. Ironically, when he first started his career, any chance of appearing with some important blues name was considered a big break; after his incredible success, many musicians now are scrambling to appear with *him*.

A self-taught multi-instrumentalist, Zucchero plays keyboards, guitar, drums, and bass with equal proficiency. Though he has never totally mastered any of the instruments he plays, his musical knowledge of each one allows him the creative room to experiment when writing his songs. There is an honesty in his playing that shines through with true professionalism.

His voice is a study in contrasts. It is not the rich voice of Pavarotti, nor is it a thin, nasal whine; Zucchero's voice is suited to the type of blues that he plays. His vocals have a soft yet convincing quality that takes the listener on a musical journey through the world he creates with his interesting musical abilities. His voice is immediately recognizable because of its distinct quality.

While his albums have sold over twenty million copies worldwide, his touring schedule is just as impressive. He is a favorite in his native Italy, appearing in different venues throughout the year. He has also appeared in Switzerland, Germany, Austria, Belgium, the Netherlands, France, Spain, Finland, Norway, Estonia, Russia, Lithuania, England, Ireland, the Czech Republic, Poland, Ukraine, Croatia, Monaco, Portugal, Tunisia, the United States, Canada, and Venezuela. He also performed at Woodstock in 1994, the only Continental artist to do so.

Zucchero is one of the few European blues artists today to enjoy such commercial success. Often, blues records are under-promoted and do not register the sales that they should. But Zucchero has found a way to present commercial material while not giving up his artistic blues identity. He plays and sings the music that comes from his heart.

Zucchero is the father of the Italian blues and, though he may stray afield once in a while, he never does leave the blues fold altogether. He is an international success story who has done as much as anyone to promote the blues on a global level. Though he may be an acquired taste in certain circles, especially to those who are more accustomed to a harsher blues sound, a careful listen to Zucchero will sweep you away with his sweet Italian blues.

## Discography

*Un Po' di Zucchero.*
*Zucchero and the Randy Jackson Band*, London 849063-2.
*Live in Moscow*, Alex 2263.
*Rispetto*, Alex 2642.
*Blues*, Alex 2641.
*Oro, Incenso & Birra*, Alex 2640.
*Zucchero*, London 849063-2.
*Misere*, Polygram 517097.
*Spirito DiVino*, Polydor 529271.
*Diamante*, Polygram 521808.
*Blue Sugar*, Polygram 559368.
*The Best of Zucchero*, Polygram 47084.
*Overdose d'Amore*, ARK 21850006.

# JAVIER VARGAS

## *Madrid Blues*

In Spain, where the classical guitar reigns supreme, other kinds of music are often relegated to a secondary role. Nevertheless, some guitarists have managed to retain the varied and rich tradition of Spanish-style guitar in their music while exploring different paths. Spain's premier blues artist has been able to meld the music of his birthright with his love of different blues textures to create his Madrid Blues. His name is Javier Vargas.

Javier Vargas was born in 1955 in Madrid. At the age of six he moved to Argentina, in Mar del Plata, near Buenos Aires. It was here that he was exposed to the music of the Beatles, the Rolling Stones and the Who on the radio; and later, in his early teens, he began to teach himself to play the guitar. Vargas followed in the traditional footsteps of the guitarists who were national heroes in Spain by adopting the classical guitar style. Once he had learned the rudiments of guitar, Vargas was eager to begin a musical career as a classical guitarist. But when he was introduced to the blues, his musical path was changed forever.

Because of the dearth of blues music in Spanish-speaking countries, Javier was forced to acquire his blues fix from imports and a close-knit group of friends who shared his passion. Thus, groups like Led Zeppelin, The Jimi Hendrix Experience, Cream, the Jeff Beck Group, all notable blues scholars, fueled Javier's desire to unlock the secrets of the genre. However, it wasn't until he moved to the United States in 1988 that Vargas could immerse himself in the authentic blues that would dictate the course of his musical career.

While in the United States, Javier lived in New York, Chicago, and Nashville. Everywhere he went he impressed older blues singers with his touch on the guitar and the power he was able to draw from the instrument. Vargas was not partial to any specific blues form; he studied them all. Slowly, a distinctive style emerged from the many forces that influenced Javier as a musician. Upon his return to Spain, in 1991, he formed the Vargas Blues Band to play the music that had inspired him while growing up.

The band's first album, *All Around Blues*, established a pattern that subsequent releases would follow. Most of the songs on the record were written or co-written by Vargas with the exception of a couple of blues classics. On *All Around Blues*, Vargas included "Rock Me Baby" and "Hideaway." But more importantly, the variety of styles he brought together was truly amazing. There were blues, Latin rhythms, rock, funk, rhythm and blues, and elements of flamenco.

Though *All Around Blues* gained the band some attention, the second release, *Madrid-Memphis*, was even broader in scope. It included Chicago veteran harmonica player Carey Bell, Louisiana Red, and flamenco guitarist Rafael Riqueni. The album kicked off with "Hard Time Blues," a true rocker. It was followed by other scorching songs like "Madrid-Memphis," "Generation Blues," "I'm Ready," "Strip-Tease," "2001 Blues," and "Del Sur." The album greatly reinforced the support that the Vargas Blues Band received in their native Spain; however, they had not yet attained true international stardom.

The third release, *Blues Latino*, left no doubt that Vargas was the real thing as his tasty guitar work sparked interest in corners that the band had not yet been heard in. The record burned with intensity on such numbers as "Rock Away the Blues," "Out of the Blues," "Hot Wires," "Blues Latino," "Magic of the Gods," "Mexico City Blues," and the outstanding medley "Pachuco Boogie/Jeff's Boogie." With the help of Chris Rea, Junior Wells, Flaco Jimenez, and Andres Calmaro, the album provided something for everyone. Vargas intelligently used the blues as a foundation from which to explore other musical ideas like rock, soul, flamenco, and tinges of jazz.

The band was picking up momentum and played festivals throughout their native land and Europe. Their appearance in Buenos Aires cemented their grip on the Spanish-language blues market. The Vargas Blues Band opened for Santana and received rave reviews. Vargas and Santana, guitar blood brothers, genuinely admired one another's abilities. The concert greatly enhanced Vargas's stature in the blues-rock community.

*Texas Tango* was Vargas's first album to be produced in the United States (Austin and Memphis). It featured guest appearances by Double Trouble, Larry T. Thurston, and Preston Shannon. It indicated the respect that Vargas had gained in the blues and world-music communities in a relatively short time. Vargas and his band proved their mettle on tracks like "Texas Tango," "Blues Pilgrimage," "Ride Baby Ride," "Black Cat Boogie," "Buenos Aires Blues," "Big Boss Man," and "Blood Shot."

With the release of each new album, a new concert venue opened up. The band played France and Portugal, and the Montreux Jazz Festival in Switzerland. Later the same year the Vargas Blues Band and Santana shared the stage together again, this time in Paris. The dual delight of seeing and hearing these two top guitar players thrilled the crowd. Back home, Vargas often opened up for bands passing through, including Santana and the artist formerly known as Prince.

*Gipsy Boogie*, Vargas's fifth album, was recorded in Madrid and Memphis, with the final mixing done in the United States. The album fused Vargas's love of blues and flamenco to create a unique sound that was all his own. With a collection of songs including "Blues for My Baby," "Back Alley Blues," "Gipsy Boogie," the Albert King classic "Born Under a Bad Sign," and "Blues Hondo," his original compositions sparkled with the brilliance of a seasoned songwriter and his cover versions were exceptional. The album also included the participation of flamenco artists Raimundo Amador, Carles Benavent, La Chonchi and the Cuban singer David Montes, as well as blues-soul-rock artists Chester Thomson, Lonnie Brooks, Larry McCray, Little Jimmy King, David Allen, and Larry Graham.

For the sixth album, *Feedback*, Vargas switched to England for the recording sessions. The album featured a veritable Who's Who of musicians, including Gary Moore, Bob Dylan, Mark Knopfler, Cheap Trick, and David Montes, the former singer of the Bobby Alexander Band. The album contained the usual number of Vargas compositions and a cover version of the Led Zeppelin killer, "Whole Lotta Love," for which, instead of the heavy blues riff of the original, Vargas chose a Latin-oriented beat as background rhythm. Other notable tunes on the album included "Back to the City," "Sangre Española," "Para Guarachar," "Spanish Fly," and "NYC Blues."

*Bluestrology* was the seventh album recorded by Vargas. It was another stellar effort and included a rousing version of the Willie Dixon classic, "Backdoor Man." Other highlights of the record were "Troubled Mind," "Wild West Blues," "Bluestrology," "Bound for Memphis," "Promised Land," "You've Got to Move," "Free Spirits," and "Traveling South." Vargas proved once and for all that he was one of the top guitar players in the world with this collection of songs. His tasty blues-rock-jazz and Latin-flavored style was pure pleasure for any blues fan anywhere in the world.

Vargas continues to perform with different musicians from around the world. One of his best efforts was with newcomer Chris Duarte, in Texas, in 1999. The two smoking guitars were a treat for all those in attendance.

Javier Vargas is a blues hero in his native Spain. He is easily and rightfully credited with the title of father of Spanish blues. But Vargas is more than just an average blues singer; he is something special. He has been able to combine elements of blues, rock, Latin, flamenco, and soul to create something that is his very own. He is one of the more interesting international blues singers anywhere.

Vargas was strongly influenced by Carlos Santana and the twin guitars often sound eerily the same. Like Santana, Vargas possesses a magical touch, an ability to fuse several forms into one cohesive sound. Though he has not enjoyed the same international success as Santana, Vargas remains one of the best blues/Latin guitar players in the world.

Guitar players who fused blues and rock together, such as Jeff Beck, Eric Clapton, Jimmy Page, Keith Richards, Mick Taylor, and Peter Green, also influenced him. The guitar wizardry of Jimi Hendrix also had a pronounced effect on Vargas's development. Later, he discovered Albert King, B. B. King, Albert Collins, Buddy Guy, and the entire legion of blues guitar legends who also had a helping hand in shaping his overall sound.

But Vargas is more than an imitator of heavy guitar riffs and clichés. He is an inventive guitarist, able to retrieve the best elements of the styles of legendary guitarists and create something fresh and new. No one combines the blues/flamenco styles better than Vargas does. He is also able to play it sweet and soft; his albums are filled with emotional instrumentals that demonstrate a more delicate, sensitive touch.

He cuts a dashing figure on stage, in the same mode as Jimi Hendrix and Stevie Ray Vaughan. His overall fashion sense of zebra vests, gangster hats, and common dress of the Spanish citizen is all part of the Javier Vargas package. He is able to project an image of calculated coolness on stage, one that adds an essential visual personality to his musical prowess.

Vargas is another example of the profound influence American blues has had on the music of the world. Though not a pure blues singer in the traditional sense, he is more of a modern bluesman, combining all forms of music he loves into his playing. As he continues to astound audiences with his easy guitar skills and genuine understanding of the subtle blues language, Vargas convinces unbelievers that his Madrid blues is a winning formula.

## Discography

*All Around Blues*, DRG
*Madrid-Memphis*, DRG
*Blues Latino*, DRG
*Texas Tango*, DRG
*Gipsy Boogie*, DRG
*Feedback*, DRG
*Bluestrology*, DRG

# YURI NAUMOV

## *Renegade Russian Blues*

In the old Soviet Union the influence of Western culture was severely frowned upon by the ruling Communist Party. The hard-driving blues-rock of Led Zeppelin, the Doors, the Rolling Stones, and other outlawed groups was deemed a tool of corruption. But, thanks to the black market, blues fever could not be totally suppressed, and it gave rise to some musicians who dared to defy the authorities. From this dark truth emerged the creator of the renegade Russian blues. His name is Yuri Naumov.

Yuri Naumov was born in 1963, in the Soviet Union. Upon hearing the blues-inspired rock of the Beatles, Led Zeppelin, and the Rolling Stones, he decided before he was ten to become a rock star. Though records of his favorite bands were difficult to obtain, Naumov managed to buy them on the black market. Despite his best intentions, however, the opportunities for becoming a full-fledged rock star in the Soviet Union were very poor.

Eventually, Naumov abandoned his dream of becoming a rock-and-roll star and instead decided to pursue a career in medicine. It was while studying to become a doctor in Siberia that the genuine blues touched Yuri. The experience rekindled an old flame and Naumov quit medical school to dedicate his life to his first love—the blues. A blues singer, a purely American-made product, was not the best career choice for someone living in a country that despised anything related to the United States. But Yuri was persistent.

Unfortunately for Naumov, the KGB was not impressed with his desire to become a blues musician. Naumov managed to stay one step ahead of the secret police, however, while spreading his particular brand of hard-edged blues throughout the Soviet Union. Like other artists, he was forced to go underground and perform discreetly. The defiant spirit of the blues—the same individual fire that enabled Charley Patton, Son House and Robert Johnson to become legends—ran strongly through Naumov's veins.

Though he was a man marked by the authorities, Naumov was a crowd favorite among his fellow countrymen. Since most of his blues training came from indirect sources—recordings by the Rolling Stones, Led Zeppelin, Cream, and other blues-rock bands—his blues contained a hard-rock edge. His secret concerts became very popular and he soon acquired a reputation as the top blues singer in the vast, cold Soviet Union.

However, his popularity was a double-edged sword: the more fame he gained the harder the secret police chased him.

Naumov sought the security of the larger cities like Moscow and Leningrad (now St. Petersburg again), but the KGB was never far behind. Finally, after spending the entire decade of the 1980s running, he moved to the United States, the original home of the blues. When he landed in New York City he realized that he had to restart his blues career. While he was a genuine rebel blues hero in Russia, in the United States he was just another aspiring blues singer with a guitar. Naumov, a self-taught musician, performed in the streets, in small clubs, and in and around public parks for spare change.

The determination and perseverance that had enabled him to outwit the KGB in his former country were two traits he took with him to America. He clawed his way from being an unknown blues musician to being one with an interesting reputation. After all, how many Russian blues singers were living in New York City at the time? Eventually Naumov built a decent following around the Big Apple. Russia's loss was the United States' gain.

Naumov, a clever individual, had one major advantage over many contemporary American bluesmen in the connections he still maintained with people in the music business all over the world. This ensured that he would always have a concert venue to play in different parts of the globe, including Israel, Germany, the Netherlands, and other parts of Europe. Also, once the Soviet Union collapsed, he could return triumphantly to his homeland like a conquering hero to play live in front of family and friends.

Even in the 1980s, Naumov was able to make a few records. The most outstanding was *1000 Days Blues*, recorded in 1986, which became available in the United States ten years later. Many of his previous recordings were made in a small studio on primitive equipment; some of the later reissues were re-mastered. Many of the albums he recorded in Russia where either destroyed, lost, or became collector's items. His first album released in the United States was *Violet*. The only other album available in North America is *1000 Days Blues*. Though he does not have a contract with a major label, Naumov still has many blues records to deliver to the world.

He continues to record and perform.

Yuri Naumov is a blues rarity. He has managed to overcome the many obstacles in his way in order to forge a respectable blues career. Though he is not yet well known in the United States, his international reputation is strong, especially in certain corners of the globe where he is highly respected. His ability to create and nurture a career under the most primitive and dangerous circumstances emphasizes not only his dogged determination but also the power of the blues.

Naumov's virtuosity is extremely well developed. He is capable of playing three guitar parts—bass, rhythm, and lead—simultaneously, making it sound as if he had a full band backing him up though he is performing solo. He shares many traits with the country-blues singers, including the use of his bare fingers, as well as being an excellent fingerpicker. Naumov also uses a number of minor and major tunings, a characteristic he shares with Skip James and Robert Johnson among others. He plays a nine-string instrument that was designed by one of Russian's leading violinmakers, Sergei Nazdrin.

Many musical elements make up the Naumov guitar style. He plays a brand of psychedelic-rock blues in the style of Cream and Jimi Hendrix, as well as a heavier rock-blues similar to Led Zeppelin, the Doors, and Stevie Ray Vaughan. He also incorporates the purer blues of Albert King, B. B. King, and Freddie King, as well as a trace of Russian folk music. His understanding of blues textures is remarkable, considering the many disadvantages he faced while developing his style.

He is an interesting songwriter who has written over a hundred songs both in English and in Russian; the majority are in his native tongue. His ability to write songs with English lyrics has greatly improved since his arrival in America. His poetic lyrics are very different from the usual blues lines because of his decidedly different point of view. As he blossoms as a blues composer there is a good chance that he may write a hit song that will catapult him to a more prominent position in the blues world.

In concert, Naumov is a real treat because of his versatility. He is a solo artist, a musician with his guitar, and performs songs in his native tongue and English. But not all of his renditions include lyrics; his instrumentals are haunting renditions that evoke spirits of Delta ghosts. Some of his concert staples include "New York, 5th Avenue," "Ping-Pong Blues," "Moscow Boogie," "Katafalk," and "Cosmos." Because of his background, his individual artistic vision, Naumov presents a totally different picture of what a blues singer sounds like; yet, like all other bluesmen, he is there to entertain the crowd.

There are similarities between the sources that inspire Naumov's songs and those of the original country minstrels. The blues were derived from one of the worst periods in American-African history when hunger, illiteracy, unemployment, lynchings, murder, and disease were common. In the old Soviet Union, conditions for many of the citizens were not much different from those endured by African Americans in the southern United States. Naumov's touching ballads of suppression and oppression stir the same kinds of emotion as Blind Lemon Jefferson's "Matchbox Blues," "Broke and Hungry," and "One Dime Blues."

Another characteristic that Naumov shares with the bluesmen of the 1920s and 1930s from the Delta and other Southern regions is the persecution he faced for playing the blues. The blues being considered "taboo" in the American South caused Robert Johnson, Charley Patton, Sun House, Big Joe Williams, and other Mississippi Delta bluesmen immense trouble from prejudiced law-enforcement officials. Naumov was considered a severe threat by the KGB for his spreading of the blues and was hunted down relentlessly. Fortunately, he survived to deliver his musical message to the world.

Yuri Naumov is the father of Russian blues. Like other foreign bluesmen—Sven Zetterberg, Hans Theessink, Shun Kikuta, Javier Vargas, Zucchero, Silvan Zingg—Naumov is the main exponent of the blues in his country. Though he currently lives in the United States, Naumov has not severed ties with his native land and plays occasional concerts there.

While his discography is slim, there exist many recordings in Russia. It would be wonderful if an American company reissued them, if the lost tapes could be found. Naumov is simply one of the most fascinating blues characters because of his background, his unbreakable spirit, and his undeniable talent. But, most importantly, like Charley Patton, Naumov has with his renegade Russian blues lit a fire in his native country that will burn forever.

## Discography

*1000 Days Blues*
*Violet*

# SHUN KIKUTA

## *Blues Made in Japan*

There has always been a market for American-made products in other countries of the world. The magic of Disney, the appeal of fast food, the allure of Hollywood, and the marvel of the American automobile are global fascinations. There is also the blues. Often, the blues created in other countries try to replicate the various American blues genres out of an admiration for the originators that borders on reverence. In the Land of the Rising Sun, one inspired blues singer has created his own blues, made in Japan to give to the world. His name is Shun Kikuta.

Shun Kikuta was born in Utsunomiya-city, a Tokyo suburb, in 1966. He developed an interest in music and at ten began to study the guitar under the tutelage of his father. During these formative years he explored different styles of music that took him away from his classical roots; he incorporated rock and roll and jazz into his overall development. By the time he was eighteen he had already decided what he wanted to do with his life. Shun—whose father owned a pickle factory—had decided against following in the family business. His heart was set on a musical career.

Kikuta moved to Boston when he was nineteen to study music at Berklee College. The institute had a solid reputation as a jazz school and Kikuta became one of its brightest students, learning the theoretical side of music. In the middle of his schooling he was turned on to the blues by a friend who played him a copy of "Live at the Regal," one of B. B. King's greatest recordings. Instantly, Kikuta caught blues fever and soon moved to Chicago in order to concentrate on learning the blues.

It was in Chicago that Kikuta began to pay his blues dues. He worked at a variety of jobs, including dishwasher, and in his spare time he played the guitar on street corners and in parks for tips. He also frequented the many blues clubs in the Windy City, waiting for the day when he would catch his first break. It came when he was invited by Louis Myers to play a weekly gig at Rosa's Lounge; Kikuta readily accepted the chair.

It didn't take long for the word to spread around the Chicago blues grapevine that a new talent had arrived in town and that he was something special. Kikuta later played with some of the legends of Chicago blues, including Junior Wells, Charlie Musselwhite, Louis Myers, Big Time Sarah, Johnny Littlejohn, J. W. Williams, Buddy Guy, and other acts like Johnny Clyde Copeland, the fire maker. In 1992, he toured Italy as a member of the Chicago Blues Night Band with J. W. Williams. The highlight of the tour was Kikuta's meeting with his idol, the great B. B. King, as the Chicago Blues Night Band opened for the legendary Chairman of the Board.

After returning from the tour, Kikuta caught another break when he was called by King Records to produce the new blues CD by the Frank Collier Band. The finished product, *Funky Blues*, included Junior Wells on harmonica and Kikuta on guitar. Though it didn't race to the top of the charts or win any special awards, the CD enabled Kikuta to expand his horizons and enhanced his résumé nicely.

Because of his previous work on the Collier CD, Kikuta was assigned as producer of a Magic Sam tribute collection. Magic Sam, the late great Chicago West Side bluesman, who, along with Buddy Guy and Otis Rush, was one of the premier stylists of Chicago blues in the 1960s, died too young. The CD, entitled *Tribute to Magic Sam*, featured performances by the J. W. Williams band, Magic Slim, Mighty Joe Young, and Eddie Shaw. It was a heartfelt project dedicated to a man who had influenced many future guitarists, including Kikuta. Some of the highlights of the tribute album were a rousing rendition of "Tore Down," an old Freddie King chestnut, and a slow, sorrowful version of "Reconsider Baby." The CD was the evidence of latter-day Chicago blues lights paying homage to a great from the past.

In 1995, after appearing as a session player, Kikuta recorded his own album. *They Call Me Shun* was released on the King label and proved that Kikuta had learned his lessons well. It was a rollicking Chicago-blues-style record that showcased Kikuta's fine guitar work and also featured J. W. Williams and his Chi-Town Hustlers. Williams handled most of the vocal chores and there were special guest appearances by Otis Rush and Junior Wells. The album boasted a few power cuts, including "Me and My Guitar," "Same Old Blues," "Let Me Love You Baby," "I'll Play the Blues for You," and the touching "Memory of Louis." Though the album did not gain Kikuta instant stardom, it was a fine debut from one of the lesser-known but up-and-coming Chicago blues guitarists.

Kikuta followed his debut album with *Chicago Midnight*, a gritty effort that certainly won him new friends. It featured the smooth guitar lines that Kikuta rolled out with relative ease and the fine musicianship of J. W. Williams and the Chi-Town Hustlers. With guest appearances by Koko Taylor singing on two tracks, Billy Branch playing harmonica on a couple of cuts, and Eddie Shaw blowing tenor saxophone on the "Rib Tips with Hot Sauce" number, the record was quite entertaining. It was also clearly evident that Kikuta had acquired a degree of respect in the Chicago blues community. Other highlights of the album included "Four Crowns," "Drinking Gasoline," "Big Boss Man," "I'm Gonna Get Lucky," and the title song, "Chicago Midnight."

By this time Kikuta was a permanent member of J. W. Williams and the Chi-Town Hustlers, one of the most promising blues bands on the scene. They toured out-of-state and became regular fixtures at some of Chicago's finest clubs, including an almost permanent residency at the Kingston Mines. They also frequently played at Artis's Lounge. The band was composed of Kikuta on guitar, J. W. Williams on vocals and bass, Johnny "Fingers" Iguana on keyboards, Al Brown on bass, Jerry Porter and Brady Williams on drums, Bill McFarland on trombone, Kenny Anderson on trumpet, and Hank Ford on tenor sax.

After making his mark in the United States, Kikuta returned to his homeland and played at the 1996 Park Tower Blues Festival in Tokyo. Once again, his good friends J. W. Williams and the Chi-Town Hustlers backed him. It was a triumphant moment for Kikuta, who has been hailed as the father of Japanese blues back in his native land. The performance was recorded and the album *Live! The 3rd Park Tower Blues Festival '96/Shun Kikuta & J.W. Williams* was released on King Records in 1997.

The album included live cuts of "Drinking Gasoline," "Love of Mine," "Blues with a Feelin'," and two medleys, "Turning Point—Turn Back the Hands of Time/Let's Straighten It Out," as well as "Big Boss Man/It's Your Thing." There were also guest appearances by two of Japan's best-known musicians, Makoto Ayukawa on guitar and vocals, and Fumio Ishikawa on harp.

Kikuta continued to record and his latest CD, *Let's Do It Again*, was released on the M&I label. However, perhaps the greatest change in the last couple of years is his departure from J. W. Williams and Chi-Town Hustlers to lead his own group, the Shun Kikuta Band. The band includes Nellie "Tiger" Travis on vocals. He performed with his band at the Japan Blues Carnival 2000, as well as on an extended tour of Tokyo, Omka, Nagoya and other Japanese cities.

Kikuta continues to perform and record.

Shun Kikuta is a rare blues jewel. He has achieved his stature in blues circles through determination, hard work, and pure talent. Though blues singers have been touring Japan for the last twenty-five years, Kikuta is the first blues artist from the Land of the Rising Sun to make an impact on the blues world. With each successive album, he has shown more promise and a growing knowledge of how to make a blues record.

The greatest influence on Shun Kikuta has been B. B. King. Like his mentor, Kikuta has developed a ringing style built on beautiful single-line runs of carefully chosen and well-paced notes. He plays with an unmatched precision and calculated coolness, rolling out solos the way Honda rolls out cars.

Magic Sam also had a strong impact on Kikuta, who has managed to blend the smooth, jazzy style of B. B. King with Magic Sam's harsher style of Chicago blues. A fan of all types of music including blues, rock, jazz, and pop, Kikuta is a master at taking the best elements of each form and forging them into his own unique sound. His patience, discipline, and constitution are trademarks of the classical-guitar approach of his native country.

Kikuta plays a Gibson guitar, pulling out pure blues from the instrument with the expertise and precision of a Sushi chef. Kikuta can make the roughest, grittiest guitar lines sound like a warm breeze on a summer night. He has a delicate yet solid touch on the guitar that makes it look as if he were barely playing while he creates a wall of sound.

Shun Kikuta is an excellent example of the way the blues have spread around the globe in the last forty years. With each new record and performance in front of a different audience from all points around the globe, he is breaking new ground. His deft touch, blues sensibility, and desire to have fun will continue to enable him to play his special blues made in Japan.

### Discography

*They Call Me Shun*, King KICP 485.
*Chicago Midnight*, King 546.

With J. W. Williams and the Chi-Town Hustlers:
*Tribute to Magic Sam*, King 441.

With Frank Collier Band:
*Funky Blues*, King 421.

---

# SILVAN ZINGG

## *Boogie-Woogie Swiss Blues*

Although the boogie-woogie craze of the 1930s and 1940s has long subsided into the pages of blues history, the reverberations continue to resound even today. The piano-thumping expertise of Pete Johnson, Albert Ammons, and Meade Lux Lewis have not been lost on the current generation of blues singers. Perhaps the best example of the influence that the three great boogie-woogie piano kings have had on future blues pianists is in the boogie-woogie Swiss blues of a young musician from Switzerland. His name is Silvan Zingg.

Silvan Zingg was born on March 19, 1973, in Lugano, Switzerland.

He showed an interest in music at an early age and began to fool around on the piano in his spare time. When he heard recordings by the three kings of boogie-woogie—Pete Johnson, Albert Ammons, and Meade Lux Lewis—he instantly caught blues fever and focused his attention on mastering the boogie-woogie piano style. Long hours of constant and solitary practice paid off when, at the tender age of seventeen, he appeared at the annual blues festival in Lugano. He entertained the crowd with his sweeping brand of boogie-woogie blues, barrelhouse, and jazz. It proved to be his big break as the promoter for the Charleston, South Carolina, Blues Festival was in attendance and was impressed enough to offer a personal invite to Zingg to play in America.

The boogie-woogie piano style that had been so popular in the late 1930s and the early 1940s was but a distant memory in the country of its origin. But on that afternoon in Charleston, the seventeen-year-old piano wizard from Switzerland transported the audience back in time and created an hour of magic. The spirits of Johnson, Ammons, and Lewis smiled down from blues heaven that day. Seemingly overnight, Zingg had conquered America with his impressive and thrilling virtuosity.

Despite his impressive concert appearances, however, the lack of merchandise on the market hurt his ability to spread his popularity and capitalize on his remarkable performances. But in 1992 Zingg rectified that situation with his first record, *Boogie Must Go On*. The CD included some classics like "Cow-Cow Blues," by blues legend Charles Davenport, and "88 Keys Boogie," an old blues standard. The collection also included an original Zingg composition, "Bye." Though it did not sell a million copies and set the world on fire, the CD served notice that the new boogie-woogie piano wizard could deliver in the studio as well as in a live setting.

It seemed that Zingg was on his way to expanding his musical boundaries; but, instead, he returned to school to study graphics. However, like so many blues musicians before him, the music was in his blood and there was no denying his true calling in life. He was meant to play boogie-woogie blues piano and entertain people all over the world.

With renewed determination he recorded his second album, *Changes in Boogie-Woogie*, accompanied by percussionist Lorenzo Milani. The album contained twenty-two compositions equally divided between originals and cover songs. Some of the highlights included classics like "Honky Tonk Train," "Pinetop's Boogie Woogie," and "Organ Grinder's Swing." His own "Blues Mood Just Before Midnight" was both a tribute to the boogie masters and positive proof that he had firm control of the style.

Zingg and his blues partner Milani performed in blues festivals throughout the world. Their combination of rollicking rhythms and expert boogie-piano thrilled audiences wherever they played. So it was with great confidence that he entered the studio once again to make another record. The result was *Double Up Boogie.*

On *Double Up Boogie,* Milani was joined by Martin Schok on grand piano, This Is Velvet on washboard, and Dion Nijland on bass to back up Zingg. The larger musical ensemble enabled Zingg to explore different avenues. There were many memorable songs on the CD, including "MFP Boogie," "The Boogaloo," "Organ Grinder's Swing," "Chicago in Mind," "12th Street Rag," and even the "Peter Gunn Theme." The ambitious project won Zingg some new fans and more respect as a young new talent in piano blues.

Zingg's most recent CD is the *Boogie-Woogie Duets Live,* with Martin Schok. The two incredibly talented pianists delivered fifteen songs with a fresh, brash flavor during a concert in Switzerland. The album kicks off with "Groovy Keys" and jumps to "Honky Tonk Train Blues." Every cut on the record has something interesting to offer as the two young virtuosos played with the fever and power of the old masters. There isn't a weak track, whether a cover version of "Pinetop's Boogie Woogie" or an original like "Double Up Boogie." One of the best piano blues releases in the past ten years, it makes a wonderful addition to any fan's collection.

Zingg continues to record and perform.

Silvan Zingg is a blues delight. His driving boogie-woogie rhythms and stomps are fun and a wild adventure. He has rekindled interest in the boogie-woogie piano style that deserves its rightful place in blues history. His efforts have not gone unnoticed and it is only a matter of time before he really breaks through on an international level.

Zingg has copied the style of the great boogie-woogie masters. He has learned how to play stride piano, thumping out basic jungle rhythms with his left hand while producing complicated runs and solos with his right. But he has also moved beyond the traditional boogie-woogie style. He injects the music with a freshness that allows him to unite the past with the present in a way never heard before. He has taken the basic elements of boogie-woogie and expanded the concept to revive the accessibility of the style.

Zingg, like Alvin Youngblood Hart, Corey Harris, Keb' Mo', Kenny Wayne Shepherd, Jonny Lang, Shun Kikuta, Susan Tedeschi, and Sue Foley, has taken an old form and modernized it to appeal to today's blues fans. This new crop of young blues artists carry the future of the blues on their capable shoulders. Zingg is definitely one of the most interesting of the new breed of blues singers, both because of his background and because of his desire to revive an old form that had been nearly forgotten in the last fifty years.

Zingg is the next link in the long history of the piano blues style. His devotion to the boogie-woogie, barrelhouse, jazz-influenced blues is a tribute to forgotten names such as Clarence "Pine Top" Smith, Cow Cow Davenport, Roosevelt Sykes, Albert Ammons, Pete Johnson, Meade Lux Lewis, Big Maceo Merriweather, Sunnyland Slim, Professor Longhair, Leroy Carr, Otis Spann, Pinetop Perkins, and Jimmy Yancey. He has duplicated the intensity of the boogie-woogie pianists, injecting his playing with the infectious spirit of a Professor Longhair and the diversity of an Otis Spann. One hopes that Zingg's career will have the longevity of a Sunnyland Slim, Roosevelt Sykes, and Pinetop Perkins.

Zingg is in the select company of modern blues pianists Lucky Peterson, Marcia Ball, and Reese Wynans. The blues piano is a genre that runs through the entire history of the blues from the pre-recording days of the 1920s to the modern era. Despite its deep history, the piano blues has seen its popularity decrease in the past few years. But with luminaries like Zingg and others, the future looks much more promising.

He has already established a reputation as a road warrior, appearing in numerous concerts in his native Switzerland as well as performing in the United States, Germany, France, Italy, Austria, Luxembourg, Sweden, Greece, Spain, Hungary, United Arab Emirates, and the Netherlands. He has played at the Charleston Blues Festival, the Blues to Bop Festival, the Schönried Jazz Festival, the Canary Islands Blues Festival, Zermatt Riverboat Jazz Party, AVO Blues Festival, Zürich Piazza Blues, and the Riverboat Boogie Woogie Party among others. His appearance at festivals, on television and radio shows, and in jazz clubs has helped spread his special blues message.

Zingg has made audiences marvel for the past seven years with his fresh take on the boogie-woogie piano blues. Along the way he has also turned the heads of many blues legends, including Sammy Price, Memphis Slim, Champion Jack Dupree, Jimmy Walker, Pinetop Perkins, Katie Webster, Peter Green, and Axel Zwingenberger. With a heavy schedule of international festivals on his tour itinerary, there is no doubt that Zingg will continue to impress large crowds as well as his fellow blues artists.

Though he has yet to reach his thirtieth birthday, Zingg has already established himself as the leader of the blues community in Switzerland. He has covered much ground very quickly and his passion for the blues is incomparable. There is no denying the fact that with his boogie-woogie Swiss blues Zingg has managed to overcome a big span of time and reignite the fire that was initially sparked by Charley Patton in another dimension of blues history.

## Discography

*Boogie Must Go On*, S7001.
*Changes in Boogie-Woogie*, Boogie Face Records BFR 96071.
*Boogie Woogie Live*,
*Double Up Boogie*, Oldie Blues OLCD 7113.

# Recordings by Three or More Blues Singers

Acoustic Disc: 100% Handmade Music, Vol. 3, Acoustic Disc 24.
The Alligator Records Christmas Collection, Alligator 9201.
The Alligator Records 20th Anniversary Collection, Alligator AL 105/6.
The Alligator Records 20th Anniversary Tour, Alligator AL 107/8.
The Alligator Records 25th Anniversary Collection, Alligator AL 110/11.
American Fogies, Vol. 1, Rounder 379.
And This Is Maxwell Street, P-Vine 5527.
Antone's 20th Anniversary, Discovery 74703.
Antone's Women Bringing You the Best in Blues, ANT-99022.
Atlantic Blues Piano, Atlantic 81694-2.
Bayou Hot Sauce, Easydisc 7044.
The Best of Chicago Blues, Vanguard 73125.
Blowin' the Blues, JWC-512.
Blowin' the Blues, Best of the Great Harp Players, Vanguard 79349.
Blues: The Language of New Orleans, Vol. 3, Louisiana Red Hot 9103.
Blues: The New Breed, EM 846-2.
Blues Across the U.S.A., Rounder CD-AN-10.
Blues Bar-B-Que, Easydisc 7030.
Blues Crossroads: Acoustic Blues, Old & New, Easydisc 7066.
Blues Deep Down: Songs of Janis Joplin, A&M 161251.
Blues Deluxe, Alligator AL 9301.
Blues Explosion, Atlantic 80149.
Blues Guitar Heaven, Delta 46005.
Blues Harp Greats, Easydisc 7023.
Blues Harp Power, Easydisc 7048.
Blues Live from Mountain Stage, Blue Plate 305.
Blues Masters, Vol. 1–5, Rhino 72027.
Blues Masters, Vol. 4, Harmonica Classics, Rhino R2-71124.
Blues Masters, Vol. 9, Postmodern Blues, Rhino R2-71132.

Blues Masters, Vol. 16, More Harmonica Classics, Rhino 75346.
Blues Masters, Vol. 17, More Postmodern Blues, Rhino 75347.
Blues Masters: Essential Blues Collection, Rhino 90128.
Blues Moods, Easydisc 7050.
Blues Power: The Songs of Eric Clapton, House of Blues 1449.
Blues Road Trip: City to City, Easydisc 7059.
Blues Summit, Charly 273.
Blues Women Today, Easydisc 7010.
Brace Yourself! A Tribute to Otis Blackwell, Shanachie 5702.
Celebration of Blues: The Best Guitarists, Celebration of Blues 97132.
Celebration of Blues: Chicago Blues, Celebration of Blues 25202.
Celebration of Blues: Great Country Blues, Celebration of Blues 2524.
Celebration of Blues: The Great Guitarists, Vol. 1–2, Celebration of Blues 97112.
Celebration of Blues: The Great Guitarists, Vol. 3, Celebration of Blues 25192.
Celebration of Blues: Great Slide Guitars, Celebration of Blues 2521.
Celebration of Blues: New Breed, Celebration of Blues 25152.
Celebration of Blues: Rock-A-Boogie Blues, Celebration of Blues 2522.
Chicago Blues Session, Vol. 12, Wolf 120858.
Chicago Blues Session, Vol. 21, Wolf 120867.
Chicago Blues Tour, Big Chicago 2.
Chicago Tour, Wolf 120861.
Chicago's Finest Blues Ladies, Wolf 120874.
Country Blues Guitar, Easydisc 7051.
Defiance Blues, A&M 161340.
Dreams Come True, ANT-0014-2.
Earwig 20th Anniversary Collection, Earwig 4946.
Elektra 15th Anniversary Commemorative Album, Elektra 78.
Essential Blues, Vol. 3, House of Blues 1451.
Every Road I Take: The Best of Contemporary Acoustic Blues, Shanachie 9012.
Every Woman's Blues: The Best of the New Generation, Shanachie 9009.
Everybody Slides, Vol. 1, Rykodisc 10344.
Evidence Blues Sampler: Two, Evidence ECD-26046-2.
Fender 50th Anniversary Guitar Legends, Virgin 42088.
Fish-Tree Water Blues, Rounder 619618.
Genuine Houserockin' Music, Alligator AL 101.
Genuine Houserockin' Music II, Alligator AL 102.
Genuine Houserockin' Music III, Alligator AL 103.
Genuine Houserockin' Music IV, Alligator AL 104.
Genuine Houserockin' Music V, Alligator AL 109.
Got Harp, If You Want It! Blues Rock-It 111.
Harp Attack! Alligator ALCD-4790.

Home of the Blues, MCA 90143.
Hot Rockin' Blues, K-Tel 6128.
Hound Dog Taylor: A Tribute, Alligator AL 4855.
House of Blues: Essential Women in Blues, A&M 161257.
House on Fire, Red House 58.
House on Fire, Vol. 2, Red House 100.
King Snake Harp Classics: HarpBeat of Swamp, King Snake 33.
Legends of the Guitar: Electric Blues, Vol. 2, Rhino 70564.
Living Chicago Blues, Vol. I, Alligator AL 7701.
Living Chicago Blues, Vol. II, Alligator AL 7702.
Living Chicago Blues, Vol. III, Alligator AL 7703.
Living Chicago Blues, Vol. IV, Alligator AL 7704.
Louisiana Spice, Rounder 18-19.
Mean Old World: The Blues from 1940 to 1994, Smithsonian Blues Box,
    Smithsonian Collection 110.
Michael Bloomfield/John Paul Hammond/Dr. John: Triumvirate, Columbia
    RC-32172.
More Heavy Sounds, Columbia 1016.
The New Bluebloods, Alligator AL 7707.
New Blues Hits, Bullseye Blues 27.
1993 Portland Waterfront Blues Festival, Burnside BCD-0014-2.
Otis Redding/Jimi Hendrix Experience at Monterey, MS 2029.
Paint It Blue: The Songs of the Rolling Stones, A&M 161315.
Prime Chops: Blind Pig Sampler, Vol. 2, Blind Pig BPCD-8002.
Rattlesnake Guitar: The Music of Peter Green, Viceroy 8021.
Red Blooded Blues, Polygram 525879.
Safe House: A Collection of Blues, Relativity 1673.
Slidin' ... Some Slide, Bullseye Blues 619533.
Songs of Willie Dixon, Telarc 83452.
Strike a Deep Chord: Blues Guitars for the Homeless, Justice 3.
Tangled up in Blues: Songs of Bob Dylan, House of Blues 1458.
Three Shades of Blues, Charly 275.
Tribute to Howlin' Wolf, Telarc 83427.
Tribute to Magic Sam, Evidence 26086.
Tribute to Stevie Ray Vaughan, Epic 67599.
White Blues in the 1960s, Elektra 60383.
Women of Blue Chicago, Delmark 690.

# Blues Societies
# and Foundations

**Alabama Blues Society**
P.O. Box 513
Tuscaloosa, AL 35402
Daytime phone: (205) 345-1876

**Arkansas Blues Connection**
P.O. Box 1271
Little Rock, AR 72201
Daytime phone: (501) 372-4642
Contact: Shirley Pharis

**Asker Blues Klubb**
Postlock: 108
N-1390 Vollen
Norway
Contact: Erik Habberstad
Tel.: 47-66 79 61 02
E-mail: Erik.Habberstad@
DNV.com
Asker Blues Klubb Web page
Located 25 km. Southwest of Oslo

**Atlanta Blues Society**
Atlanta Blues Society
www.atlantablues.org

**Auckland Blues Society**
P.O. Box 47529
Ponsonby
Auckland, New Zealand
Jan Breukkers on +64-9-376 5870

Fax: +64-9-376 4971
E-mail: Mark Herman

**Baltimore Blues Society**
P.O. Box 26250
Baltimore, MD 21210
Phone: (410) 329-5825
Fax/Phone: (410) 771-4862
Contact: Dale Patton, Marcia
Selko

**Bay Area Blues Association**
1405 Clement St
San Francisco, CA 94118

**Bay Area Blues Society**
408 13th Street, Suite 512
Oakland, CA 94612
Daytime phone: (510) 836-2227
Fax: (510) 836-4341
Contact: Ronnie Stewart

**Beale Street Blues Society**
P.O. Box 3421
Memphis, TN 38173-0421
Blues Hotline: (901) 527-4585
Fax and voice mail: (901) 525-SURF

**Bessie Smith Hall**
c/o Dr. Russell J. Linnemann
44342 Comet Trail
Nixson, TN 37343

**Bessie Smith Society**
Franklin and Marshall College
Lancaster, PA 17603
Daytime phone: (717) 291-3915
Contact: Michael Roth

**Big Wills Arts Council**
200 Gault Ave. South
Fort Payne, AL 35967
Daytime phone: (205) 845-9591
Contact: Russell Galley

**Billings Blues and Jazz Society**
3915 Laredo Place
Billings, MT 59106

**Billtown Blues Association, Inc.**
P.O. Box 2
Hughesville, PA 17737
Daytime phone: (717) 584-4480
Fax: (717) 584-4608
Contact: Bonnie Tallman

**Black Swamp Blues Society**
1455 S. Reynolds Rd., Suite 337
Toledo, OH 43615
John Henry, President

**Blue Monday**
Kronvagen 32
S-724 62 Västeras
Sweden
Contact: Leif Gaverth
Tel: +46(0) 21 11 81 82

**Blue Monday Foundation**
116 Du Bois St.
San Raphael, CA 94901
Daytime phone: (415) 457-6498
Contact: Mark Naftalin

**Blues & Rhythm—The Gospel Truth**
13 Ingleborough Dr (subscription
address)
Morley, Leeds LS27 9DT, England

**Blues Appreciation Society of Sudbury**
43 Elm Street
Sudbury
Ontario, Canada, P3C1S4
Contact: Tony Anselmo, Bob
Armiento

**Blues Association of Southeast Queensland**
P.O. Box 496
Ashgrove Q 4060
Australia
Phone: 617 3398 5475
Fax: 617 3395 4303
Contact: Helen Farley
We have a great monthly news-
letter and jams.
Membership: $Aus20 per annum
Newsletter only: $Aus10 per annum

**Blues at the Bow**
c/o Bow Island Historical Society
Box 1193
Bow Island
Alberta, Canada T0K 0G0
Phone/Fax: 403 545 2226
E-mail reyn@telusplanet.net
Contacts: Stu Couillar, Jim
Thacker, Gordon Reynolds

**Blues Audience Newsletter**
104 Old Nelson Rd
Marlborough, NH 03455-4004
Phone: (603) 827-3952

**Blues Bank Collective**
9 Towle Farm Road / TJ Wheler
Hampton Falls, NH 03844
Phone: (603) 929-0654
NH Seacoast and Southern Maine

**Blues Beat Magazine**
(32 page WNY Blues Society
magazine)

1101 Elliot Drive
Lewiston NY 14092
Editors: Sharon and Rich Schneider

**Blues Connection**
P.O. Box 161272
Memphis, TN 38186
Contact: Bill Lusk

**Blues Foundation**
49 Union Ave.
Memphis, TN 38103
Daytime phone: (901) 527-2583
Fax: (901) 529-4030
Contact: Howard Stovall (Executive Director)
www.blues.org
E-mail: bluesinfo@blues.org

**Blues Heaven Foundation**
49 North Brand Blvd. #590
Glendale, CA 91203
Phone: (818) 507-8944
Contact: Evetta Dixon

**Blues Interactions, Inc.**
2-41-10
Tomigaya Shibuya-ku
Tokyo 151, Japan

**Blues Is Truth Foundation
(Brownie McGhee legacy)**
688 43th Street
Oakland, CA 94609
www.communityace. org/BIT_
found.html

**Blues, Jazz and Folk Music
Society**
P.O. Box 2122
Marietta, OH 45750
Daytime phone: (614) 373-6640
Contact: Keith Gatto, Moon
    Mullen, and Jack Bolen

**Blues Life**
A-1030 Vienna
Kegel-gasse 40/17
Austria (0222) 723765

**Blues Live**
Keskustie 17 B
40100 Jyvaskyla
Finland
President: Mr. Heikki Heinonen
www.jyu.fi/~thrafool/steve.htm

**Blues Power**
Christian Jotter
Frankenweg 18
6716 Dirmstein
Germany 06238-2255

**Blues Society of the Ozarks**
P.O. Box 8133
Springfield, MO 65801
E-mail: janalan@earthlink.net

**Blues Society of Indiana**
6849 N. Michigan Rd.
Indianapolis, IN 46268
Office Phone: (317) 253-2421
Hotline: (317) 470-8795
Fax: (317) 253-2169
www.bluesindy.org
Contact: Doris Jackson, Executive
    Director

**Blues Society of Western New
York, Inc.**
P.O. Box 129
Buffalo, NY 14217
President: Jack Civiletto

**Boe Blues Club**
Postboks 153
N-2420 Trysil
Norway

**Boise Blues Society**
P.O. Box 2756
Boise, ID 83701

Hotline: (208) 344-BLUE (2583)
Contact: Marla Leggette

**Bonnie Raitt Foundation**
P.O. Box 626
Hollywood, CA 90078

**Boston Blues Society**
P.O. Box 15718
Boston, MA 02215

**Bozeman Blues and Jazz Society**
702 S. 7th
Bozeman, MT 59715

**Bucks County Blues Society**
P.O. Box 482
Levittown, PA 19058
Daytime phone: (215) 946-4794
Contact: Thomas J. Cullen

**Capital Area Blues Society**
P.O. Box 1004
Okemos (Lansing Area), MI
48864
Phone/Fax: (517) 349-0006
Contact Bonnie Stebbins, President

**Cascade Blues Association**
P.O. Box 14493
Portland, OR 97214
Daytime phone: (503) 283-3447
Fax: (503) 223-1850
Contact: Rick Hall, President

**Catfish Blues Association**
8 Rue Max Barel
69200 Venissieux
France
Phone: 19 (33) 72 51 17 17 (French)
Contact: Maurice Duffaud
Phone: 19 (33) 78 39 27 65 (English)
Contact Michel Boisnier

**Central California Blues Society**
1903 S. Cedar
Fresno, CA 93702

**Central Iowa Blues Society**
P.O. Box 13016
Des Moines, IA 50310
Contact: Jeff Wagner
Phone: (515) 276-0677
www.cibs.org
E-mail: drdoubt@radiks.net

**Charlotte Blues Society**
P.O. Box 172—Elizabeth Station
Charlotte, NC 28204
Hotline: (704) 331-8871

**Chicago Blues**
P.O. Box 06349
Chicago, IL 60606-0349
Daytime phone: (312) 819-1887
Contact (Editor): Jim Marshall

**Chicago Blues Coalition**
Daytime phone: (312) 744-3315

**Chicago Blues Society**
909 W. Armitage Avenue
Chicago, IL 60614
Contact: Skip Landt

**Coastal Jazz and Blues Society**
435 W. Hastings Street
Vancouver
BC, Canada, V6B1L4
Daytime phone: (604) 682-0706
Fax: (604) 682-0704

**Colorado Blues Society**
P.O. Box 130
Lyons, Colorado 80540
Phone: (303) 823-9272
Contact: Dave McIntyre

**Columbus Blues Alliance**
P.O. Box 82451
Columbus, OH 43202

Blues Hotline: (614) 470-2222
E-mail: webmaster@colsblues
  allaince.org

**Connecticut Blues Society**
P.O. Box 652
New Hartford, CT 06057
Phone: (860) 345-2432
Fax: (860) 345-7657

**Crossroads Blues Society**
420 West Locust Street
Lanark, IL 61046
Daytime phone: (815) 493-2560
After 5:30: (815) 493-2241
Contact: Liz Sarber or Craig Lang
Publication: Blueseye, pub.
  monthly
E-mail: crossblues@internetni.com

**Crossroads Blues Society**
Tva systrars vag 3A
393 57 Kalmar
Sweden
Contact: Kjell Wikstrom
Telephone: +46 480 290 78

**D.C. Blues Society**
P.O. Box 77315
Washington, DC 20013-7315
Daytime phone: (202) 828-3028
Fax: (703) 536-0284
Contact: M. LaVert—President
Music Editor—Ron Weinstoc

**Dellenbygdens Bluesforening**
Vapeng. 5C
S-820 60 Delsbo
Sweden
Contact: Mats Norin

**Delta Blues Association of
Canada, Inc.**
195 Leopold Crescent
Regina
Saskatchewan

Canada S4T 6N5
Phone: (306) 52Blues
Contact: Rae George Reid, Pres-
  ident

**Delta Blues Society**
P.O. Box 1741
Sacramento, CA 95812-1741
Contact: Johnny Nugget
Telephone: (916) 444-3102

**Denton Blues Association**
P.O. Box 2681
Denton, TX 76202
Contact: Sandy Hall
Telephone: 1-800-277-1095

**Detroit Blues Society**
P.O. Box 99549
Troy, MI 48099
Contact: Mike Mazelis
E-mail: DBSblues@flash.net

**Dutch Blues and Boogie Organi-
sation**
P.O. Box 12538, 1100 AM
Amsterdam-Zuidcost
Netherlands

**Federal City Blues Connection of
Wash. DC**
P.O. Box 55472
Washington, DC 55472
Daytime phone: (202) 828-3069
Contact: Michael Roach, Presi-
  dent

**Finnish Blues Society**
PL 157 00531
Helsinki, Finland

**Florida Blues Network**
6489 Kahana Way
Sarasota, Florida 34241
Phone: (941) 377-8220
Fax: (941) 377-8004

**Fort Smith, Arkansas, Riverfront Blues Society**
P.O. Box 8307
Fort Smith, AR
Daytime phone: (501) 784-8216
Contact: Lynn Wasson, Executive
 Coordinator
www.riverfrontbluesfest.org
E-mail: riverblu@ipa.net

**Ft. Wayne Blues Society**
P.O. Box 11443
Ft. Wayne, IN 46858-1443
Phone: (219) 428-0277
Contact: John Nitzke (Pres.)

**Foundation for the Advancement of the Blues (FAB)**
P.O. Box 578486
Chicago, IL 60657-8486
(312) 278-1352
Contact: Mike Beck, Executive
 Director

**German Blues Circle**
Postfach 180 212
Frankfurt 18
Germany, D-6000

**German Blues Circle Info**
Ringelstr. 1, 6000
Frankfurt 60
Germany

**Great Smoky Mountains Blues Society**
P.O. Box 315
Dillsboro, NC 28725
E-mail: jamhandy@hotmail.com

**Greater Cincinnati Blues Society**
P.O. Box 6028
Cincinnati, OH 45206
Daytime phone: (513) 684-GCBS
Contact: Mary Ann Kindel

**Gulf Coast Blues Society**
P.O. Box 13513
St. Petersburg, FL 33733-3513
Daytime phone: (727) 822-6615
Contact: Gene Hardage

**Hamilton Blues Society**
P.O. Box 3632, Stn. C
Hamilton
Ontario, Canada, L8N7N1

**Hamilton Blues Society (New Zealand)**
P.O. Box 4251
Hamilton East
New Zealand
Contact: Sally Cable
E-mail: nzbs@hn.planet.gen.nz

**Haninge Bluesforening**
Solhemsv. 23
40 Vasterhaninge
Sweden, S-137
Contact: Stefan Pettersson

**Hawaiian Blues Society**
#75-5680 Kuakini Highway
Suite 308
Kailua-Kona, HI 96740
Daytime phone: (808) 329-5825
Contact: Louis B. Wolfenson

**Helena Blues & Jazz Society**
Box 992
Helena, MT 59624

**Hell Blues Club**
Postboks 45
7570 Hell
Norway

**Houston Blues Society**
P.O. Box 7809
Houston, TX 77270-7809
Phone: (713) 942-9427
President: Nuri Nuri

**Humbolt Blues Society**
2098 Park Road
McKinleyville, CA 95521
Contact: Anthony Sanger

**Illinois Central Blues Club**
P.O. Box 603
Springfield, IL 62705
Daytime phone: (217) 744-3256
Contact: Steve Truesdale

**Inland Empire Blues Society**
P.O. Box 9126
Spokane, WA 99209-9126
Telephone: (509) 534-1081
Inside Blues: (509) 534-1081
Fax: (509) 534-1081

**International Blues Society**
P.O. Box 82053
Los Angeles, CA 90037
Daytime phone: (805) 267-0495
Contact: Tina Mayfield

**James River Blues Society**
P.O. Box 4064
Lynchburg, VA 24502-0064
President: Jan Ramsey
Phone: (804) 237-8080

**Jarfalla Bluesforening**
Sunnanvindsgrand 67
38 Jarfalla
Sweden, S-175
Contact: Bosse Majling

**Jazz, Blues, Gospel Hall of Fame**
600 S. Dearborn St
Chicago, IL 60605
Daytime phone: (312) 922-2433

**Kalamazoo Valley Blues Association**
P.O. Box 50507
Kalamazoo, MI 49005

**Kansas City Blues Society**
P.O. Box 32131
Kansas City, MO 64111
Daytime phone: (816) 531-7557
Contact: Roger Naber

**Knoxville Blues Society**
1610 Six Mile Cemetery Road
Maryville, TN 37803
Phone: (423) 977-6518
Fax: (423) 977-6791
Contact: Herman Long

**Kyana Blues Society**
P.O. Box 755
Louisville, KY 40201-0755
Daytime phone: (501) 456-5883
Contact: Keith S. Clements

**Las Vegas Blues Society**
P.O. Box 27871
Las Vegas, NV 89126

**Lehigh Valley Blues Network**
517 N. 6th Street
Allentown, PA 18102
Phone: (610) 437-3217
Fax: (610) 439-2103
Contact: Beverly Conklin
E-mail: lvbn@ot.com
Newsletter: Blues Net

**Lima Blues Society**
318 Boyd Ave.
Van Wert, Ohio 45891
Contact: Stuart Jewett

**Linn County Blues Society**
P.O. Box 2672
Cedar Rapids, IA 52406
Contact: Jeff Schmatt (President)
Phone: (319) 399-5105
Fax: (319) 366-0485
E-mail: jeff@lcbs.org

**Little Boy Blues Society**
P.O. Box 691
Eureka Springs, AR 72632
Daytime phone: (501) 253-9344
Contact: Rich Jones

**Louisiana Blues Society**
c/o Tabby's Blues Box and Hermitage Hall
1314 N. Blvd.
Baton Rouge, LA 70802

**Lowcountry Blues Society**
P.O. Box 13525
Charleston, SC 29422
Phone: (803) 762-9125
Fax: (803) 7629124
E-mail: emusic@mindspring.com
Contact: Gary Erwin

**Madison Blues**
P.O. Box 3202
Madison, WI 53704-0202

**Magic City Blues Society**
P.O. Box 360471
Birmingham, AL 35236

**Manhattan Blues Alliance Plus**
Town Terrace, Suite 16a
Middletown, NY 10940
Daytime phone: (914) 346-4613
Contact: Fred Jackson

**Manitoba Blues Society**
45 Sapphire Place
Winnipeg, MB
Canada R2V 4N4
Phone: (204) 334-9990
Fax: (204) 334-9989
Contact: Garry I. Frankel

**Maui Blues Association**
P.O. Box 1211
Puunene, Maui HI 96784-1211
Contact: Lou "Wolf" Wolfenson

Phone: (808) 242-7218
Contact: Kurt "Crowbar" Kangas
Phone: (808) 572-4951

**Melbourne Blues Appreciation Society**
P.O. Box 1249
St. Kilda South
Melbourne, Victoria, Australia 3182
Telephone (613) 014 869570
Fax (613) 9412 4388
Contact: Steve Fraser
E-mail: frasers@nre.vic.gov.au.

**Mid-Mississippi Muddy Water Blues Society**
P.O. Box 887
Quincy, IL 62306-0887
Contact: Julie Long
Phone: (217) 224-3041

**Milwaukee Blues Unlimited**
P.O. Box 92366
Milwaukee, WI 53202
Daytime phone: (414) 647-1725
Contact: Jim Feeney

**Mississippi Delta Blues Society**
104 Lysbeth Drive
Leland, MS 38756
Phone: (601) 686-2356

**Mississippi Valley Blues Society**
318 Brady Street
Davenport, IA 52801
Daytime phone: (319) 32-BLUES

**Missoula Blues & Jazz Society**
219 S. 3rd St. West
Missoula, MT 59801

**Missouri Musical Heritage Foundation**
P.O. Box 21652
St. Louis, MO 63109

Daytime phone: (314) 647-2447
Fax: (314) 647-2497

**Mojo Blues Society**
820 Mansfield
Plymouth, IN 46563
E-mail: MOJOWEB65@skyenet
.net

**Mon-Valley Blues Society**
P.O. Box 155
Hibbs, PA 15443
Contact: Wilbur Landman

**Monterey Blues Society**
P.O. Box 423
Santa Cruz, CA 95061

**Music City Blues Society**
P.O. Box 22582
Nashville, TN 37202
Daytime phone: (615) 383-5668
Contact: Chuck Bloomingburg

**Napa Valley Blues Society**
P.O. Box 10603
Napa, CA 94581
Contact: Michael Henry (President)

**Natchel Blues Network**
P.O. Box 1773
Norfolk, VA 23501-1773
24-hr. hot line: (757) 456-1675
Contact: Beth Jarock
Daytime phone: (757) 623-8559
E-mail: bluesbet@norfolk.infi.net

**Natchez Trace's Southern Cross Blues Society**
c/o Philip Hendrickson
Bachlettenstr. 47
Basel, Switzerland, CH-4054
Contact: Philip Hendrickson

**National Association for Preservation of Blues**
P.O. Box 894
Jackson, TN 38302
Daytime phone: (901) 424 0952
Contact: Denise LaSalle

**National Association for Preservation of Blues**
P.O. Box 3421
Memphis, TN 38103
Daytime phone: (901) 458-7151
Contact: Paul Averwater

**New Orleans Blues Society**
5520 Hurst St.
New Orleans, LA 70115
Contact: Thorny Penfield

**New Zealand Blues Society**
P.O. Box 4413
Hamilton East
New Zealand
Homepage: The New Zealand
Blues Society
Contact: Mike Garner

**Northeast Arkansas Blues Society**
206 East Nettleton Avenue
Jonesboro, AR 72401
www.bluesartistmanagement.com/
neabs.html
Phone: (870) 935-3102
Contact: Dan Ferguson, President/
Founder

**Northeast Blues Society**
Wilcock Associates
P.O. Box 2336
Scotia, NY 12302
President: Don Wilcock
Phone: (518) 347-1751

**Northwest Blues Society**
P.O. Box 91221
Cleveland, OH 44101

**Oklahoma Blues Society**
P.O. Box 76176
Oklahoma, OK 73147-2176
Daytime phone: (405) 791-0110
Contact: Marty McKinsey

**Ottawa Blues Society**
P.O. Box 708, Station B
Ottawa, Ontario
Canada K1P 5P8
E-mail: ottawablues@home.com

**Ozark Blues Museum**
P.O. Box 691
Eureka Springs, AR 72632
Daytime phone: (501) 253-9344
Contact: Rich Jones

**Permian Basin Blues Society**
P.O. Box 1981
Odessa, TX 79760,
Phone: (915) 332-7881 or (915)
520-8454
Contact: Gwen Leeper
E-mail: gcleeper@worldnet.att.net

**Philadelphia Blues Machine**
351 Pelham Rd
Philadelphia, PA 19119
Daytime phone: (215) 849-5465
Contact: Doug Waltner

**Phoenix Blues Society**
P.O. Box 36874
Phoenix, AZ 85067-6874
Daytime phone: (602)-252-0599
Contact: Bill Mitchell

**Piedmont Blues Society**
P.O. Box 9737
Greensboro, NC 27429
Daytime phone: (910) 275-4944
Contact: Jeff Farron

**R&B Rock-N-Roll Society**
P.O. Box 1949

New Haven, CT 06510
Daytime phone: (203) 924-1079
Contact: Bill Nolan

**Rhythm and Blues Foundation**
14th & Constitution Ave., N.W.,
Rm. 4603
Washington, DC 20560
Daytime phone: (202) 357-1654
Contact: Suzan Jenkins

**Richmond Blues Society**
P.O. Box 31721
Richmond, VA 23294
Daytime phone: (804) 346-3482
Contact: Andy Garrigue, Frank
Waltman

**River City Blues Society**
Box 463
Peoria, IL 61651

**River City Music Society**
Box 1109
Red Deer, Alberta, Canada,
T4N1X0
Contact: Mike Bradford, Doug
Cameron

**Riverfront Blues Society (see Fort
Smith, Arkansas)**

**Sacramento Blues Society**
P.O. Box 60580
Sacramento, CA 95860-0580
Daytime (Hotline) phone: (916)
556-5007; press 5 for Blues
business
E-mail: chevy427@jps.net

**St. Benedict Blues Society**
P.O. Box 104
St. Benedict, PA 15773
Contact: Al Slavicsky

**St. Louis Blues Heritage Festival, Inc.**
1524 S. Big Bend Blvd
St. Louis, MO. 63117
Phone: 314-644 1551
Fax: 314-644-2485
Key Contact: Maurice J. Burke

**St. Louis Blues Society**
P.O. Box 78894
St. Louis, MO 63178
Daytime phone: (314) 241-BLUE (2583)

**San Antonio Blues Society**
P.O. Box 33952
San Antonio, TX 78265
Hotline: (210) 641-8192
E-mail: bluesman@sonnyboy lee.com

**San Diego Blues Association**
17 East H Street, #A
Encinitas, CA 92024

**San Francisco Blues Resource & Research Center**
863 Waller Street, #10
San Francisco, CA 94117
Daytime phone: (415) 863-1324

**San Luis Obispo Blues Society**
P.O. Box 14041
San Luis Obispo, CA 93406
Daytime phone: (805) 772-4924
Contact: Mr. Robert Oberg
E-mail: khischke@calpoly.edu

**Santa Barbara Blues Society**
P.O. Box 30798
Santa Barbara, CA 93130
Contacts: Las Kiraly (805) 682-2982
or Steve Daniels (805) 966-2548
E-mail: sdmdsb@rain.org

**Sarasota Blues Society**
328 John Ringling Blvd
Sarasota, FL 34236
Daytime phone: (941) 388-1837
Fax: (941) 000 0709
Contact: Diane Phillips

**Scandinavian Blues Society**
S 725-75
Västeras
Sweden
Contact: Namde Mansgaten

**Shasta Blues Society**
P.O. Box 964693
Redding, CA 96099
Daytime phone: (916) 245-2117
Hotline: (916) 225-9926
Contact: Steve Lafferty

**Shenandoah Valley Blues Society**
P.O. Box 811
Fishersville, VA 22939
Contact: Lorie Strother
Daytime phone: (540) 943-0536
Hotline: (540) 946-6380
E-mail: ljstroth@cfw.com

**Sierra Blues Society**
P.O. Box 181
Grass Valley, CA 95945
Phone/Fax: 530/268-9166
E-mail: bluescon@jps.net
Contact: Thom Myers

**Siskiyou Blues Society**
P.O. Box 271
Mt. Shasta, CA 96067
Phone: (530) 926-5823
Fax: (530) 926-4749
www.geocities.com/BourbonStreet/ 8501/index
E-mail: sqblues@geocities.com

**Skylands Blues Society**
P.O. Box 857
Hackettstown, NJ 07840
Contact: Scott Acton
Phone: (908) 813-BLUS (2587)

**Sodertalje Bluesforening**
Lovlundsgade 1S-151 41
Sodertalje, Sweden
Contact: Kristina von Tartwijk

**Sonny Boy Blues Society**
P.O. Box 237
Helena, AR 72342
Daytime phone: (501) 338-3501
Contact: Houston Stackhouse, Jr./
   Bubba Sullivan

**Sonoma County Blues Society**
P.O. Box 7844
Santa Rosa, CA 95407
Phone: (707) 574-9003

**South Florida Blues Society**
420 N. Dixie Hwy
Lantana, FL 33462

**South Jersey Blues Society**
Chelsea Gardens, Apt. 2A
Stratford, NJ 08084

**South Skunk Blues Society**
415 W. 12th St. S.
Newton, IA 50208
Contact: John Yoder
Telephone: (515) 791-7473
E-mail: YoderJ@pcpartner.net

**Southern Arts Foundation**
1293 Peachtree St. NE, Suite 500
Atlanta, GA 30309
Daytime phone: (404) 874-7244

**Southern California Blues Society**
13337 South Street #249
Cerritos, CA 90703-7308
Daytime phone: (310) 495-3424

Contact: Alan Brown, Pres.,
   Melvin Eddy, V.P.

**Southern Maine Blues Society**
P.O. Box 1703
Portland, Maine 04112-4703
Phone: 207-627-7284
President: Garry Stevens

**Southern Music Heritage Society**
632 W. Dickson Street
Fayetteville, AR 72701

**Southside Blues Society**
c/o Glebe Farm House
Small Lane, Earlswood
West Midlands, UK B945EL
Contact: Ray Gardner

**Space Coast Blues Society**
P.O. Box 061323
Palm Bay, FL 32906
Daytime phone: (407) 768-8699
Contact: Goldie Daniels, Chip
   Myles

**Spokane Blues Society**
P.O. Box 427
Spokane, WA 99210

**Stichting Rhythm & Blues Breda
(Breda Blues Foundation)**
Van Goorstraat 16a
4811 HJ Breda, The Netherlands
E-mail: srbb@worldaccess.nl

**Stockholms Bluesforening**
Box 4020
61 Stockholm
Sweden, S-102
Fax: +46(0) 8 30 26 18

**Sudbury Blues Society**
46 Rio Road
Sudbury,
Ontario, Canada P3C 3A5
Phone: (705) 673-9751

**The Pittsburgh Blues Society**
5850 Centre Ave., Suite 606
Pittsburgh, PA 15206-3780
Phone: (412) 362-1328
Contact: Fred McIntosh
E-mail: BluesTunes@aol.com

**Toronto Blues Society**
910 Queen St. W., Suite B04
Toronto, Ontario, Canada M6J 1G6
Phone: (416) 538-3885
Fax: (416) 538-6559
Contact: Barbara Isherwood,
  Executive Director

**Trondheims Bluesklubb**
Postboks 4556
Trondheim, Norway, N-7001
Tucson Blues Society
P.O. Box 30672
Tuscon, AZ 85751
Phone: (520) 617-4617

**Tulsa Blues Club**
P.O. Box 702426
Tulsa, OK 74170-2426
Daytime phone: (918) 496-1011
Contact: Mark Milberger

**Uppsala Bluesforening**
Box 2107
02 Uppsala
Sweden, S-750

**Vienna Blues Society**
Alster Str. 37/18
Vienna, Austria, A-1080
Contact: Hans Thelst

**Virginia Blues Connection**
2421 Boyle Ave
Richmond, VA 23230
Phone: (804) 282-8915
Contact: Ron Smith
E-mail: CafeMojo@aol.com

**Walla Walla Blues Society**
P.O. Box 906
Walla Walla, WA 99362
Contact: Dan Glaspell
E-mail: glaspdm@whitman.edu
Phone: (509) 522-9963

**Washington Blues Society**
P.O. Box 12215
Seattle, WA 98102
Phone: (206) 632-3741
Contact: Robert Sawyer

**West Michigan Blues Society**
20 Division Avenue South
Grand Rapids, MI 49503
Daytime phone: (616) 451-3161
Contact: Sue Dodds

**Western Kansas Blues Society**
1610 Central Ave.
Dodge City, KS 67801
Daytime phone: (316) 225-2406
Contact: Tony Hornberger, President

**White River Delta Blues Society**
P.O. Box 369
Newport, AR 72112

**Wichita Blues Society**
P.O. Box 8273
Munger Station
Wichita, KS 67208
Phone: (316) 945-2583
E-mail: n2blues@netscape.com

**Wisconsin Blues Society**
2613 S. 51st Street
Milwaukee, WI 53219
Daytime phone: (414) 321-0188
Contact: Tom Radai, President

# Bibliography

Awmiller, Craig. *This House on Fire: The Story of the Blues* (New York: Franklin-Watts, 1996).

Bastin, Bruce. *Red River Blues: The Blues Tradition in the Southeast* (Urbana: University of Illinois Press, 1995).

Bego, Mark. *Bonnie Raitt: Just in the Nick of Time* (Secaucus, N.J.: Cewal, 1997).

Bekker, Peter O. E. *The Story of the Blues* (New York: Michael Friedman/Fairfax Publishing, 1997).

Brown, Ruth (with Andrew Yule). *Miss Rhythm: The Autobiography of Ruth Brown, Rhythm and Blues Legend* (New York: Da Capo Press, 1999).

Caserta, Peggy. *Going Down with Janis* (as told to Dan Knapp) (New York: Dell, 1973).

Charters, Samuel, and Ann Charters. *Blues Faces: A Portrait of the Blues* (Boston: David R. Godine, 2000).

Chodas, Nadine. *Spinning Blues into Gold: The Chess Brothers and the Legendary Chess Records* (New York: St. Martin's Press, 2000).

Cohn, Lawrence, ed. *Nothing but the Blues: The Music and the Musicians* (New York: Abbeville Press, 1999).

Coral, Gus. *The Rolling Stones: Black and White Blues, 1963* (Atlanta: Turner Broadcasting System, 1994).

Dalton, David. *Been Here and Gone: A Memoir of the Blues* (New York: William Morrow, 2000).

_____. *Janis* (New York: Simon & Schuster, 1971).

_____. *Piece of My Heart: A Portrait of Janis Joplin* (New York: Da Capo Press, 1991).

_____. *Piece of My Heart: The Life, Times, and Legend of Janis Joplin* (New York: St. Martin's Press, 1985).

Davis, Francis. *The History of the Blues* (New York: Hyperion, 1995).

Dicaire, David. *Blues Singers: Biographies of 50 Legendary Artists of the Early 20th Century* (Jefferson, N.C.: McFarland, 1999).

Deffaa, Chip. *Blue Rhythms: Six Lives in Rhythm and Blues* (New York: Da Capo Press, 2000).

Dister, Alain. *Jimi Hendrix* (Paris: Editions Chiron, 1974).

Dunas, Jeff (photographer), et al. *State of the Blues* (New York: Aperture, 1998)

Fraher, James, ed. *The Blues Is a Feeling: Voices and Visions of African-American Blues Musicians* (Mount Horeb, Wisc.: Face to Face Books, 1998).

Franklin, Aretha, and David Ritz. *From These Roots* (New York: Random House, 1999).

Friedman, Myra. *Janis Joplin: Buried Alive* (New York: Bantam Books, 1974).

Govenar, Alan. *Meeting the Blues: The Rise of the Texas Sound* (New York: Da Capo Press, 1995).

Gregory, Hugh. *Soul Music A–Z* (New York: Da Capo Press, 1995).

Giles, Mindy, and Stephen Green. *Really the Blues* (San Francisco: Woodford Press, 1996).

Gunsow, Adam. *Mister Satan's Apprentice: A Blues Memoir* (New York: Pantheon Books, 1998).

Harris, Michael. *The Rise of Gospel Blues* (New York: Oxford University Press, 1992).

Henderson, David. *Jimi Hendrix: Voodoo Child of the Aquarian Age* (New York: Doubleday, 1978).

_____. *Reach up and Kiss the Sky: The Jimi Hendrix Story* (New York: Doubleday, 1978).

_____. *'Scuze Me While I Kiss the Sky: The Life of Jimi Hendrix* (New York: Bantam, 1981).

Hendrix, Jimi. *Stay Groovy, Stay Free* (New York: Bantam, 1981).

Hildebrand, Lee. *Bay Area Blues* (California: Pomegranate Press, 1993).

James, Etta (with David Ritz). *Rage to Survive: The Etta James Story* (New York: Da Capo Press, 1998).

James, Patti. *One Man's Blues: The Life and Music of Mose Allison* (New York: Interlink, 1998).

Kitts, Jeff, et al., eds. *Guitar World Presents Stevie Ray Vaughan: Stevie Ray— In His Own Words* (New York: Hal Leonard, 1997).

Knight, Curtis. *Jimi: An Intimate Biography of Jimi Hendrix* (New York: Praeger, 1971).

Landau, Deborah. *Janis Joplin: Her Life and Times* (New York: Warner, 1971).

Leigh, Ken, and B. B. King. *Stevie Ray: Soul to Soul* (Dallas: Taylor, 1993).

Lornell, Kip, and Charles K. Wolfe. *The Life and Legend of Leadbelly* (New York: Da Capo Press, 1999).

Lydon, Michael. *Ray Charles: Man and Music* (New York: Penguin Putnam, 1999).

Major, Clarence. *Dirty Bird Blues* (San Francisco: Mercury House, 1996).

Marsalis, Wynton, and Frank Stewart. *Sweet Swing Blues: A Year with Wynton Marsalis and His Septet* (New York: Thunder's Mouth Press, 1988).

Mitchell, Mitch, and John Platt. *Jimi Hendrix: Inside the Experience* (New York: Harmony Books, 1990).

Murray, Charles Shaar. *Crosstown Traffic: Jimi Hendrix and Post-War Pop* (New York: Faber & Faber, 1989).

Nicholson, Robert. *Mississippi: The Blues Today!* (New York: Da Capo Press, 1999).

Obrecht, Jas., ed. *Rollin' and Tumblin': The Postwar Blues Guitarists* (San Francisco: Miller Freeman Books, 2000).

Patoski, Nick, and Bill Crawford. *Stevie Ray Vaughan: Caught in the Crossfire* (New York: Little, Brown, 1994).

Pearson, Barry Lee. *Sounds So Good to Me: The Bluesman's Story* (Philadelphia: University of Pennsylvania Press, 1984).

Pleasant, Joseph, and H.J. Ottenheimer. *Cousin Joe: Blues from New Orleans* (Chicago: University of Chicago Press, 1987).

Redding, Noel, and Carole Appleby. *Are You Experienced?* (London: Fourth Estate, 1990).

Rubin, Dave. *Inside the Blues 1942–1982* (New York: Hal Leonard, 1995).

Russell, Tony. *From Robert Johnson to Robert Cray* (Farmington Hill, Mich.: Gale Group, 1998).

Sampson, Victor. *Hendrix: An Illustrated Biography* (New York: Proteus, 1984).

Shapiro, Harry. *Eric Clapton: Lost in the Blues* (New York: Da Capo Press, 1992).

_____, and Caesar Glebbeek. *Jimi Hendrix: Electric Gypsy* (London: Heinemann, 1990).

Sonnier, Austin. *A Guide to the Blues: History* (Westport, Conn.: Greenwood, 1994).

Steen, Fred. *Bluesman* (Costa Mesa, Calif.: James, 1998)

Taft, Michael. *Blues Lyric Poetry: An Anthology* (New York: Garland, 1983).

Taj Mahal (with Stephen Foehr). *Taj Mahal: Autobiography of a Bluesman* (London: Sanctuary, 1999).

Tooze, Sandra B. *Muddy Waters: The Mojo Man* (Toronto: ECW Press, 1999).

Townsend, Henry, as told to Bill Greensmith. *A Blues Life* (Urbana: University of Illinois Press, 1999).

Trynka, Paul. *Portrait of the Blues: America's Blues Musicians in Their Own Words* (New York: Da Capo Press, 1997).

Vernon, Paul. *African-American Blues, Rhythm and Blues, Gospel and Zydeco on Film and Video, 1926–1997* (Brookfield, Vt.: Ashgate Publishers, 1999).

Wardlow, Gayle Dean. Edward Komara, ed. *Chasin' That Devil Music* (San Francisco: Miller Freeman Books, 1998).

Welch, Chris. *Hendrix: A Biography* (New York: Omnibus, 1982).

West, Sarah Ann. *Deep Down Hard Blues: Tribute to Lightnin'* (Lawrenceville, Va.: Brunswick, 1995).

Wilcock, Donald E., et al. *Damn Right I've Got the Blues: Buddy Guy and the Blues Roots of Rock-And-Roll* (San Francisco: Woodford, 1993).

Wolfe, Bernard, and Mike Mazurem *Really the Blues* (New York: Carol Publishing, 1991).

# Index

279